Woman's Experience of Sex

SHEILA KITZINGER

Woman's Experience of Sex

PHOTOGRAPHY BY
Nancy Durrell McKenna

DORLING KINDERSLEY

To all the women who have shared
with me their experiences
with such searching honesty
and generous openness

Woman's Experience of Sex was conceived, edited and designed by
Dorling Kindersley Limited, 9 Henrietta Street, London WC2

Project editor Pippa Rubinstein
Art editor Anne-Marie Bulat
Editor Miren Lopategui
Designer Julia Goodman

Managing Editor Jackie Douglas
Editorial Director Christopher Davis
Art Director Roger Bristow

First published in Great Britain in 1983 by
Dorling Kindersley Limited, 9 Henrietta Street, London WC2

British Library Cataloguing in Publication Data
Kitzinger, Sheila.
    Woman's experience of sex.
        1. Sex instruction for women.
        I. Title.
        306.7′024042 HQ46
        ISBN 0–86318–013–2

Filmsetting by Vantage Photosetting Co Ltd, Eastleigh and London

Printed and bound in Italy by Arnoldo Mondadori, Verona

Contents

Foreword

I could not have tackled this book without the help of many women who have enabled me to become aware of the complexity and depth of women's sexuality and to see our lives with greater clarity.

Yet every way of seeing is also a way of not seeing. (Ann Oakley, *Sociology of Housework*) We screen out that which is unacceptable, which we do not want to acknowledge or believe peripheral to what is important. In books about female sexuality women's own experiences have often been screened out in this way.

I, on the contrary, have deliberately weeded out the assumptions made about sex and our feelings which do not fit *women's* direct experience. That is, I have rejected men's explanations of our behaviour and feelings as irrelevant, except in so far as they affect our view of ourselves.

Most books about sex talk *about* women but do not speak from women's experience. They impose a view of what it is all about and generalize about emotions, behaviour and goals from that basis. And it is often a doctor's or therapist's view, too. Professional status is assumed to give an "objective" view. So both gender and professional status remove what is said from the immediacy of women's own thoughts and feelings and distort everything that we could discover about them.

Author's acknowledgments

For a book of this kind it is difficult to know how to make acknowledgments. It is all very well expressing gratitude to organizations, but I'm pretty sure that many of the individuals who will have been most helpful would not want to be thanked by name. I have learnt from so many different women's experiences and I want to thank them all for trusting me enough to talk so openly and honestly. I promised them complete confidentiality but they will know who they are and I hope I have not distorted what they said.

I should, however, particularly like to thank the Boston Women's Health Book Collective and the Oxford Women's Health Group for helpful discussions, and stimulating thinking from: Sally Haslett, Linda Hurcombe, Ann Oakley, Susan Le Poidevin, Jean Robinson, Helge Rubinstein, Elizabeth Salter, Mary Stott, Norma Swenson, Marjorie Walker and Val Wilmer.

Writing this book has taken a big slice out of my life. It has been engrossing, time-consuming and exciting. My husband has given me a great deal of emotional and practical support to be able to do this work and I want to thank him for his unfailing encouragement and confidence in my ability to write, even when I was most frustrated and despairing about it.

And daughters! How can I thank my daughters enough? They have been my guides through the maze. Their forthright criticism, clarity of thinking, the sheer gusto with which they have approached the material, has helped me enormously. The highest praise a particular daughter has ever given me about a chapter was, "Mmm, there's nothing objectionable in that." When this pronouncement was given I knew that at last the chapter would do. We have had long discussions into the night and three of them, Celia, Polly and Jenny, have worked with me on drafting and redrafting chapters. They have been stern task-mistresses, but it has been for me an astonishing educational experience.

I want to thank Polly for the research and first draft of the section on sex, past and present and for the poem on pages 179–80, which I recovered unashamedly in a crumpled ball from a waste paper basket.

Celia not only wrote the chapter on lesbianism but did the initial analysis of responses to the questionnaires which comprised the first phase of the investigation and advised me right through the book. I know that it is very different from what she advised me to write, but I hope she feels that it has been worth it all the same.

I want to thank Wendy Rose Neil, the Editor of *Parents*, for printing the questionnaires in the magazine and for the hundreds of responses which I received from her readers.

Pippa Rubinstein has been a very committed editor and has kept the lines of communication open at all times. Nancy Durrell McKenna, who took the photographs, has been enthusiastic and perceptive and works with unerring style.

I have come out of this book feeling tremendous admiration for women, their zest and courage, the way they live through the transitions in their lives and confront crises and tragedy and how they give and go on giving. This book is a testimony to what I owe other women.

Sheila Kitzinger

1 INTRODUCTION

What is sex, anyway?

I did not start writing this book with any particular theory about women's sexuality. I wanted to learn, instead, what our real experiences are and how we feel about them. My ideas have grown out of what women have told me. It is obvious that for many of us sex is not all it is cracked up to be, that many women feel guilty about sex, not because nowadays we believe we have no right to sexual expression, but because we are afraid that we are not good enough at it or, if we are not in a sexual relationship, that there must be something wrong with us because everyone else seems to be enjoying sex to the full.

This book explores women's feelings about their bodies and the many different dimensions of their sexual experience. Books which have been written to tell us "how to do it", seem to be asking "is your performance good enough?" and give instructions about how to be a sort of sexual superwoman. Sex is approached as if we learn to give and get pleasure in much the same way as we might learn to drive a car or use a computer and the emphasis often seems to be on excelling, proving that we can do it as well as, or better than, anyone else. Techniques and methods are often discussed with only passing reference to what is, after all, the most vital thing of all – the emotions our experiences arouse in us, our identity as people, our values, our relationships with others, and the social context in which all our private behaviour occurs and which is reflected in our most intimate acts.

For women sex is not something restricted to bottoms and breasts. We cannot talk about it with any sense of reality just in terms of what we do with our genitals. Whatever it is for a man, for a woman sex consists of a whole range of experiences that are not just genital. Sex involves the whole body and is expressed in different ways at different times in a woman's life, during her ovarian cycle and with the varied and complex bio-social experiences of pregnancy, childbearing, menopause and aging. We are only just beginning to share with each other what sex really is in terms of a woman's unique experience.

One view of sex is that it is what a man does to a woman on a Saturday night in bed. We have been conditioned by a society that sees the be-all and end-all of sex as intercourse and that devalues all the other aspects of female sexual experience.

Sex can infuse the whole of life. It includes things like the excitement and sense of physical well-being that comes from walking in the country when autumn leaves are falling in the crisp air, gold, scarlet and rust. Picking up a baby from her crib and feeling the little body's firm plumpness in your arms. Or a baby hungrily seeking the nipple, finding it and latching on in utter contentment. Sitting holding hands with a lover, or even not touching at all, on an evening when frost and snow have islanded you together in the warmth indoors. The companionship and closeness of women joined together in a common cause, working for peace and to change society.

Even at the level that is most obviously physical, sex can be a whole range of different experiences, too. It can be romantic, all rosy sunsets and soft music. It can be passionate, with longing forcing its way in to every pore in your body. It can be witty and intellectually stimulating. Sometimes it is basic – Tarzan wants Jane or Jane wants Tarzan. Sometimes it is funny, a puppy romp in which the climax is helpless laughter. At different times it is casual and relaxed, desperate, sometimes even like a game or a contest.

For each woman sex may be all these things at different phases in her life or with different partners. But even that is an over-simplification. Sex changes as our moods and attitudes change, and depending on whether the sexual experience is shared or we are alone. It is also profoundly affected by all the other things that happen to us in life. Money worries, anxiety about our parents or children, problems at work, all drain the joy out of sex. When other relationships are going well and we can enjoy life, the radiance pours through into our sexual experience, too.

Sex and self-worth

This is because sex is linked with our sense of self-worth. Though sex is usually discussed as if it existed independently of all the other things that happen to us in life, the evidence from women is that sexual feeling depends to a large extent on other things that are happening to us and our feelings about our own identity and how we value ourselves. The strains of living in a high-rise flat with small children or having a partner who drinks heavily or elderly parents, for example, often means that a woman feels entirely drained in coping with problems and serving the needs or demands of others.

We live in a society in which men get serviced and women provide the service. Women are the nurturers. It is assumed that men go out to work and provide economic support in return for housekeeping, child-rearing and sexual availability and they are active and dominant, while women are relatively passive and submissive, having been led to expect men to know best how to satisfy them. Many people do not live like this, of course, but everything we believe and do is affected by that basic template from our culture which shapes and limits our choices, and which often makes nonsense of them because, as social beings, we find it hard to act completely independently of it.

Our relationships with our partners, children, and with others outside the family, intimately affect our personal sexual experiences.

A woman on her own

Our society is organized for couples, heterosexual couples. The single woman, the single man, are odd ones out. Living accommodation, mortgages, even the family railcard, are directed towards a man and a woman living together with perhaps a couple of children. If a woman does not link up with a man she is at a social disadvantage. Even if she does, as soon as he goes away on a business trip, or after he dies, she discovers herself in an anomalous situation. Documents are signed by him. The car is insured and taxed in his name, plumbers, builders, decorators and electricians may all await his written orders before they do any work. An invitation comes for them as a couple and though if she could not go, he would be welcome as a single male, single women are awkward to seat and the invitation may be withdrawn. She may be seen as a sexual threat by other women within couples in her social circle. She may even begin to feel guilty about a sexuality that, simply because she is on her own, must be on offer. She knows it is risky to be walking on the street after dark alone or with another woman and this limits leisure activity. If she goes on holiday alone and can afford it she must pay extra for a single room.

Women as child-rearers

If she goes out to work a woman has to cope with all the obstacles put in her way by a society in which it is assumed that women are housebound or child-rearers. There is no crèche at work, no nursery places available and it is difficult to find anyone suitable to take responsibility for the children. The man who said "Do what you want" now says, "I should pack it in, if I were you – you look worn out! You're doing too much!" (He means the job, not the house-work or the children or washing his shirts.) Housework is not "real" work. It is not real work *because* it is women's work and therefore undervalued. To many women home becomes a trap and after 10 years or so of marriage *feels* like a trap.

Anything that is said about sex between a man and a woman and our feelings about it has to take this into the reckoning. For it is not just a question of what happens when two bodies are intertwined in the darkness but of everything that occurs right through the 24 hours and of all those things that each partner takes for granted about the other.

Sexual stereotyping

Women are often unhappy and frustrated, too, because it is implied that each woman will fall in love with one man, marry him, have children and live – or so the myth goes – happily ever after. Our society assumes that the nuclear family, with mother, father and two or maybe three children, is normal and that anything else is in some way a deviation. We prepare our daughters for this and though we accept that there needs to be a phase of experiment, perhaps to try out different partners, we still want girls to "settle down" and fill the traditional female role of wife and mother, even if our own experiences of marital life have not lived up to the ideal. Many of us have learned our lesson so well that we are not even aware that our lives are constricted by a male view of who we are and how we should see ourselves. We grow up in a society and impose on our children stereotypes about what it is to be male and female. However enlightened we are and however much we seek to escape from these stereotypes, they are so much taken for granted that we have to be constantly on our guard in order to actively resist them directing our lives.

A man learns to	A woman learns to
control	do what she is asked/told
"score", to achieve	be pleasing to a man
pursue goals	hurt no one's feelings
discuss women's bodies part by part	look good
shoulder burdens	be taken care of by a strong man
work as a team	compete with others for a man's attention
push himself	
take risks, challenges	care for others before herself
make the rules	make no trouble, "be nice"
be virile	follow the rules
be a "man", grow up	be compliant, say yes
make decisions	enjoy being a "girl", forever immature
put women on a pedestal	
expect service from a woman	let others make choices for her
belittle "girlish" things	expect a man to make her happy
take charge	be friendly and helpful
	be helpless
	accept her status
	expect someone else to "fix" things

(Adapted from Helen Seager, *Not For Fun, Not For Profit: Strategies for ending sexual harassment on the job*.*)

*Titles mentioned in the text are contained in the Bibliography.

Every woman has a right to choose who, and how, she loves . . .

Such stereotypes of what it is to be a man and a woman are not only stifling but have a profound influence on our attitudes to sex. For sex is defined largely in terms of male experience. It is seen as intercourse. And orgasm is seen as the goal of intercourse, a kind of "hitting the jackpot" and all other sexual pleasure merely a preliminary to that. There is even a word for it: foreplay. Sex is also seen as an activity taking place between two organs of the male and female bodies, the penis and the vagina.

Masturbation is considered a kind of substitute for sex with a man, and, largely as a result of the work of Masters and Johnson and the modern sex therapists, as a way of learning how to do it better. In these pages I want to challenge such assumptions and explore women's sexuality much more widely and deeply.

I shall not, for example, define sex as only a heterosexual activity: this book is about lesbian experience, too. This is another way of loving that brings happiness and fulfilment to many women, and, for some, a way of making an important statement about our patriarchal society and woman's place in it.

The emotions

I shall be questioning the central role of orgasm in sexual experience. Though it is an exultant outpouring of energy, there are times when a woman does not seek it and there are women who are happy without it. Most important of all, a woman can have an orgasm, even a multiple orgasm, and yet not feel *emotionally* satisfied. Sex is more than orgasm.

Alex Comfort (*The Joy of Sex*) compares sex with food and recommends gourmet feasts of sex but this analogy is a restricted one. We do not need sex to survive, but we do have to eat. Even so, if sex is really like food, the last thing we want is fine cuisine and fancy dishes every day. Sometimes we prefer a picnic or snack. Often we want to skip a meal or not to eat at all for a while, and often good, wholesome, plain food is what we need. We can bring the same selectivity to sex that we take for granted with food. We can work to free ourselves from the constraints which other people put on us about when and how we should enjoy sex and how we ought to feel about it, just as when we grow up we escape from similar parental constraints about when, how and what we ought to eat. We can begin to find out what we really want.

If we are to begin to gain control over our bodies and lives we need to look at the way in which male attitudes to sexuality are imposed on us and we are permitted to see the world only through male eyes. Though in these pages I am writing about where we start on all this in our most intimate private lives, in one sense this aspect of our personal behaviour expresses social values that control how we see ourselves and others, and what we do. Through the centuries women have been invested by men with roles of compassion and caring. Men have found it very convenient to do this. We have reared the young, tended the sick, cared for the elderly and sustained men right through their lives.

. . . sex is about relationships not just intercourse.

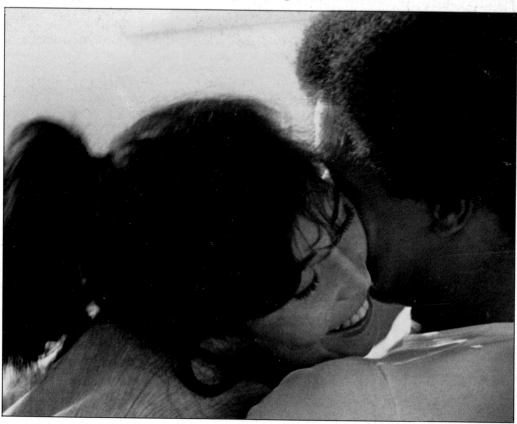

A woman first learns what love is from her mother ...

The role of love

Yet it is these very qualities, traditionally associated with being a woman, that the world needs most urgently. To throw out tenderness, sympathy, capacity to nurture, because they are linked with women's subordinate social position is to ditch almost everything that enriches life emotionally and makes for a caring society.

I am, quite unashamedly, writing about love, too. Even though we love it may be difficult to *show* love in a way that has meaning for the other person and in these pages I explore some of the forms in which love can be communicated.

Making decisions about sex involves thinking about who I am as a woman and what I want to get and give. My relationships with my mother, father, partner, children, with other women and men outside the family, intimately affect my personal sexual experiences. If I leave out these I neglect the whole setting in which I see myself as a person. To understand what sex means to a woman we need to talk about it in terms of our everyday lives, the network of relationships in which we are caught up, the flow of changing experiences through time, and to consider the implications of our personal relationships on the kind of world we live in and the kind of society in which our children will live.

Sex, past and present

Women's sexual expression through the ages is obviously an enormous subject – much too wide-ranging for me to attempt to cover here. All I can hope to give in these pages is a kind of entrée to the historical and anthropological studies that offer much more insight into this fascinating area.

Throughout history women's sexuality has either been demeaned as trivial or seen as dangerous, even life-threatening to men. The early writers of the Christian church taught that there were two types of women: mothers and prostitutes. Mothers had no sexual desires, but submitted gladly to sex in order to bear children. Prostitutes were quite different: they were so intensely sexual that, driven by lust, they ravaged men's bodies and souls. This dualism persisted through Medieval times, was an unwavering theme in both Catholic and Protestant England, and was a basic tenet of the Victorian value system.

For most of us, our historical awareness of changes in attitudes to sex covers a fairly short time span. We can compare our own ideas with those of our mothers – perhaps even a generation or so further back. And we have a fairly clear idea of the prejudices which we associate with Victorian attitudes.

Victorian attitudes: "Close your eyes and think of England"

In the nineteenth century there were powerful influences and assumptions about what women were and the nature of sex, which, in one way or another, affected most women's lives.

It was assumed either that women did not have spontaneous sexual feelings, but might perhaps be gently introduced to sex by their husbands, or, on the other hand, that they had fallen from grace and from the pedestal on which pure women were adored by men. The good woman suffered sex for the sake of her marriage. In the bestselling pamphlets, *Wives of England, Women of England,* and *Daughters of England* ("Every husband should buy one for his wife, every brother for his sister, every father for his daughter") Sarah Ellis instructed women about their relations with men. She said that "a woman without the love of a man is a lone, lost thing" and stressed that an important part of woman's nature is gratitude, which is unfulfilled if it is not expressed to the men who guide and cherish her through life. Another book advised:

With grace to bear even wrath and peevishness, she must learn and adopt his taste, study his disposition and submit in short to all his desires with all that grateful compliance which in a wife is the surest sign of a sound understanding. (*Woman as She is and Should be*, 1879, quoted in Carol Adams, *Ordinary Lives: A Hundred Years Ago*)

Knowledge sullies woman's innocence. She must simply trust the man who loves her to tell her what to do. Happiness cannot be sought and found by a woman for herself. It must be bestowed by a man. With this gift a good man becomes almost God-like: "He for God only, she for God in him." (John Milton)

One Victorian surgeon, in the standard book on sexual matters of that time, said that to attribute sexual feelings to women was "a vile aspersion". Another medical work of the same period described the woman who responded to her husband's advances with any physical sign of pleasure as "lascivious".

On the other hand, romantic friendships between women were not only tolerated but warmly approved, perhaps because the possibility of any sexual element in them was denied. (Lillian Faderman, *Surpassing the Love of Men*) Lesbians, therefore, had a freedom that in many ways they lack today. Love letters between women survive uncensored and form an extraordinary contrast to the hostility with which lesbianism is often viewed nowadays.

Dual standards of morality

In the nineteenth century there was an accepted double moral standard for men and for women. Men could "sow their wild oats" but women had to be chaste. The sanctity of the family and the virtue of wives and mothers as guardians of their husbands' honour was built on the exploitation and degradation of another group of women, prostitutes. Virtuous women were not supposed to know about the existence of prostitutes, but men accepted them as an unpleasant "necessity" in order to uphold the morality of the family. W. E. H. Lecky, in his *History of European Morals from Augustus to Charlemagne*, describes the prostitute as:

the vilest of her sex. . .doomed. . .to disease and abject wretchedness and an early death . . . the perpetual symbol of the degradation and sinfulness of men. Herself the supreme type of vice, she is ultimately the most efficient guardian of virtue. But for her, the unchallenged purity of countless happy homes would be polluted and not a few who, in the pride of their untempted chastity, think of her with an indignant shudder, would have known the agony of remorse and despair. On that degraded and ignoble form are concentrated the passions that might have filled the world with shame. She remains, while creeds and civilizations rise and fall, the eternal priestess of humanity blasted for the sins of the people.

Men were warned, in terms which implied that their own sexual vices were entirely due to having been tempted by the fallen daughters of Eve, not to do anything that could lead to sexual arousal in a wife:

It is a delusion which many a previously incontinent man suffers to suppose that in newly married life he will be required to treat his wife as he used to treat his mistresses. It is not so in the case of any modern English woman. He need not fear that his wife will require the excitement, or in any respect imitate the ways of a courtesan. (Lord Acton, quoted in Steven Marcus, *The Other Victorians*)

If a woman became pregnant outside marriage it was the consequence of her depravity. It was understandable for men to have strong sexual desires which they needed to control, but unnatural for women to have any at all. So a woman who became pregnant had either surrendered to her ravisher as a consequence of moral weakness or had wickedly tempted and seduced the man.

Warnings against birth control

Victorian women spent much of their lives in a state of child-bearing, lactation or ill-health following miscarriage. Many fictional heroines of the time died in childbirth. The frailty which was considered an innate quality of the well-bred woman was to a large extent a consequence of the drain on her health of repeated pregnancies. To escape this debilitating process was to avoid sex.

In the latter part of the century the literature on contraception was growing. But, even so, birth control was considered by the great majority to be disgusting and injurious to morals and to health, and this by doctors as well as by churchmen and other guardians of public morality. In 1869 the *Lancet* thundered this advice:

A woman on whom her husband practices what is euphemistically called "preventive contraception" is. . .necessarily brought into the condition of mind of a prostitute. . . . She has only one chance, depending on an entire absence of orgasm, of escaping uterine disease.

The only acceptable way to avoid frequent pregnancies was abstinence. Yet families were becoming smaller and "secret remedies" were discreetly advertised in the press. Doctors warned against "sexual fraudulency and conjugal onanism" and a certain Dr Routh threatened that the consequences would be:

death, or severe illness from acute and chronic metritis, leucorrhoea, menorrhagia and haematocele, histeralgia and hyperaesthesia of the generative organs, cancer, in an aggravated form, assuming in such examples a galloping character so rapid is its course . . . ovarian dropsy and ovaritus. . . . Lastly, mania leading to suicide and the most repulsive nymphomania are induced.

The publicity given to the trial of Charles Bradlaugh and Annie Bessant for publication of a pamphlet on birth control, which by 1881 had sold 277,000 copies, played a large part in making women aware that contraception was feasible. Only when sexuality could be separated from constant childbearing, miscarriages and the pelvic diseases and injuries associated with these could most women begin to think about sex as a possible source of pleasure.

Old myths in a new guise

Havelock Ellis, who made the great breakthrough in teaching about sexuality, in his books, *Studies in the Psychology of Sex* (published between 1897 and 1928, though till 1935 these were legally available only to doctors), still saw men primarily as guardians and educators of their wives. They were enjoined to fan the tiny spark of ardour in a woman so that she would accept the conjugal embrace. That was the goal. Female sexuality did not, could not, exist apart from this. He lamented that:

The civilized woman, under the combined influences of Nature, art, convention, morality and religion, has often tended to come into her husband's hands, usually at a rather late adult age, in a condition inept for the conjugal embrace, which, if the bridegroom is lacking in skill or consideration, may cause her suffering or disgust, or merely leave her indifferent. . . . Even on the physical side of sex, the organs are by no means always so ready to respond normally to the exercise of their natural functions. (Havelock Ellis, *The Psychology of Sex*)

His teaching reflected the power of the Sleeping Beauty myth. The princess is asleep till kissed by the prince who, on approaching the forest, sword in hand, discovers that, as if by magic, clearings appear in the thicket and blossoms replace thorns. The myth encapsulates male attitudes to female sexuality. Not only is the woman to be woken by the man but the triumph is made possible by his sword-like penis.

Penis envy?

The works of Sigmund Freud were first published in English between the early 1900s and the 1930s. He brought sex out into the open and claimed that it should be viewed as the basis of human personality and relationships.

He believed, and the whole of psychoanalysis has been built on this theory, that the little girl is shocked to discover that she has no penis and thinks that she must have possessed one but has lost it by castration. This castration is seen as punishment. A girl is, therefore, a mutilated and biologically inferior boy. She envies the boy his possession of a penis and is never able to recover from this feeling of inferiority. Because experiences in early childhood mould the individual character of the adult, this early trauma makes her narcissistic and she tries to compensate by embellishing her own image. The symbolic castration creates a pattern which is repeated throughout her life so that she masochistically delights in suffering. She wants to be a man and seeks to avenge herself on men for having something she lacks. Consequently men live in fear of women. A woman copes with her penis envy in one of three ways: she wants a baby as a replacement for the lost penis, she becomes neurotic, or she develops a "masculinity complex" and denies that she lacks anything.

Freud subscribed to a theory of male superiority basic to the culture in which he lived. His phallo-centric views were tightly bound to a specific culture, that of Vienna under the Austro-Hungarian Empire. Women psychoanalysts since, acknowledging his deep and perceptive thinking, criticize him for theories that were derived entirely from middle- and upper-class Viennese ladies in his practice. (Karen Horney, "The flight from womanhood: the masculinity complex in women as viewed by men and by women", and "The problem of feminine masochism"; Clara Thompson, "'Penis envy' in women".) If society values the possession of a penis above anything a woman possesses, it is only reasonable for a woman to want one. There is nothing psychologically fundamental about this. It is a position into which women are forced. Freud's theory of "penis envy" probably says more about men and their values than it does about women.

Though there is a whole male literature in which the penis is extolled and its activities recounted with admiration and wonder (D. H. Lawrence even made women kneel in front of his "purple penis" and worship it), women who have written to me about sexual excitement do not describe the penis in any detail. They talk about their own emotions and the feelings sweeping through their whole bodies. A woman is stimulated by seeing or feeling her lover's erect penis because it is evidence of his longing for her and of her power to affect him.

The 1920s

The First World War came and went and by the 1920s the old order seemed to be crumbling. With ideas and customs shaken by the disruption of the war, an era seen by many as one of greater sexual freedom unfolded. It was not a sexual revolution, for though pre-marital chastity was no longer as important as it had been, everyone knew the rules they were breaking. Whereas in the sexual revolution of 1960s the very rules were challenged, too.

Bright young things

These were the days of the flapper, cropped hair, no corsets and a boyish figure and stance. Women had been employed in munitions factories, on buses and trams and in jobs that previously they had been thought too weak to do. They were demanding a new autonomy and sexual openness. The dances of the period, epitomized by the Charleston, give some idea of the feverish activity, the rushing from place to place, that became the stylized model for how bright young things behaved. There was a veneer of wry cynicism and a frenetic search for pleasure, exemplified in the songs of Noel Coward and the novels of Scott Fitzgerald.

Birth control became available to more and more women. But those most in need were untouched by the new technology of contraception. They relied on withdrawal, waited each month for a period to come and still only had recourse to such things as hot baths, gin and lead pills.

In 1921 Marie Stopes's first birth control clinic opened in Manchester and the whole issue of contraception became a matter for public discussion. Newspapers accused those who ran the clinics of being "overdressed" and "overfed", brazen hussies forcing contraception on the poor.

One whole issue of the *Practitioner*, in 1923, was devoted to the subject of contraception. Birth control, it claimed "has now become a commonplace of conversation at women's clubs and mixed tea-tables" and that "women of unblemished virtue espouse the cause", though one eminent contributor warned his colleagues that men would be rendered sterile and driven to insanity if they used contraceptives. Several shared the view that birth control was justified for the incurably insane, but that since the flower of the nation's manhood had been killed in the war, it was the responsibility of those in the educated classes to repopulate the nation.

In different countries of the Western world the new sexual expressiveness took different forms. For example, in Germany in the 1920s men were in very short supply. Many women had only their memories of dead lovers and husbands. War cripples begged for food in the streets and there were shortages of everything: jobs, money, homes. The cartoons of the day by George Grosz, the songs of Kurt Weill, convey a bitterness and hate, a raw violence and exploitation of the poor by the rich and the helpless by those in power, that were explicitly sexual. Sexuality, in a manner which may have been more flamboyant than ever before, became a way of commenting on social injustice.

Sexual liberation

The first part of the Kinsey Report, *Sexual Behaviour in the Human Male*, was published in 1948, the second, *Sexual Behaviour in the Human Female*, in 1953, presenting a monumental body of statistical research based on what 18,000 men and women said about their sex lives. But the full social effect of these studies was probably not felt until the 1960s, when the Pill provided a more reliable means of communication than had ever existed before. Kinsey showed that there were enormous variations in sexual behaviour and that many practices that previously had been thought abnormal were perfectly normal, in the sense that many people engaged in them. (Wardell B. Pomeroy, *Dr Kinsey and the Institute for Sex Research*) Increasingly, masturbation, homosexuality and oral sex all got talked about with new openness, though with a *frisson* of excitement about what had been previously taboo subjects of conversation.

The sexual revolution of the 1960s would not have been possible without the contraceptive pill. It first came on the market, following its trial on Puerto Rican peasant women in 1956, as the 1960s dawned. It has been estimated that by the middle of 1966, 10 million women in different countries were on the Pill. (Clive Wood and Beryl Suitters, *The Fight for Acceptance: A history of contraception*) It was the Pill that at last promised, if it did not actually provide on the spot, a separation between sex and reproduction. At last women could have intercourse without the threat of an unwanted pregnancy hanging over them.

Flower power

In California, the Flower Power movement started as young people came together in emotional and physical communion, making love not war, and highly critical of the world of violence their parents had made, together with the bureaucratic structures and bourgeois institutions such as marriage, which shaped their lives. Soon, however, Flower Children, who blossomed in sweetness and light, were to be swallowed up in another, more drug-oriented, hippy culture that was often violent and that treated women as sexual pets or "chicks", there for men to do whatever they wanted.

The drug culture of the 1960s also added a new dimension to sex – sex when you are gently stoned or dreaming of sex (but unable to engage in it) when very stoned. Its apotheosis was reached in the

Manson murder case. Charles Manson dominated a "family" of women who worshipped him in sado-masochistic slavery.

The Esalen movement initiated a more general search for the discovery of physical sensations and emotions and a new "togetherness" between couples and in groups. In the communion of the bath, glistening bodies touched with the thrill of enlightenment. Men and women, naked or wrapped in sheets, explored palms, rubbed backs, coiled like serpents and climbed all over each other in a quest for communion.

Writers about sex introduced a whole new repertoire of bed exercises and party games intended to guarantee and improve orgasm. A woman could excite her man by spreading whipped cream on her nipples or maple syrup on his penis. You had to have a sweet tooth in those days! "Swinging" and "wife-swapping" now also offered a new kind of sexual adventure. Clubs mushroomed where swinging couples could go and find new partners for the evening. Under strobe lights bodies writhed in communal delight. They said it improved their marriages: (Duane Denfeld and Michael Gordon, "The sociology of mate swapping: or the family that swings together clings together")

William Masters and Virginia Johnson published their first book, *Human Sexual Response*, the result of an 11-year study, in 1966. It was sold out three days after publication. (Fred Belliveau and Lin Richter, *Understanding Human Sexual Inadequacy*) From studies of the physiology of orgasm, using film and measuring equipment, they concluded that the basic theories of sexual arousal and of orgasm were the same for the female as for the male. The clitoris, they revealed, is both the source and transmitter of sexual arousal.

This was followed by the publication of *Human Sexual Inadequacy*, also by Masters and Johnson, the study which described rapid two-week sex therapy in St Louis, and the use of "replacement partners" (if your real partner did not want to come along you chose another). As a result of their work sexual dysfunction has become as much a subject of matter-of-fact treatment as astigmatism or dental decay. Masters reckoned that: "A conservative estimate would indicate half the marriages (in the USA) are either presently dysfunctional or imminently so in the future."

Sexual cures

When it is claimed that a certain kind of behaviour is a disease or disability, when doctors and therapists start to treat it and men and women seek a cure for it, we need to look at how to define "illness". In medicine the definition of what constitutes illness is constantly changing. Sometimes it shrinks: homosexuality is no longer an illness. Often it expands: children can be "hyperactive" and be given a special diet or sedated out of this state. Pre-menstrual tension has now acquired the status of a disease. Cigarette smoking is fast on the way to becoming a disease, too, and to being treated like other kinds of drug addiction.

The concept of illness

Not only does the definition of illness change historically, but in different cultures illness is defined and its severity rated in different ways. The concept of illness and of what illness consists is value-

23

laden. It is not just a medical matter. Are we, for example, to work out a statistical norm and define disease as anything that deviates from that? If so, we are taking it for granted that the majority of people are healthy. Does less usual behaviour need "correcting"? Is the "normal" a consequence of stereotyping? This has always been important in defining illness in women. Should behaviour which does not fit with how women are expected to behave in their social setting be classified as illness? Doctors often treat women's marital unhappiness with tranquillizers. They could not cope with the number of women who come to them anxious and depressed, unless they did so. Sex therapy is not just a matter of whether techniques work. It raises questions about a society's *values*.

Masturbation used to be thought to cause insanity and doctors would lop off a woman's clitoris in an attempt to cure mental illness. Thanks to the research of scientists like Kinsey, and Masters and Johnson, and to changing social attitudes towards women and towards mental illness, this would be unacceptable today.

Masters and Johnson treat sexual "dysfunction". The wheel has swung full circle and now anybody who does *not* masturbate, or who cannot masturbate to orgasm, may be thought to need treatment. If a woman does not get orgasms with masturbation they call it "masturbatory orgasmic inadequacy" and have devised a cure for this, even though the woman may "reach orgasmic expression during coital connection". (Masters and Johnson, *Human Sexual Inadequacy*) You are only healthy, they imply, if you masturbate and if you have orgasms when masturbating. If you only have orgasms when making love there is something wrong with you. The radical psychiatrist, Thomas Szasz, commenting on this, says:

The discovery of this disease is an inversion of the old doctrine of masturbatory insanity. In the nineteenth century, masturbating was an illness and not masturbating was a treatment; today, not masturbating is a disease and masturbating is a treatment." (Thomas Szasz, *Sex: Facts, Frauds and Follies*)

Though Masters and Johnson state that homosexuality is not a disease, simply a natural expression of sexuality, they also offer "treatment" for homosexuals who want to become heterosexual. It is very confusing.

Virginia Johnson, William Masters's co-researcher, and later his wife, has emphasized throughout their work together that the quality of the relationship between a couple is important and the attempted treatment of sexual problems without reference to this may be totally ineffective. (Belliveau and Richter, *Understanding Human Sexual Inadequacy*) Other therapists have often disregarded this and been busy treating symptoms without regard to the person who presents the symptom or to the social setting in which behaviour is defined as requiring a cure.

Sexual surgery

Though doctors in the West no longer cut out a woman's clitoris to change her mental condition, there are surgeons who operate on the clitoris, claiming that to remove its hood or to reconstruct a part of the vagina makes the clitoris more accessible to stimulation by the penis during intercourse and, therefore, produces better and more frequent orgasms. They claim that this fits with Masters and Johnson's teaching about the female orgasm and is directly derived from their research.

An American surgeon appeared on television who had performed this operation on 4,000 or 5,000 women wanting to improve their sex lives. He presented his wife, on whom he had also operated, to testify to the effectiveness of this surgery. Her orgasms during intercourse had previously been "random". Now she has them all the time.

Women with whom I have talked, have sought surgery because they believed that their vaginas were ugly and doctors have operated to trim and tidy the inner and outer labia and to detach the clitoris from its hood. The operation of episiotomy – the surgical incision of the perineum to enlarge the vagina during childbirth – has often been done on the grounds that having it sutured after delivery makes a woman's vagina tighter and intercourse, therefore, more exciting for her male partner. A doctor often sews her up a little smaller than before. In the USA obstetricians sometimes mention this with pride to their patients. They even call it "the husband's stitch".

Surgery is obvious because it mutilates and reshapes. Since sex therapy involves the mind and affects relationships, it may be thought relatively unimportant. Its results are less susceptible to measurement except in terms of frequency of orgasms before and after, yet, used inappropriately or done badly, it can be just as harmful, and ethically just as wrong, as unnecessary surgery.

Sex as a cure

Whereas the Victorians treated female sexuality itself as a disease, modern society puts heavy emphasis on sex as therapy. Not only is sexual activity a sign of health, but it is advocated as treatment.

Therapists sometimes claim that a major problem in helping someone is that they are distracted by their sexual partner. So sex surrogates may be used. "For patients who have no partner or a partner who is unwilling or unsuitable for participation in a treatment programme clearly the provision of a surrogate. . .is of utmost importance", Martin Cole writes. He goes on to say that "with a new partner high levels of arousal can be achieved more readily", and recommends sex with a stranger, because "there is no, or only a 'mini', relationship." ("The use of surrogate sex partners in the treatment of sex dysfunctions and allied conditions")

Group sex, sado-masochism, fetishism – anything goes, it seems, except celibacy. The person who enjoys being celibate is seen at least as potentially sick. The freaks and oddities are not those who engage in unusual sexual activities but those who aren't particularly interested in sex or who don't have sex. And the implication of this is that the person who is unhappy or depressed has only to find a partner and to get sexually active in order to be all right. Although many people do not think like this, many women, and men too, feel coerced into having casual sex. There are social and internalized pressures to use sex to "grow" and develop as a person, and the implication is that you are unlikely to be able to do this in a monogamous relationship and are much more likely to do so in multiple relationships.

Images of sex today

The "total woman", we are told, is permeated and radiant with sex, whatever her age. She thinks and breathes sex. And it is this that keeps her young, "feminine forever": "The elimination of menopause (through hormone replacement therapy) is perhaps the most important technical advance by which women may equip themselves for an enduringly feminine role in modern life." (Robert A. Wilson, *Feminine Forever*) (see pages 236–7 for more on this.) The woman who does not have orgasms is incomplete. Though she must not think of herself as frigid, she is "pre-orgasmic". If only she would try hard enough, orgasm is just round the corner and she can be cured.

Lest children grow up not enjoying sex to the full a psychiatrist advises mothers to produce a stimulating sex education for the young. Since a woman who does not enjoy looking at a penis is suffering from a condition which "reflects a long-standing inhibition of sexual response" (Alayne Yates, *Sex without Shame*), to avoid this, she claims, a mother should help her daughter by admiring the penises on Greek statues and illustrations in *The Joy of Sex*, and should give her a subscription to *Playgirl* magazine. The adolescent who lacks a "firm erotic foundation" needs to be told how to masturbate. The mother hands the girl a book on how to get orgasm "and offers to discuss it and to provide lubricants and mechanical devices". It is as if we had made sex obligatory.

There is a lot of talk today about the freedom of our sexuality as compared with the repression of sex in Victorian England. Foucault considers that, for the last three centuries, we have progressively been talking more and more about sex. We tell the story of the past, seeing Victorian sexuality as repressed and distorted in a style that suits us because it legitimates our present urgency to bring sex out, full-frontal, into the open.

The question I wish to pose is not: why are we repressed, but why do we say, with so much passion and so much rancour against our most recent past, against our present and against ourselves, that we are repressed? By what spiral have we arrived at affirming that sex is denied, showing ostentatiously that we hide it, saying that we silence it. . .? (Michel Foucault, *La Volonté de Savoir*, p. 16)

We should examine critically our society's much vaunted sexual "freedom" and "honesty" in terms of our own experiences as women. For a woman sex is much more than whether or not she is in a sexual relationship or whether or not she is having orgasms. It has to do with the way she expresses herself through her body, with her closeness with the bodies of her children and her friends, as well as lovers. It springs from her feelings about her body as it passes through all the changes of puberty, the ovarian cycle, childbearing and menopause, through grieving and loss and into old age. It is inextricably linked with the way she gives and receives love.

Genital sex is just one small part of this rich experience. Reducing sex to something limited to what happens to a clitoris is to drain from it much of what makes female sexuality exciting and alive with longing, tenderness, passion – and strength. It is time we reassessed widespread assumptions as to the overriding importance of genital sex in our lives.

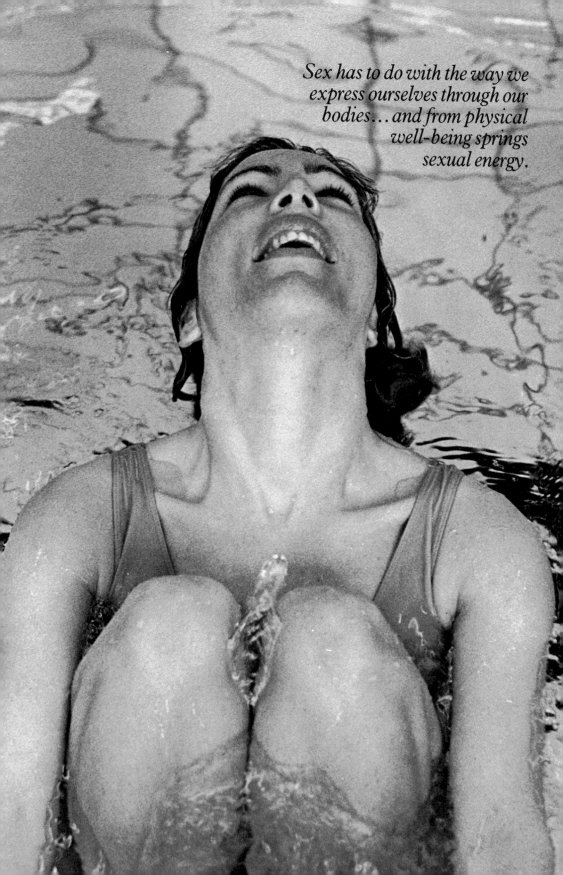

Sex has to do with the way we express ourselves through our bodies... and from physical well-being springs sexual energy.

Sexual ideologies

He slipped the ring on, smilingly looking into her eyes. He tilted up the oval face above the rose-petal blouse. 'Home is the sailor, home from sea, and the hunter home from the hill.' He reached her lips, and thereafter was only silence and ecstasy. (Essie Summers, *A Lamp for Jonathan*)

That is one view of sex – the romantic view. It is a very popular one. Sex is tinsel and stardust packaged as part of the romantic story. When his trembling lips touch hers, when his hands reach out to explore her reed-slim body, we know, or, rather, it is implied, that somewhere out of focus there is an enormous erection and that this great, gentle yearning brute of a man is about to take for himself. Ultimately the novelette romance is all about *possession*, a man having and owning a woman – for keeps. And a woman being safe in his arms for ever.

Behind the romantic myth

This, the romantic myth indicates, is why people get married. The goal is attained: the woman is held, contained, secured.

Falling in love, and trusting you will stay in love for ever and ever, is an essential ingredient of the romantic ethos that is part of our Western cultural heritage. It is inculcated in childhood, reinforced in the form of the pop idol as a girl grows up, and gets mistier round the edges in the love stories of popular fiction, ranging all the way from the romances published by Mills and Boon, written for an exclusively female readership, through to Barbara Cartland's tales of virtue rewarded, and all the other novels in which at the end the woman is enveloped in the male hero's arms – including even Cathy and Heathcliff in *Wuthering Heights*.

The power of this romantic view of sex is such that almost all the women who wrote to me about their experiences said that they would tell their daughters to wait for the right man to sweep them off their feet, and that then they would get married and live happily ever after. In fact, what these women were communicating to their daughters was usually not their own lived experience but a cultural myth. Another common theme is the taming of a wayward, headstrong girl. Jo in *Little Women*, the heroine of *What Katy Did* are among those who learn grace and gentleness, develop "feminine qualities" and submit to the better judgment of a man.

While women read romantic novels, men read pornography. While romance packages sex with love, fidelity and marriage, pornography packages sex with violence, possession and promiscuity. This means that women and men often have very different views of sex and what it is all about.

Romance and monogamy go hand in hand together. Even falling in love, marrying and then divorcing over and over again cannot, for many people, shatter the romantic ideal. In fact, serial monogamy in that way endorses the myth. Each time "it's for keeps"; each time "the right man at last!"

Regulating sexual relationships

Traditionally the concept of a woman's fidelity to one man lies in the organization of relationships to control inheritance of property in a patrilineal society. A man needs to know that he is the father of his children so that his sons may inherit his lands and other wealth. Only by restricting sexual intercourse to a properly sanctioned relationship between one man and one woman, or, in some countries, one man and a group of wives, can it be ensured that an inheritance is not passed on to some other man's son. Women are the property of social groups controlled by men and are valued because of their uterine potential. The ideology of romantic love obscures and legitimizes a political and economic system directed by men, in which, as in the majority of kinship systems all over the world, a woman is handed over in marriage by her father to a husband who then owns her body and can expect to use her reproductive capacity to continue his lineage. Underlying the glossy photographs and the fairytale glamour, this is the story of even those apparently most fortunate of women held up as an example to the rest of us by the media, like Princess Diana, filmstars and the wives of millionaires. Men are perceived in terms of their work and achievements. Women have a social role and identity merely because of their relationships with men, and the sexual tie is a key one in defining who a woman is.

Defining a woman

The men at whose disposal a woman's sexual and reproductive functions are put dictate her role in society. She is someone's wife or mother. Otherwise she is a prostitute or "loose woman" who has sexual relations with many different men. Or she may be a nun who is married to Jesus. In spite of changes in sexual fashions, women are still expected to "settle down" eventually, with a clearly defined sexual tie with one man. The "Cosmo girl" or "liberated" woman can enjoy varied sexual relationships for a few years, but by the age of 30 or so, even she has to watch out if she is not to be seen as on the road to becoming an "embittered old maid".

The limitations of romance

The ideology of romance is for many women a burden which subjects marriage and other sexual partnerships to intolerable strain and prevents couples acknowledging each other as human beings. The thrill of sex, the snatched romantic moments, are supposed to compensate for all the other feelings of being trapped and, for the woman, of having surrendered her autonomy and her very identity as an individual. Romance and sex together can serve as balm and band-aid in a relationship only for so long. There comes a time in most partnerships when there has to be more than that, more even than loyalty, if they are going to be able to grow together.

The romantic ideology also means that some women who do not really want to be monogamous at all are forced into explaining and apologizing for the fact that they are not tied to one man. They call it "looking for the right person" or "searching for love". Some feel that every sexual encounter must be justified in terms of "being in love", and convince themselves that each one-night stand is a great passion. This has been described as "love at first sex". (Jill Johnston, *Lesbian Nation: The feminist solution*) It means that sex cannot be enjoyed simply because it brings pleasure or as an element in friendship, but must always be elevated to be the seal set on love. The price of sex is seen as nothing less than a lifetime spent together in undying devotion.

Sexual liberation

The sexual revolution of the 1960s and 1970s was a reaction and challenge to all this romance. Alfred Kinsey produced his first report, *Sexual Behaviour in the Human Male*, in 1948 and this was followed, in 1953, by a study of women's sexuality, *Sexual Behaviour in the Human Female*. They kindled a public response that was part of a widespread change in attitudes to sex which now spread like a forest fire.

In the sexual liberationist philosophy sex is a drive that requires regular expression for healthy, fulfilled living. It is also a leisure activity – and an important one. We owe it to ourselves to turn on, tune in, drop out and let our hair down, to explore our sexuality, act out our wildest fantasies and pursue bigger and better orgasms. The sexologist, Albert Ellis, writing in 1969, said: "I would call the preservation of virginity an overt display of arrant masochism." (*The Journal of Sex Research*) According to the philosophy of sexual liberation, moral, religious or ethical considerations about sex are symptomatic of sexual repression or inadequacy. Women who are not particularly interested in sex, or who are celibate, are asked "What are you repressing?" Those who reject the "swinging chick" image are accused of frigidity, puritanism and prudishness.

Alex Comfort's *The Joy of Sex* was at the top of the bestseller list. A variety of primers drawing on the research of Masters and Johnson hit the bookstalls. There came the *Hite Report*, the *Cosmo Report* and a host of sex manuals to show women how to have better and more frequent orgasms. The way to get to know someone and to feel good about yourself was seen to be through sex and the recipe for social success was to surround yourself with warm, sexy people who shared your capacity for uninhibited sexual expression and fulfilment. For women it often seemed that going out and having intercourse with someone could be a statement of independence, that it was a powerful blow for freedom and equality with men. Commitment, promises, fidelity all carried with them the implication of being "just a housewife and mother", being taken for granted in the way that women saw that their own mothers had been by their husbands. A series of affairs with no ties, no illusions was a way of saying they were liberated.

The Pill and the IUD were seen by many as making intercourse "safe". Suddenly the old taboos had been lifted and, provided you did not get pregnant, everything was all right. One major disadvantage of more reliable contraception, however, was that women no longer had a legitimate way of saying "No". It was understandable that the threat of accidental pregnancy had scared many away from intercourse. But now a woman had actually to tell a man that she did not fancy him, or be sufficiently assertive to say that she did not want intercourse and face up to accusations of being labelled "narrow-minded" or even "frigid".

There are other problems with contraception too. Gradually at first, and then with startling rapidity, evidence mounted demonstrating dangerous side-effects of the Pill and the IUD (some are discussed on pages 184–7). The Pill may enable a woman to avoid pregnancy but can also shorten her life. The IUD may prevent the cell cluster implanting in the uterus but is also likely to cause pelvic

Sex is inextricably linked with the way we give and receive love…

infection and some women discover as a result that they can never have a baby after all.

Though fertility control was seen as a major issue in heterosexual behaviour, it proved to be by no means the only obstacle to free, untrammelled, spontaneous sexual relations. As men and women mixed and matched and coupled more and more, they carried with them infections which, though often dormant at first, flared up to produce irritation, sores and, sometimes, open lesions. New diseases were diagnosed and, to avoid overtones of Old Testament retribution for sin, the venereal diseases were rechristened "sexually transmitted diseases" (STD). We are experiencing the full impact of this only now. Thrush, herpes and the rest act as very efficient antaphrodisiacs.

There was a minefield of other problems with the sexual liberationist approach. It didn't take into account the very important and central place of morality or religion in many people's lives (it merely sneered at it) and it labelled people as sick for not having sexual relationships, just as, in the past, those who did have multiple sexual relationships had been labelled sick, "nymphomaniac" or "emotionally immature". And because the so-called sexual revolution was actually the *male* sexual revolution and gave men more access to women's bodies, sexual liberation legitimated male promiscuity, the male separation of body and emotions and the split between sex and caring. For many women it turned out to be a delusion and a con-trick. As one woman said: "I felt used and alienated in a notching up game."

One legacy of this period is that today women are beginning to ask searching questions about the place of sexual relationships in their lives. They are also asking whether they want to continue with those which may have been good in the past but from which the life has drained. Why am I doing this? Do I really want it? Is it just that it is expected of me?

Feminism

Feminism starts by exploring and questioning all those ideologies that have formed the bases of relationships between men and women. It examines, for example, what passes for male sexuality in our own culture – the desire to dominate. Feminists say this is no more "natural" than what is often seen as the female desire to submit passively.

Feminists are looking at sex in the context of history and ideology, at all the things women have been conditioned to think about sex and at conventional male and female roles in society. They feel that women need to look at themselves and work out what they really want in life and who they really are. They are concerned to break down barriers which separate women from each other and create a sense of sisterhood.

A feminist perspective on sex

Because feminists challenge commonly accepted norms, they are often lumped together with sexual liberationists. If they are against linking up with one man it is taken for granted that they must be promiscuous. If they are opposed to the institution of marriage, the conclusion is that they must be into a sexual free-for-all. The "liberated woman" has become a term descriptive both of feminists and of a woman who is seen by men as being "an easy lay".

Radical feminists, in fact, are saying something very different from the sexual liberationists. Sexual expression is for many one vital part of freeing yourself from the constraints of a male-dominated society. Psychiatrist Carmen Kerr, writing about women's orgasm, says: "For some women to break down their sexual inhibitions is a first, indispensable step in claiming power in respect to men, and ultimately the world". (Quoted in Eleanor Stephens, "The moon within your reach")

Sex, however, is not the *goal*. And where the liberationists say that sex is tremendously important for healthy functioning and personal fulfilment, feminists believe that it should be possible to incorporate sex into friendship rather than "falling in love" and restricting it to just one individual. Sex might be better seen simply as one way of relating to people. Thus sexual friendship takes the place of romance and exploitation (though it doesn't always work out this easily in practice). Sex is one element in caring and continuing relationships. It is not something that takes over a woman's life, nor the bait to lure her into marriage, but a loving expression of friendship.

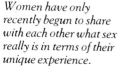

Women have only recently begun to share with each other what sex really is in terms of their unique experience.

Feminists stress the importance of friendship with other women. Many are critical of exclusive "couple" relationships which can become claustrophobic, and in which one partner may get very dependent on the other. These can form barriers between women, alienating them from one another.

Feminism makes a strong link between the way we think and how we behave, between the personal and political. Our most intimate, private thoughts and actions are statements about society and the way we see relations between men and women. On pages 81–3 you will see that sexual fantasies, for example, often vividly express male power and female submission.

Some feminists assert that a woman cannot be truly a feminist and continue to have sexual relations with men. The only "real" feminist is a lesbian. These women are "out on the frontier" (Linda Hurcombe, author of *Dispossessed Daughters of Eve*, personal communication) and their commitment is not to be envied by those of us who know from our own experience that marriage can be a loving and nurturing relationship. It can be difficult for a committed feminist to defend her decision to marry or to have sexual relations with men. And within the Women's Movement it is now those who are living with men who are "coming out of the closet" and defending the validity of their own personal experience.

For most of us there seems to be no choice about whether to be anything other than heterosexual, since we adapt to the dominant culture and values to which we have been conditioned since babyhood. But it is important that we all examine the social structures which dehumanize us as women and men and work to create relationships in which human beings can grow and which themselves nurture life.

Sex and language

The words we use about sex, and those we avoid using, reveal our attitudes to it. There is no way in which we can escape the expression of social values in language.

There is often a time lag between a dictionary definition of a word and the values that are attached to it when it is used in everyday life. Most editions of *The Oxford Dictionary*, for example, still define masturbation as "self-abuse".

Language and social control

All language is a powerful agent of social control. It not only colours our thinking but actually shapes our thoughts. Words we hear on the TV or read in our papers, words used casually in conversation and those which, though we do not express them aloud, mould our thinking, our feelings about and attitudes to what is happening around us. A "terrorist" is seen differently from a "freedom-fighter", though it may be one and the same person. We express different values when we say that someone is "queer" or "gay", a "nigger" or a "black".

If we are uncomfortable with a subject there is usually a range of terms we can use to avoid mentioning the offensive or difficult words connected with it. Because we do not want to talk about death in a way that upsets us or other people there are many euphemistic ways of saying that someone has died. Look at the inscriptions in a graveyard next time you pass. We talk about excretion in a similarly round-about way: we "spend a penny", "relieve" ourselves, "visit the bathroom" and so on. Many swear-words and insults deal with death and excretion directly: "drop dead!" and "shit!", for example.

Like these other highly emotive subjects, sex is a taboo topic that draws around it, like iron filings to a magnet, a number of euphemisms and swear-words. And, as with death and excretion, the only alternative to using coy and unspecific terms or crude language to talk about sex is medical terminology. Many of us are uncomfortable with all three options. Coy words can be really confusing. Talking about sexual intercourse as "sleeping with" or "going to bed with" is fairly harmless, but, because it is so vague, may bewilder the other person and leave them wondering what we are really talking about. One woman told me that her husband's only way of telling her that he wanted sex was to say, "I'll take a shower this evening." And that was the full extent of his sexual communication with her.

Many women feel that the "four-letter words" about sex (fuck, screw, bang, score and so on) are unpleasant. Because they are often used as insults, they seem inappropriate as descriptions of a warm, loving, tender sexual relationship. But there is more to it than this. These words also portray sex as an aggressive act performed by a male on a passive female. Since the words are often violent, they imply that the woman is harmed. So we are left with medical words. And because they are primarily the tools of anatomy and physiology, they cannot begin to express the wealth of feeling contained in sexual experience. They are often heavy, cumbersome terms whose proper place is the dissecting room or the laboratory and they never come alive to be anything other than a faint echo of real human emotions and relationships.

Word associations

We may be able to get closer to how we think about sex by looking at the way we use words and the associations that they have for us. To find out some of the meanings that words connected with sex have for you, take a large piece of paper and divide it into two vertical columns. In the left-hand column, write the following words, well spaced out, so that each stands alone: sex, love, clitoris, enjoy, wife, orgasm, penis, guilty, husband, need, sanitary pad, oral sex, nipple.

Then, very quickly, without stopping to judge your thoughts, write down in the right-hand column the first word or phrase that comes into your head as you read each of the words you have put in the left column.

Now look through your list of words. Do any of them surprise you? Think about *why* you have given the responses you have. How do they relate to your feelings about your body, your sexuality and the people who are closest to you?

Some women who have done this find that they have given opposites each time: "husband" for "wife", "hate" for "love" and so on. If you have done this it may be that you didn't have any ideas about these words, or you might have been avoiding thinking about what the words mean to you. Other women have felt that their responses were quite revealing. Pam wrote "masturbate" in response to the target word "guilty" and then talked about her feelings of "self-indulgence" in enjoying her own body.

Though the meaning of what you have written may not be immediately clear to you, notice those things to which you responded with really positive associations and those that produced negative words. Then think why this is. In response to the target word "clitoris", some women wrote "pearl", "rose", "warm", "wet", "soft", "lick", "stroke", whereas another wrote "nothing". Some women produced neutral or "medicalized" words like "pubis" or "vulva". You may react to these target words in a different way on another day, depending on your mood at the time.

Penetration: the predominant theme

One thing all words about sex have in common, the four-letter words, medical words and euphemisms, is that they include the idea of penetration of a vagina by a penis. You haven't really "made love" unless this has happened. Sex without penetration is considered to be "foreplay" or "petting". No matter how exciting sex is, or how many orgasms a woman has, the process is not complete without penetration. This use of language reflects and reinforces the idea that the goal of every mature sexual encounter should be penetration and orgasm. For example, some people find it difficult to imagine what lesbians can possibly do in bed without some kind of penis substitute.

Though many women enjoy the feeling of a full vagina and choose to enclose a penis, fingers or some other object during sex, others do not particularly like it. If women were free to choose, many might like to have sex with vaginal stimulation sometimes and other times without it. But there is not much choice because women and men both expect penetration to take place.

A woman who does not want to "go all the way" may be called a "cockteaser" (there is, incidentally, no similar word that applies to a man). A man who ejaculates before penetration is a "premature ejaculator". A woman who may have had every other sort of sexual experience, including orgasm, with another person, is still a "virgin" until she has been penetrated. Thus language is structured around the idea that every time a man and a woman have a full sexual relationship they must have intercourse. Otherwise, it is implied, there is something wrong with them.

We ought to look critically at this assumption. Mandatory penetration as the goal of every sexual act may be as boring and restricting as it would be if every sex act had to include oral sex, or was viewed as incomplete without a backrub. There are other words for sexual behaviour, like "going down" or "tossing off", but these activities are usually seen as "extras" to the main business of having sex – penetration.

So language is one important way in which our thinking about sex is socially controlled. Language is man-made and expresses men's views of women's bodies and sexuality. This means that women's feelings and experience remains unspoken, because it is, quite literally, unspeakable.

Body labels

There are, in fact, very few words for women's genitals (can you think of other words for the clitoris?), whereas there are a great many other terms for the penis, such as "prick", "tool", "dick", "weapon", "willy", "John Thomas", "cock" and so on.

Communicating is an important part of lovemaking...

The clitoris is such a tiny organ in the growing girl that she may have to depend on seeing it represented in a textbook in order to visualize it. Yet a girl growing up is often given diagrams in which the clitoris is not labelled, or even drawn. Much more prominent are the organs of reproduction: fallopian tubes, ovaries and uterus. So she is presented with a reproductive rather than a sexual view of herself. She usually learns the name for her clitoris much later than a boy learns words for his penis. And when she wants to talk about what she feels she will discover that there is a poverty of language to describe clitoral sensation. When what happens is discussed in books about sex it is almost invariably presented in terms of what occurs to the penis and is felt by a man during sexual arousal and ejaculation. The male body and male experiences are seen as the norm from which a woman's body and female experiences are derived. The male is the standard against which the female is judged. Because the clitoris can be stimulated it has, says Freud, "a male character". He even described the vagina as "an asylum for the penis". (Sigmund Freud, *Collected Papers*, vol. II).

When the penis is engorged it is said to be erect. When, however, the blood vessels in the clitoris fill with blood it is described as "congested", a word with connotations not only of passivity but of injury. The warm wetness of a sexually excited woman is called a vaginal "discharge" or "mucus" – both terms that may suggest a polluting flow of body fluids – or it is referred to as "lubrication" for the introduction of the penis, as if based on an engineering model.

The term "vagina" comes from the Latin for "sheath" or "scabbard". This male encoding represents the vagina as a passive receptacle awaiting penetration as a scabbard awaits a sword. If women had the power to name and give meanings, the images associated with the vagina might well be much more active, creative and strong.

Language and female body processes

Even the language we use to talk about an exclusively female experience, menstruation, is based either on men's perception of what is happening to us or on our own reaction to their perception. (P. Shuttle and P. Redgrove, *The Wise Wound*) The common description of it as "the curse" reflects a medieval view of menstruation as the curse of Eve, her lasting punishment for eating the forbidden fruit.

In many cultures menstrual blood is perceived by men as threatening their virility, potency, health, success at work and in battle and even their lives. So men must be protected by the withdrawal of women during menstruation. This may seem a far cry from how we behave in the West today, yet I remember that I used to take a note to school, two or three times a month if I could get it, saying I was "unwell", so could I be excused gym? The implication was that menstruating girls must draw back from normal activities because they were both vulnerable and unclean. The worst shame of all would be if they should accidentally reveal a spot of blood. Menstruation was secret, dirty and debilitating.

There is very little language to describe the physical and emotional sensations of childbirth. It has to be drawn from other experiences and is often defined in almost exclusively medical terms because that is the only language we have. The fallopian tubes are named after their male discoverer of the same name, and the tightenings of the uterus which take place in late pregnancy have to be called Braxton-Hicks contractions, perpetuating another doctor's name.

The body as sex object

Although women do not have the language to describe parts of their own bodies or their own sexual experiences, those areas of their anatomy that men enjoy looking at and handling are constantly referred to, and are important elements in, the social definition of the body as female. Men appraise women's bodies and make comments about their physical appearance: "Give us a smile, dear", "Look at those tits". No wonder we are self-conscious about how we look! Magazine articles tell us how to dress to catch a man and advertisements underline the message even more clearly: "If it was a lady it would get its bottom pinched"; "Underneath we are all lovable". There is a steady barrage of propaganda from men, and from the media, to remind us all the time that our bodies are objects for male consumption.

We may even find ourselves described as tit-bits or delicacies on offer to men, seen as plates of food – "cheesecake", "crumpet", "tarts", "a juicy piece", "a tasty bit", "sweetie-pie", "honey" or "sugar". On the rare occasions when men are described in terms of something to be eaten, the food is much less frivolous – "beefcake" or "hunks of meat".

Insults often refer to our sexual organs in slang terms – "cunt", for instance – or to a sexual activity engaged in by women, as for example "cock-sucker". To insult a man, a woman, usually his mother, is implicated. "Son of a bitch" reflects not on the man so much as on the woman who bore him. The insult "bastard" similarly reflects, in its original meaning, on his mother who "got herself into trouble" by conceiving an "illegitimate" child. But to insult a woman no man in her life need be implicated. It is simply suggested that she is a prostitute. There is a wide range of words for a sexually promiscuous woman: whore, trollop, tart, tramp, harlot, floosie, and so on. There are very few for men who use prostitutes and these mostly refer to those who control prostitutes, as for example, pimps. No word exists to describe a woman who functions in a sexually healthy and vigorous way. If a woman has more sex than is considered appropriate she is a "nymphomaniac". If she has less than is considered normal she is "frigid". But there is no female term corresponding to "virile" or "potent" in a man.

In many ways, then, language is either silent about women's bodies and sexuality or condemns them. Not only are our bodies described as tit-bits for men's delight and our own organ of pleasure left unreferred to, but sex is defined in terms of an aggressive act perpetrated upon a passive woman. The language insists that a woman wants and needs penetration in every sexual act. It is almost impossible to free ourselves from the preconceptions and prejudices with which language lumbers us. It can sometimes even be difficult to notice that these preconceptions are there because they are embedded in our culture and thinking.

2 OUR BODIES

Genital geography

In each woman the vagina, the shape formed by the lips of the vagina and the size and form of the clitoris are different, just as our faces are different. There is no one "right" way to be.

You can explore your genital organs with your finger and look at them in a mirror, too. We examine our faces in a mirror almost every day – sometimes several times a day. Think of the amount of time a woman spends looking at the reflection of her face, yet how little she spends getting to know her genitals by touch and sight.

When you have some quiet time alone, sit comfortably with a mirror and a small table lamp or torch, and take an opportunity to understand how you are constructed and the exact configuration of flesh folds and the relationship between the different organs and their relative sizes. You can aim to do two things: first to see exactly what is there and second to explore the feelings you get when you touch yourself in different parts of the genitals.

What you can see or touch

The curved slope in front, which in some women is hairy and in others is only lightly covered, is sometimes called the mound of Venus, a nice classical association. Hair may spread quite a long way up your abdomen and down the insides of your legs too. After the menopause this hair, together with the hair which grows under your arms, becomes much sparser in growth.

The outer lips

At the bottom of the curve, tucked behind it, you can feel the hard ridge of the pubic bone that forms the front of the pelvis. Move your hand down between your legs and you come to the hair-covered outer lips or labia, formed very irregularly, like the thick, fleshy lips of a tropical flower. They do not look neat and tidy like the drawings in many anatomy books.

The inner lips

When you part the lips you come to another set of lips inside. These are thinner, smooth and silky and they glisten with moisture, especially if you are sexually aroused. If you look closely you can see

41

through the outer tissue a network of veins. The inner lips often curve out and over the outer lips so that there is a lighter shaded strip projecting from within the outer labia, producing a shape like a conch shell.

These lips, like our mouths, do not form a standard cupid-bow shape. You may even think they are ugly. Perhaps it is significant that a woman sometimes spends a long time tidying up her mouth with lip-liner and lipstick, hoping to make it conform to an ideal and regular shape. With the vaginal lips we obviously cannot do this. Confronting them in a mirror they may look very "primitive", even savage, compared to the regularity we superimpose on a cosmetically decorated "public" face. Yet if you think of other forms in nature, you realize that these curved and convoluted petal shapes often occur in orchids and other flowers.

Notice the colours of the outer and inner lips, shades of violet, dusky pink, crimson, tawny brown, gold and blue. The outer lips are darker than the inner ones. They may be a deep brown or black, whereas the inner lips are in the pink and red shades of the spectrum. In pregnancy added blood supply in the pelvic area causes these colours to become more dramatic, the red shades to brighten.

After a baby is born, they change again and there is more blue. Following the menopause shades get paler again and the inside lips are softer, rosy grey – the colours often seen on a pigeon's breast.

The hymen

In childhood a hymen, a fine layer of tissue, closes the entrance to the vagina partially or completely. In some women this is strong and resistant and makes intercourse difficult. Very occasionally it needs to be cut under local anaesthetic. Usually the hymen is torn easily when a tampon is first inserted, when a woman slides her own finger in or sometimes as a result of sports that put the whole area under stress. There may be slight spotting of blood when this happens. Most women probably do not notice when the hymen is first torn, and there is no reason why it should be painful. If you look closely you may still see the frilled edges of the remaining hymen. The presence or absence of a hymen has nothing to do with being a virgin. Though the exhibition of a blood-stained sheet following the defloration on the wedding night forms a part of wedding ceremonies in some peasant communities in the Mediterranean, this is a purely ritual act and does not reflect physiological reality. (To get the blood a chicken is often slaughtered.)

THE LABIA

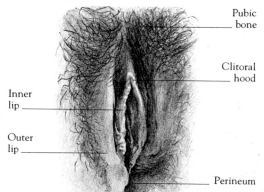

Pubic bone

Clitoral hood

Inner lip

Outer lip

Perineum

The formation of the labia varies widely in different women as can be seen below left and centre. You can look at your own labia with a mirror and, if necessary, a light, far left. The perineum, below right, has become distorted by the scar tissue from four episiotomies following childbirth.

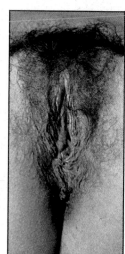

*It takes quiet, uninterrupted
time to find out
about yourself…*

The clitoris

The exquisitely sensitive clitoris lies at the upper end of the vagina between the folds of the labia, with its smooth, curved tip, the glans, projecting like a pea, looking a little like the kind of pink india-rubber that is sometimes stuck on the end of a pencil. There is often quite a thick fold of skin like a hood or wimple over the clitoris and you may not be able to see it till you pull your inside lips aside with your fingers.

Many women who have never before looked at the clitoris might think that men, at any rate, would have a fairly good idea of what it looks like. But men often say they have never actually seen the clitoris. Shere Hite, in her *Report on Male Sexuality*, said that most learned about the clitoris from books and their idea of it is derived from illustrations encountered in manuals of sex or biology textbooks. When they did describe it, however, those who had actually seen one produced some vivid and often tender descriptions: "a small nipple"; "a pearly little head"; "a tiny titty jelly bean"; "like a red pea coming out of its shell"; "like a baby clam – very ripe and inviting"; "a small leaf"; "a cross between a small shrimp and a small appendage with an excitable tip"; and even "like an ice cream cone in a raging storm".

If you slip a finger down a little further, to the entrance of the vagina, and press it inwards, you will be able to feel the root of the clitoris lying beneath the glans, the part you can see. When you squeeze it repeatedly you will notice that the glans plumps up in response to the stimulation.

Slide your finger in further still and press forward and you can feel a pad of thick, spongy tissue between your pubic bone and the urethra (the urethral sponge). Then press down and you will discover another pad of thick, spongy tissue between your vagina and your anus (the perineal sponge). These spongy tissues surrounding the vagina obviously protect it and when you are sexually excited they become engorged and thicker still.

SIDE VIEW OF THE CLITORIS AND ADJACENT ORGANS

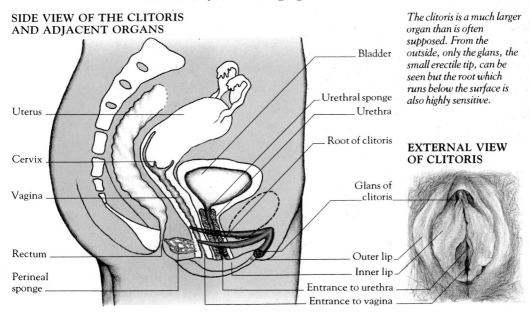

Uterus

Cervix

Vagina

Rectum

Perineal sponge

Bladder

Urethral sponge

Urethra

Root of clitoris

Glans of clitoris

Outer lip

Inner lip

Entrance to urethra

Entrance to vagina

The clitoris is a much larger organ than is often supposed. From the outside, only the glans, the small erectile tip, can be seen but the root which runs below the surface is also highly sensitive.

EXTERNAL VIEW OF CLITORIS

45

The cervix

The opening in the centre of the cervix, the os, is closed prior to ovulation.

The os gradually dilates and there is more mucus.

The flow of mucus is at its highest and the os fully open prior to ovulation.

The uterus

If you kneel and slip a finger deeper inside your vagina you may be able to feel the lowest part of the uterus, the cervix. If you have not yet had a baby it feels like the tip of your nose, except when you are ovulating, when it gets softer. If you have ever had a baby it feels more like a chin with a deep dimple, and when you are ovulating the dimple may feel like a soft, relaxed mouth.

This dimple is a small hole or slit in the centre of the cervix, called the os. At ovulation, the os opens and mucus from the cervix bathes the vagina, keeping it clean and slightly acid. This mucus is usually white but changes so that when a ripe ovum is waiting to be fertilized it is of a clear slippery consistency which encourages the movement of sperm up into the fallopian tubes where fertilization takes place. There is more and more mucus, until the day before you ovulate you feel really damp. After ovulation the quantity of mucus decreases. You have least mucus during a period and feel driest immediately after the period is over.

Some women like to use a speculum to examine their cervix and get to know how it looks when it is healthy and at different times in the menstrual cycle, and to learn about deviations from the normal. If you want to do this, you can buy a speculum so that you can examine yourself. Try to get hold of a plastic speculum, not a metal one. It is much easier, lighter and more comfortable to use, and also costs less. It is a kind of plastic "beak" which you insert into your vagina when it is closed. Once it is inside you open it and the two halves separate the walls of your vagina so that you can see inside, using a mirror. It will be easier if you use a torch but shine it on to the mirror, not on to the cervix, to get the best view. (A plastic speculum can be ordered from Sisterwrite, see page 312.)

You will not be able to feel the main part of your uterus. It is shaped like a pear or fig, with the stalk end tilted down into your vagina. Sometimes this "stalk" is tilted forwards, sometimes backwards. It is often said that a backward tilted uterus makes it more difficult to conceive, but this is not so. The uterus is an active, contracting organ from the first menstruation at least until the menopause when, as many post-menopausal women know from experience, it sometimes contracts.

The uterus is not just a bag hanging there, but a living network of muscle fibres which, though not under our conscious control, tightens and releases regularly in response to certain stimuli and at special times within the menstrual cycle. The cramps which are often felt during a period are simply tightenings of the uterus. When you have an orgasm your uterus probably contracts then, too. Sometimes it goes on contracting after an orgasm, and occasionally this causes a painful abdominal cramp. During pregnancy the uterus contracts regularly as a kind of rehearsal for the birth. The uterus also contracts when the breasts, and particularly the nipples, are stimulated. There is a connection between the uterus and the nipples and any woman who has breast-fed knows that when a baby is sucking steadily in the first few days after birth it is almost as if the mouth was pulling an invisible string in the uterus, producing "after-pains". These contractions tone the uterus so that it quickly returns to its previous shape and size.

PELVIC FLOOR MUSCLES

The pelvic floor muscles are shaped like a figure of 8 around the vagina, urethra and anus. When the upper circle, about half-way up the vagina, is contracted, the circle of fibres changes from an "O" shape to an almond shape. Deeper layers of muscle support the bladder and uterus and when they are contracted you can feel the pressure against your bladder and cervix. The muscles are rich in nerve endings which record pleasurable sensations so that contracting and releasing them sometimes produce sexual arousal.

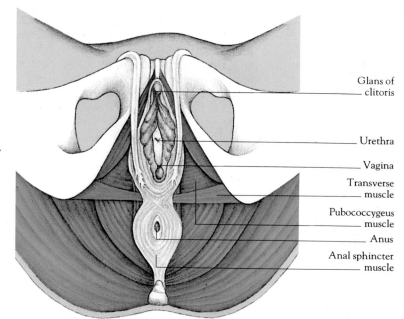

Glans of clitoris

Urethra

Vagina

Transverse muscle

Pubococcygeus muscle

Anus

Anal sphincter muscle

Pelvic floor muscles

When you put your fingers inside your vagina you will find that you can squeeze them with the muscles surrounding the vagina, about half-way up inside, and so discover the position of your pelvic floor muscles. If you are not quite sure whether you have located them you can feel these muscles working by squeezing as if you wanted to prevent urine flowing. Those you can feel with your fingers are the ones nearest the outside. There are others further up inside that you will not be able to locate with your fingers.

During orgasm these muscles contract at 0.8-second intervals, pressing on the clitoris, the vaginal tissues and the inner layers of the muscles that support the bladder and uterus. You can also tighten the muscles deliberately in a steady rhythm to increase your sexual arousal.

Pelvic floor muscles form a figure 8 round the vagina and anus. They support everything in the bony pelvic girdle and, at one remove, everything in the abdominal cavity. They are probably the most important muscles in a woman's body. The biggest muscle, which is called the pubococcygeus, sweeps across from the bone forming the front of the pelvis to the one at the very bottom of the spine. There are layers of muscles like coiled springs surrounding the urethra (the tube leading from the bladder) as well as to the vagina and to the anus.

Changes in shape and size

The structure of the female genital organs, however, is like a theatre in which is enacted a dramatic cyclical pattern of change which starts from the time just before a woman's very first period until the end of the menopause. And even after that, the vagina and uterus undergo dramatic changes as the woman becomes sexually aroused and experiences orgasm.

This is largely because many of these organs are constructed with a good deal of "slack", like a very loose weave, pleated muslin dress,

CHANGES IN THE UTERUS AND VAGINA

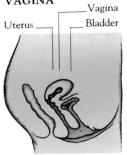

Vagina
Uterus
Bladder

Unaroused state

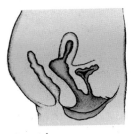

Aroused state

The ovaries

and also because of the quantity of blood vessels, like rivers with hundreds of tributaries, that etch a wide band surrounding all the genital organs.

In response to thoughts and feelings the folds of convoluted tissue which surround the vagina can spread and open out so that the whole shape of the vagina changes. One of the most significant things about the female genital organs is that they are pliable and able to change their size and form in this way.

The rich network of blood vessels criss-crossing the outside of the vagina, the uterus, the fallopian tubes and ovaries means that increased or reduced blood flow to these organs also results instantaneously in a change in their shape and size.

When we blush, feel self-conscious and go pink, our faces do not radically change their shape. The equivalent flow of blood to the vagina, however, results in a plumping up and opening which is more like a bud bursting into full flower.

Examining anatomic structure gives very little idea of the immense variations and changes of which a woman's genital organs are capable. The entire process, throughout life, is one of ebb and flow, folding and unfolding, opening and closing.

This happens not only in the parts where obvious changes can be felt with your fingers – the lips, the vagina and clitoris – but deep inside – in the uterus, the fallopian tubes (sometimes called oviducts) and the ovaries. There is no other part of our bodies where such enormous changes take place without causing damage.

The ovaries are like egg-producing factories. Each ovary is about the size and shape of an almond in its shell. If one is not working, the other usually takes over its function. During the part of her life when she has a menstrual cycle, a woman produces a ripe egg, an ovum, every month – usually about two weeks before her next menstrual period. The extraordinary thing is that though the ovum bursts out of the ovary through a swelling 1.5 cm across (roughly the size of a hazelnut), no wound is produced, no scar is left by ovulation, and it happens again and again and again, without causing injury. In the average woman's reproductive cycle this may occur over 300 times.

Pelvic floor potential

The tone and vitality of the pelvic floor muscles is very important to a woman's sex life. If they are slack and you do not know how to use them, you are missing out on one whole aspect of sexual experience – that involving the deep layers of muscle that surround the vagina and rectum and press against the uterus and bladder.

An easy test to discover whether your pelvic floor muscles are strong is to interrupt a stream of urine and see if you can stop it completely. Then let urine flow again. Then interrupt it again and so on. If you can do this they are in good condition. Even so, you can go on from there to learn how to use them more actively. There are ways of exercising these muscles to give you added sexual pleasure, and perhaps also to delight a partner.

Movements to increase sexual pleasure

The first movement is very simple. It is the vaginal kiss. Imagine a ring of muscle fibres about half-way up inside your vagina and tighten it. The "O" shape will change to a smaller almond shape. Hold it for a few seconds and then release. We often do this spontaneously when making love. During orgasm this movement occurs at split-second intervals as a sequence of rapid vaginal kisses. Now imagine a small, soft fruit – the size of a cherry – inside the circle of muscles and use them as if you were chewing and eating the fruit. You will probably find that you are using the muscles of your mouth too. Then "swallow" the fruit with a smooth movement as if you were drawing it into your uterus. Rest a few seconds and then "eat" another piece of fruit. And rest again. You may find this quite tiring at first, so allow for regular rest times.

Then imagine a much larger soft fruit – a peach or apricot perhaps – with a smooth, velvety skin. With your pelvic floor muscles, "scan" the whole curved surface of this imaginary fruit in a sweeping, stroking movement. This is a much slower, larger movement than in the previous exercise.

Now imagine that the fruit is crushed and the juices flowing from it. Slowly suck in the juice with your muscles. Again, you may find that you are making similar movements with your lips, mouth and throat. And now rest.

As you have been doing this you will have realized that you were contracting not only the muscles of the vagina but also those which encircle the rectum, anus and urethra. When you tighten the vaginal muscles the others tighten too. This is normal. The muscle fibres are all interconnected, so that when you firmly contract any part of the pelvic floor other parts automatically contract as well.

Taking it gently

When a muscle is not strong enough to cope with a sustained contraction it starts to tremble. This may have happened to you with some of the longer, firmer contractions. This is why it is a good idea, if your muscles are not well toned to start with, to practise light, short movements at first and to build up activity gradually. When a muscle is contracted hard the flow of blood through it is reduced and hence its oxygen. When it is released the blood flows through faster. So when you deliberately contract and release in a dance-like movement you increase the oxygen supply to the muscle and avoid straining it.

In lovemaking other muscles work with the pelvic floor and become caught up in the same interplay of movement. Muscles connected with one's breathing are affected, so that when you contract and release your pelvic floor you are probably also sometimes catching your breath in little gasps. You may spontaneously squeeze your thighs or press your buttocks together. This has the effect of further gripping the hand or penis.

When you are very excited pelvic floor movements spread to whole body movements. The most characteristic of these is a movement in which the pelvis rocks forwards and backwards. When your pelvic floor is contracted you tend to rock your pelvis forward, press down the small of your back and flatten your abdominal muscles. When the pelvic floor muscles are released the lower back is slightly hollow and the abdominal muscles relaxed.

The pelvic rock

Lying on your back with your knees drawn up and feet flat on the floor, tighten your pelvic floor muscles, press your buttocks together and also press the small of your back against the floor, then release your pelvic floor and all the muscles of your lower back and abdomen. Let the tightening and release flow right through the whole pelvic area. Do this about 10 times.

You may have noticed that other muscles get involved in this movement, too: shoulders, hands, muscles of the face and feet, for example. Now let all these other muscles join in the activity and *exaggerate* the movement. Contract the muscles of your pelvis and anything else you want to contract. Then release and contract and release and contract and so on. But all the time let what is happening flow from the activity of the pelvic floor. Let the pelvic floor be your pacemaker. Then relax completely for a few moments and think of your vagina being soft and warm.

This is one way of "waking up" a pelvic floor that is not tuning you into sex with enough excitement.

The lift

The best all-round exercise for toning the pelvic floor muscles is the lift. Think of your pelvic muscles as a lift in a building with five floors. You are going to gradually tighten the muscles as if the lift were moving first from the ground up to the first floor (remember to go on breathing!) and then go to the second floor. By the time you reach the third floor you will already feel a good deal of pressure against your bladder. Now tighten and pull the muscles up even more. (Don't try and do it with your shoulders.)

Contract the muscles still further and bring the lift up to the fifth floor. Hold for four or five seconds and then go down, little by little, till you reach the ground floor again. Now finish by going back up to the first floor so that you complete the exercise with a toning action.

This exercise is best done daily whenever you go up and down stairs or in a lift, if you have to wait at the supermarket checkout or for the traffic lights to change, and in those boring parts of the day when you are not getting anywhere with anything else! If you do this exercise regularly over a period of six weeks the result will be a general toning of the pelvic floor muscles and an increase in their natural vitality.

Hormones

As chemical messengers in the blood stream, hormones play an important part in sexual maturation, sexual arousal and the physical changes that go with it, and in reproduction. Hormones have, however, an even more fundamental role. Like the nervous system, and in partnership with it, they have the task of keeping the organism developing and functioning as an entity, right through our lives. Together with the nervous system, they link up different parts of the body, co-ordinating them into a whole, making us individuals and not just a set of disconnected organs. They span the invisible space between mind and body and without them activity could not be organized.

The endocrine system

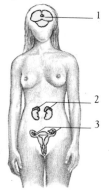

SOURCES OF HORMONES
1 Pituitary gland
2 Adrenal glands
3 Ovaries

Hormones are secreted by the endocrine glands. These glands keep our bodies working at a normal rate and level. Some are made up of just a few cells. Others, like the thyroid and pituitary glands, can be clearly seen without a microscope. Glands may function as long as we live or they may have a temporary existence. The egg follicle of the ovary, for example, and the placenta which is the tree of life for a developing fetus, are both temporary endocrine glands, while the pituitary gland, at the base of the brain, is a permanent gland.

Some hormones, such as those secreted by the thyroid gland in the neck, affect every cell in the body. Others serve specific organs. Ovaries secrete oestrogen which has a specific action on a woman's genital system and breasts, though it also maintains the health of the skin, mucous membranes and other body tissues.

How the ovaries work

Ovaries manufacture the hormones oestrogen and progesterone. These are both steroids: hormones derived from cholesterol. All steroids can be changed into each other by the agency of enzymes – soluble proteins produced by living cells to act as catalysts.

SEQUENCE OF OVULATION

1 *Follicles, like little bumps, appear on the ovary. Some of the bumps become larger and the outer wall of each follicle thickens.*

2 *One of the follicles grows larger still, and bursts to release the ovum.*

3 *The fringed end of the fallopian tube curls round the ovary and wafts the ovum into the tube.*

4 *The walls of the ruptured follicle collapse and the cells accumulate a yellow pigment called lutein. This becomes the corpus luteum which produces hormones.*

5 *The tube's muscular contractions squeeze the ovum along and fine hairs called cilia waft it into the uterus.*

6 *The ovum comes to rest for a few days in the tube. Here it may be met by sperm.*

7 *Fertilized or not, it is then propelled into the uterus. If fertilized, the cell cluster implants itself in the lining of the uterus. If not, the lining breaks down and the ovum leaves the uterus with the menses.*

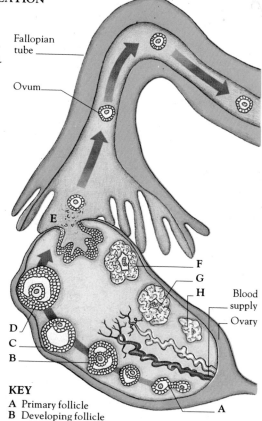

Fallopian tube

Ovum

E

F

G

H

Blood supply

Ovary

D

C

B

A

KEY
A Primary follicle
B Developing follicle
C-D Follicle approaching maturity
E Follicle ruptures to release ovum
F-G Corpus luteum forms in place of burst follicle
H Decaying corpus luteum

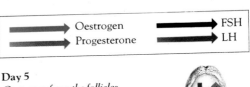

→ Oestrogen	→ FSH	
→ Progesterone	→ LH	

THE MENSTRUAL CYCLE

The menstrual cycle is controlled by hormones whose output is controlled by a special part of the brain, the hypothalamus. This sends a chemical message to the pituitary gland, which regulates growth and metabolism.

Day 1 to 4

Follicle stimulating hormone (FSH) travels from the pituitary gland to the ovaries where it creates a chemical change in the follicles which make egg cells. As these grow they manufacture oestrogen.

Day 5

Oestrogen from the follicles, too, passes into the bloodstream and is carried to the pituitary gland. Once oestrogen has reached a certain level the pituitary secretes less FSH and starts to produce luteinizing hormone (LH).

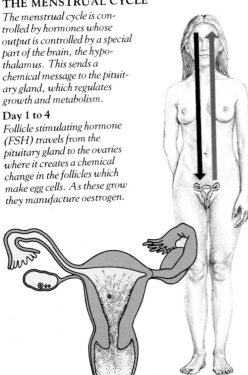

Day 14

LH flows into the blood stream and travels to the ovary where it stimulates the growth of one follicle. The ripening follicle then releases an egg – the ovum. It bursts out of the follicle like a pea out of a pod and is sucked into the fallopian tube. This is ovulation. The empty follicle turns into the corpus luteum or "yellow body" and starts to manufacture another hormone, progesterone, as well as oestrogen.

Day 28

After 7 days the ovum has reached the uterus. When the pituitary records a high level of progesterone in the body it triggers a shut-down mechanism and LH is no longer produced. Without LH, the corpus luteum withers and disintegrates. When the level of progesterone is lowest menstruation occurs. After a couple of days of bleeding the pituitary starts to secrete FSH all over again and a new menstrual cycle begins.

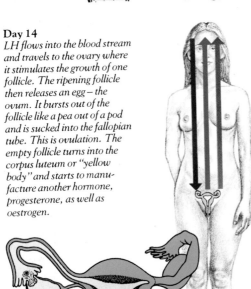

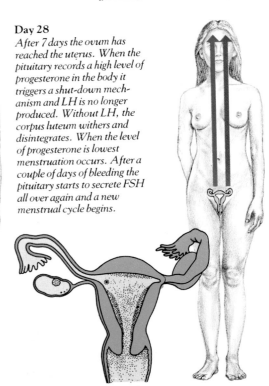

Oestrogen plays a major role in a woman's body in all the physical changes of puberty, menstruation and pregnancy. It is produced every month by the ripening egg follicle and levels change at different times in the cycle.

Progesterone is also secreted in a monthly rhythm. It is important in ovulation, the rebuilding of the lining of the uterus when a period is over and in enriching the wall of the uterus so that it offers a nourishing "broth" for a fertilized ovum to feed on.

At the end of a menstrual period the oestrogen level rises. It reaches its peak just before ovulation. Oestrogen stimulates the cervix to secrete mucus which is at first thick, sticky and opaque, but which gradually changes to become thin, slippery, clear and stretchy, like raw egg white. When mucus is like this it allows sperm to swim easily through up into the cervix, and from there into the uterus and fallopian tube.

After ovulation the level of oestrogen drops steeply. Progesterone thickens the mucus again to form a plug in the cervix until the next period starts. With menstruation, levels of both oestrogen and progesterone drop. Lacking hormonal support, the surface of the uterine lining disintegrates and is discharged with the menses.

The contraceptive pill works in three ways. It suppresses ovulation. It prevents the entry of sperm into the uterus by thickening the mucus. And it prevents implantation of the cell cluster by changing the lining of the uterus. The oestrogen-progestogen pill (see page 188) works mainly by suppressing ovulation. The mini-pill works mainly by changing the mucus so that sperm cannot penetrate it and also by preventing implantation.

Medical books usually take a 28-day cycle as the norm. You can be perfectly healthy and have a cycle which is of a quite different pattern. If you are under psychological stress or not having good enough nutrition your cycle may change dramatically. When you come off the Pill it may be about a year, sometimes even longer, before your cycle develops a regular pattern again.

Changes in the vaginal mucus

Natural secretions keep the vagina moist and clean, and you can become aware of where you are in your own menstrual cycle by getting to know the state of the mucus. In the first days after a period has finished there may be very little mucus and you feel that the vagina is dry. This usually lasts five to seven days. Then a thick, non-stretchy mucus starts to flow from the cervix.

As the oestrogen rises the mucus changes to become watery and stretchy. The vagina feels slippery and wet. You may notice that there is glistening mucus on your pants. When you take some between a thumb and forefinger it can stretch up to 10 centimetres. Occasionally it is pinkish because of the presence of blood. This is highly fertile mucus. Ovulation occurs at the time when there are copious quantities of this type of mucus.

The mucus then gets thick and sticky for a day or two and this is followed by a run of dry days till the next period begins. Some women notice a thickening in the mucus just before a period comes. You may have cycles in which no ovum ripens, or you may ovulate more than once in a cycle. The general pattern, though, is that an ovum becomes ripe at three- to six-week intervals.

By exploring sensations of touch you can discover more about your own sexual feelings…

Genital response to touch

Most of us develop a fairly clear idea of what we like and don't like to eat and don't mind saying that we hate pears or oysters, quite like porridge or enjoy fresh raspberries and cream best of all. We probably have equally strong sexual likes and dislikes, but many of us feel inhibited about expressing them or find it difficult to put these things into words, or have general ideas, but cannot be specific about sexual feelings.

When you know how you are constructed, go on from there to begin to explore the sensations touch gives in different parts of your genitals. Choose a place where you can be quite alone and unhurried. Use a mirror and torch again if these help you, though they are not really essential.

The pubic mound

Start with the pubic mound and gradually trace the whole area lightly with one or two fingers. Then do the same thing using pressure. Then alternate between light stroking and pressing. Decide if there are any parts of the pubic mound where you prefer light touch to pressure or vice versa. When you stroke, does the direction of the stroking affect the quality of the sensation? Take your time over this.

The outer lips

Go on to the outer lips. Do exactly the same, exploring different kinds of touch, varying the direction in which your fingers move. Observe the different sensations you get when you cover a small or large area. Experiment with varying speed of touch using some feather-light, darting movements and then some much longer strokes. Feel how it is when you use your whole hand or the side of your hand rather than your fingers.

The clitoris

Now slip a finger up to the clitoris and notice the different sensations of touch on different parts of the clitoris. Observe how touching the tip produces a different effect from touching the base. The clitoris is richly equipped with nerve endings. Sometimes it can become *too* sensitive, so that continued touch is irritating. Notice what happens when you move your fingers in different directions, try various kinds of touch and observe the effect of rubbing as distinct from stroking. Experiment with continuous movement as compared with intermittent touch. How would you describe what you have learnt?

Men sometimes think of the clitoris as a "magic button" which only has to be pressed or rubbed to produce instantaneous arousal. For most women there is more to becoming sexually excited than that. The clitoris can also be stimulated indirectly by touch or pressure against the inner lips. This causes movement in the part of the lips which connects with the clitoral hood and the base of the clitoris. Touch the inner lips and notice the location and kind of touch that produces a clitoral response.

Another misconception often held by a sexual partner is that the most effective technique is to use friction against the *tip* of the clitoris. This can become painful. Sometimes it is merely boring and your lover might as well be polishing silver. If you have discovered that the base of the clitoris is especially responsive, a partner may need to be told about this. Indirect routes to clitoral stimulation can be more effective than direct attack.

The buttocks and anus

Then touch your buttocks, moving your hands to different parts of them and trying different kinds of touch. Slip a finger between the cleft of your buttocks and part them. Observe the effect of touch around and over the anus when you press.

The perineum

The part between the anus and the vagina is known as the perineum. Explore the effects of touch there. If you have had a baby in the last year or so, especially if you have had an episiotomy (a cut), there may be a tender area which feels particularly vulnerable and which may hurt. It is important that your partner knows this too. When you slip your finger inside your vagina, press firmly and notice how the angle at which your finger is pressing affects the sensations in this tender area. If it is painful, experiment with varying the angle of your finger until there is no pull on these tissues. It is important for a sexual partner to know this too.

You can experience the effects of touch not only by using your hand, but also by tightening and releasing muscles around your vagina, urethra (the tube leading from the bladder) and rectum to produce different kinds of pressure on these parts of your body.

The urethral sponge

The urethral sponge lies between the front wall of the vagina and the urethra and expands with blood during sexual arousal. It was first described by Ernst Graffenburg, though he did not give it this name. It is one of those nameless parts of the woman's body which we often do not know about simply because we have no language for it. Now it has been popularized as "the G-spot". (Alice Kahn Ladas, Beverly Whipple and John D. Perry, *The G-Spot*) Some women spend time searching for a special magic spot, but, in fact, it is simply this little cushion on the anterior wall of the vagina. And every woman has it.

Graffenburg himself wrote about it as a specially sensitive area "along the course of the urethra . . . surrounded by erectile tissue" and went on to say: "the most stimulating part is located at the posterior urethra, where it arises from the neck of the bladder." (Ernst Graffenburg, "The role of the urethra in female orgasm")

This spongy area is particularly swollen at and immediately after orgasm. Kinsey and his team only discovered areas of erotic arousal which responded to light touch in very small areas because to test sexual reactions they used soft-tipped sticks like cotton buds. Firm pressure is needed against this sponge. But even under these conditions Kinsey remarked that there was an area "on the upper wall of the vagina just inside the vaginal entrance" which he considered was sensitive in some women. (Kinsey *et al.*, *Sexual Behaviour in the Human Female*)

The fanfare about the G-spot which set women looking for it as the key to sexual fulfilment was the claim that women, too, could ejaculate in orgasm, that it was pressure on "the G-spot" that triggered this, but that only an élite minority could do it. The liquid which is produced – just a few drops – is not urine, may be colourless or milky and appears to change its consistency at different times in the ovarian cycle. Some gynaecologists are sure that it must be urine and women who experience it are often anxious that it is. Others say that it is simply the normal vaginal lubrication of a sexually aroused woman. Because it spurts out during orgasm, the authors of *The G-Spot* assert that it cannot be simply vaginal. But they also add that they have observed that "female ejaculation occurs mostly in women with strong pubococcygeus muscles". One explanation of female "ejaculation" could, therefore, be that a sexually excited woman with a vagina which is copiously lubricated shoots out her own lubricant as a result of the powerful, rhythmic contractions of her pelvic floor muscles.

The perineal sponge

The pad between the vagina and the rectum gets larger in the same way when a woman is sexually aroused. Concentration on the "G-spot", as if its discovery promised ecstasy, could mask the importance for some women of this other spongy pad, too. Many women enjoy stimulation of the anus and pressure against the posterior wall of the vagina and the lower rectum during lovemaking. Maybe this "magic" spot will be heralded in yet another book as the key to female sexual fulfilment!

When fingers, tongue or penis are introduced into the vagina during lovemaking pressure is usually produced against both the urethral and perineal spongy areas. This is one reason why women may enjoy penetration. Women's sexuality is not located "in" the clitoris or the "G-spot" any more than it is located in the back of the neck. A woman who is paralysed from the waist down may still have strong sexual feelings. A Sudanese woman who has suffered the mutilation of clitoridectomy and infibulation (having the clitoris excised and the labia sewn together so that only a small hole remains for urine and menses) can still become sexually aroused and – though this might seem incredible given the importance of the clitoris – may experience orgasm.

Genitally mutilated women who have had sexual relationships before marriage tell me that they have sometimes had anal intercourse until the ritual defloration takes place. In these cases, the focus of sexual excitement is shifted to the perineal sponge. It seems that women who have had clitoridectomy and infibulation are aroused only when this area is stimulated. This must make us think again about the emphasis that today, in the West, is put on the clitoris as the sole organ of sexual arousal and the only means of reaching orgasm.

It seems that, in fact, women are extraordinarily adaptable, and terrible as it is to cut out the clitoris of a little girl, there are other parts of the genitals which can then be developed so that a woman experiences intense sexual arousal and climax.

To tell a woman that everything depends on her having a clitoris in working order and that all sexual pleasure stems from it, may be just as restricting as when, in the past, women were taught that the only "real" orgasm is a vaginal one. We need to explore our feelings and to learn from our own direct experience what is possible for each of us, rather than simply limiting our understanding to what scientific research teaches us is possible.

3 FEELINGS

Sexual rhythms

Though many women expect to be more easily aroused when they are ovulating, because this is what they are told they will experience, most of those who have told me about their sexual feelings describe peaks of desire immediately before and during menstruation, with a second, less pronounced, peak at ovulation.

Menstruation

During a period many women find it difficult to cope with their heightened sexuality. "I am aroused far more easily," Annie says, "and not only from touch. I find myself aroused all day without any help from my boyfriend". She starts to feel "tense and sexy" a few days before and "thinks of nothing else" by the end of her period.

Women often express surprise at the increase of libido in the middle of menstruation. "It seems irrational", one says, "that I'm interested in sex then." Another comments that "There doesn't seem to be any 'biological logic' behind it." We are so conditioned to provide a reproductive justification for arousal that some women are not even aware that they are usually sexually excited at this time until they stop to think about it and it is only when asked about sexual rhythms that they realize this pattern exists.

When the flow is unusually heavy a woman is less readily stimulated, probably because she is uncomfortable and preoccupied with not soiling clothes and bedding. But even women who have considerable blood loss may enjoy intercourse more at the beginning and the end of menstruation, perhaps because there is natural lubrication even before localized stimulation occurs.

One element in sexual excitement for some women is that they feel they should not have sex during a period: "I want sex because I know I can't have it." For many women there is a prohibition which has all the force of taboo on intercourse during the flow. Others just say that it is "too messy" or "doesn't feel right". Many say their partners are put off by menstruation and are "disgusted" or "nauseated" at lovemaking then. One woman says that even though she feels "randy" right through her period her husband "has always been queasy about blood", so she masturbates then. Women who use the contraceptive cap seem to cope most easily with this, since it acts as a barrier to and container for menstrual blood and can be removed after intercourse. Many couples think of sex as analogous with penetration and that not having intercourse means ruling out all lovemaking during a period.

When a woman feels especially sexy during her period but feels she should not have intercourse, tension tends to build and she is then likely to be more readily aroused in the week *following*: "I am really randy immediately after a period. It's the days of enforced abstinence that do it." "I know I can't enjoy sex during this time for fear of mess. The thought of no sex for four days is like torture. I just can't stop thinking about when I can resume it."

Pre-menstrual tension

Although sexual arousal usually starts two or three days before the period, severe pre-menstrual tension reduces libido and often makes a woman feel she cannot stand being touched during that week. Women say they get "terribly ratty", argumentative, have headaches, feel bloated and if intercourse occurs it may be very painful. Some are particularly aware of a swollen abdomen or enlarged, tender breasts. Others just find it difficult to relax so that they can enjoy lovemaking during this time. Taking vitamin B6 tablets sometimes helps this condition and may make all the difference not only to your general feeling of well-being, but also to your capacity for sexual arousal.

For *mild* pre-menstrual tension has the opposite effect and is associated with heightened sensuality and increased skin sensitivity, especially of the breasts, which respond to the lightest touch. Some women also experience more feeling deep inside the vagina at that time. This does mean, however, that the partner has to adapt sexual techniques and be responsive to the woman's greater tenderness. Penile thrusting in the week before a period, as well as during it, can be painful. The cervix may be especially sensitive and some women say that in spite of feeling aroused they "hold back" or "want to take things more gently". We often take it for granted that women understand each other and that none of this applies to lesbian lovers. This is not necessarily so. Women, too, need to be sensitive to each other's ovarian rhythms and to realize that a partner will not always want the same kind or degree of stimulation. The border line between feeling irritable and over-reacting to stimuli — picking quarrels and smacking the children — and being acutely responsive to sexual stimulation is a narrow one.

Other women feel luxuriously sensuous and dreamy and would lie in bed all day making love if they could. One woman comments that she wants extra sugar in her diet then, is "totally lethargic" but very sensuous and organizes her work around her cycle. If you experience these kinds of psycho-sexual arousal, the few days before menstruation can be an exciting time, if the setting is right and the lover considerate and tender.

Ovulation

The second peak, that about 16 days before the start of the next period, is when ovulation usually occurs and when fertility is greatest. It is a common experience for sexual urges to build up to the day of ovulation and then subside gradually. Some women who

LIBIDO AND THE MENSTRUAL CYCLE

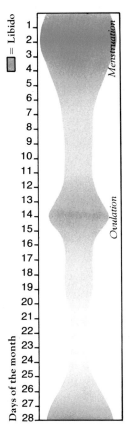

do not feel aroused during menstruation may only experience this one peak. It seems to occur especially with those Jewish women who observe religious prohibitions against any contact with a man during and immediately following menstruation. One Orthodox Jewish woman said to me, her face shining at the thought, that after the ritual cleansing bath she felt overwhelming desire for her husband and "every time I come to him as a bride." The same thing happens when a woman is longing to conceive and the thought of making a baby gives special meaning to lovemaking. With some women this means that libido is greatly reduced at other times of the month: "I am only interested in sex for those few days. I don't want it unless it is my fertile time, and then I think of nothing else." Another woman says: "I tried desperately to get pregnant for a year and literally dragged my husband to bed to conceive. I always felt down the week before my period was due because I knew that it was another month wasted." It is hardly surprising that a woman who very much wants a baby is not sexually aroused during menstruation, which each time is like a little death.

Women who are avoiding intercourse during and immediately after ovulation because they have an unreliable method of contraception or are using the rhythm method, may find it inconvenient and frustrating that just when they reach a peak of desire intercourse is forbidden. But this rhythm of arousal often adapts to the exigencies of the situation, evidence that sex is more in the mind than the genitals. "I attribute any difference in feelings to whether or not there is a risk of getting pregnant," one woman says. "If there's no risk, it's no holds barred!"

During ovulation some women have pain which reduces libido. In medical books this pain goes under the name of "mittelschmerz". It may be very slight and merely disconcerting, but those who experience it tend to say that it dampens sexual pleasure.

Understanding your own rhythms

Not all women experience these fluctuations at different times of the month. If you are on the Pill you may not notice any difference in libido, though here again, women often say that they feel sexy during the days they are off it when they have bleeding. A woman who is breast-feeding may not ovulate or menstruate and she, too, may experience no variation. Even when she starts to menstruate again, she may feel few changes in sexual arousal during the cycle and many women say that libido is reduced throughout the time they are lactating (see page 230).

Getting to know your sexual rhythms and the way in which they may fluctuate during the menstrual cycle not only helps you understand your body better, but also makes you more aware of what you like and when you like it. Though some of us are about equally sexually aroused all the time, or hardly ever get excited anyway, most of us experience variations of mood and feeling and to go through the menstrual cycle is to travel up hills of desire or down into calm, peaceful valleys. There are times when we relish intense stimulation, other times when the single light touch is enough. When we become aware of these variations the knowledge can be shared with a partner. In this way understanding is deepened and the relationship enhanced.

Masturbation

Nearly every woman has masturbated at some time – giving herself sexual pleasure by touching herself or moving her body in a special way – and though some cannot get an orgasm this way, most of us can easily bring ourselves to orgasm because we know what we like.

Many of us learn how to guide a partner in giving us orgasm through understanding what we do during self-pleasuring. By exploring the movements we make and the kind of touch we most enjoy when masturbating, we can know what to suggest to a partner during lovemaking – especially for the many women who have orgasms during masturbation but rarely during lovemaking.

But masturbation does not have to be justified by being "useful" in a relationship with a partner. Even if it reveals nothing at all of value in a sexual relationship, a woman has a right to enjoy masturbation and it can help her get on much better terms with her own body and be more aware of her own sexual identity.

Sex as assurance to your partner

A popular American writer about sex, Dr Joyce Brothers, teaches women that sex is "Mother Nature's way of keeping a man around the house" (*What Every Woman Should Know About Men*) and advises, in a rather odd mixed metaphor, that "an ounce of prevention is better than locking the barn after the horse has gone". A woman's orgasm is, according to her, what most men need as "a seal of approval". They "love it when a woman gasps and groans and squeals, and when she tells how great they are." A woman's sexual behaviour is geared to keeping a man happy and has little or nothing to do with her own sense of fulfilment. If she achieves satisfaction it is to be gained as an automatic consequence of pleasing a man. The woman should invent sexual innovations to grab his interest, though they should be introduced "the way one introduces a baby to solid food" – gradually.

From this view of female sexuality, intercourse is mainly a way of preventing a marriage breaking up ("the more often a couple make love", Dr Brothers claims, "the less likely they are to end up in the divorce court"). Orgasm holds the promise of a meal ticket for life if you are good enough at it. And masturbation has no part in the picture at all.

Masturbation and body image

Women often feel they have no right to sexual experience apart from that which a man provides. Sex is like a gift we must receive from him, not something radiating from us which we do for ourselves. We expect to come alive through *his* sexuality. It is often very difficult for us to accept that a woman's feelings in solo sex are just as valid as those with a partner. We tend to denigrate our most personal sexual experiences in favour of how we feel we *ought* to be as satisfying sexual partners.

In many ways a woman sees her body as a container. She parts her legs to receive semen. She carries a fetus, bears the child, is heavy with the milk which feeds the baby. She enfolds her children in her arms. She shops for, carries home, cooks, prepares and serves food for them, clears away the mess and starts on the whole process again. It is as if she is weighed down with her responsibility to nourish and sustain, to meet the needs of other people. As a housewife and mother she is like an open chest-of-drawers, spilling over with all the things her family needs in order to go out into the world. And when they have gone she may feel empty, like a discarded piece of furniture.

Many women feel alienated from their own bodies. It is not only that they often do not know how to get sexual fulfilment, but that they actively dislike and despise their bodies. One of the most striking things in the discussions that women have had with me about their sex lives, is the way in which they apologize for their bodies, for all the parts which do not measure up to some external standard of female beauty. Many seem to be waging a constant battle against fat, spots, unwelcome odours, sagging muscles, flabby thighs and breasts, underarm hair and hair in other unwelcome places (such as on the breasts and face), vaginal discharge – but fat most of all. And all for the benefit of men. They are under pressure to deodorize, smooth, trim and decorate, to disguise their "bad" parts and stress the "good" ones, and thus to package themselves and their bodies like boxes of chocolates and iced cakes available for male consumption.

Feeling guilty

Guilt about masturbation tends to be linked with guilt about other aspects of female sexual experience and with a negative body image. One woman who says: "Without being bigheaded, I think I have quite a pretty face with lovely eyes. It's the body that lets me down", feels "guilty and disgusted" about her masturbation, especially if she allows herself to have an orgasm. She also tries to "control" orgasm during lovemaking, "because I've always been a bit embarrassed by it . . . I was brought up not to talk about sex . . . even now I couldn't mention periods to my mother. It's something you just wouldn't talk about to her, or sex". She would hate her husband to find out she masturbates but invariably does so when she has a period because she then feels sexually aroused: "I wouldn't want to make love then because I think it is dirty. In fact I feel embarrassed if I have to tell my husband I have come on." Though this is an extreme example, it points to the generalized anxiety about female body functions and sexuality which tends to be expressed by women who feel most guilt about masturbation.

"I feel dreadful about it after. I tell myself it's normal and natural but I still feel really nasty afterwards."

Female sexuality, together with our body products – menstrual blood, sweat, lochia after childbirth, vaginal mucus – has always been considered "matter out of place" (Mary Douglas, *Purity and Danger*) and because it is out of place and inappropriate in the relations between men and women, it has also been treated as dirty and dangerous. In terms of the social structure and of the reproductive task with which society enjoins women, solo sexuality drains vitality from our main duties: satisfying men and rearing children.

My overriding impression is that women not only feel guilty about masturbation but now also feel guilty about being guilty. Sex therapists urge us to be free, to know and understand our bodies and sexual responses. Most of us probably feel we have worked out our own ideas about masturbation and that it is a normal part of sexual experience. But for some it isn't that easy and being instructed to be free makes them feel worse than ever.

Carol, for example, is 27 and remembers being told off for masturbating when she was three. Though she realizes that her husband masturbates, and is able to accept that he needs to, she says she feels dreadful when she does so herself. She masturbates occasionally as a release from tension, and then attributes anything that goes wrong during the next few days to the fact that she masturbated. In this way she manages to produce regular punishments for enjoying a perfectly natural activity.

Though in the twentieth century we talk much more openly about sex and every women's magazine has its share of articles about cunnilingus and fellatio and how to get an orgasm, the personal experience of masturbation is still rarely discussed and the subject tends to be aired only as a therapy for sexual dysfunction. In that context, as a result of the work of William Masters and Virginia Johnson (*Human Sexual Inadequacy*) and Helen Singer Kaplan (*The New Sex Therapy*), it has gained a new respectability. It has even become part of a woman's *duty* in order to be a satisfactory sexual partner. Perhaps our attitudes to masturbation are not so enlightened after all.

Anxiety about masturbating

Fears about masturbation can be powerful: "What if I get to like masturbation so much that I can't enjoy sex with a partner?" or "Suppose I get so dependent on it I can't stop and have to do it more and more frequently?"

Let us look more closely at some of these anxieties. Some women say they are afraid of "being used up". Louise, for example, says: "I feel it would be self-indulgent and injure my ability to give myself in sex." The first and most important thing is that a woman's capacity for sexual arousal is not limited in quantity, so that if you get excited with masturbation you will have no energy left over to become excited with a partner. Though a man can ejaculate only on a limited number of occasions within a certain time and after that cannot go on, women are very different. You can continue to be aroused and have orgasms over and over again *if you are sufficiently stimulated*. So, in fact, feeling your body more alive with masturbating can increase your arousal in lovemaking.

Women who do not understand how other women's genitals are formed and that we are all of slightly irregular shape, with the inner vaginal lips spread through the opening between the outer lips, rather like a Madeira cake's soft centre which has oozed through the outer crust, sometimes think they are deforming themselves with masturbation and that a doctor or nurse will immediately notice. One woman told me that she could not recover from the shame she felt in childbirth when the midwife "stared" at her genitals and "obviously" saw that she masturbated. She got in touch with me because she wanted to find a gynaecologist who would operate to reduce the size of her inner lips and make her "normal". It is understandable that if you feel frightened and guilty about what you are doing you may think that you are causing your body permanent damage. But masturbation does not enlarge or deform the genitals. The most it can do is to produce a temporary swelling in the labia and clitoris which, since the genitals are composed of very flexible tissue, goes down once sexual excitement has abated.

It is sad that any woman should be so isolated from knowing how other women's bodies are constructed that she should bear this burden of guilt. The neat line drawings in biology books and sex manuals misrepresent the female genitals because they tidy them up and give them an appearance of similitude and regularity which is quite incorrect. It is easy for a man to see and handle his external genitals and to notice other men's in the shower and locker room. Women do not usually see other women's genitals and in this we are at a disadvantage.

Women's experiences of masturbation

Most women who masturbate experience orgasm. More have orgasms with masturbation than in sex with a partner and these orgasms are often much more powerful than those experienced with lovemaking. (William Masters and Virginia Johnson, *Human Sexual Response*) Women who have multiple orgasms when masturbating may never achieve this in sex with a partner. Women also often find it easier to fantasize when self-pleasuring than in sex with a partner. The immediacy of someone else's needs actually inhibits the expression and satisfaction of their own. Some also say they have to imagine that the person making love to them is not the person they know so well.

Women's masturbatory experience fills a wide spectrum. Some only masturbate when other forms of sexual pleasure are missing, a partner is away, or if things are going very wrong in a relationship. Others do so at phases of their lives when the sex drive is strong, before there is a regular partner or when a relationship has split up or a lover has died. Some masturbate at times in the menstrual cycle when they are especially "turned on" and when the other person is not aroused to the same degree. For many women this is during the menstrual flow because they themselves or their male partners are disgusted by the idea of intercourse, or sometimes even cuddling then. Sexual arousal at this time is a result of increased blood flow in the pelvic area which produces engorgement, pressure and resulting stimulation.

'Masturbation is the best treatment for period pains but it's more than that, it's me loving myself.'

Many women also masturbate during the last weeks or months of pregnancy, when intercourse in conventional positions is uncomfortable, if their partners are anxious that they can harm the baby or induce labour, and when some find the physical changes of advanced pregnancy repulsive.

Some women only masturbate when particularly sad, lonely or under stress, perhaps using it as a last resort and getting it over as quickly as possible. A great many masturbate to get to sleep ("It's nicer than sleeping pills") and as an effective treatment for menstrual pain. Some women masturbate because they are angry with their partners. Ann says she does so because "when we were trying for a family he was highly enthusiastic about sex, which made me furious". She is now completely unresponsive in lovemaking and masturbates to relieve the frustration she feels and "to pay him back". But most of us seem to masturbate simply because we enjoy it, though often with very conflicting feelings about the practice. When women write about it they often add phrases like: "I feel it's cheating"; "It's just a safety valve"; "I don't feel guilty about it: why should I?" or "I could *never* let my husband know I do it".

'I discovered the joys of masturbation after my husband died. First for solace and to relax and get to sleep and now for sheer pleasure.'

A masturbatory orgasm usually occurs much more quickly than during lovemaking and you may climax after 40 seconds though taking up to two hours when making love with a partner. This, of course, does not make the masturbatory orgasm "better", since the pleasure of the journey to orgasm is just as important a part of sexual experience to women as orgasm itself, and it is for this reason that some comment that it is "not so fulfilling". "It gives me a thrill", says one woman, "but a very quick one." You may feel there is something missing when making love to yourself and that a less powerful physical climax with a partner has more meaning and produces deeper satisfaction. As one woman says: "With masturbation it is totally physical, the feeling of satisfaction not so deep or long-lasting, though physically much stronger." Another says that when she and her husband make love it results in "an ecstatic pulsating of not only the clitoris and vagina but also of the mind", which does not happen when she masturbates.

Quite a number of women, in fact, are discontented about masturbating if it goes on for any length of time without the possibility of lovemaking, because the relationship with another human being is lacking. Sometimes this other person is loved and needed from the depths of one's being. Sometimes it is an urgent desire for a phallus. Leonie says that when she stimulates herself she becomes very excited, has a "sort of" orgasm, but then longs for a man to enter her. So masturbation makes her more sexually frustrated than before.

There are no rules – just follow your feelings.

Self-pleasuring can help you get on better terms with your own body and make you more aware of your own sexual identity…

Self-pleasuring together

Those women seem to be happiest with masturbation who have drawn on their experience of self-pleasuring to enrich their sexual relationship with a loved partner. They may show each other, through self-stimulation, what they find exciting. For some this is an astonishing breakthrough. They have masturbated since they were children but have never incorporated this pleasurable experience into lovemaking. When they are courageous enough to do so, a whole new range of lovemaking opens for them. Some have their first orgasms as a result and weave into lovemaking the kinds of touch and movement which makes this experience possible for them. Lucy says : " We do it in front of each other for extra sexual excitement", and Sarah: "I tell him about my masturbating. It arouses him. Then we do it when we make love and watch each other. It turns us on, especially my husband when he watches me. It turns *me* on because I know it's driving him wild. He can have an orgasm just watching me!"

A major difficulty with intercourse is that the clitoris is not situated where it is automatically touched during penetration and ejaculation. A lover has to learn how to provide the appropriate stimulus with hands or mouth. A man can do this either before or after he has had his own orgasm, or in place of it. Many men never learn how to do this. It is up to a woman to show her partner how to elicit her sexual response and she cannot do this unless she has learnt about her own body reactions. So through masturbation a woman can help her partner learn how to arouse her sexually. Early on in a relationship it may not be obvious that the couple need to learn anything about each other's bodies and feelings, because they are so excited anyway that the subtleties of arousal are overlooked. But there comes a time when they do need to learn about these things, to explore together the art of lovemaking in place of the sheer tempestuous passion of the first encounters. In many relationships this fails to happen and women look back with nostalgia to the days when there was the spice of novelty and they were swept through sex by the thrill of the chase, the delight of conquest, the surprise of discovering that the other person existed, and wanted and needed them – and lovemaking was new and sweet in its never-to-be-forgotten intensity.

Helping a relationship

When a woman is rooted in herself, with the confidence to get as well as to give, everything she learns about her sexuality from self-pleasuring adds to, rather than detracts from, sexual relationships with others. As she grows in self-awareness she can both give to, and receive more from, her partner.

When Rebecca started to live with Peter, she decided never to masturbate again because now she had what she saw as "the real thing". But because they wanted to be completely open with each other about everything, she told him that she used to masturbate and mentioned that to have an orgasm she had to keep her legs together. He was glad to learn this because it taught him how to make love to her better. But she adds: "Peter made me realize, too, that it's not an inferior substitute, just different". Now they have incorporated masturbation into their lovemaking and use it as a source of discovery about each other's bodies and sexual responses.

Rosemary says she has masturbated as long as she can remember. When she was four she used to lie on her front and rub the bedclothes between her legs until she climaxed. She fantasized about swimming naked in "vats of jelly, jam or other gooey stuff!" This seemed such a bizarre thing to talk about with anybody else and masturbation so "self-loving – and I don't love myself" that she avoided the subject even when Richard asked her about masturbation as they tried to sort out the sexual problems which emerged soon after they were married. For though sex with him was good before marriage, when they used to have intercourse in the open air, in the back of the car, or on the big couch in the sitting room when her parents were out, and there was always the risk of "being caught", once this element of excitement was removed it soon became "boring" and she rarely had an orgasm. She felt she could not talk to him about this because he would be "upset and think he had failed". It was not until she became desperately unhappy and sought help from psychotherapy and marriage counselling that the way was open for her to share this with Richard. And to her great surprise she found him interested, entirely non-judgmental and really pleased that she could talk to him about her sexual feelings. Rosemary says: "I know my body and exactly what to touch now and Richard does too."

Self-discovery

Pam has two children and a husband whom she describes as a "stodgy lover". She is overweight and says she has come to hate the body in which she feels trapped. Her husband never talks to her during intercourse and does not caress or touch her either before or after penetration. The relationship has lost its life and they are only sticking together "because of the children". She had no idea what an orgasm was until she discovered how to masturbate recently: "It's out of this world! Like a volcano erupting!"

For her, learning to masturbate is part of a process of self-discovery and beginning to feel that she is a person. From this, further growth is possible which may improve the relationship or lead her to choose another kind of life or another partner. Either way, she is escaping from the despair she was experiencing before and is now making decisions about what she wants.

Learning from masturbation

If you want to be able to learn from and enjoy masturbation the first requirement is some leisure time when you can do whatever you want without interference and in complete privacy. However busy you are, you have the right to insist on this.

If you have children they ought to learn that adults need space away from them and that it does not mean that you love them any the less. A little solitariness is important for every one of us, adult and child alike. This is difficult to organize with under-three-year-olds, who are now past the earlier baby days when you usually have a rough idea of their main sleeping times. Even so, when a toddler is snuggled down in her cot you usually have a choice of whether to get on with the ironing, get a casserole into the oven or take a little time to relax and enjoy yourself. It is some of these spaces in a busy life which can be used for exploring sexual feelings and learning from masturbation. At first you will probably feel guilty about it. But there is no need to behave as if you were a child doing something naughty. You can choose what you want.

You may also feel reluctant because deep inside you are afraid of losing control in case terrible things happen. This anxiety is often very diffuse so that you would be hard put to it to say exactly what you fear. Some of us are afraid that if we "let rip" we shall get completely out of control, saying and doing awful things, and that letting go is to lose identity, no longer being the kind of person we have so carefully and conscientiously trained ourselves to be.

Girls are taught as they grow up to control themselves and not let boys "go too far". They learn to be kind, considerate, gentle, tender and caring with animals and children and to exhibit qualities which are thought of as quintessentially "feminine". "I was taught" says one woman "that it is a girl's responsibility to restrain a boy's animal nature, that men always want sex and a girl has to be permanently on her guard". If you have learnt this lesson well it is hardly surprising that you continue to hold back in this way when you are supposed to start enjoying sex.

The feeling of not being able to surrender is one which women who become sexually aroused with lovemaking during masturbation, but who never manage to leap off into the unknown sensations of orgasm, often experience. They almost get there, but not quite. Just as we can never learn to swim practising on dry land, so we never let an orgasm happen until we actually allow sexual feelings to flood through us without keeping anything back. The first task, though, is to learn the strokes which will allow you to really trust the water.

In surrendering to the sweep of physical sensations and powerful emotions which culminate in orgasm we need to be able to focus entirely on our own feelings, not to be distracted by other concerns or worries, or a partner's needs. If you think you have to put on a performance, prove that you can have an orgasm, are anxious about pleasing a partner you cannot focus in this concentrated way.

Exploring feelings

So when you have the opportunity, choose a quiet time and place where you will be undisturbed and use your fingers to find out where and how the most pleasant sensations are produced. You will probably discover that the best feelings come when your fingers are lubricated. If you are already aroused you can use the secretion from inside your vagina to let your finger slide over your labia and clitoris. Or you can try a little warmed oil, gel or lotion. Anything you use should be unscented or lightly scented, or you may cause tissue irritation. That can sometimes feel quite exciting but if you do it a good deal the tissues will become sore and swollen.

You may find that the light pressure from a hand-held shower feels good. Occasionally something very cold, like a sliver of ice, may bring a shock of excitement, or you may want to use several different kinds of stimulating touch.

You can also experiment with fabrics of different textures against your breasts or thighs. At times you may like something soft and smooth as an aid to arousal: velvet, silk, or satin, for example. Or something hard and firm may feel good. Some women like to slide an object into the vagina so that it presses against the clitoris. Never introduce anything into your vagina which you would not willingly put in your mouth. It is easy to harm the delicate tissue.

You may like to punctuate touching by making the pelvic floor movements described on pages 49–50. When you are ready to stop, whether or not you have experienced orgasm, call it a day for now. There is no reason to turn it into a drill session or feel that you have to accomplish anything. One of the problems for some women who want very much to have an orgasm is that they are so concerned with the goal that they neglect to enjoy the way there.

Arranging a series of sessions like this is not merely self-indulgence. It is part of a journey of discovery about yourself, and about what may be a neglected area of the body, so that you can grow in understanding and awareness of your sexual feelings.

Extra stimulus

After two or three sessions of this kind, choose some extra things to help you enjoy yourself more. You will already know that you find certain things stimulating: reading an erotic novel, perhaps, dancing to sexually arousing music, or just listening to it, thinking of a scene from a film, remembering passionate lovemaking in the past or using a fantasy about which you feel good (one that does not result in guilt) in the way described on pages 80–91. Spend some time in your next session doing one or two of these things.

Sex therapists often speak of "orgasm triggers". They consist of different kinds of muscular contractions, movements and breathing and some of these may work for you.

You may use a mirror to watch yourself masturbating. If you feel uncomfortable, simply imagine the mirror is there, since this in itself can be sexually stimulating. Or imagine that someone is watching you, carefully observing and learning from what you are doing. You will see in the chapter on fantasies that many women find it exciting to fantasize that they are outside their own bodies watching themselves or that someone else is watching them.

If you usually sit or lie down, select a different position this time. If you were on your back before, try lying on your front, perhaps with a pillow or two under your hips. Or lie on your back with your head and shoulders low and your hips raised on firm pillows.

It can help to change position after you have become aroused, turning so that your head is lower than your pelvis. Try lying across the bed with your head hanging over the side, for example. If you put a pillow on the floor and you have a low divan bed you may be comfortable with your hips raised on the bed and your head and shoulders on the floor. A polystyrene-granule-filled bean bag is useful for this as you can fold it into any shape you want. You can use it for lovemaking with your partner, too.

Experiment with contracting muscles in your legs, abdomen and arms. Some American sex therapists suggest that since body tension (such as pointing your toes or clenching your hands) can be an automatic part of sexual contact, increasing this tension often triggers orgasm. (Julia Heiman, Leslie LoPiccolo, Joseph LoPiccolo, *Becoming Orgasmic: A sexual growth program for women*)

They also suggest experimenting with holding your breath for a while, or panting heavily or lightly. Another thing you can do is to

EXPLORATION IN SELF-PLEASURING

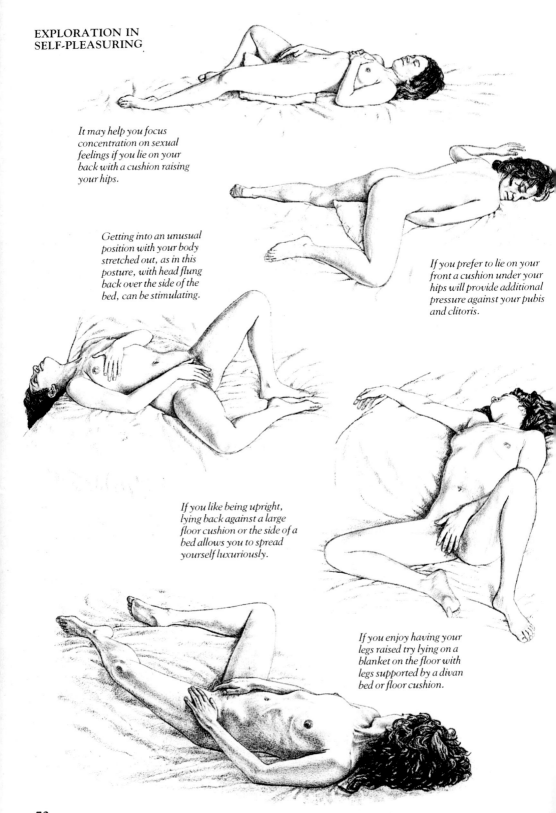

It may help you focus concentration on sexual feelings if you lie on your back with a cushion raising your hips.

Getting into an unusual position with your body stretched out, as in this posture, with head flung back over the side of the bed, can be stimulating.

If you prefer to lie on your front a cushion under your hips will provide additional pressure against your pubis and clitoris.

If you like being upright, lying back against a large floor cushion or the side of a bed allows you to spread yourself luxuriously.

If you enjoy having your legs raised try lying on a blanket on the floor with legs supported by a divan bed or floor cushion.

"tease" yourself. When you have been stimulating your clitoris, move to your inside arms or your breasts, then go back to your clitoris again and, as you become increasingly aroused, move your fingers away again to another area of your body.

In spite of the term "orgasm trigger", which suggests a rapid firing, the idea is to prolong pleasure as long as you can. You will soon find that you get very good at this.

Discovering many different ways to pleasure yourself and extending the time before you get highly aroused is not just a matter of producing a barrage of physical sensations in the genitals. It involves your whole body, your mind, you as a person. You can call on intense visual images, music, great poetry, all the loveliest ideas about human longing and sexual desire. You are starting out on an adventure of the senses which allows you to feel as if you were following a long, winding path through a forest, that reveals exciting new scenes. It is as if you encounter a dappled clearing, soft grass and tall ferns, a waterfall, the shock of cold water in the stream, the luxury of hot sun pouring down on your skin, brilliantly plumaged birds and the velvet darkness of night with stars netted in the branches of the trees.

Orgasm

Orgasm is not just a vague feeling. Masters and Johnson (*Human Sexual Response*) have shown that there is a clear sequence of physiological events leading to orgasm that always have to occur for a climax to be reached.

They divide the physiological process into four stages: excitement, plateau, climax and resolution.

Excitement

In the excitement stage, which may last anything from several minutes to several hours, a woman's heart rate and blood pressure go up, her nipples harden and become erect, her breasts plump up and the areola (the darker circle around the nipples) swells too. Her abdominal skin is flushed and mottled and this flush may spread to the breasts as well. She breathes more heavily. Within 10 seconds to half a minute from the start of effective stimulation her vagina becomes moist with a natural lubricant produced by the blood vessels in its tissues. These vessels expand as extra blood pulses through them. The part deepest inside the vagina, the walls of which usually rest against each other, opens up like a tent. The outer vaginal lips draw apart as the result of increased blood flow. The inner lips become plump with extra blood. In some women the clitoris becomes erect, but not in others. The extra flow of blood affects the uterus, too, which expands, starts to lift up from the pelvic floor muscles and tilts forward.

Reaching the plateau

The plateau phase comes just before orgasm. The breasts, nipples and areola get larger still and her body may now be hot and flushed. Muscle tone is increased and she may make involuntary shuddering

ORGASM

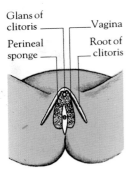

Glans of clitoris — Vagina
Perineal sponge — Root of clitoris

Non-erect phase

Excitement phase

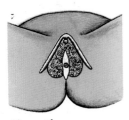

Plateau phase

Orgasm

or jerking movements. Her heart rate and blood pressure are further raised and breathing gets faster and may be irregular and gasping. The inner vaginal lips are engorged and become scarlet or wine red and the entrance to the vagina now swells up further to form what Masters and Johnson call "an orgasmic platform". They make it sound rather like a sexual launching pad, which, in a way, it is. It may feel as if the inner lips have risen and enlarged so much that they are able to clasp and enfold. When this happens the outer third of the vagina becomes tighter, making a narrower entrance. At the same time the inner two-thirds of the vagina are opening and the folds of tissue lining it spread wider and wider, rather like a balloon. The uterus completes its lift-off from the pelvic floor. The hood of the clitoris swells, together with the lips surrounding it, which means that it usually disappears from view.

Attaining climax

It is difficult to talk about climax without describing emotions. It is a very one-sided view to define orgasm as something that merely happens to our bodies, and not to *us*. But there are clear physiological events which occur. The skin becomes still more flushed, the breasts, nipples and areola firmer and larger and then a series of muscle contractions occurs involuntarily in the pelvic floor. These contractions spread from the circles of muscle which are near the base of the spine and around the rectum, right through to those which form a circle about half-way up around the vagina and deeper inside, in the muscles which are nearer the uterus. These contractions are rhythmic and very fast – each lasts about one eighth of a second. The muscles in the lower abdomen contract too and the whole perineum clasps and unclasps in a wave of lightning-quick embraces. The uterus contracts, each squeezing movement beginning at the top of the uterus and flowing down into the vagina. Blood pressure and heart and breathing rates are highest of all.

The female orgasm, unlike male ejaculation, need not be a one-off event. A woman is capable of reaching climax over and over again if further stimulation follows. Though it is sometimes suggested that the first orgasm is always the best and that others are less exciting, this is by no means always true. Sometimes orgasms seem to climb higher and higher or reach their peak half-way through and then subside gradually. But the important thing to know is that many women have multiple orgasms and that if stimulation is suddenly stopped you may be left feeling that the act is curiously incomplete. (There is more about this in the sections about our feelings in lovemaking on page 142.)

Resolution

The final phase is that of resolution. The clitoris goes back to its usual position and the orgasmic platform returns to its previous size. The heightened colour of the inner lips fades. Blood pressure, heart rate and breathing slow down within a few minutes of orgasm. The lowest part of the uterus, however, the cervix which hangs down in the vagina rather like the clapper of a bell, remains open for about half an hour following orgasm. It is not until then that the uterus finally resumes its normal position.

Clitoral or vaginal orgasm?

The female orgasm always starts in the clitoris, Masters and Johnson say, though the main sensations may be felt deep inside you, in the vagina. The clitoris and its underlying structures are criss-crossed by a network of nerves and blood vessels which are vital for sexual arousal and climax. When you are sexually excited the nerves record touch and pressure and blood vessels swell with increased blood flow to the area, so that the external clitoris – the part which you can see – and the whole clitoral system become engorged. This often occurs without direct pressure on the clitoris, especially if we are already emotionally aroused, since pressure on the labia and the pubic mound stimulates the clitoris underneath.

The action of the clitoris

Stimulation of the clitoris results in erection of tissues. When a woman is highly aroused and the entire clitoral system is fully engorged, the clitoris, together with the network of veins and arteries serving it, is about 30 times bigger than the clitoral glans – the part which, because it is outside the body, can actually be seen.

It is often claimed that the clitoris "triggers" orgasms. Yes, in a way it does, but it is odd that we should need to use this male image of a gun going off to describe a female sexual process. The idea of "triggering" also suggests only a part of what is happening. Stimuli in the clitoris and its underlying structures are conveyed to the vagina and the whole pelvic region, including the pelvic floor muscles coiled and enclosing the anus, rectum, urethra and the vaginal barrel, supporting the base of the bladder and uterus. In fact, as the clitoris registers touch it sends out waves of sexual pleasure which spread to all these interconnected organs. The process is much more like water flowing, breaking down boundaries, rushing into every part and flooding the genitals with erotic sensation, than like a revolver being triggered off. Every organ involved is showered with sensations which pour through them evoking a physiological response in each.

When all these different parts of the genital organs are caught up in the same activity, patterned into a harmonious whole, the muscles which form a figure 8 round the orifices of the anus, urethra and vagina start to contract in rhythmic spurts. The orgasm which results may be experienced by a woman as occurring in her vagina or deeper in her body. But without clitoral stimulation the flood of sensation would never be released so powerfully.

The complexity of orgasm

The source of an orgasm, then, is clitoral. But a woman can *feel* orgasm mainly in her clitoris or the area beneath it, or in her vagina, or both, or in the whole pelvic area including her uterus, or – indeed – flooding her whole body. An orgasm obviously cannot be clitoral for women in the many parts of the world where the clitoris is excised in childhood or at puberty – and many of these women experience orgasm too. Because Masters and Johnson's work was restricted to the USA they may have missed out on understanding still more complicated female sexual responses.

Talking about orgasm as if it were located entirely in the clitoris is confusing and frustrating for many of us who have feelings which are much more widespread. We may think there is something inadequate about our experience and that it does not match up to the sharp, intense, overwhelming sensation centred in the clitoris which other women say they have. Equally, if sensation is concentrated in the root of the clitoris and the immediately underlying structures, we may feel we are not measuring up to some standard because we cannot feel anything happening in the uterus, for example. So asking whether orgasm is in the clitoris or in the vagina is really the wrong question. And there is certainly no "right" or "wrong" kind of orgasm.

How we think and feel

Orgasms vary, both between women and for the same woman at different times. We experience different qualities of orgasm depending upon the degree and kind of stimulation we receive and also on what is going on in our *minds*. Experience of orgasm is inextricably linked with how we feel about ourselves, our bodies, our sexuality. To isolate one psycho-sexual process from the rest of our lives is to falsify it and make it meaningless.

What orgasm feels like

It is difficult to describe the feeling of an orgasm with any accuracy, because it is different with different women and much depends on the particular occasion. Just as no two kisses need be alike, so no two orgasms are necessarily similar.

Orgasm has been described as like a sneeze. You know it's coming, you can't stop it and there's a sense of relief when it's over. But although the analogy with a sneeze takes into account the mounting pressure that builds up just before the act of release, the inevitability of the action once it has been set on course and the way it involves your whole body, not just the organ where it is occurring, many women think it falls short of being an accurate description of orgasm. For one thing, the excitement of rising to orgasm is usually greater than that of sneezing!

But there is more to it than that. For many women orgasm is a very diffuse experience. It does not have the sudden, sharp, dramatic ending which a man has with ejaculation. It is more a sensation of erotic flowing and flooding.

A woman who expects orgasm to be like climbing to the top of a hill and jumping off may be terribly disappointed to feel a tide of sensation which comes in waves of intensity until it is as if she is filled and tingling with liquid light. It is not that the experience of orgasm has escaped her. It is just that the male climax is different from the kind of orgasm which many women describe.

Faking orgasm

Women sometimes fake what they think orgasm ought to be to reassure a man. They may do this because the man gets impatient or even angry if they do not appear to climax. One woman, for example, tells me that her husband gets irritated when she does not have an orgasm and mutters: "Come, damn you, come!"

Some sex therapists believe that a woman who does not have an orgasm which is clearly recognized by the man should pretend to have one. One male therapist, Hans Giese, claims that *acting* orgasm can ultimately lead to orgasm and that it is, therefore, an important educational experience for a woman: "The woman who simulates has a better chance than the one who restrains herself from such simulation, of finding and reaching" – and he then goes on to say, not "orgasm", – but "the 'correct' position *demanded by the imagination of her man*" (my italics). (Hans Giese, Paul H. Gebhard, Jan Raboch, *The Sexuality of Women*) This is fine, he believes, because orgasm does not come naturally to women and "one might think that orgasms in the human female were a kind of invention of the male, i.e. a potency specially developed in the female *so that she can co-operate*" (my italics). He does not explain why women should be expected to play this elaborate game of deception which allows a man to use a woman as he pleases.

These and similar theories about female sexuality derive from a male-dominated and directed therapy which perceives women's psycho-sexual experiences as basically stemming from, and a distortion of, a male model of sex. They are an expression of a social system in which women are subordinate to men and are conditioned to serve their needs.

Women's experiences of orgasm

Women talking about their experiences stress that orgasms do not always feel the same and vary depending on who you are with, what you are doing, and your mood at the time: "It depends on the circumstances. If I reach it fairly quickly, it is just like a quick physical spasm where I can't control the muscles involved. If it takes a long time with my husband really trying and me being on the verge of getting there for a longish time, it is usually very satisfying and gives a good feeling all over."

There can be a great difference in orgasm when you are relaxed and refreshed and when you are overtired. Some women have good orgasms when they masturbate and less satisfying ones with their partners. It is this variability that accounts for the uncertainty of some as to whether they have orgasms at all: "It sounds stupid, but I cannot be sure that I have experienced orgasm. Surely I would know if I did have one? Why isn't it the mindblowing burst of sheer ecstasy I have read about?" "It never seems earthmoving as my friends describe it." It is understandable that you feel disappointed, resentful, even perhaps a bitter failure, if you do not have the experience you read about in books and which you believe almost every other woman is having. Some women even begin to suspect that orgasm does not exist. It certainly is true that a woman may have a good warm feeling when making love which she thinks is orgasm until suddenly she really does have an orgasm and realizes that it is quite a different experience.

When you have an orgasm the pelvic floor muscles always contract. If that does not happen you are not having an orgasm. For most of us there is also a rise in body temperature. We feel a warm flood flowing through the whole body. This may be a warm glow or a sense of burning. Many women start to tremble and may experience what one woman describes as "a huge, tingling shudder" or "quivering", but this does not accompany every orgasm.

There is also very often a change in the level of consciousness, producing a sense of faintness and numbness. Some of us actually do faint when we have a very powerful orgasm. Or you may just feel, as one woman put it: "on the brink of a delicious faint".

Both the faintness and an accompanying feeling of numbness over the surface of your body, as you concentrate on the intensity of the inner explosion of sensation, are connected with the way you breathe when you are excited. As you rise in crescendo to orgasm you probably breathe very heavily and fast. This overbreathing leads to hyperventilation, a state in which carbon-dioxide is flushed out of the blood stream. When this occurs you experience peripheral anaesthesia, losing feeling in your hands and feet and often also around your mouth, and you may get very dizzy and even become unconscious. It often feels, too, as if your body has suddenly become lighter and is floating away: "My hips feel as if they are floating off the bed"; "It's like being wrapped around and floating in the softest cotton wool cloud."

Women describe other feelings too. Some get a sensation of inner fluttering: "like a clutch of butterflies let loose inside" as one woman put it. Some have very strong rectal and anal feelings with orgasm. It is, one woman says, like "having a good strong bowel motion". Another woman has more complicated feelings about it: "Just like going to the toilet, or wanting to and not being able and not wanting to control it."

"Orgasm is much overrated, unless you love the other person."

Orgasm can involve intense sensations in other parts of the body too and there is often a connection between what is happening in the vagina and sensations in and around the mouth. For some women orgasm is rather like yawning. You have to do it and feel yourself opening wide: "The feeling builds up to a lovely long climax to be continued for as long as possible." One woman says that her orgasms "are like long satisfying yawns" and that they also "come in colours".

Longing to have an orgasm which does not yet come can be highly irritating. Perhaps this is why some women consider orgasm to be like scratching an itch, though this is a very prosaic way of describing an experience which they may still find enormously satisfying. It suggests something of the stress, even the pain, of wanting something very much and having to wait before you can have it: "It's a lovely itch in every part of your body you can't scratch." "A sharp tingle you want to squash", says another woman "like resisting rubbing an itching mosquito bite as long as you can until it's almost unbearable, then having a good scratch."

Women who have had babies sometimes compare orgasm with giving birth: "It's like having a baby: you build up to a climax (labour pains) then you push the baby's head out. It's the most wonderful feeling in the world. I guess it doesn't 'hurt' as such, but the end feeling is the same." Another woman says that the release she feels can only be compared to the sensation she felt when her waters broke and she delivered her son.

Pleasure and pain

You may feel orgasm as a bittersweet *pain*: "Orgasm is like a pain, a sweet pain that gets bigger and bigger and fills you up. Then as it ebbs you're left feeling content and throbbing." One woman feels it is "sensuous bordering on painful", while another says that "sometimes the pleasure is so acute that it is almost too much to bear, almost painful." For many women there is a narrow, almost razor-edge separation, between intense pleasure and sharp pain.

Orgasm is a paradox: "A painless pain, an ecstatic agony, a paralysed movement." When women talk about orgasm in terms other than those of corresponding physiological states they nearly always introduce the idea of tension increasing to "explosion" – a word used by many when describing the peak experience – and followed by relaxation and a feeling of tiredness or heaviness. They talk about orgasm as like bursting balloons, twanging rubber bands, exploding bombs or erupting volcanoes. Time and time again they introduce images of waves crashing on to the beach.

For many women orgasm is also essentially a giving and a flowing: "like squeezing juice from a lemon". For some it is a rhythmic kind of blossoming: "A flower opening." For others it is experienced as movement, achievement and bliss: "like dancing on a sort of spring – getting higher, slipping back a bit – getting higher still and back a bit and so on until you reach 'the top' – the sort of explosive release which comes – like a broken honey pot with honey spreading through your body. It's lovely!"

A sense of danger

For some women there is a half-hidden danger implicit in the feelings they experience: "An orgasm builds slowly and bubbles before it finally explodes then returns to a simmer once again. I would describe it as a kettle boiling." One says, for example, that it is: "A high build-up of electric power. When you have an orgasm it's like just before the fuse blows", and for many there is a sense of urgency, having to put something right, "like a car screaming out for someone to change gear". Sometimes orgasm is associated with an increasing sense of constriction – mounting anxiety or of being lost or blinded, for example – and then a sudden feeling that you have escaped from the anxiety, have found your way, are able to see with remarkable clarity or that you soar, or fall, into freedom. One woman expresses this feeling of constriction followed by release when she says that, for her, orgasm is "like a train going through a tunnel and suddenly emerging into bright daylight".

If you do not have orgasms

'By far the best orgasms are masturbatory ones – complete self-indulgent pleasure.'

Orgasms are natural, but intercourse is not, for many of us, the easiest way to have them. If a man is too hurried, if his sole aim is penetration, or he concentrates on foreplay just as a brief preliminary to his more important ejaculation, a woman may never be sufficiently aroused to experience orgasm during lovemaking. Or she may be aroused, but find that she is left stimulated but unfulfilled because the main action has moved to the vagina, and the clitoris is left like a stranded and neglected island of excitement. This is why many women have better orgasms with masturbation, for example, than with intercourse. They can take their own time. They know exactly the area which needs to be stimulated and how to do it most effectively. They can concentrate on their own sensations without having to make suggestions about how they would like it or shift position so that they can better share in the excitement.

Women making love to each other sometimes discover that each of them has more orgasms than in lovemaking with men. Angie says: "Sex with men was hopeless. All they want to do is thrust into you and pump in and out, and then it's over and they couldn't care less. I hardly ever had orgasms with men. With Sue it's much more relaxed, warmer, gentler, and incredibly exciting. We spend more time making love and I almost always have an orgasm, several orgasms, with her."

Discovering what it is you need

If you have orgasms when you masturbate you are obviously capable also of experiencing orgasm during lovemaking. It may be a matter of changing the tempo or where you are touched, of trying a different position and of avoiding doing things which cause you discomfort or which you find off-putting. (Sometimes, of course, if that is to be achieved, it may mean changing the partner.) But you are not "frigid". You are not even "pre-orgasmic". You are a sexual being who has not been excited in that particular way.

Only about half of all the women who have told me about their sexual experiences say they usually have orgasms during lovemaking. The others either do not have orgasms, or find that they usually have an orgasm only when masturbating.

Orgasm has been set up by our culture as something women should strive for, a gift men must offer women and the proof of sexual success for both partners. Sex researchers – Kinsey and his team and Masters and Johnson, for example – all assume that orgasm is the measure of sexual satisfaction. Even Shere Hite who provides a new focus on women's sexual experiences, still accepts orgasm as the sole index of sexuality.

For most women orgasm does not have this central role in life. And if it does, it tends to be for a small part of their lives, and often to melt into the background against other significant experiences and other expressions of their sexuality. When a woman is persuaded that she ought to want orgasms or that she could have better orgasms, or more of them, the pressure to perform sexually, to achieve, to excel, is often just one more stress in a life already burdened with difficulties in sorting out relationships, serving others and finding space to be herself. For some women lovemaking without orgasm is unsatisfying and they feel they have missed out on something precious. For others the journey holds more richness and delight than the getting there. For others again, the love they feel for another human being contains a deeper satisfaction even than orgasm. Each woman has a right to define her own sexual identity and the nature of her sexual fulfilment.

Sexual fantasies

Sex is composed of friction and fantasies.
(Helen Singer Kaplan, *The New Sex Therapy*)

Whether or not we agree with that statement, many women enjoy fantasizing. Kinsey's report (Alfred C. Kinsey, Wardell B. Pomeroy, Clyde Martin, *Sexual Behaviour in the Human Female*) shows that about two-thirds of women say that they have sexual fantasies. Those who discuss women's fantasies often talk about them as if they consisted solely of explicit sexual scenes and stories. Nancy Friday, in *The Secret Garden*, records fantasies as if they are, by definition, meticulously detailed anecdotes formed around what is done to the female genitalia. The dark, handsome salesman comes to the door with his vacuum cleaner and shows what else he has on offer; the brown-eyed doctor, his lower face hidden behind a green surgical mask, ties the women into stirrups and stimulates her into a state of sexual ecstasy; the blonde chambermaid in a frilly apron has intercourse with an enormous black man in the Louis XV-style hotel bedroom; the affectionate sheepdog slowly licks a woman's buttocks and genitals with his rasping tongue. Many women do have this kind of sexual fantasy. However we feel about fantasies, it is clear that sex is not, for most of us, just a rubbing together of bodies, but involves our minds and that they sometimes play extraordinary tricks on us and often bring themes and images of which we disapprove or are ashamed. We take our minds with us into each sexual encounter. They may be loaded with all sorts of distracting impedimenta: shopping lists, problems in the office, difficulties with relatives and money worries. Or the mental focus on sex may be blurred by the sudden sound of a baby's cry, someone coughing in the next room or a teenager coming in late.

Making space for fantasy

Though we may want to summon up fantasies, when we are tired or anxious it may be difficult to let them flow. Early on in a relationship, when we are still discovering a great deal about each other and revelling in the excitement of everything new, there may be no room for fantasies of any kind. Some women say they never have fantasies at all. They may even wonder whether they are sexually inhibited or if they are missing out on something.

Women sometimes enjoy fantasies with masturbation but not during lovemaking. It may be easier for a woman to let fantasies come with masturbation because in lovemaking the immediacy of someone else's sexual needs denies her her own, and, apparently for many women, because rushed intercourse and inadequate clitoral stimulation allow no opportunity for the use of the imagination. Women say, for example, that they would like to have fantasies but that there is little chance during lovemaking because the man is so fast that there is "no time". In such situations a woman may feel that she is being used for a man's pleasure as a passive sex object. Laura says that during intercourse she makes shopping lists and decides what she is going to do the next day. She is both bored by her husband and resentful of him and says she wishes he would "talk to me, touch me more, make it last longer". Jean says she tries to relax and let sensual thoughts come into her mind but that her partner is quickly aroused, penetrates, ejaculates soon after and then is no longer interested in anything else.

Some women think it is wrong to indulge in any form of make-believe. They deliberately avoid fantasy because for them it is sheer self-deception and they feel it would not be fair to their partners. Maggie, for example, says, "I would *never* fantasize. It would be disloyal to my husband." Or a woman may say that just as she would not want her sexual partner to fantasize about any other woman in her place, so she would not dream of replacing her partner with some fantasy figure. Barbara says: "When I am making love with someone it's with *that* person, not a fantasy in my head."

"How can she make love to *me* if something entirely different is going on in her head?"

81

*Fantasy can be the poetry
of sex …*

Fantasy and reality

Some fantasies draw us away from what is actually happening in sex and can be a deliberate attempt to block out the reality of the sexual partner. A woman may dream of a vacuum cleaner salesman because she finds her lover rough, crude, inept or interested only in his own sexual release. She may let fantasies take the place of a dull or disturbed reality as if she were plugging a decayed hole in a tooth so that she does not have to feel the pain. In order to be compliant sexual partners and keep a marriage intact many women seem to use fantasy in this way.

Fantasy can also be used to blot out reality in a rather different way, to enhance a relationship by changing its setting and help you concentrate on lovemaking. A woman may use fantasy like this to forget about problems at work – she is lying on moss in the depths of a forest – or to shut out the noise of the hi-fi next door – she is in a sunny field, miles from anywhere, with an orchestra playing. When fantasy is used in this way it does not mean that there is anything wrong with your sex life. Nobody has 100 per cent thrilling and passionate sex all the time, but the dividing line between using fantasy as an anaesthetic so that you need not take any action to change the circumstances in which you find yourself and using it to enrich reality is a hazy one, and what feels right to you depends a lot on where you see that line drawn.

Many women have fantasies which they find exciting at the time but afterwards feel ashamed and guilty about them because they degrade the female body and make women the victims of male brutality. Those involving bondage, cruelty and rape are of this kind. They often say they feel they must be "over-sexed" or "perverted" in having such thoughts and feel at the mercy of their imagination, as if the fantasy itself was a rape of the mind.

"It's just fantasy – we all need dreams."

There is a startling gulf between fantasy and what a woman is really seeking in a sexual relationship and she may find this very disturbing. Women stress that though they enjoy dreaming of group sex or being made love to by their husband's best friend, they would hate this actually to happen and because they are often so surprised at fantasies that come without bidding, may be appalled at admitting to thoughts which are immoral, exhibitionist or "dirty". Isobel says: "I like to imagine I am walking through a wood and a gang of Hell's Angels attack me. I am made to do every conceivable degraded and perverted thing, but am not allowed to reach orgasm until the leader has his turn . . . but I wouldn't like this in reality!" Another woman fantasizes that she is a nude model in front of a photographer who puts her in various positions, eventually telling her to lie over a stool, and in this position, where she cannot see him, he enters her from behind. She was obviously disconcerted – even disgusted – at having this particular fantasy, though it is one shared, in various forms, by a great many women.

Fantasies of domination

One significant element in many sex fantasies is that something is done to you for which you cannot be held responsible because you could not see, you were bound down, overpowered or it happened by "accident". This is how in our dream worlds, we try to make peace with conscience and our sense of propriety. Perhaps it is one reason why violence plays such a large part in many women's

"My rape fantasies were disgusting but they turned me on. But now I'm like a theatrical producer with my fantasy life – I make it be what I want, what I can accept morally."

fantasy lives. They imagine being "forced into sex with other men by my husband" or "tied, blindfolded, to a brass fourposter bed and raped". It does not mean that the woman wants her partner to be rough. It is much easier to imagine that you are enjoying being taken by force when your partner is considerate, gentle, subtle and gives you plenty of time in which the fantasy can develop!

The essence of a rape fantasy may be that you are so irresistibly attractive and your lover so overwhelmed with passion that control is lost. A woman who was worried and disgusted by rape fantasies which crept into her mind as she was making love discovered that the element in these fantasies which was most significant for her was that her lover completely and passionately surrendered to the experience, taken over by a force too great to control. When she worked out a new fantasy for herself in which she vividly imagined her lover reaching orgasm, and deliberately switched on this picture during lovemaking, it took the place of the rape fantasy, was much more satisfying for her and produced no nasty after-taste.

Many of us are uncomfortable with fantasies involving violence and being overpowered because we are aware that, like dreams, they reflect and interpret our view of the world. If we had recurrent fantasies about torturing animals or battering a child, for example, we would probably get alarmed. Our fantasies are not isolated occurrences, detached from the rest of existence. Our most private dreams reflect, in a distorted and caricatured way, social reality. They arise out of, and are influenced by, the sexual standards of the society we live in and reflect our attitudes to those standards. Though it does not help merely to be horrified at our fantasies, we ought to think of their implications for the kind of world we live in.

Women seem to have fantasies about being dominated and brutalized, for example, far more than men do, and this mirrors something about the relations between men and women in our society. The fantasy material on sale for men in newsagents typically depicts them overpowering women who are either virgins ("nymphets", schoolgirls and nuns) or whores (prostitutes and "nymphomaniacs") and magazines like *Playboy* talk about sex using military metaphors – surrender, dominance and mastery. Pornographic pictures include things like a woman's legs and vulva upside down, her head and waist having gone through a mincing machine, or a workman drilling into a woman's vagina with a road drill. Porn shops sometimes sell whips, chains and locks, straitjackets, "tit clamps", executioner-style masks (black hoods with eyeslits and zippered mouths) and even a "meat tenderizer" (a harness with protruding nails, worn around the man's middle, which is driven against the woman during intercourse).

Men have rape and domination fantasies. Women have fantasies about *being* raped and dominated. Because we live in a violent world in which women really are raped and battered by men, it is understandable that many of us feel bad about our masochistic fantasies. Andrea says: "Rape fantasies are nothing but an obscenity. How can you read in the papers all the sordid details surrounding a rape case and then enjoy a pleasant little rape fantasy? That bothers me a lot. I wonder, for example, how it affects my behaviour and my feelings towards women who have been raped. I can't permit myself to enjoy that kind of fantasy. I mean, I banish the thoughts immediately, but it disgusts me that I found them arousing at all."

The image of being an innocent girl, a virgin, seduced by an older man or woman, often occurs in fantasies. It is striking how much this kind of masochistic fantasy is also directly related to male masturbatory material. It is as if women as a whole were playing a game the rules of which have been dictated by men and in which they have imprinted on us their view of the world. But this kind of fantasy has another function too. We can opt out of responsibility for what is happening in a way these women describe: "I am a young girl who knows nothing about the 'facts of life' and my wicked uncle is determined to teach me a few things", or "I am very young and innocent and the man is a casual pick-up." In this way, too, some women try to re-create the excitement of sexual experience earlier in their lives and this fantasy is frequent among those who are bogged down in housework with young children and who feel that sex has lost its thrill.

Many women find themselves in a double-bind between fantasies which are sexually arousing and their awareness that such fantasies exist as a sick parody of relations between men and women in our society. They realize that in nourishing these thoughts of being raped and dominated they are willingly accepting roles that are scripted by men.

Kitchen-sink fantasies

One way in which women permit themselves fantasies is to tie them tightly to the conventional social role of housewife, making them part and parcel of the duties they are expected to perform. The wildest excesses of sensuality are then given the seal of domestic approval. Marge says her favourite fantasy is to imagine her legs wrapped round her husband "and him to be sunk to the balls in me" and while the reader might think that having achieved this, further exciting things would happen, she goes on to describe her fantasy as "for him to carry me about" (still inside her) "doing the household chores and shopping". Perhaps the element of incongruity between sexual passion and cooking and cleaning provides an extra relish for this kind of fantasy. The restraints of duty can actually impose the sexual activity. One woman, who explains that they are very short of money, says she enjoys imagining having sex with "a man who has called at the house to sell or mend something. I pretend I am making love with him instead of paying the bill." Sexual intercourse with a repair man is an extension of wifely duties.

In many fantasies the husband plays an important part, giving permission, as it were, for the events which are taking place. The woman is being restrained while he directs operations: "Other men are looking at and touching me, and my husband is showing them my internal parts and what I enjoy most." Even when he is not physically present he may have arranged the fantasy scene. Sharon says her favourite fantasy is that her husband comes home with an invitation to a "wife-swapping party". She goes in a slinky dress with sexy underwear, has a few drinks, dances: "Then, because we are new, the initiation ceremony takes place. The other women take my husband off to another room. I am dancing with one of the men and he undresses me. Then they all take it in turns to have sex with me." Sometimes the fantasy is given therapeutic and professional sanction, as in the one that a doctor is making love to the woman on his couch, with her husband watching happily.

The photographer's model

Some women enjoy fantasies in which they imagine they are doing a job of work. The fantasy may be that they need the money so this is why they are doing something which they would otherwise find unacceptable. A woman may act the part of a prostitute ("a very high-class one" they often add) or imagine they are being paid to present their bodies in different ways or have things done to them by men, other women or occasionally animals. The "photographic session" or making a "blue" film is a fantasy shared by many women and one which, since it fits so well with men's views about women's bodies, they often say their partners join in describing: "Someone is taking photographs because I am so imaginative that they have to publish it in a book", says Susan. Many women who describe these scenes escape from their own bodies by turning them into ideal, model-girl or playboy bunny figures. The idea of total strangers becoming so sexually aroused that they have to seek immediate relief is a stimulating one often linked to the fantasy of the photographic session: "I would love to be the centre-spread in a girlie magazine and to think that men masturbated over me", one woman says.

As women, we are used to turning ourselves into anything that men want of us, to accepting and incorporating into ourselves *their* way of seeing us. It is as if we become the frisky playboy bunny with her little cotton-tail, the plastic inflatable doll, passive and available, the centre-fold girl in her wet T-shirt, her hand cupped around her silicone stiffened breast and a look of astonished rapture on her face as if she had just discovered it for the first time. Many women are themselves turned on by these male images of what women are, and the excitement they experience is that of putting themselves at the disposal of men in exactly the way that men have dictated and expressed through porn magazines and in blue films.

Fantasy idols

In fantasy the male partner can also be turned into another synthetic celluloid figure. Some women seek images of actors and pop stars clothed with the personality the media has given them – the Beatles, Steve McQueen, Jeremy Irons, Oliver Reed, find a role in these fantasies. Others (far fewer) imagine being made love to by characters from fiction – Mr Darcy from *Pride and Prejudice* emerges in one woman's fantasy life, which might be a surprise for Jane Austen. One of the recurrent characteristics of these fantasy lovers is that they are "faceless strangers", shadowy, symbolic male figures who have no hold over you and who disappear back into the darkness as soon as you have got your pleasure from them. A woman does not have to make their beds or clean up the bath or cook and tidy up after them!

Multiple partner fantasies

They also tend to come in twos, threes or even larger groups, naked men in the changing room into which you have wandered by mistake, for example, "with big, hard pricks ready for a good fuck" and in spite of their advanced state of arousal each lover concentrates on an assigned erogenous zone so that there is long-drawn-out total body stimulation. This is often very different from the kind of stimulation the woman is receiving from her real-life lover, since one of the things women criticize most frequently about lovemaking is that the man confines his attentions to nipples or vagina, neglecting all those other parts of her body which would be responsive to his touch. Not so in fantasies, however. The problem is solved in the fantasy world by having more than one man. In this way both breasts can be sucked at once, vagina, anus, mouth, thighs, all stimulated simultaneously.

Many women fantasize about having sex in situations in which they are very likely to be discovered, or in full view of a shocked but admiring audience. The venue may be public transport – a plane or train – a cinema or "in the car with the risk of getting caught".

Masturbation in fantasy

Fantasies of masturbation while actually having intercourse with a partner also introduce some of the guilt still attached to masturbation and thus seem to add to the pleasure of lovemaking. Many women who cannot have orgasms with their partner without difficulty, but who know exactly how to give themselves orgasms when masturbating, discover that their capacity to do so is increased if they imagine a masturbation scene. They say things like "I am using a plastic penis in front of an audience."

"A man is watching me as I masturbate."

Some women also say that they like to imagine their partner is masturbating and this often in response to intolerable stimulation from a woman who is exhibiting her body. In these fantasies the man is often seen as very young and inexperienced and is being taught about sex by her. It is as if she can only express her own sexuality when with a less confident and unassertive male. The woman who fantasizes the man as "a virgin of sixteen" tends to have a partner who is the very opposite. She often seems to be a woman who feels dominated by a man who imposes his sexual rhythms on her and in her fantasy she changes the scene so that she becomes the sexual initiator. An important element in many fantasies is that the woman stands outside the scene enacted, as if detached and watching herself being pleasured. "I imagine what his penis looks like as it goes into me", says a woman who fantasizes that she is standing observing the couple having intercourse. The partners may be recognizable as yourself and your lover or may be idealized so that they seem to be other people. In fantasies in which there is a "voyeur" the woman may be the onlooker or may slip into the skin of another imagined character who becomes the onlooker. This seems to be what is happening with all those fantasies in which an audience is an important part of the action. The woman stands outside herself, becoming at once actor and onlooker and in the reactions of the audience a whole range of emotions can be expressed. Women sometimes say that they find it stimulating to think of watching their partners from behind making love to another woman. In some fantasies other women play a prominent part: "A woman is being restrained (not me) whilst a man explores her vagina with his fingers and pushes a vibrator up inside her". Voyeurist fantasies draw a good deal on pornographic images.

"I watch us making love. I'm outside and inside at the same time."

Fantasies about being made love to by other women or feeling or exploring another woman's body are frequent, and often there is a male figure watching and becoming excited by or controlling the action. Women often describe the pleasure of breasts in recounting these fantasies and if they themselves have small breasts dream of the other woman with large ones. Sometimes the dreamer feels she is possessed of a penis: "While I am coming I often imagine that I am doing the penetrating"; "I am the man with a large, powerful penis ejaculating into my partner." Jan says that she likes to imagine that her male partner has a vagina and slips a finger into his anus as he penetrates to add to this fantasy: "His penis is a vibrator shared between our two vaginas."

Pornographic images

Few women who tell me about their fantasies say they use photographs to titillate, in the way that men do, though some say they would like to. One unhappily married woman who apologizes for having "a sex hang-up" says she plans the menus for the following day, since her partner tries very hard but is lacking in preliminaries – "just bed and get on with it". She masturbates to obtain relief, while looking at his pornographic magazines and imagining that she is the centre-fold model.

Another scenario, almost entirely missing for these women, is that with animals. Unlike Nancy Friday's collection of sex fantasies (*The Secret Garden*), which includes many involving dogs, domestic animals are noticeably missing. Strange, when the British are supposed to be a nation of dog-lovers! Only one in 340 women who talked to me fantasized about sex with a dog, though some dreamed that they themselves turned into cats or tigers when aroused.

Childhood experiences

While some fantasies come cling-film-wrapped, with all their props, from commercialized pornographic images, others are gradually constructed over months or years. They contain unconscious elements which draw on early childhood experiences. The many references to a lover's smooth skin and softness may be of this type. It is as if the adult woman derives comfort from a mother's arms and her soft breasts. Later childhood experiences which were sexually exciting may be woven in, too. Annie says her masturbatory fantasy of being bound and dominated started when she was about eight. She found it very exciting to day-dream of submitting to a captor and loved the Enid Blyton books because the heroes and heroines were often tied up and held prisoner. Another woman says her earliest erotic fantasies, before she was six years old, were about Peter Pan and Tinkerbell. Tinkerbell's wings got caught in a drawer where she was fluttering helplessly. She was at first angry and defiant and then reduced to pleading for release.

As you start to think about your fantasies, and perhaps remember some of which you were only dimly aware because they were fleeting, or because you rejected them morally or aesthetically, you may begin to understand the different elements on which you draw in your own imaginative life. It is just as important to observe what mental images you find erotic as to know what you find physically stimulating. Discovering this helps you to be more aware of who you are as a person. Sex is more in the mind than in the genitals.

The images in our minds can be as important as the physical sensations we enjoy...

We may feel unwilling to accept uncritically anything and everything that comes into our minds, even when it does violence to us as women. The disturbing thing about so many fantasies is that they are heavily spiked with masochistic images of male power over women. Most of the women who have such fantasies and talked to me about them feel tremendous sexual excitement which merges with self-loathing and disgust. Perhaps the hostility towards the captors and persecutors gets turned in on *ourselves*, so that instead of criticizing the pornographic view of women and their sexual exploitation we hate and further denigrate ourselves. In enjoying those very images we become collaborators in the sordid game.

We have the power to create fantasies of our own choosing and to shape them, if we wish, so that they are really ours, not merely a reflection of male pornography.

Memory and imagination

In any loving and close relationship between two people memories contribute a special flavour to the partnership. A chance word or phrase conjures the same association for them both and they may not need to finish the sentence. They laugh at the same things, not because they are wildly funny in the here and now, but because they trigger remembrance of other things which were funny in the past. It is as if through shared experience there is a split-second communication between minds which does not depend on words alone. Sounds, smells and tastes stir these associations. The band strikes up music which immediately captures another place and time. There is the smell of hot sun on hay or the taste of a food or wine and in their minds the whole setting and mood of that occasion springs alive. It happens especially when they have been together a long time, and even after death for the surviving partner, in a way which can be both poignant and erotic.

Fantasies are part of this life of the imagination. While memory draws on imagination to evoke something which has already occurred, fantasies may never have actually happened and probably never will, but have the same power to stir emotion. Sensual images can be conjured in a profusion of shapes, colours, cadences, tastes which can in a second flood us with erotic arousal. Fantasies can be the poetry of sex. They provide the imagery which gives it its different flavours. Sometimes this poetry is lyrical, sometimes it has the beat of jazz or blues, sometimes it has a heavy rock rhythm.

It is clear that fantasies are often defined as episodic scenes of sexual encounters. Nancy Friday certainly defines them in this way. I am not happy with this very restricted view of fantasy, because it seems to me that there is a much wider potential and for the use of our imagination in ways which are quite different from that of male pornography. She does not include anything which is not like a pornographic strip-cartoon story. Though women do have this kind of fantasy, it is not the only kind and by limiting the definition we miss out on all the other kinds of fantasy which, though not explicitly sexual, are yet highly erotic.

When they draw on experiences they have shared a couple can, if they wish, develop this kind of fantasy together. To do this they need to be able to talk about how they feel. Women often say that their partners do not talk during lovemaking and that one very effective way of stimulating fantasies is thereby lost. Time and time again they say things like: "If only he would speak, if only he would say what he is about to do, what he is doing, describing my body, telling me about the pleasure he feels." Leonie, for example, says she plays over in her head a passage in a book or magazine that she has found exciting as a substitute for words from her husband. Love talk obviously does not have to be great literature. A few words or a phrase can stimulate fantasy.

Creating an imaginary setting

One way you can fantasize is to use your imagination to change the setting in which you are making love. You may be lying under a clear blue sky in long grass by the side of a river with the hedges smothered in wild roses, or decide to be on a fantastically beautiful, white-beached, aquamarine-bayed, tropical island. Or you may prefer a luxurious hotel: Zoë gets in the mood by thinking of "black satin sheets, sheepskin carpets and large mirrors on the ceiling". Francesca and her partner pretend they are in "a large fur-covered bed with champagne and soft music", and another couple are in "a bedroom with mirrors and red velvet and gold fitments every-where". Sue imagines that she is making love to Katie underwater, "in one of those marvellous coral reefs with brightly coloured fish and shells, and we move weightlessly and effortlessly through the warm green sea, like in Jacques Cousteau films".

"There's a game we play together . . . I imagine I'm testing lovers."

Fantasies are often funny and in many good ones there is an element of joking. You recognize them for what they are – play-acting. An Arabian Nights scene in which a queen chooses lovers from among her slaves or in which a prince selects a willing slave-girl is quite obviously make-believe, with all the splendour and colour of exotic fable. You are both aware that the last thing in the world you want is to be confronted with a lover with a penis the size you are imagining or to lie, covered with bangles and slave bells, on marble paving wet and slippery from a splashing fountain.

The kind of fantasies we enjoy may change as we ourselves change. With fantasies, as with jokes, we may get tired of them because they are too familiar. Our view of ourselves changes too, and with it the kind of fantasies we enjoy. Many fantasies, like jokes, involve stereotypes and these can do violence to the way in which we perceive the world and to our sense of right and wrong. There are some jokes you may not feel comfortable about telling, those about Jews, mothers-in-law, Irishmen and "the bird with big tits", for example. You may feel exactly the same about fantasies.

As you have read through women's fantasies in this chapter you have probably encountered some which are sexually stimulating even though you find them distasteful. You may have become aware that there was a split between the sexual response and your emotions, as if you felt something *in spite of* yourself. We should feel happier if there were no such contradiction between sexual feelings and our values. We need to bridge this gap. It is one which to a large extent has been created by the impersonal, mass-produced commercial and media representation of women's bodies as mere objects with sexual responses which can be triggered, rather than as whole people with emotional responses. We have to decide who we are before we can really know what fantasies are right for us.

4 SEXUAL LIFE-STYLES

Loving men

It is difficult to write about heterosexuality because for many women it is the unstated and implied basis of our sexuality. Most of us assume that we will fall in love with one man or a succession of men. We do not question it. It is "natural". It is a view of human sexuality based on reproduction. And since the baby who is born has to be reared, we also take it for granted that the man and woman stay together to care for their offspring and that each child has a mother and father. We see the family as founded on a couple's monogamous commitment to each other.

The monogamous ideal

When things do not work out this way we think of the consequences as social aberrations and believe that the individuals concerned ought to be punished, treated as sick or protected because they are particularly vulnerable. The unmarried mother, women who are promiscuous, men who beat up their wives or assault their children, people who stay single and those who are separated or divorced, all these seem like the exceptions to prove the rule that the most fulfilling kind of partnership is between a woman and man who come together to share each other's lives and have a family.

We have seen already that many women are questioning this view of the relations between men and women and the function of sex, and are certainly no longer accepting monogamy as God-ordained. If we are to commit our lives to a man we need to have good reasons for our decisions. Some of us will give an explanation in terms of the romantic ideology: "I'm in love". Some in terms of sexual liberationist ideology: "He's terrific in bed". Or for some, a simple social explanation: "Everybody wants to get married, don't they?" But those of us who are not happy with any of these explanations as a foundation for spending the rest of our lives with one man have to think again.

The reality

Part of the attraction towards a man is being drawn to different physical characteristics and qualities of character which may seem at first to be the polar opposite of a woman's own. There is friendship, shared ideas, interests in common, but the extra spice comes from the stimulus of otherness. When a woman and man are newly in love the air seems almost to crackle with the excitement of this difference. Once the partnership is established this difference often seems to disappear. It is as if their two personalities have mixed and merged. Many things never need to be said because they know each other so well. Although it does not happen like this for everybody, in what is generally accepted as a "good" marriage there is minimal conflict. Differences, opposed viewpoints, incompatibilities are all submerged in love.

There is a price to pay for this. And almost invariably it is the woman who pays it. For in contemporary Western culture she is expected to fit into his life. She is sucked into his orbit, often away from her own interests and her own social life and at the expense of her own goals. She may have to move to where his job is and have to spend time entertaining his friends and business acquaintants, and often has to give up her own. For many women it feels as if they are running on railway lines dictated by his goals and interests.

An ideal marriage?

In the "ideal marriage" all conflict disappears and the man and woman see everything as if with the same eyes. But, "In the deep intimacy of the couple", Simone de Beauvoir writes, "...no exchange is any longer possible." (*The Second Sex*) There is harmony – but then there may also be a wearisome dullness. And, worst of all, the woman may never stand back to look at who she is and what she really wants in life.

Thus a "good" marriage has its own hidden dangers. When a couple know that their partnership is not working out, when it is shattered by conflict, at least the woman has no choice but to examine what the relationship means to her.

There are satisfactions along the way, many rewards for the woman in a good marriage if she adapts accordingly. She feels safe, protected, is economically supported and cherished, surrounded by a loving family and has status reflected from her husband. The couple nurture each other emotionally so that both feel content in their roles. She may think that there is nothing more she wants.

We have inherited a marriage system in the Judaeo-Christian tradition in which the man is seen as head of the household and the woman as his companion and helpmeet, the mother of his children and guardian of his property. Traditionally women are powerful inside the home but have no power outside it. The wife's control of domestic territory is important because family life can then be regulated to add to a man's esteem. It is a "model family". He is "proud" of and admired for it.

This is clearest of all in the traditional Mediterranean family, where the man is evaluated by the wife's character and reputation. She, and the children she bears him, embellish him. He is rewarded or disgraced by them. It is as if they are extensions of himself.

In many contemporary marriages women are often completely isolated from each other – in marked contrast to the network of female friendships in peasant societies, rural communities, and inner-city slum communities. The suburban dwelling and the high-rise can seal a woman off from other female friendships. The door is closed, the blinds down, to the emotional support that can come from other women. She is alone with her problems and feels that if she is not content, it is her own fault.

When she can stand it no longer she goes to the doctor because she is depressed or anxious and is given anti-depressants or tranquillizers to enable her to cope better. But nothing else changes. When her husband has an affair with another woman or her children become disturbed or delinquent she blames herself for not having loved or cared for them well enough.

Marriage in a changing society

Many women, concerned to retain their own autonomy, are asking if marriage can now adapt to the new social roles of men and women. Is it possible to love a man, enter a partnership with him, and perhaps have children and bring them up, without accepting the whole, ready-made package?

A woman who maintains her own identity gives of her strength to a partnership.

We want to develop the good things in marriage and reject everything that prevents us from seeing ourselves as human beings in our own right. We know we need to clear personal space for ourselves so that we are not crowded out by the demands being made on us by all those whose needs we serve. Not to be submerged by this, but to maintain a sense of self, an awareness of our own needs and goals is vital. Sometimes it may seem almost impossible unless we can afford to get other people to do things for us, or there is genuine shared partnership between a man and a woman.

In many marriages a woman is employed outside the home and still does most of the housework and child-rearing. She has two full-time jobs instead of one. Her husband may "help" but takes little initiative or responsibility for domestic decisions. He often avoids jobs by saying he was never any good at ironing, anyway, or has not been taught how to do that particular thing. Or does so, but half-heartedly, or makes such a great show about doing a task that the woman claims: "It would be quicker and easier to do it myself," and thereafter lets him get away with doing nothing.

The challenge to marriage today is whether couples can create a relationship in which each accepts equal responsibility for domestic work and child care and has equal opportunity to work and achieve outside the home in separate worlds. This is much more than the practical matter of the fair distribution of effort. It has to do with a woman's identity, her own belief in her worth as a human being and with the way in which she wants to be perceived, as against the way in which society would like to stereotype her role.

Women have been, with rare exceptions, invisible even to themselves except as wives and mothers. When they have tried to be visible it has usually been a solitary struggle.

Marriage and motherhood do not have to destroy a woman's autonomy. A relationship with a man can be one in which both partners are mutually supportive and cherishing and in which each gives space for the other to grow. But this rarely happens by chance. It needs frank discussion and working at. It requires effort on both sides and often a lot of initiative on the woman's part, and there is no point at which you can let things slide and hope that the relationship goes on developing well. As circumstances change, perhaps as a woman stops working outside the home, or has a baby, or when the second child is born, when children go to school and as the couple grow older, it is important to examine together what is happening and remind each other of the needs you both have for self-expression and for private space. It is all too easy to allow conventional male–female roles to infiltrate our relationships, and to drift into a life-style in which we accept cultural norms because it appears simpler not to question them.

Breaking with the past

We always bring into marriage ideas that we have absorbed, often without realizing, from our own parents and the way they lived. Sometimes we are determined our relationships will be quite different. But often we re-create a very similar pattern in our own lives, not because we want to – we may not even be aware of it – but because we cannot be bothered or do not have the courage to create anything else that would suit us better.

Loving a man is not just a private, personal experience. To talk about heterosexual relationships we have to take into consideration this whole framework that shapes the interaction between men and women. Though its core is marriage, even in the freest sex, the most semi-detached partnership, it is a framework which forms the background to most male–female relations. Sex can never exist in a vacuum. In any kind of sexual partnership we implicitly make a statement about society and our place in it as women, both in the present and as we want it to be in the future.

Part of the attraction towards a man is being drawn to qualities and characteristics different from our own.

Loving women

In this chapter my daughter **Celia Kitzinger**, *a psychologist doing research on the experiences of lesbian women, who has worked in a gay counselling organization and is herself a lesbian, describes how it feels to be a lesbian and the process by which different women may come to think of themselves as lesbians. We both strongly believe that every woman should have the right to choose who, and how, she loves. Lesbian relationships reveal a facet of loving in which women share joy and fulfilment. They can be a powerful comment on a society that is organized for the benefit of men. And passionate friendships between women can teach us all to understand better the nature of love.*

A lesbian is a woman who loves women. In a society in which women are supposed to give emotional energy and practical support primarily to men and to their children, just being a lesbian is being political, since lesbians are showing that relationships between women are important.

Explaining away lesbianism

Many people try to avoid confronting the issues raised by women loving women. We are dismissed as pseudo-men, with kinky genes and imbalanced hormones, portrayed as a butch and femme parody of the heterosexual couple, or as acting out mother–daughter relationships. Psychiatrists have described us like this, and many people – some lesbians too – believe them.

In fact, lesbians are not in any way biologically different from other women (in genes, chromosomes, hormones, genitals, or general body shape), and scientists have never been able to demonstrate that lesbians have different family backgrounds, upbringings, relationships with parents, childhood experiences or psychological make-up from heterosexual women. It is simply convenient for people to believe these ideas because then they can "explain away" the lesbian as a different kind of human being, whose life-style does not have to be taken seriously as a possibility for every woman.

However well-intentioned these sorts of "explanations" of lesbianism might be, they serve to deny lesbianism any validity, and they affirm people's belief in the "naturalness" of heterosexuality as the normal state for most women. In believing this, we forget that building relationships and experiencing our sexuality are social activities in a social world. We do not live our lives blindly driven by innate biological impulses, forced by genes, hormones, or the dark forces of our subconscious along predetermined channels. We make choices; we create new possibilities for ourselves; we define who we are and make decisions about who we will be.

Becoming lesbian

In any society certain choices are encouraged and are easy to make, while others are not. Most of us, as small girls, were given dolls with bridal outfits, or wendy houses to play mummies and daddies in, or read stories in which the prince and princess always ended up happily married. Blatant and practising heterosexuals confront us every time we turn on a television, open a newspaper, or just walk down a street. It is assumed that one day we will fall in love with a man, that we will have boyfriends and husbands, and the possibility of choosing other women as passionate friends and lovers is systematically closed to us. Because of this massive social conditioning into heterosexuality, many women experience their heterosexuality as "natural"; they may feel distaste for other women's bodies, or reject women as "bitchy", "gossipy" or "silly". Many other women accept a heterosexual life-style but maintain important and loving relationships with women friends. Other women choose a lesbian identity and life-style.

This choice can be very painful to make. Rachel, who began to think of herself as lesbian when she was 14, says: "It dawned on me as an awful problem that I had better hurry up and grow out of, because otherwise my life was ruined, you know. I would go to see a film and come out much more attracted by the women than the men, and then I'd think 'Oh no, I'm going to have to forget this.' It was a real sort of hell on earth."

Penny was in her thirties, married with two small children, when a dream led her to begin thinking about being lesbian: "I had a dream one night, and I woke up after the dream and I remembered it immediately, and in the dream I was making love with Jillian, and it was lovely. It was a lovely, beautiful dream – one of the nicest I've had for years! And when I woke up I had two thoughts simultaneously, which were 'Wow!! How lovely!' and 'Oh no, I'm *not* that.' I mean, I was brought up either not to think about it, or to think about it as deviant. So accepting that I was still me and could acknowledge these feelings about Jillian took quite a split."

Choosing the friendship and love of women can be a joyful and liberating experience.

Passionate friendships help us to understand better the nature of love…

When you first begin to think of yourself as lesbian, you may feel very isolated, as though you're the only one in the world, although in fact we all know lesbians, as friends and colleagues, next-door neighbours, teachers, sales clerks, doctors, secretaries, sisters, daughters and mothers. Lesbians who wear badges like "Lesbians Unite" or "How dare you assume I'm heterosexual?" are trying to make themselves visible to isolated lesbians who often feel cut off, lonely and without hope of meeting others.

Tina says: "I didn't even know such a thing existed until I was about nineteen – that it was even possible. I mean, I must have known that it was the kind of thing that maybe one or two women in Paris got up to, but it wasn't anything that anyone you might ever know would do; not anything 'our sort of person' did. I felt very very lonely, not knowing how I would ever meet another lesbian. It seemed to me that they must be incredibly rare."

Alison says: "You feel you must be such a weirdo and a freak, and you think 'Oh no, that word doesn't apply to me.' I spent about a year of misery, feeling completely isolated."

Meeting others

Many women first meet others they know to be lesbian by phoning a lesbian befriending service and going along to a lesbian group. There are some telephone numbers and addresses at the end of this book. This first move can be frightening because it means admitting to yourself that you are, or might be, lesbian, and it entails taking a first tentative step into a world that you have probably been told is populated by the jealous, aggressive, pipe-smoking, tweed-suited lesbian monsters of the psychology textbooks and the popular films. The lesbian who answers your call will know exactly how difficult this can be because she will almost certainly have gone through the same experience herself. She will not force you to say or do anything you do not want to; she is there to listen and to help you sort out how you feel about things.

June phoned Lesbian Line after seeing the number on a sticker in a train. She says: "First I thought, 'Oh, I'm not phoning them. I don't know that I'm completely gay, and I hate that word "lesbian".' But I was really lonely. I was crying every day. I carried the number around on a bit of paper in my purse for about six weeks and sort of took it out and looked at it every day, and thought 'No, I can't.' Then I phoned a couple of times, and I was shaking so much I could hardly hold the phone, and this woman said 'Hello, this is Lesbian Line', and I couldn't say a thing. I just couldn't think of anything to say. No words would come out. So I just put the phone down again. But the third time I rang I just squeaked out 'I think I might be a lesbian,' and we had a really long chat. And after I'd talked to her several times I got up the nerve to go to a meeting, and I was quite shocked. I thought I would be able to tell that they were gay, and I couldn't tell. They just looked like people in the street. And I thought, 'Well, *anyone* could be a lesbian.'"

Problems don't miraculously go away just because you've made contact with other lesbians, but it can help tremendously to share your difficulties with other women who've gone through similar experiences, and find out how they've coped with them. Lesbian groups can offer a warm supportive and relaxing environment.

Sharing ordinary, everyday tasks is part of the give and take in friendships between women.

There are real difficulties with letting it be known that you are lesbian. Jamila keeps her lesbianism secret because she says it would cause a scandal in the Indian community: "Sex is really taboo. Anyone who talks about sex or who wants a relationship outside marriage is anyway promiscuous and immoral and a bad influence. If my family knew about me, people would talk, and the family estimate would go down, and prospects for the future would be affected by that. I may be spoiling the chances of the children for marriage. So I say nothing, and meet no one."

One Jewish woman's father read "Kaddish", the prayer for the dead, after she refused to renounce her love of women: her family now treat her as dead and even refuse to speak to her when she tries to telephone them. (Quoted in Sasha Gregory Lewis, *Sunday's Women: A report on lesbian life today*)

Mandy's father sent her to a psychiatrist to be "cured"; Sally was expelled from her convent school; Liz was raped by her sister's boyfriend who told her "All you need is a good fuck". Other women have been sacked from jobs, or refused promotion. Some women feel social outcasts and are ridiculed, taunted or ignored altogether by people they had thought were friends.

Lesbians who have, or would like to have, children often encounter a lot of prejudice because of the notion that lesbians cannot be good mothers. All the research that has been done on the children of lesbians indicates that they grow up to be distressingly normal. They choose the toys, games and dress expected of their gender, and rarely become homosexual themselves. But, as Susan Hemmings, herself a lesbian mother, points out:

The assumption is, of course, that we ourselves do not want our children to be different, but I will not blow the gaff. We do. We are not crazy about the world as it is, and we'd like our boys not to grow up into bomber pilots and our girls into animated aprons. All-American boys and girls leave us rather cold. ("Horrific practices: how lesbians were presented in the newspapers of 1978")

Dawn and Katy have two children each, but Dawn's husband won custody of her children because of her lesbianism, and Katy's ex-husband pays for her daughters to go to boarding school rather than let them live with Katy and Dawn. Katy says: "I feel as though they're being punished for my behaviour, but if I protest, my husband will fight me for custody, and I know I'd lose that, so I put up with it. I see them in the holidays."

We have to acknowledge the risks involved in being open about our lesbianism.

Being secret

But it is far too easy to let ourselves be frightened into thinking that these sorts of responses will inevitably occur if ever we let anyone know about our lesbianism, and in believing this we forget that concealing our lesbianism has its own problems and brings its own losses, too. The sheer time and energy that can go into pretending to be other than one is can be exhausting. You may find that you become very self-conscious, constantly on your guard in case you let something slip; you may publicly deny your lover, talk vaguely about relationships with men, move her belongings into the spare bedroom when your mother comes to visit, monitor everything you say over the phone to her, never touch her in public with even the lightest caress, never say with the same easy assurance adopted by heterosexual women, "*We* did this. . . ." or "*We* went there. . . ." And you're always wondering "Do you think they've guessed?" Dropping this pretence is not being "blatant" or "flaunting your sexuality"; it is assuming for yourself the same rights that heterosexuals have, and affirming that who you are is OK, too.

Telling people

There is no "right" way to tell someone important to you that you are a lesbian, no way that will *guarantee* their understanding. People who want to will find ways of rejecting you whatever you say, and however well you express yourself. But you are most likely to get a positive response if you feel genuinely happy about being lesbian and can convey this to the person you're talking to. If you break the news, shrouded in guilt or through streaming tears, in sentences that begin: "You're not going to like this, but. . . ." or "I've got something awful to tell you. . . .", you can hardly be surprised if the other person in turn becomes distressed. Blurting it out during a blazing row with a parent: "I don't care what you say; you've never really loved me anyway and it's because of you I'm a lesbian", or, during a fight with a husband: "You're no good for me anyway; I'm having an affair with Jane", will practically guarantee rejection and trauma. Indirect approaches such as "accidentally" leaving love letters or a diary where people will read them, or leaving the bedroom door unlocked "by mistake" can be appealing because you don't have to face up to the responsibility of telling someone openly and honestly about yourself, but it's a brutal method of communication, and one that often leads to recriminations and reproach.

If you feel positive about your lesbianism, you will want to tell the people you care about in a way that lets them know that you are happy about it, in a situation where they can ask questions and express their own doubts and hesitations. Debbie says that her 17-year-old son, Michael, "finds it very difficult to cope with, mainly because he's been under a lot of pressure from his father. I said, 'Look, Michael, try and remember the last seventeen years of your life, what I've been to you and who I was. The fact that I love Linda now doesn't make any difference to you and me. Being lesbian doesn't make me any different. I'm still the same person.'"

Sarah is very pleased that she told her mother: "I was about thirty at the time, and I said to her that when she was my age she was married with two children, and that my life must seem very different to hers. She said yes, that she thought I was doing things with my career and stuff that she'd never had a chance to do. It was quite a woman-to-woman talk, of a kind that I hadn't had with my mother before. And then I said that Kathy was a woman who I wanted to live with, and who I loved very much, and that it was a choice I was making and that I felt happy about it and I hoped she would learn to understand it. She seemed to. I got quite a different view of my mother when she talked with me about how she felt as a young woman and the choices she'd made, and it was good. It was really very good."

When Jenny told her father about being lesbian, "it was about a year before his death, and he was really ill. This one afternoon I was looking after him while my mother was out, and he started to talk about my sister. He said she was settled, and married, and had children, and what was happening to me? I told him. At that time I was living with Helen and was fairly happy, and I think I told him mainly because I'd always wanted to, but also because he was worried about me. And he said, 'Well, that's OK; as long as you've got someone to keep an eye on you.' There wasn't any difficulty."

Penny describes how she told her five-year-old daughter about her love for Jillian at a time when she was very unhappy about the failure of that relationship: "I was so upset, I was left in pieces, in shreds, and I couldn't stop crying. My daughter was very perplexed, and my explanation to her was that I loved somebody very much, but that I wasn't able to love them in the way that I wanted to and that made me very sad. I talked about her security blanket, because she has a little blanket that she carries around, and if she loses it, she's absolutely desperate and desolate, and I said, 'It's just the same for me. I've lost someone I want very much and I'm very sad, and that's why I've been crying.' She understood that. I mean, she was able to see that, because it's a part of family life; you know, when the blanket is lost then aaaaah!, it's a real sort of crisis!"

These women have not *apologized* in any way for being lesbian, and they have made connections between their own experience and the other person's. They have made their feelings intelligible by linking them up with things that the other person knows about (motherhood, wanting freedom, security, a child's blanket) – everyday, understandable human awareness that doesn't readily translate into textbook pathology. They have communicated their lived experience instead of using the label "lesbian" as a punishment, a threat, an apology, or even an explanation.

Listening and learning

If someone tells you that she is lesbian – it could be a sister, a daughter, a friend – try to listen to what she is saying to you. Do not assume that you know in advance what it means to her to be a lesbian, and don't leap in with advice, suggestions and information. She knows more about being lesbian than you do, because it is her lived experience; she is the expert. Don't try to shut her up by saying things like "what you do in bed is your business" or by giving premature reassurance that you know exactly how she feels and you're not at all prejudiced, so she needn't say any more about it. It's important to keep the topic open for discussion, because you can learn a lot from her. If you feel angry, upset or disgusted by her lesbianism, ask yourself why that is, and try to deal with your feelings honestly. Virginia wrote a letter from college to her mother telling her that she was lesbian. This is an extract from her mother's sympathetic reply:

Thank you for your letter – it can't have been easy to write and I'm happy and proud that you trust me and care enough about our mutual honesty to take the plunge. I love you – always – and believe I can truly accept you as you really are, at any time.

It would be dishonest of me to pretend that I liked the situation you described, even if I didn't have purple fits. All I can say is that I'm trying to understand. It seems to me that probably anything said now will seem wrong, but believe me I must, if we're to be honest, let you know some of my thoughts. ... Anyway, whatsoever, I'll try to be really *with* you, to understand. (Virginia Hoeffding, "Dear Mom")

Blocking the way

Because people are uncomfortable with lesbianism, they have invented a very rigid and narrow definition of the lesbian, so that as few women as possible fulfil the criteria and count as "real" lesbians. Almost all the women I spoke to had been told by someone that they weren't "real" lesbians. Lots of women, especially younger women, are told that it's only a phase and they'll grow out of it. Middle-aged women may be told, as Jessica was, that "it was just because my marriage hadn't worked out, and what a shame I hadn't met the right man yet".

Older women may have Debbie's experience: "My husband said it was the menopause. He actually got textbooks out of the library with cases of women who had thought they were lesbian during the menopause and who subsequently turned out not to be, after they'd totally wrecked their lives."

Sharon has been told she is not a real lesbian because she hasn't had intercourse with a man, so how does she know sex with a woman is better? Lucy *has* enjoyed sex with men, so is told she must be "really" bi-sexual. Josie has never had sex with a woman and says: "You wouldn't say to a heterosexual woman, 'how do you know you're heterosexual if you haven't had sex with a man?', or, for that matter, 'how do you know you're heterosexual if you haven't had sex with a woman to compare it with?' You really have to go out of your way to *prove* you're a lesbian."

Natalie finds that she doesn't have orgasms with women lovers, and she makes the important point that: "Lesbianism is not about sex, not about having orgasms. It's about how you want to live your life, and I want to live my life surrounded by women and knowing women closely, and getting all my sexual and emotional pleasure and comfort from women. I think probably the core of lesbianism is a strong *emotional* attachment to women."

When people deny that we are really lesbian, when they say we're "going through a phase", that we're too pretty or too "feminine" to be lesbian, that we must be bi-sexual, or depressed, or confused, or that we're just saying it in an attempt to shock and annoy, we should understand that this is really a way of denying the existence of alternatives to heterosexuality. These statements are defences against accepting our lesbianism, and they act as subtle (and not so subtle) pressures to conform. Because it is difficult for us to acknowledge our own lesbianism, we often wonder these things about ourselves too.

The question of choice

In choosing lesbianism we are making a choice that other women could also make, and many women and men feel very threatened by this possibility. They try to make us seem as different from them as

Being lesbian is about how you want to live your life . . . finding your sexual and emotional fulfilment with another woman.

possible. This is where all the theories about genes and hormones and early childhood experiences come from; they draw a dividing line between lesbians ("the third sex"!) and other women.

Many lesbians also believe that there was always something different about them. Looking back over their pasts, they remember sex play with a little girl in kindergarten, a best friend in primary school, or a crush on a woman teacher as a teenager. Jackie remembers having dreams about women when she was three years old. Andrea says "I always felt different from other girls. I never wanted to play with dolls or skipping ropes. I played football with the boys." Sarah remembers her first orgasm with a girlfriend at boarding school when they were both 11. It can seem, from stories like these, as though a woman's whole life was an unconscious acting-out of her lesbian destiny, only now apprehended as such. But in fact, loving and erotic relationships between girls and between women are part of almost all women's experience. Women who later identify themselves as heterosexual have learned to forget or ignore these feelings, to put them into a different perspective alongside their feelings for men, or think of them as mere adolescent preparations for the serious business of heterosexuality; a relationship with a man is a sign that they are at last adults.

To many women who identify as lesbian, however, there are good political reasons for telling the story of their pasts in this way. Autobiographical details demonstrating early childhood lesbianism are important to some women because they "prove" to other people, and to the woman herself, that, whatever she is told to the contrary, she *is* a real lesbian, and that being lesbian is "natural" or "normal" for her. Debbie says: "I don't believe it's a choice. Well, some people may be able to choose it, but in my case it chose me. I tried for twenty years to turn away from it, and in the end I had to follow it. If I'd had a choice, believe you me, there's no way I would have turned my life inside out and upside down and put everything at risk. I had a joint appointment with my husband, and we had a house which we jointly owned. I was a pillar of the local community; I was involved in the Family Planning Clinic and I was a regular church-goer. I had to risk all that – that was the package I was going to throw into the balance."

Diana, too, says she didn't choose to be lesbian: "Who in their right mind would *choose* to be a lesbian, for heaven's sake? It is so much easier to be straight, and acceptable and not have to hide and pretend all the time. I think it's something to do with my father being away a lot when I was little, so I didn't learn to relate to men. But it's been done now, and I can't help being lesbian. There's nothing I can do about it."

Debbie and Diana are both at a loss to explain why anyone might choose to give up the security and acceptability of a heterosexual life-style, although this is what they've both done. So they have come to believe that they had no choice, that their lesbianism was forced upon them. This belief is in some ways similar to the experience people often have after making a difficult decision (especially if we're not sure it's the right one), when we say things like "There was nothing else I could have done", "The choice was made for me", "I was forced into it", or "There really was no alternative". The desire to relate to women, and to love and live with women can seem, in the face of the tremendous pressure to the contrary, completely overwhelming and compelling. Instead of giving long explanations and justifications to people who want to know *why* we are lesbian, it is just easier to say – to them, and to ourselves – "Oh, I've been like it since I was two".

Not just sex

A large part of the social definition of the lesbian is in terms of her sexuality. Very few women see their lesbianism primarily as a sexual preference, yet this is exactly how most people think of it. A lesbian is often seen as a woman who just happens to prefer sex with women instead of sex with men, the way some people prefer vanilla ice cream to chocolate. There are a lot of myths about sex between women. It is sometimes seen as a refuge from male abuses – two pitiful creatures crawl into each other's arms for solace. Or lesbians are presented in the pornographic image as sexual superwomen, indulging in bigger and better orgasms day and night, without interruption. And because many people's idea of sex is limited to heterosexual intercourse, the notion that one woman must play the part of the "man" and the other the part of the "woman", so as to be able to mimic a heterosexual relationship, is also widely believed – even by some lesbians. These myths distort and caricature our lives as women relating to women. Sex between women can be intense, passionate and loving, warm, caring and friendly, and also, disappointing or destructive. But lesbianism is *not*, for most women, centred around sex. Lesbianism is a way of experiencing reality, a way of being in the world.

Bi-sexuality

We all have the potential to love and feel sexually attracted towards both men and women. But society usually decides *for* us, directing the teenage girl towards boys as suitable love objects. She is told that loving another member of the same sex is just a "phase". If you are bi-sexual you are obviously not happy to be pigeon-holed in this way and may see it as a gesture of liberation.

Women who describe themselves as bi-sexual are often told that they are really lesbians who are unable to accept it, or that they are really heterosexuals looking for a bit of excitement on the side. A woman can find that both her gay and straight friends pressurize her to stop "sitting on the fence"; they may insist that she "come to terms with" her sexuality, one way or the other, and encourage her to "make up her mind". But it has less to do with making decisions than with the perception of self.

Women who identify as bi-sexual often say things like "It's the person, not their gender that matters to me. I might fall in love with a man, or I might fall in love with a woman." In this way, the concept of bi-sexuality suggests someone capable of more subtle and varied experiences than those who limit themselves to just loving women or just loving men.

Bi-sexual women are showing that the rigid categories "heterosexual" and "lesbian" are much more fluid than they sometimes appear. People are not so easily boxed up into one or the other. Like lesbians, bi-sexual women reject exclusive heterosexuality, and sometimes choose to emphasize their lesbianism instead. Alison says, "Well, I'd say I was bi-sexual really, in that I would just as happily have sex with a man as sex with a woman. But I usually say I'm lesbian because it's lesbianism that's oppressed and attacked, and if there's a side to be on I want to be on that side."

There can be a lot of problems in being bi-sexual. Some women talk about the danger of *using* people: using men as meal-tickets, as husbands and fathers to their children, getting all the benefits of being heterosexual in a heterosexual society, and using women for warmth, comfort, and sensual gratification – all the benefits of being lesbian with none of the social discrimination attached. Other women feel that they sometimes use the word "bi-sexual" as a justification for an affair: "I love you a lot Sarah, but I had to sleep with Michael because I'll always need a man as well as a woman – it's the way I'm made." In this situation it might be more honest to talk about the role of monogamy and exclusive coupledom in relationships, instead of using the notion of "sexual orientation" to explain everything away.

Bi-sexuality is not the problem-free, liberated, answer-to-all-ills it is sometimes made out to be. We are all potentially bi-sexual, but we need to think very carefully about why we choose to apply that label to ourselves, how we use it, and its meaning in a social context. It is almost as if describing ourselves as "bi-sexual" serves as the justification for any romantic encounter that is in the offing and for embarking on sexual adventures just for the kick of it. It thus becomes one of the ways in which a philosophy of sexual liberation is given expression. We need to think whether this is what we really believe and whether it is what we want.

Life by yourself can be complete and satisfying…

Celebrating celibacy

"You can say, 'I'm not very musical' or 'I'm not particularly interested in
    ballet'. But you can't say that about sex."
"Windsurfers do it standing up"
"Glider pilots do it quietly"
"Young farmers do it with their boots on".

We live in a sex-oriented society. Whereas in the past women were
likely to be denied sexual feelings and were deviants if they wanted
to be sexually happy, nowadays we are considered deviant if we do
not. There is a great deal of pressure on us not only to have sex, but
to have the best possible sex and prove that we are sexually
successful. For many of us it is almost as if sex is evidence of being
alive, as if we have to prove that we exist, that we can feel, that we
are healthy, by being sexually stimulated and genitally active.

   Books are written counselling geriatric sex in order to delay
aging and even to put off death itself. We are warned to keep up
sex like jogging lest our insides shrivel. Women are told that if they
do not have intercourse or masturbate they may atrophy.

Obligatory sex

Advertisements for a wide range of medicaments, foods and vitamin supplements, ranging from vodka to Ginseng, imply that by
taking them we can stimulate libido. New experiences, even new
sexual organs, are discovered. After the clitoral orgasm and the
vibrator comes the "G-spot" on the anterior wall of the vagina and
a woman who is incapable of ejaculating feels herself inadequate. It
is, as Shere Hite suggests, like the search for the Holy Grail. And
the most difficult thing in all this welter of sexual activity is to say,
"No thank you. This is not what I want" and choose to do
something else instead. People can confess to almost anything else,
and there is bound to be a sympathetic ear, somebody who understands their particular line of sex, whether it is little boys or great
danes. But to admit that you do not want sex, that you do not care
to live with anybody, that you do not even particularly want to
masturbate, is to suggest that you are really odd. One woman,
describing how she lost her virginity at the age of 24, said she was
"so relieved". At last she no longer felt abnormal. Our society has
imposed on young people a new and onerous burden, that of always
being sexually successful and having more and better sex.

   But in some ways those who were young during the sexual
revolution of the 1960s and who are now growing older, who feel
abandoned by lovers, or who look again at the excitement of that
time and find it has all turned to dust and ashes, have suffered most
from the pressure towards sexual experience at every available
opportunity, and the frightening feeling that if they do not have
sex they will "dry up". Voluntary celibacy is, of course, very
different from celibacy forced on a woman because there are no
alternatives, or because those alternatives are distasteful.

*The unwilling
celibate*

Rowena is 44 and for her, in her twenties and thirties, sex was an
ordinary expression of friendship and of casual encounters. She
would meet a man, they would have sex, he would walk out: "It was

just a performance! It meant absolutely nothing to him." But now she is alone and the things which she finds most troubling about her life today are what she sees as disordered personal habits and self-centredness, together with black depression and intense loneliness: "I've a peculiar life-style. I sleep in my clothes. I work any time, in the sloppiest way. When the work stops I go into a kind of fog. I make no *demands* on myself. I don't clean the bath.

"My friend Sophia said, 'Why don't you get a boyfriend and we'll all go to France for a weekend?' That hurts! There isn't anybody I could ask. I go to the opera and there's no one to talk to about it. I don't have anyone with whom to discuss the *continuity* of life. That's one of the things you look forward to in old age. I worry about it."

Rowena feels trapped in celibacy from which she cannot escape. But it *is* possible to choose celibacy as a way of making personal space, of tidying life up so that you can do the things you really want to do and pour your whole energy into them.

Positive celibacy

If we are to be truly sexually free, and refuse to be pressured into doing things we do not wish to do, we must have the right to be celibate, either all the time, or for a part of our lives, without feeling we are failures or that we have to justify it in any way. Karen says: "I suppose I'm celibate, but I wouldn't call myself celibate. I know it's the official feminist name now, but it doesn't sound anything like me! It sounds like what those quirky, self-denying hermits were supposed to be under their hair shirts. I mean it sounds like it's a strain, but for me, well it's just my natural state at the moment. You know I've got all my friends, and I've got Becky [her daughter] – I need a few hugs and cuddles from them now and then, but I'm not desperate for sex."

The sexual revolution of the 1960s not only liberated many people to express and feel what they wanted, but made sex mandatory. And for women it entailed something far short of sexual freedom: their bodies were up for grabs. For many the sexual rat race resulted in a kind of numbness, an inability to feel anything, rather as if you'd eaten a whole box of chocolates and were left unable to taste anything except sugar. Women have felt coerced to have sex, and this often by the demands they have made on *themselves*, as the result of social values about sex which they had internalized and made their own.

Defining ourselves through sex

In many ways feeling that you are sexually desirable and that somebody wants your body, and that, because of this, you are valued, is important for many of us because society gives women a very limited range of ways in which we can gain self-esteem. Where men gain a sense of power and significance in business, industry and politics, for many women a feeling of self-worth comes from men wanting their bodies. And even if we do not really enjoy sex it may still be important for us, and give enormous reassurance, to play the sex game.

Through giving their bodies women can wrest from men, for themselves and their children, economic support, a home, security. It does not always work like that, of course. But our society

…and the deci
to be independent can br
a new freedom and a new stren,

conditions girls to expect to use their bodies in this way. A woman who does not do so may be pitied, ridiculed or despised. She may be described as a "bachelor girl" until she is about 30, but after that people start wondering what is "wrong". Is she a man-hater, frigid, domineering, or simply "on the shelf"? In the past the word "spinster" aptly described her state – according to the Oxford Dictionary "an old maid", "a prudish fuss-pot". Whereas a man can be described as a bachelor with some aura of glamour, there is no way in which the word "spinster" can suggest a similar carefree and pleasure-loving state of existence.

In the Middle Ages the main targets of witch hunting were spinsters and widows, women without male sexual partners who were an anomaly in society. One study of the witch hunt in Germany explains its function as being that to delineate the "thresholds of eccentricity tolerable to society" (H. C. Erik Midelfort, "Witch hunting in South Western Germany") and its psychological hold as that of "fear of a socially indigestible group: unmarried women." Single women, he says, were "a socially disruptive element" and the witch hunt an attempt to purify society from their influence.

Prejudice and disbelief

Today women still have two main uses: as sex objects and for reproduction. Women who do not fit into these two sexual categories are an aberration. A man may find it impossible to understand that a woman does not *need* men. Nicky left her husband because she was so unhappy with him: "When I walked out on him I decided I wasn't ever going to sleep with a man again. For as long as I was alone, he refused to believe it was a permanent thing. He kept coming round to 'check I was OK' and persuade me back. He was very paternal and sweet about it and he brought my mail, but it was that he just couldn't believe that we were finished. He treated it all as some kind of momentary, regrettable lapse.

"So, after I'd had enough of this, I started sleeping with another man – just to keep my husband away. Getting rid of *him*, though, was just as difficult! But what really freaked me out was when he went round and told my husband that we'd split up and that I must really be pining to get back to him! It sounds like they had a real good talk about me! Ugh! In the end I had them both at the door demanding that I choose one or other of them . . . I told them both to go to hell. I moved house, leaving no address."

It is obviously very difficult to be celibate and be taken seriously. Only a religious calling seems to many people an adequate excuse for a woman to choose celibacy, and even that is suspect. We need to accept that it is perfectly possible for a woman to live a whole, satisfying and creative life *with* love but *without* sex. That most of us prefer not to do so may be evidence of society's stamp on us rather than any intellectual conviction on the one hand or intense sexual drive on the other. Perhaps there is the niggling fear that without sex we shall miss out on love and that nobody will want us.

The advantage

Yet for many women there are obvious advantages in being celibate, at least for spaces in their lives. Some stress the freedom from fear of unwanted pregnancy and the hassle of having to use contraception. They find they have more time and can regulate it themselves. This gives them the opportunity to do different things and, once they have coped with the strong emotions which may have been triggered by the very act of becoming celibate – leaving someone or having him walk out on you, or after a death, for example – they often find that fresh energy is released. This is partly because they can start to do things *they* want to do instead of being mainly occupied with servicing someone else, or, whether the partner was a man or a woman, compromising the sense of self to sustain the partnership. It is as if you had become "John-and-Mary" – in other words half of a couple, rather than a woman in your own right. Breaking out from that, however painful it may be, means that she can start to feel an individual instead of being moulded in a composite identity.

Another consequence of this new autonomy is that a woman can make friendships which would otherwise be subordinated to the sexual partnership. Many women say that when they were committed to one other person they tended to sacrifice other friendships to sustain the sexual relationship. There is a general social expectation that you spend free time with your sexual partner.

Coping with freedom

New and varied relationships provide an opportunity for discovering new aspects of yourself and there is an astonishing, if at first alarming, sense of personal space. This new or rediscovered sense of personal space can be difficult and challenging to cope with. A woman recently widowed says: "Freedom is not always easy – decisions about what and when to eat, from whether to clear off to India again, or accept an invitation to share a cottage holiday, are not cosy. Juggling around with relationships, recognizing what you need from each of them, and getting all one's bits together to make a whole me, is a continuing process."

Janet is a single parent with three children who has been without a partner for almost a year. She left a sexual relationship in which she felt completely taken over by a man "who needs for his own security to have control of everything". She did not, she says, "want to be rescued" from being a single parent, though that is how he saw it. "For four years I had discovered that the quality of life alone was good. It was a struggle. You either go under or come through it. You find and use your own resources. But I found myself." Once she broke with her lover: "I was back to me again. I realized that I don't *have* to live through someone else. There is a strength in myself which gives me confidence, a feeling that I am part of the world again, that I belong and can make life happen. I know I can make life happen for other people too. I am able to generate a kind of energy that starts a chain of events and I have become more conscious of it since I was on my own." Though a woman may find it very difficult to cope with celibacy at first – even be frightened of being alone – the decision that she does not want a sexual partner can sometimes be a way of gaining in strength. The realization that she does not need anyone to lean on often brings a surprising sense of power. Independence, standing on her own two feet, facing life as her own self, not as one half of a partnership, can bring a new freedom and creative energy.

115

5 RELATIONSHIPS

Talking to a man about sex

Many women find it very difficult to talk about sex with their male partners. More than a quarter of the women with whom I have discussed the subject say that they never talk to their partners about things they might do to improve lovemaking. Sometimes this is because they feel it cannot do any good. Sometimes it is because they feel it is all "their fault". Sometimes the social situation in which sex takes place, living with in-laws or having to cope with family problems, for example, seems to rule out any possibility of solving sexual difficulties. One woman says she has given up trying to do anything about her sexual dissatisfaction because they have a 10-month-old baby: "Just as things would be getting interesting she would wake up. Have you ever tried making love with a baby's crying as an accompaniment!?" Sometimes a woman's own reservations about what is suitable behaviour for a woman make it almost impossible for her to start talking about sex. One woman, whose husband repeatedly hurt her during intercourse, said: "I put up with it because it doesn't seem right for *me* to be telling him what to do. It is not a woman's role and I wouldn't feel feminine."

Frustration

Women who describe their sexual frustration or complete lack of erotic feeling say that they experience complicated and mixed emotions, ranging from sadness and regret through resentment at being simply used for someone else's pleasure to intense anxiety and distress. But the overriding conviction they have is that *they* are failures. One woman who has never had an orgasm during lovemaking says: "I just wish I could relax and enjoy it and have the release of an occasional orgasm. I usually have no feeling at all, or end up going to sleep frustrated because I have taken so long to find any kind of feeling." She sees it entirely in terms of her own failure.

Fear of hurting his feelings

Most women who say they have never discussed the subject with their partner say that they feel too shy, embarrassed or inhibited, that they don't want to make a mountain out of a mole-hill and threaten the relationship in any way by complaining about what the man is doing or are afraid that he will "take it personally". The feeling that he will be hurt or angry is very common: "I am afraid I may upset his sense of masculinity." "I do not like to say these things for fear of upsetting him and making him feel inadequate." "I can't find a tactful, non-hurtful way of mentioning it at the time and the opportunity to discuss it in a non-sexual context doesn't often arise." "I don't want to hurt him. He thinks he is very good at making love."

"I wouldn't want my husband to think I was criticizing him."

In heterosexual relationships the old image of the man as attacker and the woman as passive recipient of his passion lingers on. As a result many men are not aware that there is anything wrong with their sexual technique and continue in what they have always done in the belief that what worked in the early stages of a relationship still works, or that techniques which were effective with other women must also excite the present partner. If men are really to get the accurate information they need, we must have the courage to step out of the traditional Sleeping Beauty role, waiting for the kiss from the prince to produce ecstasy.

On the other hand, it is true that some women who try and talk about improving sex do find that their men react defensively and either get angry or refuse to discuss it: "He finds it very difficult to talk about our problems constructively and generally turns my sincere efforts to talk into criticisms of my house-keeping, life-style or pre-marital affairs." "He gets annoyed if I ask him to do things differently at the time. Somehow the opportunity to talk about sex at other times is shelved by both of us." "He refuses to discuss it and changes the subject."

"You cannot talk to my husband about sex at all. He says I'm trying to tell him how to do his job."

Some women also say that when they tentatively make suggestions to improve sexual technique a man often cannot understand what he is being told. They say things like: "He tries and is getting to know *a bit* better what I like." "When we have discussed it he tries. Still he doesn't get it quite right and I don't persist with explanations." Many say that these tentative suggestions have not really improved the situation at all and most women seem to resign themselves to it. In just the same way as women feel that if they do not have an orgasm it must be their fault, so they often explain these break-downs in communication as due to something they must be doing wrong: "I must have rubbed him up the wrong way."

The subject women most want to discuss with their men is that of what is often called "foreplay", and the need for greater all-over body stimulation before penetration. This is probably because "having sex" is usually defined in terms of penetration and ejaculation so when we ask a male partner to make love to us and to our whole bodies, not just one part of them, it tends to be thought of as something extra, a favour to the woman that the man will offer if he can be bothered and if he can control himself long enough.

The "encouragement" approach

When women tell men that they would like something done differently it is often seen as running the risk of "upsetting his masculinity" or "slighting his manhood". And because so many women feel that their male partners will either be annoyed if they try to talk about sex or will quickly lose confidence, many resort to what one woman calls "the encouragement system": "Sometimes he is clumsy and hurts me. I have never made an issue of it as he tries his best and a woman's labia are very intricate I suppose. When he was gentle I said at the time how gentle he was and how it turned me on and that method seems to have worked. But sometimes when he strokes my clitoris he scratches my pubic hair. This is a recent development. I wait till he stops and praise what he does next. My husband *hates* being told what to do in bed. We once had a ferocious argument about it. He feels I am criticizing him, however gently I try to put it, which is why I have developed this 'encouragement system', which works, but, oh so slowly!" Another woman says: "I try to communicate by sound or gesture, pulling his hands to where I would like them, making sounds of pleasure or saying 'Mmmmn, that's nice' when he does it the right way."

Women who have been effective in telling men what they want often say that it is best not to make suggestions about changes in lovemaking when a man is highly aroused. To interrupt his passion with a discussion of techniques can be a bit like talking about diets in the middle of a delicious meal and is guaranteed to reduce pleasure. It is important to find a time when you are comfortably together, cuddling and feeling close, perhaps. (Though it is precisely this kind of non-sexual touching and affection which most women who are unsatisfied sexually say is lacking in their lives.) A woman might say, "I want to talk a bit about my sexual feelings" or

Finding the right time to talk about your feelings can make all the difference.

"Can we make some time to talk together about sex?" Or she can use the opportunity provided by a hand on a leg or arm or any kind of friendly stroking to say, "I love it when you do that when we are making love, and especially if you . . ." and go on to explain the kind of touch she enjoys. Or she may herself use a touch which she knows her man likes and relate the pleasure he experiences to the kind of touch she is giving him and point out that this is what *she* would like him to do to her, too.

The use of encouragement as a style of persuasion is one often recommended to those asking advice on sexual problems in the pages of women's magazines. Dr Philip Cauthery, who answers readers' problems in *Parents*, for example, recommends to a woman who writes that her husband only wants to masturbate in front of her, that she should "involve" herself in his masturbation, discover what sexual thoughts excite him and then try to fulfil them: "Respond ecstatically, so as to encourage him to greater efforts. Be patient, loving, understanding and subtle, flattering and seductive." When she has somehow got his penis inside her, which she is counselled to do by climbing on top of him when he does not expect it, she is told she must "encourage" him, and an important part of this is for her to have an orgasm while his penis is in her vagina. She is advised to "keep trying, and avoid resentment". Dr Cauthery does not disclose how she is to ensure that she gets an orgasm following penetration but tells her that she should "make him reach orgasm and ejaculate before his anxiety has built up". Perhaps he means that she is to simulate orgasm if she cannot get one spontaneously. One suspects that though her husband will enjoy all this, she will very likely be left with her problem.

Confrontation v. manipulation

On the other hand, some women feel that it is demeaning for a man to be treated, "the way you train a dog with a chocolate drop when it does the right thing". They feel that this traditionally approved "feminine" way of doing things is extremely manipulative. Men ought to be treated as equals and this entails frankness and openness about sex, not manipulation. Many women who reject this manipulative kind of approach sometimes feel that the only alternative is direct confrontation and criticism. Yet when sharing thoughts and feelings about sex it is very important to stress positive aspects if a partner is not to be left bewildered and hurt. Men *are* sexually vulnerable. From boyhood they are taught to believe that sexual performance is an index of masculinity. To criticize their performance is to strike at the roots of their sense of self. On the other hand, when a woman only hints at a dissatisfaction, when she is so tactful as to be inscrutable and fails to be definite about what she wants, a man cannot learn how to please her.

Emphasizing your own feelings

The answer is always to stress *your feelings* rather than his performance. Then when you know that the message has been received you can reinforce it during lovemaking and be even more specific.

It is not always like this, of course. Some couples find it easy to talk and share together, to explore different ways of making love and discover what each wants. Women who describe this kind of relationship often comment on its quality as a whole, rather than

*There is tension in every sexual
relationship at some time...
it needs to be worked through.*

just its sexual aspects. They say it is easy to talk with their partners about *anything*. Discussing how sex can be improved is just one aspect of sharing freely with each other.

This may provide a clue to what needs to be done if sex is not to become just one more skirmish on the battle-ground of a relationship. Talking together about other things, rediscovering or getting to know each other for the first time as people, not as sexual protagonists or potential providers of orgasms, is vitally important if a couple are going to be able to talk spontaneously and easily about sex. When a sexual relationship is not going well either partner, or both, may see it as the central problem, but it is almost invariably part of a larger pattern. Learning new techniques to trigger off orgasm is not going to provide a solution to these other difficulties, though it does, undoubtedly, sometimes ease the path.

Once past the first fine rapture of excitement in a relationship, most couples need to work out a sexual repertoire that suits them. It is not simply a matter of discovering what "works" and then sticking to it for the rest of their lives. They change or a new kind of stimulus is needed and they build on what they have already learned about each other and develop new skills. The process of sharing feelings, the discussion and rehearsal involved, can be part of the build-up to sexual excitement. Talking together about sex can be an integral part of arousal, rather than a discouraging end-of-term school report in which you tell him that he "doesn't try hard enough" or "could do better". In every man's life there have been powerful women – mothers, teachers, perhaps others, too – and in the situation when a man feels he is being reprimanded and directed he often responds exactly as if he were trapped in these earlier relationships. He reacts like a small boy. It is as if the sexual partner has become the mother controlling his bowel and bladder behaviour or the schoolmistress criticizing his sums and spelling. Throughout life men, and women too, regress to these earlier patterns of response in situations of stress.

The impact of early experiences

Women often bring to sexual relationships early conditioning which leads them to feel that they cannot be truly feminine if they ask for what they want and take the lead in sex. So it can be important for both partners to recognize the possible long range effects of childhood experiences, to talk together about their childhood and get to know each other, not only as they are now, but as they were then. It is something that people living in village communities probably had almost as a matter of course, since not only was the past spun into the present without any break, but everybody knew everybody else. In contemporary Western culture we encounter each other more or less in isolation from all the earlier formative influences in each other's lives and have to work at learning about and understanding each other.

Maureen

Take Maureen, for example. She comes from an Irish Catholic background: Right through her adolescence, Maureen says, there was a conflict in her mind between an intense curiosity about sex and dread of the consequences of "indulging" in it. She was taught that boys had "insatiable passions". It was a girl's responsibility to "keep things cool". "We were told about the 'point of no return' which I pictured like a high-speed film." She grew up scared of being attractive to men and that things would get out of control.

She did not have sexual intercourse until she married and then discovered that, instead of the heavens opening and choirs of angels singing, it was all rather tedious and boring. She had some sexual tension, and occasionally masturbated, but even then could not let herself go and stopped short of orgasm: "I feel so guilty and dirty afterwards." During her first pregnancy she sometimes had an orgasm with lovemaking. She says this was because the fear of conception was removed and she could relax and enjoy it. As she relaxed, fantasies shaped in her mind about being made to submit to intercourse by a gang of youths on motorbikes or making love on the top of a bus or in some other public place where they might get "caught", but she never told Geoff about these fantasies and was careful not to let him see that she was excited: "I'd feel ashamed to let him see me come." With a complete absence of sharing, neither partner knowing what the other was experiencing, sex became a mechanical routine. Geoff never varied his techniques, only used the "missionary position", and over the years restricted sex to Saturday nights, as regularly as clockwork. Now, with three young children, Maureen is frustrated and unhappy. She says Geoff acts as if she has no feelings, but that she could not possibly talk to him about this because it would be "unfeminine". Though he polishes her clitoris assiduously for a few minutes before penetration, she feels she cannot possibly tell him how to bring her to orgasm as he would then realize that she had masturbated. Over the last year they have had intercourse less and less often and she wonders whether there is another woman. If there is, she says, "I don't blame him." This is just one example of a couple who cannot possibly begin to work out their problems unless they see the difficulties they are facing now in the perspective of the past and open up discussion.

But even when they have done this, they need to move on from that understanding to realize that what we learn from our parents is derived from much more widely imposed social values. Parents are the medium through which social ideologies are inculcated in the young. Mothers are often blamed for their children's problems. But it is much more complicated than that.

When a woman is unhappy in sex it is not really her mother's "fault", any more than it is Geoff's mother's fault that he does not know how to bring his wife to orgasm. Our mothers, too, were trapped and moulded by the culture they passed on to us and we merely evade the challenges facing us if we try to explain them by accusing our mothers of being responsible for our misery. It is for us to come to terms with our past and to deal with our problems.

A couple need to look at their total relationship and at the assumptions they make about their roles as man and woman.

The evidence from women talking about their sexual problems is that a couple who are not communicating well *generally* are not able to communicate about sex. And when they cannot talk about sex the woman is far less likely to experience orgasm, or, even if she does, feels that it is merely a physical mechanism of climax and remains *emotionally* unsatisfied.

We grow in self-confidence by becoming aware of our needs... and daring to be honest about them.

Developing self-confidence in sex

Self-confidence is the best basis for a relationship if it is to grow and develop and give space for a woman to be herself. Many of us lack confidence in sexual relationships. Few of us start off entirely confident but it is something we learn with positive experience.

Women often find themselves on the serving, passive side of sex, primarily concerned with meeting a man's needs. When we love someone we long to give ourselves entirely. This giving of self is beautiful and we lose ourselves to find ourselves. Or that is how we would like it to be.

Discovering what you want

In fact, it does not always work out like that. A woman often gives herself but cannot find the space to stand back from the experience to discover who *she* is and what *her* needs are. She may see her roles as those of loving wife and mother, efficient house cleaner, cordon bleu cook, skilful courtesan, politician, gardener, charming hostess, "sex kitten", chauffeur, imaginative house decorator, psychologist, discerning shopper – and a host of other things – but she has lost *herself* in the process. A woman in this situation feels frustrated and resentful, yet guilty about being discontented because she believes that, with a nice home, a loving husband and gorgeous children, she ought to be happy. But she has been typecast into playing standard roles that can become boring and repetitive. This scenario varies for different women, of course. But there is a common pattern in many of our lives which is that of caring for others and as a result failing to acknowledge what we really want ourselves. (Anne Dickson, *A Woman in Your Own Right*)

The resulting feeling of having no identity apart from the people we love and care for is much more threatening and all-pervasive than any dissatisfaction as a result of difficulties in sex. Changing sexual techniques offers no solution when the underlying reason for unhappiness is this sense of being completely used up by other people's needs.

Miserable as many women are made by this, they are also often trapped by their own longing to be valued by and necessary to those they serve. They may honestly believe that their families could not possibly manage without them (they usually *would* manage, of course, but in a different way), but deep down these women derive satisfaction from other people's dependence. And all too often there is the fear that without their dependants needing them like this they would crumble away and be nobody at all.

When this happens it is not only the woman who is trapped. All those whose needs she serves are trapped *with* her, too. They begin to resent her and the more she tries to make them happy, the more stifling the relationships can become.

This is when the "zipless fuck" (a phrase used by Erica Jong in *Fear of Flying*) can seem an exciting alternative to the tight and throttling bonds of marriage and family. Yet since not only self-respect, but any remaining shreds of identity, depend on continuing to meet the expectations of those with whom one is caught in the trap, many women could not allow themselves casual sexual encounters. Many, too, feel themselves unattractive and lack the sexual confidence, or verve, to go on adventures of this kind.

The answer, in fact, is that a woman has to change the nature of the social group in which she functions day by day. This means that, though she may not want to change the actual *people* in her group, the relationships and her role in it have to be changed. And she cannot do that unless she first defines what her *own* needs are and develops self-confidence by discovering she can change her life to accommodate them. Once she has done this, she can decide on ways in which she might be assertive and state what she wants.

Preparing yourself for change

It may be difficult for a woman to make this break when her children are still small. But as they grow up and can tie their own shoelaces, and can help themselves to snacks from the 'fridge, it will become vital for her to clear a space for herself and refuse to permit others to rely on her all the time. It takes direct action to get the image of "Supermum" down off its plinth. Idealization of women as mothers has, over the centuries, been a cleverly contrived way of preventing them from defining their own identities. However, it is no good erecting a statue when there is a real woman trying to find herself.

It is often hard for a woman to accept that ultimately she is responsible for her own life. A society designed mostly for the convenience of men puts women under such pressure that the only emotional release we may have is the kind of inturned anger that allows us to feel very sorry for ourselves. Being trapped can also mean that we are paralysed and unable to change not only the big things in life but also to make any move to alter smaller everyday things. You may not want to ditch the family, change your job, stop cooking supper, go on a holiday alone, or to refuse ever again to scrabble under the bed for your husband's dirty socks. But the important thing is to recognize that you do *have that option*. Getting to this point of decision-making is important. Otherwise you may simply leave yourself immobilized in swamps of self-pity.

Strategies for change

Select just one of the things you would like to alter in your life and work out a strategy for change. Decide the most effective method of making it clear to everyone that this change is going to take place, of reminding them that it has occurred when they conveniently forget, and also of reminding yourself.

How do you think *you* will react emotionally when you do not get the approval of people who really matter to you – the "significant others" in your life? Getting steamed-up with anger against them or with self-loathing on the other hand, or collapsing with pity for them, will make it much more difficult to tackle the problem rationally. A simply prepared strategy as to what to say and do to meet their objections and criticisms will help you avoid these pitfalls. You will have to accept that you may not be able to win their approval for what you are doing. For some women this may be the first time in their lives that they have not been dependent on the wishes or esteem of other people.

Different people will obviously make different choices about what course of action will best help them establish a bit of independence and, as a result, self-confidence. One woman, for example, decided to set aside time each week for voluntary work. Another took a part-time job. For both of their families it meant a reorganization of daily life and acceptance of new responsibilities by the other members. Yet another woman came to the conclusion that she needed a holiday on her own for two weeks each year, just to be by herself – away from everyone.

Josie's husband disapproves of public protests. They are, he says, "always an incitement to violence and it is no wonder that police are heavy-handed in order to preserve law and order, and that people get hurt". It was, therefore, a big decision for Josie to visit a peace camp outside a nuclear missile site.

Whatever you decide to do, remember that you are doing something for *yourself*, that *you* want. And you do not have to give yourself or anyone else any other justification.

Obstacles to assertiveness

As you work through the options you have for changing your life, take note of your emotional reactions. How you feel can guide you to identify and understand some of the greatest barriers to change – those you produce from inside yourself. We often block the way to being assertive about sex, just as we put blocks in the way of being assertive in our other relationships. Which, if any, of the blocks in the descriptions which follow apply to you and are stopping you from being sexually assertive?

Many women's inability to be sexually assertive arises from a low sense of self-worth. Felicity, for example, is ashamed and apologetic about her body and so grateful when any man shows an interest in her that she offers herself on a plate. She usually finds herself in bed with older men with a "macho" image, who have a good line in talk and make her feel desirable and feminine.

Not recognizing that one has a right to decide one's own sexual identity is often linked with this low sense of self-worth. Some women accept a partner's assumptions about who they are and how they should be treated without ever questioning what is happening, or realizing that, like the many women today who are critical of the old male power relationships, they have the capacity to change what they don't like.

Saying, as one woman did, "You can't change them, men, can you?" is resigning oneself not to the fact that men cannot be changed, but to the fact that one is not prepared to try.

Being passive also devalues the partner because it involves drawing back from full involvement with the other person on equal terms. The woman who says, "I can't say I enjoy it. I just wait till he's finished. He's really very understanding and asks me if I like what he is doing and I usually say 'Yes' and things like that to please him," is being passive. She is also cheating herself of what, with a little bit of assertiveness on her part as to how things could be improved, could be a more satisfying relationship.

For many women there can be the feeling that they do not want "to make a fuss", and that if they only wait long enough a problem

127

will go away or a relationship sort itself out automatically. There are women who continue to fake orgasm because they started pretending years ago and it would now be too awful to let their men know that they have hardly ever experienced one, but have been putting on a performance. If a man has been led to believe that something he does gives a woman an orgasm he keeps on doing the same thing, in the belief that this is an effective sexual technique. He is not going to change that unless she dares to be open and honest with him. To wait in hope is merely to reinforce his habitually poor sexual technique.

Anxieties about being assertive

At the heart of many of the reasons that prevent women from asserting themselves sexually can be the fear of being "punished" – directly by their partner's ill temper, or indirectly by other things going wrong in their lives as a result of what they have done. It is true that society often punishes people for daring to step out of line, but if women behave like children waiting to be punished they actually reinforce the situation in which men are the rule-makers and punishers and women simply become victims.

There can be times when anxiety is based on bitter experience. A battered wife may have good reason to believe that being sexually assertive will cause trouble. But often anxiety is more a worry about how the other person will react if you do or say anything which breaks the established pattern of the relationship.

Another element in not being assertive may be embarrassment or shame: "I couldn't ask him to do that. . .I don't like talking about down there." A woman may be very reluctant to ask her partner to change a sexual technique, leave the light on during lovemaking or make love to her in front of a mirror, even though she would very much enjoy these things, because she has a feeling that the whole process is slightly indecent and this makes her reticent about expressing any sexual preferences.

Assessing one's own reactions

We may try to handle our inability to be assertive in a variety of ways. Knowing how we react can sometimes enable us to see situations in which we could have been assertive but have failed to be so. If you find yourself, for example, criticizing your partner, feeling very angry or turned-off sexually, you may be able to look a bit further back in time and discover that you missed an opportunity to be assertive and that tension has built up in your relationship because of this.

Sexual assertiveness

When you know that you can make some changes, however minor, in your everyday life by making decisions about what you want and sticking to them, go on from there to think about your sexual needs. Men usually take it for granted that they have the right, even the responsibility, to be sexually assertive. Women need to learn how to be. And one element in this is the recognition that you have the right to say you do not like things your partner enjoys or that you feel uneasy about something – it is important to be aware of your feelings and honest about them. After all, nobody else is a better judge of how you feel and what you want than you are.

As before, think of some of the things you would like to change in your sexual relationship. Be sure to select only aspects that can be affected by some action on your part. Does your partner really know that something he thinks must be exciting is actually a big turn-off for you, for example? What could he do that you would enjoy much more? Think of how you will tell him or lead him to do this. Is there something you want to do that your partner rarely or never does? How could you set the scene for it? It is important to be constructive if you are going to tackle a sexual problem, to suggest alternatives rather than just criticize what he does do.

Being sexually assertive is quite different from being aggressive. A woman who exclaims: "You're a rotten lover! I've never had an orgasm. I've been faking every time just to satisfy your silly pride!" is being belligerent, not assertive. It might be a salutary shock for her partner but she is not telling him what he can do about it and he will almost certainly feel humiliated and angry, and it is unlikely that anything positive will come out of this confrontation.

You do not need to become "a castrating woman", someone who is always giving directions or who is unable to savour and enjoy sex. Assertiveness means refusing to be passive and it involves learning to express how you feel in a constructive way. Aggression can only provoke hostility and a defensive or attacking response in your partner. Assertiveness in sex means entering into a partnership and giving both of you the chance to make it a going concern or deciding that this is not for you and putting an end to it. Saying honestly how you *feel* is a good basis for assertiveness. The validity of your feelings cannot be disputed. The woman who says, "I need

You can start being assertive just by saying what you want.

Assertiveness in sex means entering into a partnership, and expressing how you feel in a constructive way...

more time before you come inside. I'm just beginning to feel a rosy glow, especially when you do *this*. . . ." or who takes her lover's hand to guide it to where she wants stimulation, is being assertive.

Ladder of assertiveness

Being assertive is easy in some situations, difficult in others. Starting off by trying to be assertive in a really threatening situation may mean that you give up trying after the first attempt. It is best to tackle easier things first. Developing self-confidence in sex is a matter of gradually getting more control about what you do and who you are. It is unlikely that you will become assertive at one fell swoop. So start with small things which matter to you and then build on them, as if climbing a ladder of assertiveness. You will gain confidence from your success in coping with relatively easy, non-threatening situations and will be able to develop your skills.

Then think of being assertive in a way you would find slightly more difficult and do exactly the same thing. This forms the second rung of your assertiveness ladder. Have a look at the ladder constructed here by an imaginary person we can call Deborah.

When you have made your own ladder of things about which you want to be assertive, look again at those at the bottom of the ladder and think of ways in which you could be assertive – the words you might use and what you might do – starting with the easiest situations and working up.

AN ASSERTIVENESS LADDER

17 Suggesting that we use a sex aid

16 Suggesting that I show my partner by masturbating how I can get aroused most easily

15 Saying I want to make love without intercourse

14 Telling my partner that I have often pretended to have orgasm

13 Asking my partner to delay penetration

12 Telling my partner that I did not have an orgasm and that I do not want one just now

11 Asking my partner to talk when making love

10 Telling my partner that something he does is really uncomfortable

9 Saying I don't want to make love

8 Suggesting changes in sexual techniques

7 Saying that I don't like something my partner is doing

6 Getting my partner to realize how switched off I am when one of the children wakes up and cries

5 Describing the effects of something we are doing together

4 Saying what I would like my partner to do

3 Describing my sexual feelings

2 Explaining to my partner changes in desire at different times of the month

1 Saying I enjoy something my partner is doing

Deborah

Deborah, for example, wanted to be able to say to her partner: "I like it when you stroke the small of my back very lightly." It was fairly easy for her to do this, but often she did not ask her partner to do something she specially enjoyed because she was reluctant to interfere with *his* pleasure. In fact, he found it exciting when she told him what she liked. When Deborah thought about describing her sexual feelings she at first found it quite difficult to put her thoughts into words, but then decided that she would like to say to her partner: "When you touch me like that it feels like hundreds of sharp little flames spilling through from my clitoris to deep inside me and then turning into a pulsing sun." She was anxious about hurting her partner by saying she did not like something, but several things he had been doing regularly interrupted her flow of sexual feeling and what she wanted to say was: "I don't like it when you give me smacking kisses on my ear and scrunch up my hair."

When Deborah thought about how she would say that she did not want intercourse she decided to say: "I don't want you inside me tonight but I love being stroked and cuddled." And on an occasion when she was not in the mood for lovemaking she made up her mind to say: "I don't want to make love, darling. I feel I need a bit of space round me and I don't want even to be held." Explaining that something your partner does actually hurts you can be threatening, especially if you have put off saying this for a long time. Deborah plucked up courage when her lover next did what she disliked and said: "It hurts when you bite. Please don't do it."

Suppose that, like so many men, Deborah's lover was strong and silent during intercourse. To tackle this in an assertive way Deborah decided to say: "One of the things I want is for you to talk about your *feelings* when we make love and to say tender love words and what we'll do now." It can be difficult for a man to understand that a woman does not want orgasm and can be satisfied without one. "I don't always want one. Sometimes I enjoy making love without orgasm. I feel a warm glow and flood of energy, and that's just right for me then."

Perhaps her partner took it for granted that as soon as she was lubricated he would penetrate. Deborah wanted to say: "No, don't come in yet. Go on doing that. It's lovely. Coming in would spoil it. I enjoy doing that for a long time." Asking her partner to do something which was not a regular part of their lovemaking proved even more threatening, but what she wanted to say was: "I'd love you to gently lick my clitoris with your tongue." Deborah had been simulating orgasm and found it difficult to tackle this subject. She wanted to explain to her lover why she had been pretending. It was because she wanted to please him: "I want to make you happy and I realize you are happy when you know I have an orgasm. That's why I've pretended all along. I'm not finding it easy to tell you this, but I've never had an orgasm with lovemaking, only sometimes when I've masturbated. So there are things I want to change about the way we make love. I'd like you to help me discover how to have an orgasm." And the next step was for her to show her lover, by guiding his hand, how she wanted to be touched: "The right kind of touch for me is soft and gentle, like this. I need steady stimulation from your fingers."

The most difficult thing of all was for her to suggest that she wanted to use a sex aid: "I think it would be exciting to try a vibrator and for you to hold it between my legs while you kiss me."

Your own ladder of assertiveness may be very different and the way in which you will want to express your preferences and dislikes may be different too. This is certainly not intended as a model of how you should put things into words, only as one person's way of working out how to be assertive. And even when you have a strategy and know what you want to say it is not always that easy to take effective action. You may have to be very determined and persistent in order to be sexually assertive. The first time you state your wishes you may find that you are ignored. It is then necessary to pluck up courage and to repeat what you want. Sometimes a woman has to do this over and over again before her partner actually hears her. It is called the technique of the "cracked record". (Pamela Butler, *Self-Assertion for Women*) It consists of saying how you feel and what you want, quietly but firmly, over and over again till the message is clear.

Anticipating difficulties

If you understand your partner well you probably have a fairly accurate idea of what the response may be. This will obviously vary according to the situation and your lover's mood at the time. It can help if you think out the most likely reactions and plan what you might do and say. How can you cope with negative reactions in an assertive way? Let us imagine that Deborah, having decided to tell her partner that she would like to use a vibrator, meets with the response, "You must be joking!"

The conversation might go like this: "I know it comes as a surprise, but I really would like to try using a vibrator."

"Aren't I good enough for you?"

"You're a *very* good lover. That's why I would enjoy doing something else together, too – using a vibrator."

Or she might have decided to say: "I like you to make love to me very slowly and to stroke very gently – like this." Suppose he then went on to say:

"Ssssh . . . don't talk. This is *my* job."

"It isn't just your job. I like it when I can ask you to do things for me. I like to say what I enjoy."

"You are making me lose my erection."

"I'm sure it can come back quick enough! But actually that's rather nice for me because that way you make love for much longer and much slower. It's wonderful when you make love really slowly."

"Why don't you just lie back and enjoy it?"

"Because I want to feel alive and active, not passive – at the receiving end. I enjoy it most when I suggest where and how you touch me and it's very exciting when you touch me like that."

Thinking ahead can help to sort out how you can deal with negative responses that come in the form of attack or evasion. It is often not too difficult to make a first statement assertively, but it is easy to get rattled at your partner's response and discover that what you intended to be a calm, reasonable conversation in an atmosphere of warmth and caring has turned into a battle, or that it seems better to give up and just let things go on as they were before.

Using your imagination in this way can also help you think ahead to the right *setting* in which you plan to be assertive. Announcing something at breakfast, or when your partner is feeling very passionate, or is just about to drop off to sleep after an exhausting day, is likely to provoke a very different response compared with something you say when you are cuddling in front of a fire, sunning yourselves in a garden or having a lie-in on a Sunday morning. It is easier for you both if your partner is relaxed but still attentive.

Discovering self-assertiveness in sex starts with looking first at your own needs, learning more about your sexuality and getting on better terms with your body and going on from there to find words in which to express how you feel, what you want and how you would like lovemaking to change. The result can be a new sharing, and a deeper understanding between lovers.

Touch and timing

He was finished in a matter of seconds . . . He pulled away, sat up, guzzled half a beer and lit a cigarette . . . .

"Maybe some day, if we keep this up," she murmured "you'll even learn how to screw."

"You don't like how I do it?"

"What's there to like? or dislike?"

"What do you mean?" He was always the first to come during the circle jerks in junior high. He had the biggest dick in the whole school. What did she want anyhow – a telephone pole?

"You are too fast. A girl likes it slow, with a lot of hugging and kissing."
(Lisa Alther, *Original Sins*)

This chapter focuses on what a woman can teach her partner about making love to her. Many of us are reticent about saying what we would like and a lover often feels that it is humiliating to need to be told anything. We have seen already that men are often extremely defensive of anything that smacks of criticism of their sexual technique. But this is a difficulty encountered not only with a male partner. Though a woman may feel she should instinctively understand another woman's responses, even lesbian lovers may need to learn these things. All loving, in both its physical and emotional aspects, involves learning and touch and timing are vital in this process of discovery.

A man once told me that making love to a woman is like playing a musical instrument and that once you know the techniques they can be applied to any woman with equal effectiveness. All the evidence coming from women themselves about what is important to them in lovemaking suggests that this just is not true. Each new relationship requires its own artistry and lovers need to discover how to construct their own patterns of lovemaking and find a harmony that is right for them. It is a creative process quite different from the idea of being programmed for orgasm. There is more in it even than that: people change and mature and a way of making love that was fine for a woman in her twenties may need to be adapted to the different person she has become when she is 40.

The two subjects of touch and timing must be discussed together, for a touch which is absolutely right at one stage of lovemaking can be completely wrong at another. As one woman says: "I like being touched everywhere in different ways. It's the order of the procedure that matters, not how or where: flirting, kissing, cuddling must come before stroking, fondling, undressing."

Complete body stimulation

By far the most frequent criticism women make of male partners is that they concentrate almost exclusively on the genitals and do not give enough all-over body stimulation: "He sticks to the so-called erotic areas – fanny, breasts, etc, when I like to have other parts of my body caressed – my back, sides and legs." "He rushes straight to my genital area before I feel in the mood." "I want to give and get comfort, not just pure lust." "He is intent on being the thrusting, probing, domineering male. Quite often he will forget my needs and think I just want a penis pushing hard inside me. I do not like it when he forgets the rest of my body."

Much of the advice men get and share with other males about sexual skills seems to be in this "magic tricks" department. Many men continue to operate at this level when all the evidence they are getting from a relationship points to its ineffectiveness. Jean says she wishes her husband would take more interest in her as a *person*, "all day as well as in bed . . . the TV is the most important thing in his life until he wants sex" and her words come in a rush: "and I wish he would wash oftener and not be all spotty and dandruffy with smelly socks!" Godfrey has no idea at all of the effect he is having on Jean and will be very surprised when she leaves him.

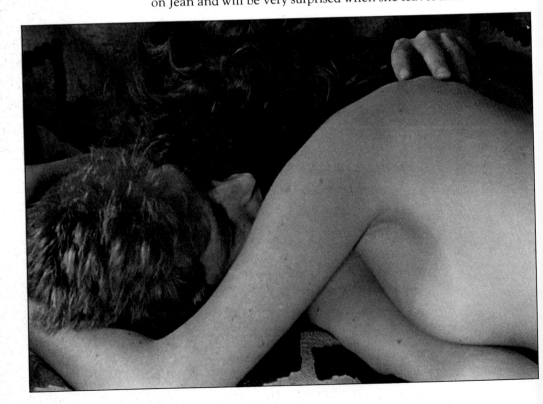

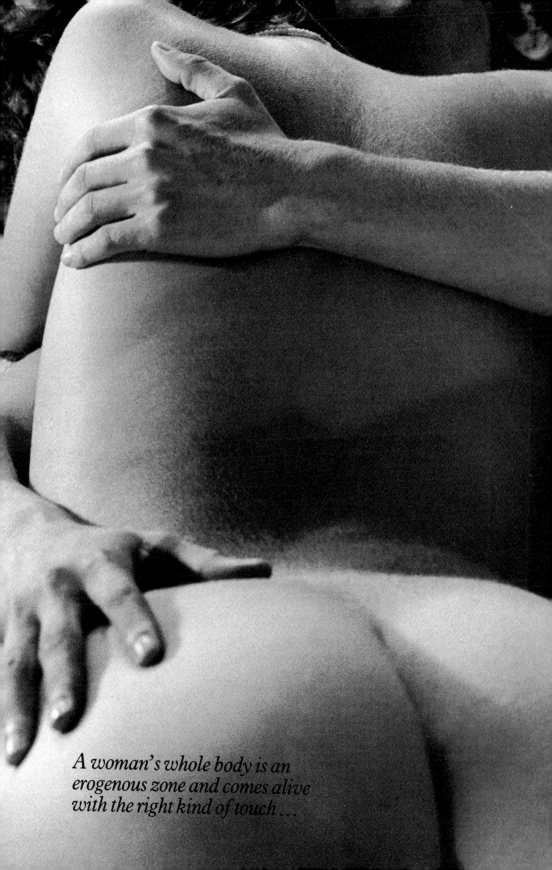

A woman's whole body is an erogenous zone and comes alive with the right kind of touch . . .

Efforts to please

Women often feel bound to take trouble to please men. They are brought up to believe that they need to make themselves more attractive through dress, cosmetics and dieting. They pluck their eyebrows, varnish their nails, put on make-up, wonder if he likes the blue dress better than the green, the silver earrings or the gold necklace, the musky perfume or the flowery scent. When they have been together with a man for a few years they realize that men take far less trouble to be attractive to them. The un-deodorized, unshaven male with a grubby collar, scratchy toenails and calloused hands can be pretty revolting! Women say their partners have unpleasant habits, many of which interfere with lovemaking, such as "burping", "breaking wind", "scratching", "snorting with catarrh", smoking ("I wish he would give up smoking. I can smell the faggy smell even when he has brushed his teeth a couple of times and rinsed with mouthwash") and drinking ("If my husband has been drinking I don't like to kiss him because he has stale breath"). A little self-reflection about such matters may be even more important for some men than improving sexual techniques.

Cuddling, gentle stroking, kissing and back-rubbing are all ways in which a woman can be aroused. The rest of her body then automatically goes with her, instead of seeming to be target practice for an exclusive male activity. Women also are sensually aroused by being caressed without being made to feel that it is always the prelude to intercourse. Some become so alerted by the predatory sexual approach of a partner, knowing that it is seen as foreplay to intercourse and must have one inevitable conclusion, that they tense up the moment he starts to touch them. It is as if the man is proffering some minor pleasures as payment for getting down to what he really wants to do. "I can't feel responsive to kisses which are supposed to lead to lovemaking when I know that that's their intention", one woman says.

There are still men who do not understand the importance of the clitoris in female sexual arousal or who do not bother about providing any clitoral stimulation. They go straight to penetration, often before the woman is excited at all and when her vagina is not lubricated. Many women can enjoy satisfying sex and have full arousal without any kind of penetration.

But even when a man realizes that he should delay penetration, or that the woman may not want it at all, he sometimes makes straight for the erogenous zones or the clitoris, with a hand or mouth, ignoring every other part of the body. There is a right sequence for every woman and this must be adapted to her mood, the time of day and the situation in which lovemaking starts. Women need plenty of time in which to unwind and begin to feel desired and desirable.

Loving touch

The first phase of touching should be designed simply to relax the woman and help her, step by step, to smooth out muscle tensions and enjoy her body. Sometimes this will be enough and she will not want to go on to more embraces and intercourse. This kind of touch is pleasurable in itself and should never be considered "foreplay".

Even when caresses become more passionate and she responds with arousal, emphasis should be on teasing, and stroking all over

her body, not just the obvious erogenous zones. Concentrating on these alone can make a woman feel as if she is one of those cookery book diagrams about how to choose a joint, with her body divided into "rump", "haunches", "sirloin", "underbelly", "ribs" and so on. She may like her neck stroked very gently and lightly, may enjoy the feel of a hand seeking sensuous pleasure from the texture of hair, the curves of her face traced with a finger, perhaps a slow, comforting head massage or long, slow stroking on the insides of her arms or legs. One woman who says her husband does not take enough time over lovemaking comments, "The problem is that men's sexual excitement is concentrated in the penis and they imagine that a woman is similar and that just by giving the clitoris a quick rub she will get very excited and ready for intercourse." Some women enjoy breast stimulation fairly early in lovemaking. Others, whose nipples are very responsive, like it to be kept till later: "I am not awfully keen on a lot of attention being given to my breasts till I am near orgasm. I especially dislike my nipples being fiddled with." The responsiveness of the breasts varies with the time of the month and for some women nipples may feel too tender to be touched just before a menstrual period. Other women find that they can be most readily stimulated then.

Stimulating the clitoris

There comes a phase in lovemaking when a woman longs for her clitoris to be gently, subtly touched with a tantalizing, deft stroking movement. The kind of touch is important, for if the clitoris is treated as a "magic button" which only has to be pressed to elicit sexual arousal, she feels that her partner is employing mechanical techniques of stimulation that are the very opposite of tenderness or genuine eroticism. Jean says of her lover: "He thoroughly overstimulates my clitoris with too much direct digital pressure." Men are often rather heavy-handed with the clitoris in this way, treating it as if it were a smaller version of the penis, instead of an exquisitely sensitive and unique female organ. Some are rough without realizing it, putting a painful weight on the clitoris, pinching and sometimes pulling it at an angle that causes further pain. They also make fast rubbing movements and continue doing this in an effort to arouse sexual response until the woman is feeling physically irritated and sore. In the penis many of the nerve endings which convey intense sexual stimuli are above the coronal ridge, around the mushroom-shaped tip of the erect organ. In the clitoris the most satisfying kind of touch is one provided by stroking or licking the *root* of the organ or by not touching the clitoris itself at all, but rather *the inner vaginal lips* that connect up with the hood that slides over the clitoris. When sexual stimulation is at its greatest, the penis sticks out. When the clitoris is most responsive to sexual stimulation it also becomes erect, but slips *under* the tissue surrounding it.

The clitoris can be stimulated lying or sitting facing each other and it may help for the lover to gently part the outer vaginal lips with the fingers of one hand to locate its exact position. Light stroking of the outer and inner lips stimulates the hood which passes over the clitoris and this may itself cause the clitoris to grow firm and responsive. Since with many women the clitoris is readily

139

overstimulated, movement should always be teasing, sliding away for a little and then back to it. Sometimes it feels best to stroke only the area immediately *above* the clitoris, rather than the organ itself.

You can also suggest that your partner lies or sits behind you, a hand slipped over on to your pubic area, or between your legs. If a hand is introduced between your legs the wrist should be about level with the base of your vagina or there is a chance that the fleshy part of the fingertips which provide most delight do not reach to the clitoris. Especially if you have had suturing of the perineum after childbirth, your partner should avoid any dragging on the tissues at the base of the vagina and in the small triangle, called the fourchette, between your vagina and anus.

Another position many women enjoy is to lie on their front with the partner's hand introduced between their legs. A pillow can be used under your pelvis so that there is a little more space for manoeuvre. You can add to the effect of the fingertip touch by slightly moving your pelvis or by squeezing your buttocks together and then releasing them in a rhythmic movement.

For the majority of women clitoral stimulation is the high point of sex and it is only when the clitoris is stimulated – directly or indirectly – that they can achieve orgasm. Many can experience full sexual arousal and deep satisfaction without penetration.

If it is to continue to be effective and to generate intense erotic arousal, not just a pleasant, ticklish, sexual sensation, skilled touch and timing must find a place in an equal sexual partnership in

**CLITORAL
STIMULATION**

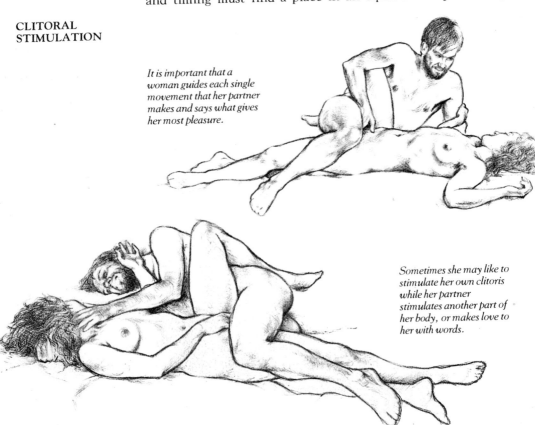

It is important that a woman guides each single movement that her partner makes and says what gives her most pleasure.

Sometimes she may like to stimulate her own clitoris while her partner stimulates another part of her body, or makes love to her with words.

which a woman is acknowledged as a whole person. It is fairly easy to produce a sexual itch. It demands much, much more to meet and greet the whole person in a lover.

Oral stimulation

Oral stimulation of the clitoris and vagina (cunnilingus) is often mentioned by women when asked what they like best in lovemaking: "My partner very rarely does oral sex, but when he does, it's heavenly"; "He's only done it once and it drove me wild. I climaxed immediately." Some women say their partners expect them to take the man's penis in their mouths (fellatio) but refuse to make love with lips, tongue and mouth, caressing the clitoris, labia and vagina. One woman says her husband told her that if he did so it would "shame him as a man". He thought the vagina was dirty. To put his mouth against it was a kind of pollution.

There are women, too, who dislike the idea of oral contact with their genitals, usually because they are afraid they are "smelly" or "dirty". Their anxiety about being unclean is an expression of a very common attitude to the female genitals. Whereas the penis is seen as strong and brave, a soaring, clean shape, a noble tower, a pillar from which stores of rich, life-giving semen are propelled, a woman's genitals are hidden, irregularly shaped like some dark underwater creature. Menstrual blood, clots, secretions from uterus and cervix, seep through it. The penis is seen primarily as representing power, the vagina as a container for it and an orifice for the excretion of waste matter.

This is why some women are only happy for a lover to have oral contact with their genitals when they have spent a long time bathing beforehand and feel quite sure that there can be no offensive odour. Many of us have been brought up to think that all genital scents and any kind of natural lubrication are unclean. As soon as a woman who is self-conscious and embarrassed about this starts to lubricate with sexual arousal she may draw back and "switch off" because she is aware that she smells different. It's not only her feelings about oral-genital sex but about her whole body in lovemaking. She has been socially conditioned to distrust and hate her own body. For some women it is an obstacle to sexual surrender.

One thing a woman may dislike is having her partner blow into her vagina. Though it is fine to blow on the clitoris, it can actually be dangerous to introduce air into the vagina. Air embolism, though rare, may lead to sudden death.

Penetration

If penetration occurs, contact with the clitoris should be maintained either by hand pressure or fingertip touch. Or you may like to touch and stroke your clitoris in the way you know is exciting while your partner is inside you. In a position in which the man is uppermost he should be careful to avoid putting his weight on you. Some women say their men drop down on them so that they can hardly breathe. Any position that completely immobilizes the woman by the man's weight also means that she is unable to make the pelvic movements that help bring her to orgasm.

A woman often enjoys having her bottom held too. "I like my hips and bottom stroked gently first and later, in passion, gripped more strongly." The buttocks can be held during penetration

Being on top may give the woman more mobility. In this position she can also guide her partner in how she wishes to be stimulated.

A lover may need to be shown exactly how to stimulate the clitoris. After doing it herself she can guide her partner's hand.

in many positions and some women are further excited by having them slightly parted and light anal stimulation provided.

Most women who have talked with me about what they like and dislike in lovemaking say they do not enjoy anal intercourse. If the penis is inserted into the anus it should be done gradually, after gently dilating the anus with an oiled finger, and the penis itself should be liberally oiled before inserting. The woman should guide the man in and should stop at any point at which she finds it uncomfortable. The penis should not be put into the vagina after it has been in the anus, as bacteria from the rectum can cause vaginal and bladder infections.

Afterglow

Women also like to be caressed and cuddled *after* intercourse. Many say their partners go straight to sleep: "As soon as my husband ejaculates he is down to earth and I am on cloud nine. I would prefer him to hold me longer and say loving things." This is particularly remarked on by women who do not have orgasm with intercourse, but even those who do are often distressed when the man rolls over and falls asleep immediately he has ejaculated.

For, in spite of the contemporary emphasis on the importance of the female orgasm – and for many women orgasm is a vital part of sexual fulfilment – *orgasm alone does not satisfy most women.* Whether or not a woman relishes lovemaking depends much more on how much interest a lover shows in caressing her entire body, in kissing, stroking and cuddling and responding to *her* needs as a whole person. No orgasms, however deftly they are triggered, make up for the absence of that passionate cherishing.

Massage and sensate focus

Plan ahead for a massage session, choosing a time when you are not overtired and have an uninterrupted hour ahead. Make sure the room is warm. You may enjoy some background music and soft lighting. Your partner may like to use an oil or lotion so that hands slip more easily over your skin and can do quite deep massage without your skin becoming sore. Some people enjoy massage with both people naked from the beginning. Others like the active partner to be clothed while doing the massage.

The aim of this session is to learn how to achieve release from tension, and simply to enjoy your own and your partner's body, not to stimulate one another. So during these sessions avoid touching the genitals or breasts. The most important thing is to remember to touch slowly. You will also want to vary the kind of touch you give or receive, ranging from feather-light stroking to firm massage. Sometimes you will use the fleshy pads of your fingers, sometimes the palm or the side of the hand, occasionally even your knuckles and perhaps your mouth or tongue. It is also important to tell your partner what you are doing as you massage and to listen to what the person being massaged would like you to do.

In their system of sex therapy, Masters and Johnson talk about "sensate focus". This means keeping in touch with that part of your body and the precise stimulus you are receiving there, almost as if a white light was shining on that spot. Whether you are being touched or are the partner giving the touch, concentrate on the sensations you are receiving and on the pleasure you are giving.

Starting the massage session

Unless your mattress is really firm, use a duvet or blanket on the floor or a couple of floor cushions to lie on. Undress and lie down on your front. Begin with an exercise to make you feel warm and relaxed, to be aware of your whole body and let your feelings flow.

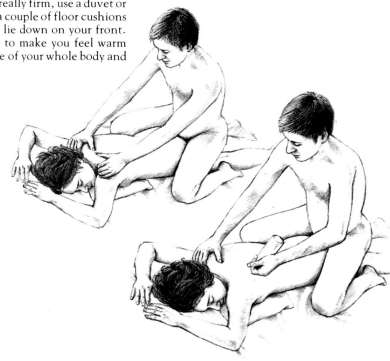

1 Rest your hands on her shoulders and slowly and firmly circle your thumbs in the little valley at either side of her spine. Work down her back. Ask her where she wants it heavier and where lighter and let her guide you. Finish with your hands massaging either side of her pelvis, just where the cleft in her buttocks starts.

2 If you want to take extra oil, always keep one hand in contact with her body as you do so. Take hold of the bottle by the neck and tip some oil into the palm of the same hand, or, better still, use a plastic squeezy bottle.

3 Using the palms of your hands, start again at her shoulders with a deep kneading movement of the whole palm and massage in circles, emphasizing the movement out and away from her spine. At the end, let your hands slide gradually down her back until eventually you are massaging her buttocks in the same way. Do this up and down her back four or five times.

4 Now try some variations in the kind of touch and explore the effect of using the heel of your palms, pressing deep into the muscle and leaning well forward so that your weight passes down through your arms into your hands.

5 Experiment with moving down beneath her bottom, and over her thighs, and then up from her shoulders over her neck, under the curve of the skull and up the back of her head, pressing with the fleshy pads of your fingers and thumbs. She may find lying over a small cushion raises her shoulders to provide some height for her head, making it easier to massage her head and neck.

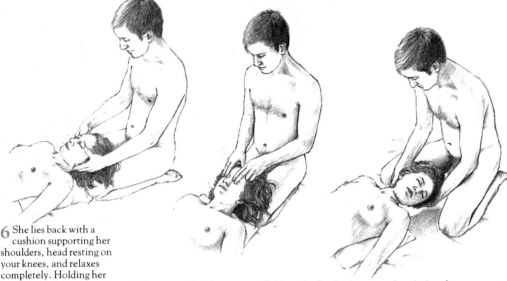

6 She lies back with a cushion supporting her shoulders, head resting on your knees, and relaxes completely. Holding her head in your hands, massage all over her skull with your fingertips very slowly, moving the flesh on the bone. Then move forward over the bridge of her nose, her eyebrows, and temples.

7 Now move firmly on her temples with your thumbs inscribing big circles, and finish by resting your fingertips *lightly* on her closed eyelids for about a minute.

8 Move further back, spreading your knees apart. Cradle your hands beneath her head, supporting its whole weight, and very slowly roll her head in your hands. Let the movements get larger. If at any time you feel tension or resistance remind her to release her jaw. Finish by cradling her head in the palm of your hands.

Touch relaxation

This is a way of becoming more pleasantly aware of your body as your partner helps you through touch. The idea is very simple; you respond to touch by releasing tensed up muscles. Letting the tension go allows feeling to flow in.

We often guard ourselves against feeling by tightening muscles. It is like a body armour we build in reaction to the stresses we meet in life and inside which we try to protect ourselves.

This body armour is individual to each of us and gives us our characteristic physical stance, gestures and facial expressions, dictates the way we stand and sit and even how we lie when asleep. It is this hard shell we have constructed which can cut us off from loving touch, from erotic sensations and from the full flood of feelings.

You are going to deliberately tense muscles in different parts of your body, noticing the feeling that comes when you are tight there; then your partner is going to rest a hand over the contracted muscles. The moment you feel the touch, you release all the tension and let it flow out into your partner's hands.

Two kinds of stimuli help you to do this: pressure and warmth. Every time you feel pressure and warmth from touch think of it as a message coming to you saying "relax *here – now*". Take a little time to notice the different sensation once the contraction has been released. It helps to give a long, slow breath out as you relax and then to give yourself space simply to listen to the sound of your own, slow breathing.

Face and neck

The face and neck are parts of the body which are often stiff with tension as we try to cope with everyday difficulties. We jut our chins forward, stiffen the backs of our necks and tighten muscles around our eyes, automatically clenching our jaws at the same time. This kind of tension is responsible for many of the frowns and other signals of facial stress.

Sit facing one another. Your partner needs to be able to move easily. You should be well supported, knees flopped out and the soles of the feet towards each other. Make sure your head and neck are supported, too. A Chinese neck cushion or other small cushion is good for that. Your head should feel like a large, heavy crystal ball which you can let gently roll from side to side as you relax all tension.

1 Begin by screwing up your eyes and forehead as if you had a headache and were in a very bright light. Notice how it feels when you tighten muscles in that way. Where else do you feel tight?

2 Now your partner rests two fingers of each hand firmly on the bony ridge of your temples and as soon as you feel the warmth and pressure of the fingers you relax, letting the tension flow out at either side of your head into the hands.

Shoulders

We often bear life's burdens on our shoulders. As we tackle crises, we brace them for action. We may feel bowed down by responsibilities or other people's needs – and our shoulders sometimes feel that they are going to crack under the strain. All this means that for many of us it is difficult to let the tension go from our shoulders. So here is an exercise to get them relaxed.

1 Still facing your partner, pull your shoulders right back, as if you could make them meet at the back. Hold them like that for about 15 seconds, noticing how you feel and what other muscles in your body are affected.

2 Then your partner rests firm hands on the front of each shoulder and leaves them there while you relax, and flow out towards the warmth and pressure. Notice the changes in your body and the completely different feeling now in your shoulders.

Arms and hands

In Indian dancing arms seem fluid and floating, to be different physical organs from the kind we use in our everyday lives. We bump around and drop things, yet if you watch a potter turning clay, hands and arms are used with confident precision and flowing movement.

If arms and hands are to convey messages which are erotic, sexual energy needs to flow through our arms and into hands, palms and fingertips. This means that we need to be able to let tension escape from them so the next exercise is particularly important for both partners.

1 Tense up one arm without lifting it from the floor. Observe the feelings that come when you do this and other muscles which may be contracting in sympathy with your arm muscles.

2 Now your partner leans one hand on the front of your shoulders as before, the other over the inside upper arm so that it is curved over the biceps. As soon as you feel the touch, let the tension go. Notice the different feelings now the tension has gone.

3 Then with one hand on your shoulder, your partner slowly moves their other hand down towards your lower arm, firmly moulding it to the shape of your arm, and slowly slides it down over your inside arm to sweep out any residual tension. When the arm reaches the wrist it circles it and for another 10 seconds you both stay like this and notice the different physical feeling.

Abdomen

Abdominal tension is a spontaneous reaction to something which frightens us. If we are in a permanent state of anxiety we may go around with abdominal muscles contracted all the time. When abdominal muscles are tight in this way it is impossible to breathe easily. The most relaxed kind of breathing flows down through the abdomen and into the pelvis. It is like a wave which sweeps through the body, down even as far as the vagina, and then sweeps away from you, to be followed by another wave, in a steady rhythm.

1 To be aware of lower abdominal tension, pull in the muscles of your abdomen. Notice how you feel. Has it affected your breathing at all?

2 Now your partner rests both hands over the base of your abdomen and you release all the tension the moment you feel the warmth and pressure of the hands. Keeping the hands there, listen to the sound of your breathing and let it flow through your abdomen in a wave-like rhythm. You may feel that you can "breathe" with your vagina. Notice how this affects your mouth and other muscles of your face, and your whole body.

Legs and feet

Even when the upper part of your body is relaxed you may not be aware at the time that there is tension in your legs and feet. Especially when we are alert to tackle difficulties, legs and feet may be ready to leap into action, and when we feel insecure and threatened we may pull the inner thighs together in an attempt to protect ourselves.

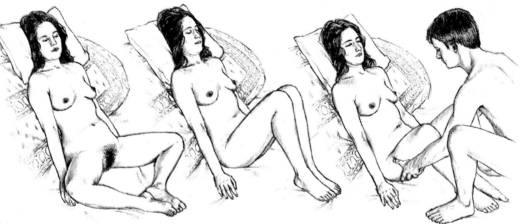

1 Starting with your knees flopped apart and relaxed, pull them up and towards each other until they are so tightly together that they could hold a sheet of paper gripped between them. Notice how you feel. Have any other muscles tightened?

2 Now your partner rests a firm hand on the outside of each thigh, moulding the palms to your legs. When you feel the warmth and pressure of the touch you release and let your legs drop apart. Observe the different physical sensations now.

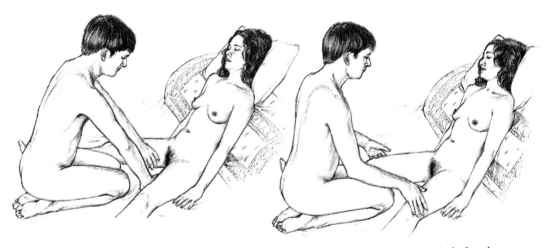

3 Then your partner kneels forward (it may be easiest for their legs to be between yours) and, with fingers pointing down to the floor, holds your inside upper thigh firmly. Let the warmth of the hands flow into your legs.

4 Then, very slowly and firmly, your partner strokes down towards your knees, coming up again over the top of your legs with fingertip touch. Each time the hands hold your inside thigh and move downwards, focus on the feelings in your vagina and let the tissues in and around it soften and open, like a soft, relaxed mouth. Talk together about how you feel and what kind of touch is most effective.

5 Keeping one knee bent and flopped out, straighten the other and press the heel down to the floor, tensing your whole leg and foot. Hold this for a few seconds.

6 Your partner then rests one hand on the outside and the other on the inside of the leg which you have contracted, moulding the hands to the shape of your leg. The contact should be firm and definite. The moment you feel the warmth and pressure from the touch, relax your leg completely, letting tension flow out towards the touch. Your partner keeps the hand on the outside leg quite still, but slowly slides the palm of the other hand down your leg to help any residual tension. As the hand reaches the foot it is important that it grips strongly, or you will find the movement ticklish and irritating.

7 The hand slides on to the sole of your foot, and one thumb is pressed centrally against the spot immediately below the ball of the foot. When the finger is in the right position, you get a satisfying, tingling sensation and will also feel very safely held. Release any tension elsewhere.

Back

The next exercises are done in a position in which your partner can easily reach the whole length of your back. You may like to experiment with different postures for this. Kneeling and curved over a large floor cushion can be good, or with knees wide apart and your body curved over so that you are on all fours, or lying three-quarters over with a cushion under your head and another under your upper knee. Avoid tucking an arm underneath you, as then it becomes more difficult for your partner to gain access to your shoulders and upper back. In any of these positions it helps if you have your legs well apart and your back rounded, not straight. Start by giving a long breath out and relaxing completely.

Your partner stimulates your back by slapping it with a light touch with hands which are relaxed and floppy from the wrist, keeping to either side of the spine and avoiding slapping the spine itself. If this action is attempted with stiff hands it can be quite painful, so get your partner to practise a similar movement first. Guide your partner as to where you like the slapping heavier and where lighter. When your whole back is tingling and warm, move on to the next phase of the exercise.

2 Using two fingers of each hand, your partner presses at either side of your spine, starting at the very bottom, and you rock away from and then back towards the pressure with a smooth, rhythmic movement. The fingers must stay quite still so that you have a firm stimulus against which to push. Allow the breath to come slowly or fast, deep or light, just as you feel. You will also discover that breathing varies according to the level of your spine which you are unloosening at the time. When your back is really relaxed you will move like a cat stretching in the sun. Finish the exercise by lying for a minute or two enjoying the feeling of relaxation, with your partner's hands resting wherever on your back you like them best.

3 When sitting up, you explored the effects of shoulder tension and release. Now you are in another position you can try a different shoulder tension and release. Shrug your shoulders towards your ears. This is something we do automatically when trying to protect ourselves. Hold it for about 15 seconds and notice how you feel. Then your partner rests the palms of each hand firmly at either side of the spine above the shoulder blades, leaning the weight of the body down through arms and hands on to you. As soon as you feel the warmth and pressure, you release, flowing towards the touch.

149

4 So this time tense up your whole back as if it were freezing cold. Observe what happens in the rest of your body, too. Then your partner rests two hands firmly on your upper back as in the previous exercise and you relax. Once all the tension seems to have gone, your partner slowly and firmly, with a deep massage movement, strokes down either side of your spine till the hands rest below your pelvis. This helps to draw out any residual tension.

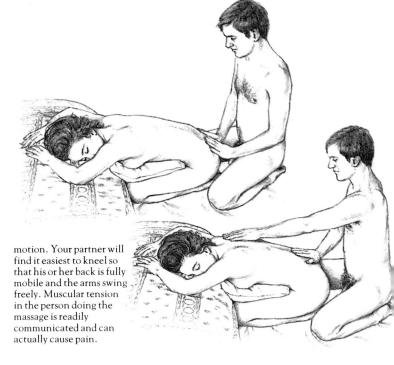

5 With one hand, your partner starts massaging down one side of your back and as it reaches your buttocks, the other starts at the top on the other side, with long, sweeping strokes, so that there is always one hand in motion. Your partner will find it easiest to kneel so that his or her back is fully mobile and the arms swing freely. Muscular tension in the person doing the massage is readily communicated and can actually cause pain.

Pelvis and buttocks

The tensions held in pelvis and buttocks may be built up as a result of anxiety or fear. It is as if by clenching muscles in the lower abdomen, pelvic floor and buttocks, we could protect ourselves or somehow neutralize feelings in the whole pelvic area. Some of us actually hold that part of the body tight all the time, making it completely out of bounds to feelings. We may think that by letting muscles become soft and loose we will allow something dirty to escape. This usually means that breathing becomes strained and shallower, too.

1 Hollow your lower back and notice what happens to your neck and throat, head, shoulders and upper back. Hold it like this for several seconds. Your partner rests the palm of each hand on your pelvis and either side of the sacrum and you release.

2 Using pressure from the heels of the palms, not the fingers, your partner then massages away any further tension, exerting a pressure which sinks deeply into your muscles. This massage is best done with the hands staying in the same place, not just sliding over the skin. It helps if weight from the body is allowed to pass down through the arms into the hands.

3 Tension in the buttocks is often linked with tension in the muscles deep inside the vagina. When they have relaxed you may be aware that you have released your jaw and that your mouth has become softer, too. Imagine that you are sitting on an icy cold bench in a thin dress and contract your buttocks tightly together. Notice how you feel and exactly what muscles tighten elsewhere in your body. Has your breathing changed? Now your partner rests a firm hand over the lower curve of each buttock and immediately you feel the warmth and pressure, you relax and flow out towards the touch.

4 Your partner now helps smooth out any remaining tensions in the buttocks by firm, deep, slow massage, as if kneading bread dough, but using the fingers and thumbs as well as the palms of the hands. You may be aware that your breathing becomes slower and deeper. Notice how different your body feels now and spend a few minutes enjoying the sensation. This massage can produce sensuous – even erotic – feelings, but only if it is done slowly and firmly.

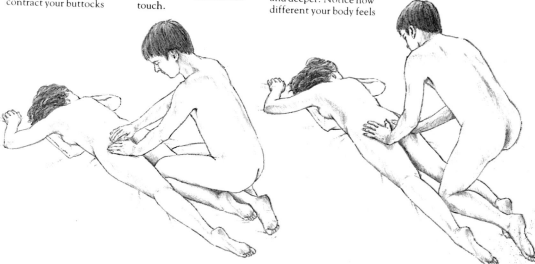

Revitalizing our sex lives

All this discussion of relaxation may seem odd because when you are making love you do not want to be like a big, floppy sponge merely soaking up the sensations or like a dollop of whipped cream, all sweetness and goo and nothing else. You want to be active, giving as well as getting, communicating and sending out your own electric sexual signals, not merely absorbing someone else's. The aim of massage and sensate focus and the kind of psycho-physical relaxation that I describe in this chapter is to unbuckle the muscle armour in which we try to shut ourselves off from sensation and to hide and guard ourselves, so that feelings can flow. Unless we do this we do not give ourselves a chance. But when we demolish that protective structure around ourselves the verve and energy of sex comes quite naturally. It all starts with daring to let both the mental and physical barriers down. And then we discover that inside, though soft, vulnerable and exposed, we are filled with sexual vitality and the richness and colour of sensual experience.

For power flows from relaxation. If we can let tension go we open the door on a new psychosomatic harmony. Just 10 minutes spent really relaxing brings new energy, not only physically, but also for the fantasies that shape and pattern sexual experiences. Without that precious space in our lives we may go on, day in day out, doing the same old thing in the same old way. With it, the slightest touch of a hand can cause rivers of light to pour through the body. It is this creative energy that we draw on when we know how to relax.

Intimacy, closeness, and a shared sense of fun — these are all vital ingredients in our sexual relationships…

The physically challenged

The word "handicapped" is often nowadays replaced by another – challenged. A handicapped person is one with a challenge. This can be anything from a disability which other people can see and recognize, like blindness or being paralysed, to a condition which is not obvious to anyone else, like wearing a colostomy bag or being scarred from an operation. We *all* face challenges, whether or not we are labelled as handicapped. A challenge often makes us look at things in a fresh way and releases new energy to cope with it.

Overcoming other people's inhibitions

A woman who is physically challenged by not being able to use certain parts of her body or her senses, or who does not look like other women, has the right to full sexual expression, like anyone else. But she, and her partner, if she has one, need to develop specific skills. Women say that it can be difficult to talk with their GP about this. Doctors often have the same inhibitions about sex as their patients and many have no special training to know how to discuss these matters. When a woman has had a serious accident or a stroke, a doctor may assume as a matter of course that she no longer has any sexual needs. When she has been handicapped from birth, or from childhood, no one, doctors included, may be willing to help her explore her sexuality, or even to acknowledge it.

A woman who had cerebral palsy as a child says, "By and large, forget doctors and nurses! They're grossly handicapped by their training. They can just about cope with 'normal' sex performed by 'normal' people." Though there have been studies published on sexual rehabilitation of men with spinal injuries, women are usually not considered to have the same sexual drive. The paraplegic woman, for example, may be seen simply as a passive, receptive sex object if a partner wants to use her in this way.

Parents and care-givers often try to protect the disabled teenager from emotional experiences, from the opportunity to learn through living and from others of the same age who are able to experiment with sex in a different way. A girl in a wheelchair may be thought out of place in a disco and seems to intrude on the little knot of girls at the back of the school bike-shed. The girl who has been disabled from childhood may pretend she is not interested. She may develop a tactic of avoiding any emotional commitment in relationships. Yet it is important for all of us to take risks, to feel, to experience – and to deny a woman this, together with the suffering that may be entailed, is to deny her life.

Sexual arousal

We are so accustomed to think of sex as being located *in* certain organs – the vagina, the clitoris and the erogenous zones – that we may forget that every part of the body can be aroused and become sexually aware. When touch receptors are not functioning in one area of the body, new areas for sensory stimulation need to be discovered. And finding out, by stroking yourself or by a partner touching you in all these other places, can be a lovely way of exploring feelings.

Most of what makes sex exciting and magnificent is in our *minds*. It is fantasy, ranging all the way from remembered lovemaking, through poetry, novels and other romantic and erotic literature, films and pictures to loving, sexually stimulating words, in order to nourish sex-in-the-mind. People are sometimes frightened of doing this because they are anxious that if they allow themselves to become sexually alive they will be aroused without any chance of satisfaction. But a woman with even a severe physical disability can often still discover a way in which to masturbate or stroke and caress parts of the body which are exquisitely sensitive to touch, such as her breasts, inner arms or neck and through kissing, too, she can experience a warm flood of sexual fulfilment. Sexually a woman is infinitely more complex than just a body with a vagina and clitoris.

If you have a partner you can find out together where you are sensitive to touch and where you have no feelings. It is impossible for a lover to know this unless you communicate about it.

Preparing for lovemaking

If you cannot use all of your body, getting ready for lovemaking can be difficult because it takes a long time, and a non-disabled partner has to tune in to your rhythm and pace. Some women say that these preparations can be incorporated into lovemaking so that undressing, bathing or showering, positioning yourself, even using a contraceptive, can be a part of the lovemaking – just as it can be, after all, for a woman who is not disabled. You may want to take your bath or shower in candlelight and turn on soft music. And you can use scent or place a perfumed candle beside the bed. If you have had a colostomy and urine is collected in a bag which needs changing you may find that it is impossible to make preparation a part of lovemaking. It is difficult to make changing a colostomy bag anything to do with the build-up to sex. Yet it is important to be scrupulously clean if you have a urine-collection device or an indwelling catheter. So you have to work out whether there should be an interval between preparation and lovemaking or whether it can be a continuous activity. Sometimes another person will be available to help you get ready so that you can come to your partner fresh and clean and can both feel in the right mood.

A sexual ally

Some severely disabled people living more or less independently say that they can, with the right aids and environment, manage with much less help than others might think. Someone understanding and matter-of-fact about it who can be a "sexual ally" may be important. A blind woman, for example, may find it difficult to get access to books about sex. There may be no one who she feels she can ask to read them to her and no Braille versions.

If you are not in a socially acknowledged relationship with a sexual partner you may especially need a "sexual ally". Books and magazines about sex are often on the top shelves in shops. If you live in an institution or with your parents you may also have no privacy and it is difficult to explain parcels arriving in the post. It is bound to be embarrassing at first to seek help, but it is up to the disabled person to overcome that embarrassment.

Sexual aids

Cushions of different sizes and shapes can be a help in getting into and varying your positions. A bean bag or big floor cushion could give firm support in a semi-upright position if you have difficulty when lying down. If you are able to make very few movements of any kind you may find that a heated water bed is right for you, so that as the water moves it moves you a little, too (but water beds are very heavy and you must have a strong floor). Mechanical sex aids are used by many people nowadays, often because they find the idea a turn-on. Discovering what is on the market which can help you with your specific disability can be fun, especially if you have a sexual "ally" to help you. You may enjoy a vibrator, which you can get through the mail order pages of a magazine like *Spare Rib*. One kind can be strapped to a hand (or even to an ankle) and is useful if you have limited hand movements.

Sometimes a disability reduces the amount of natural vaginal lubrication produced. Anxiety about whether you are going to be able to cope has the same effect. A water-soluble lubricant gel is useful and with a catheter in place this is important.

Oral stimulation

Being kissed and caressed by your lover's mouth exploring your body and stimulating your clitoris and vagina with a tongue is a way of making love which works well for some women who find all movement difficult. And if you cannot move your body you can use your tongue and lips to excite your partner. A woman who has no sensation in her clitoris and vagina may enjoy stimulation of the anus. Your partner's finger should be well lubricated. If anal intercourse takes place the anus should be gradually and gently dilated first of all with a well-lubricated finger.

Planning ahead

In the early stages of a relationship which is obviously likely to become sexual it may be a good idea to tell your partner what you feel your limitations are. Paraplegic women with whom I have talked say that being disabled can be not only frightening for the woman herself when she is on the threshold of a sexual experience with someone, but often for the sexual partner, too. Sometimes the other person cannot cope with the anxiety aroused by considering what they might do if there are sudden muscle spasms or incontinence, but if you don't panic and present it in a matter-of-fact way, your partner will probably take it in their stride. "Take it one step at a time", the women I have spoken to advise: "Don't burden your partner with a long list of all the things that might happen. They are always worse when you think about them in advance. If it actually happens you can cope." Christine says: "The biggest worry of all is incontinence. The first time I went to bed with a guy I didn't say anything about it. We let it all happen as naturally as possible, and let all the mistakes happen, too. But we discussed them afterwards, when we already felt really close." If this is likely to be a problem you can always have a towel at hand.

Women who have a scar from an accident or operation such as a mastectomy, or a disability that is not immediately obvious to a casual observer, are often anxious that a lover will be disgusted or appalled at discovering them. Those who have been through this experience nearly always say that their worries were unnecessary. Only in the most superficial of relationships is it an obstacle, and if it is that superficial it may be better to discover before you have made a big emotional investment in this.

Contraception

If you are in a heterosexual relationship you will need to consider contraception. The Pill may not be right for you if you are more or less immobilized since not being able to move about increases the risk of thromboembolism. If you have no feeling in your legs you may not be aware of circulatory problems that can be produced by the Pill, so it is important to check your legs regularly for signs of redness and swelling.

An intra-uterine device (IUD) is often recommended for women who have spinal injuries. But those who have pelvic deformities may find it painful to have put in. If you want to have a diaphragm you need to be able to use your fingers to get a good grasp. When pelvic floor muscles are not well toned a diaphragm can slip out of place and if you do not have any feeling in your vagina you may not realize that it is malpositioned. A woman who needs to empty her bladder by putting pressure on her abdomen could actually shift her diaphragm the few millimetres that mean it would no longer be an effective contraceptive. A condom combined with spermicidal foam may be the method of choice. But you must be careful if you have an indwelling catheter, because friction between the catheter and the latex of the condom can tear it.

Natural family planning methods (see pages 192–4) involve careful record-keeping, and things like examination of mucus and taking your temperature can be very difficult if you do not have much movement in your hands.

Making love

Whatever kind of disability you face, it is important to develop the erotic imagination and invent variations on a sexual theme. For any two people making love, however adept and agile they are, there is always a good deal of thumping and groping, and to Martian eyes the whole procedure might look preposterous. When we see lovemaking in films usually only the most elegant and graceful parts of the process are shown. In real life clothing gets twisted and buttons stuck, you get cramp in your leg or pins and needles in a hand, are lying uncomfortably with a hair grip under your neck, find the screw top of the massage oil in the small of your back or biscuit crumbs on your bottom – and then the wine tips over.

So laughing together, sharing the same sense of fun, is also important. Lyrical romance, comedy, wit, high passion and quiet content all have their place in a sexual relationship.

Many people who would not think of themselves as disabled have to cope with some of the problems that those that are more severely disabled know so well. If you are very fat you may be relatively immobilized when flat on your back, as any woman in the last month of pregnancy knows. I remember a man saying to me about his wife, who had an enviably slim figure, that it was "like making love to a step-ladder". I had never thought before that being thin might actually be a disability, but I could see what he meant. Someone who is deaf in one ear will only be able to hear sweet nothings whispered in the other. Icy cold feet, calloused hands, chilblains or indigestion can all be a turn-off.

There are many conditions, too, that we may develop as we get older, and illnesses with which we live without necessarily feeling disabled, that we need to take into consideration in a sexual relationship. Arthritis, suffered by many women as they grow older, puts a severe limit on sexual acrobatics. Legs, arms, hands and pelvic joints may be stiff. And it can be difficult to stroke and caress with the tenderness you feel. Partners can explore new kinds of touch using lips, tongue, cheeks and little finger – or any part of the body that is not stiff – to give and receive messages of sexual longing and love. Variations in posture for intercourse, and a need to find ways in which a partner's weight is not pressing on aching limbs or immobilizing you further, may open up new possibilities.

For an asthmatic, bed is often the place where the worst asthma attacks occur and it is difficult to feel sexy when wheezing or coughing up mucus. The temperature of the bedroom should be constant and the air as free as possible of dust and any of the organisms that trigger off attacks. An electric air filter right by the bed might help, but be sure it does not have a scented pad inside. These "hyacinth" and other room scents not only smell like powerful lavatory cleaners but can cause a really bad asthma attack. A mass of coloured cushions so that you can be well propped up not only looks inviting but increases comfort when making love, and a large boomerang pillow can support the upper back and shoulders. The asthmatic, like the person with arthritis, may find intercourse most comfortable in the "spoons" position, since then no pressure is put on the chest wall or rib cage, or may enjoy lying with legs crossed over the partner's (see page 205).

A woman with multiple sclerosis or cerebral palsy may find it difficult to part her legs when on her back, so may prefer sitting up and sometimes a comfortable chair gives her the best support.

Monica has had cerebral palsy since childhood. Her spine is twisted and she is now only four feet tall. She says she used to be terribly afraid of letting sexual feeling come and that society forced her into a sort of emotional straitjacket, ostensibly to shield and protect her. She was not disabled in the same way as a woman who cannot use her arms or legs. Yet, she says: "With every limb and orifice in perfect working order, I felt like an outsider. . . . Why should I have been so afraid? I suppose because we think predominantly, subconsciously, of sex as being something which happens to the young and attractive. The disabled and disfigured fall into the same category as the old, but with even stronger taboos. We are taught that beauty is good. Ugliness could only be an embarrassment. And we the disfigured, the disabled, the unusual, are frequently made to apologize for our presence by trying to blend into the background as much as possible. To challenge, to reveal 'indifference' requires a rare talent – a hardness of soul.

"And so we protect even our closest friends from our real selves. What can they do if we say 'what I need is sex', 'what I want is a lover'? It would be a social gaffe. Therefore we talk about their boyfriends, not ours; their marriages, not ours; their sex life, not ours. It is protection of themselves by us. Up to the age of about 35 almost 100 per cent of my friends and family were so protected. In one or two I lightly confided my current 'crushes', both a relief and a danger. If they saw these as more they would have questioned further – and so the rightness of silence was confirmed. But if allowed, the spell of that silence can last a lifetime."

6 CHILDREN AND SEX

Childhood sexuality

Even babies have sexual experiences. Boys often have an erection at or shortly after birth and the vaginas of baby girls lubricate. Erections have been recorded in the male fetus well before birth. We cannot really tell what babies are *feeling* when these things happen, but they certainly like to have their genitals handled and will coo and babble when their nappies are changed or they are rubbed between their legs, if it is done gently and lovingly.

Rita has two boys aged two-and-a-half and seven months. She says that Julian, the older boy, first began to masturbate when he was about six months: "When he was between one and two he used to point his penis out to me when he was in the bath and say, 'it really goes hard, doesn't it Mummy'. Our little one has just discovered the pleasure of it. He had nappy rash and spent a lot of time without a nappy. Rubbing relieved the itch and he found that when he rubbed his penis it was very nice!"

In some peasant communities mothers regularly caress and stimulate the penis of a baby boy and tell him what a fine man he will be. Any kind of fondling of a baby may produce the excitement followed by relaxation which is essentially sexual.

Rhythmic rubbing, patting, stroking, kissing and cuddling all have sexual elements which can be pleasing to the baby. The massage used by Indian mothers on their babies, done for up to two hours at a time, first seems to stimulate the baby, then produces a delicious state of peace, almost of ecstasy, as is shown clearly in Frederick Leboyer's film *Loving Hands*. A modified version of this massage is described on pages 163–6.

Breast-feeding can also be a highly sexual experience, not only for the mother but also for the baby, involving the whole body from top to toe. It is approached with excited anticipation and the baby who has learnt what it is all about gets down to it eagerly. Feet and hands curl and uncurl in vigorous delight and the steady rhythm of contented sucking is interspersed with short pauses, after which the baby eagerly grasps the nipple again, submerged in warm waves of satisfaction and sleepy bliss.

Loving touch   The way we touch our babies and our emotional responses to their sexuality play an important part in the later development of a warm, loving sex life. The parent who is afraid of stimulating the baby conveys the message that these delightful feelings are to be avoided or only indulged in secretly. The parent who handles the child like a lump of meat gives the message that she does not enjoy the child's body and that it is not something which the baby should enjoy either. Any amount of positive talking about sex or careful sex education is unlikely to make up for this lack of warm, loving touch and it may be left for the growing boy or girl to discover that first from some other human being.

It is sometimes very difficult for a mother to touch her child lovingly because she has never "fallen in love" with that child though she may find other of her children easy to love. This can happen when her experience of birth and the first meeting with the baby at delivery takes place in an unloving environment, or, and this amounts to the same thing, when a rigid hierarchical and bureaucratic system of care takes over the baby as if it belonged to the hospital and not to the mother.

Sometimes, too, we find it difficult to love a child because in that child we see reflected aspects of ourselves which we reject, or reflections of qualities in other people to whom we are hostile: "he's just like his father" or "she takes after my sister".

It is a static view of motherhood to assume that a woman mothers in a single uniform style. She may mother different children in different ways, being very protective of one and forcing another to be brave and independent (sometimes that is part of the pattern of gender differences we impose on our children, encouraging a girl to be gentle and a boy to be tough, for example). She also mothers the same child at different ages in a completely different way. And this is appropriate. The enveloping love for a newborn baby needs to be different from the love she gives a five-year-old going to school for the first time, or an adolescent trying to find her own identity apart from her mother.

Mothering is sometimes treated as if it were a "science" which, along with home economics and nutrition, is a fit subject for study by girls in the less bright streams of comprehensive schools. The assumption is that there is one "right" way to do it and that if you are assiduous enough you will acquire the skills.

But loving a child and relating to that child, like loving a man or a woman, is chock-a-block full of so many emotions, shot through with so many meanings and so dependent on the quality of other relationships, that it is a much more complicated matter than doing the "right" thing. The technical skills are far less important than the quality of interaction between mother and child.

Being sensitive to your child's needs

The mother receives and responds to messages coming from the child. And since each child is a unique individual these messages are special to that child. Some children love being cuddled, moulding themselves to your body, revelling in skin contact; others don't "give" in this way. You get the feeling they are watching you rather critically. These children do not provide the immediate warm reward that cuddly children bring to a relationship. When a baby stops crying and accepts caresses, sucks contentedly at the breast, relaxes in your arms and sleeps, it is for the mother an affirmation of her successful mothering. It is like lovemaking in which everything goes well, feelings flow and both partners climax and fall asleep knowing that they love each other. When a baby cries – and goes on crying – or refuses to mould herself to your body, it is not only rejecting, it is like an act of love which goes terribly wrong. Children can make love very easy or very difficult for their parents. Any general guide-lines to the importance of touching and cuddling children must come second to respect for the individual child and acknowledgment of her or his unique personality. To do anything else, to impose on children rules about freedom and self-expression, nudity and physical contact, is to intrude on that child's privacy and commit a kind of psychological violence.

As children grow up there are times when they withdraw a little from contact, pulling up the drawbridge, as it were, demanding privacy. To be aware of this demands great sensitivity and *all* parents make mistakes about it. It can happen long before we are ready for it. Caroline told me how she was bathing her two-and-a-half-year-old son and he suddenly put his hand over his penis and said, "Mummy, get off my penis! that's mine! you're not supposed to touch that." This is why many of the lovely ideas about keeping close to your children, being lavish with physical affection, having them sleep with you in a large family bed, even commitment to breast-feeding, perhaps for two years or more, will take on the characteristics of dogma if we ignore the messages, some spoken but the majority non-verbal, conveyed by the child. To be "in touch" with another person is to know when that touch is *not* the right thing, to deny yourself the reassurance of a caress, to realize that it is not the time to question or even to discuss a subject which you may see as very important, but rather to give space and silence, because that is what the child needs. Physical affection is a vital part of mothering but you need a light hand, cooling-down at times and knowing when to let well alone.

When a mother is able to be at home in the afternoon and is not rushed off her feet with work, a good opportunity for spontaneous physical contact is provided by taking a nap together. This may depend on a younger baby being willing to go to sleep at that time or the phone not ringing. (Take it off the hook for half an hour, if you can.) Some women enjoy sharing rest time with one child and some say they like having all their children in the bed. In practical terms, hoping to get any rest with more than two children beside you is unrealistic. They wriggle, bump, sing tuneless tunes, grumble, startle, get cross with each other, compete to cuddle next to you or decide they want a story instead – and wake the baby. So if you have more than two it may be best to let them take it in turns to have the afternoon nap with you.

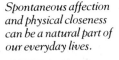

Spontaneous affection and physical closeness can be a natural part of our everyday lives.

This casual physical contact with our children is unselfconscious and is like that which little children have always had in peasant societies, where they sleep in the same bed as their mother, and perhaps other brothers and sisters, too.

Baby massage

One of the things you can link with an afternoon nap together is a baby massage session. An older child can learn with you how to do this for a baby to enjoy. And an older child may like to be massaged too. But you will need to remain very sensitive as to how a child of over three or so really feels about this and there is no point in attempting it unless the child enjoys it.

Think how you feel about massaging a little boy. You may be very comfortable about this until, say, he is two or two-and-a-half and then be concerned that you could over-stimulate him or turn him into a "mother's boy". Since in the West massage of children is rarely done, other family members may also be critical of this. Yet boys often learn so little about loving! No wonder that many adult men are rough and insensitive when they have had very restricted experience of delicate loving touch in childhood.

You have to bear in mind that stopping any kind of expression of loving *suddenly*, whether it is breast-feeding or the loving physical contact of massage, can be painful and traumatic for the child. So it is important to think in advance about your feelings and how your child may feel. One way of enjoying warm physical contact with a baby boy is to suggest that his father joins in whenever possible, at weekends, for example, and on holiday, even if he is not at home on weekdays at a suitable time.

You can start gentle massage with a baby at any time from birth onwards. If your baby was in an intensive care unit after birth or has been separated from you, extra touching is especially important. It helps you both to get to know each other and for you to develop trust in handling your baby. Sometimes it can help make up for all the unpleasant experiences a baby has had at the beginning of life.

This massage can also be very helpful if you have a baby who cries in the evening and seems to have "colic". Make this a regular evening massage. After the bath is a good time and if you do it at about 6pm you may be able to each take it in turns, one getting the evening meal while the other is with the baby. (And it should go without saying that it is not always you who gets the meal while father can play with the baby.) The room must be warm, but if you have a garden, in sunny weather you may be able to do it out of doors in the fresh air.

Make sure your hands are comfortably warm before you start. Take off any rings or dangling jewellery. You may want to take off your shoes, too. Undress the child and sit on the floor with your back supported by a bean bag or big cushion, with the baby on your legs facing you or on your lap, or lie the baby down on a towel on the floor. Whichever way you have the baby, it is a good idea to spread a nappy under the buttocks, and with a little boy to have a flannel or towel to hand as well.

Start by talking to your baby and go on talking as you massage. You can let it turn into singing, humming or any sing-song sound, nursery rhyme or poem that feels right to you. You will discover that the sound of your voice and the movement of your hands make a synchronized pattern which, as the baby relaxes, may be matched by coos and gurgles.

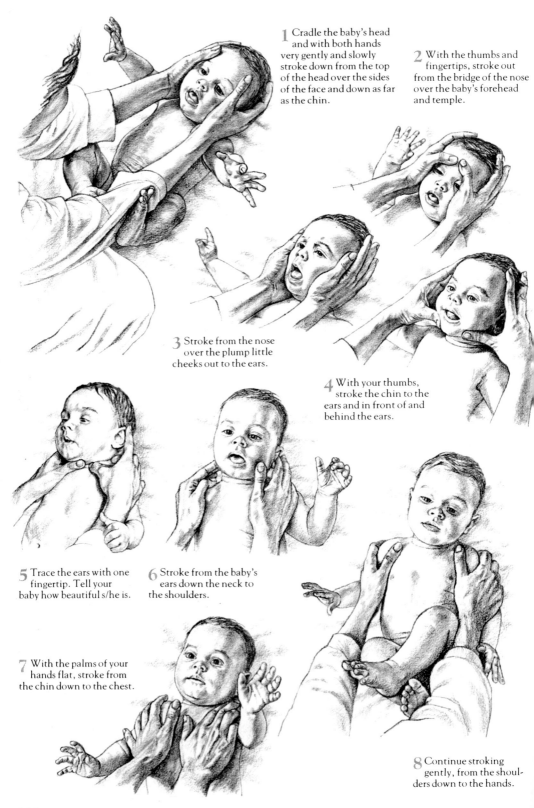

1 Cradle the baby's head and with both hands very gently and slowly stroke down from the top of the head over the sides of the face and down as far as the chin.

2 With the thumbs and fingertips, stroke out from the bridge of the nose over the baby's forehead and temple.

3 Stroke from the nose over the plump little cheeks out to the ears.

4 With your thumbs, stroke the chin to the ears and in front of and behind the ears.

5 Trace the ears with one fingertip. Tell your baby how beautiful s/he is.

6 Stroke from the baby's ears down the neck to the shoulders.

7 With the palms of your hands flat, stroke from the chin down to the chest.

8 Continue stroking gently, from the shoulders down to the hands.

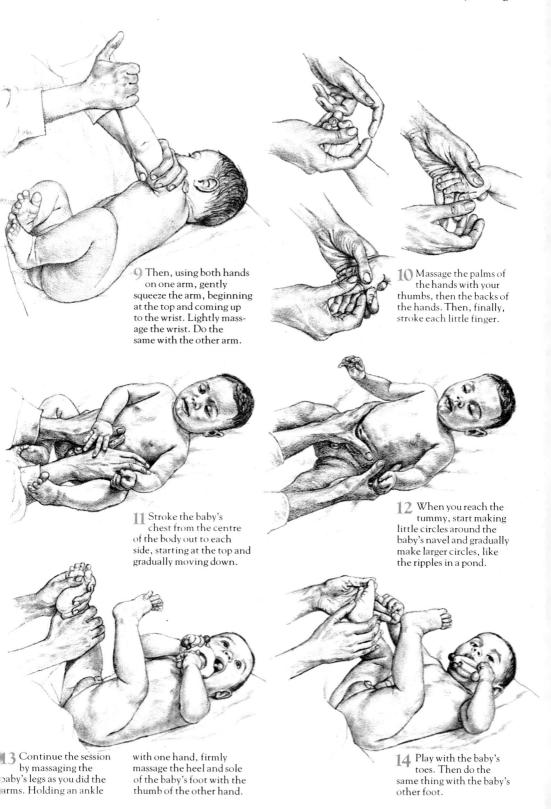

9 Then, using both hands on one arm, gently squeeze the arm, beginning at the top and coming up to the wrist. Lightly massage the wrist. Do the same with the other arm.

10 Massage the palms of the hands with your thumbs, then the backs of the hands. Then, finally, stroke each little finger.

11 Stroke the baby's chest from the centre of the body out to each side, starting at the top and gradually moving down.

12 When you reach the tummy, start making little circles around the baby's navel and gradually make larger circles, like the ripples in a pond.

13 Continue the session by massaging the baby's legs as you did the arms. Holding an ankle with one hand, firmly massage the heel and sole of the baby's foot with the thumb of the other hand.

14 Play with the baby's toes. Then do the same thing with the baby's other foot.

165

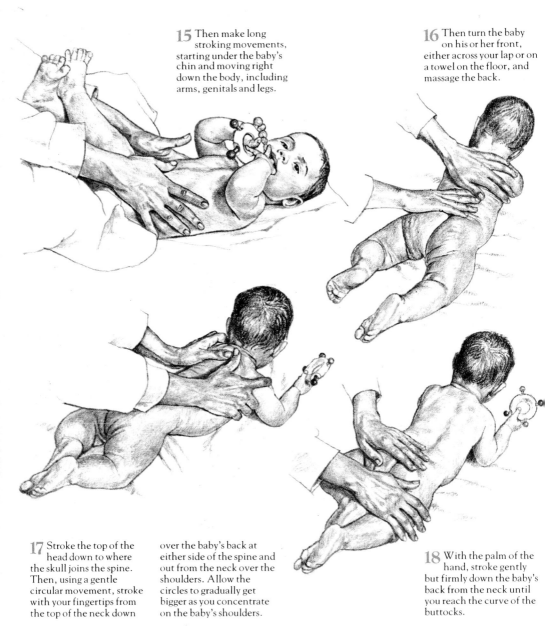

15 Then make long stroking movements, starting under the baby's chin and moving right down the body, including arms, genitals and legs.

16 Then turn the baby on his or her front, either across your lap or on a towel on the floor, and massage the back.

17 Stroke the top of the head down to where the skull joins the spine. Then, using a gentle circular movement, stroke with your fingertips from the top of the neck down over the baby's back at either side of the spine and out from the neck over the shoulders. Allow the circles to gradually get bigger as you concentrate on the baby's shoulders.

18 With the palm of the hand, stroke gently but firmly down the baby's back from the neck until you reach the curve of the buttocks.

Timing when to stop

As a child grows you will be aware that there comes a time to let the massage time get shorter and gradually peter out, because you feel the child has outgrown this particular experience of babyhood and because it is obvious that he or she has other interests. Just as with going on to solid foods or moving from a cot into a bed, there comes a transition to a new phase of life with a new competence. This awareness of the timing for transitions is as important in a mother's relationship with her child as it is when you plant hyacinths for Christmas, and need to judge exactly when to take them out of the dark and bring them into the light for the leaves to grow green and glossy and the flowers to push through.

Leaving sexual education of boys almost entirely to the father means that a woman misses out on the opportunity to help a son grow up to be aware of female sexuality as it really is, not as men often like to think of it. Yet mothers often hand over boys' sex education, feeling that it is too much for them to tackle and that they do not know enough about male sexuality to answer all the questions that a boy is likely to ask. Sometimes it happens simply by default. Liz, for example, is a single mother and says: "There was a guy who lived downstairs – we were lovers for a time – and when he was about twelve Jason got friendly with him. I found a stack of *Playboys* under his bed that this guy had given him. They used to spend a lot of time together. I think that is where he got most of his sex education from."

There is more to it than that because Jason visits his father, too: "He is always picking up girls and forcing Jason to talk about them. He picks up waitresses and says, 'Have you seen *that* one?' Jason is mortified beyond belief."

It sounded at first as if Liz had opted out, but a very important aspect of Jason's sex education is that, instead of trying to pretend that this does not happen or condemning it outright, Liz discussed it with him, both how his father behaved and Jason's feelings about it: "We talk about *why* he does it and try to understand it. I try and do it without teaching him his father is inadequate. I explain it was the fashion in the sixties when he was young and that his father just hasn't changed."

Exploring values and interpreting behaviour in terms of our understanding of what motivates it is a vital part of sex education for both boys and girls. This cannot be dealt with in formal learning sessions but is one aspect of the way we can stimulate the need to question and has to be woven through our everyday life.

Early sexual experiences

Learning about sex involves much more than talking. It means becoming aware of your own and other people's feelings of arousal. It is also about the way in which society defines and interprets sexuality and imposes upon us attitudes which we should question and test against our own experience and our own values. This has not much to do with getting knowledge about anatomy and physiology. Information only has relevance when it sparks off increased awareness.

Everything that we tell our children takes second place to the attitudes and emotions we convey. When women have talked to me about their first awareness of sex as children, they have always described *feelings*. Things they have been told by parents and teachers are remembered in terms of the emotions with which the information was conveyed. And those who have been given little or no factual information still gained a pretty clear idea of attitudes to sex through the emotions communicated by adults.

What is said, the carefully selected information fed to children, is often discarded, while the emotional messages, embarrassment, amusement or disgust, for example, are learned. This is why we need to develop a searching honesty in sex education.

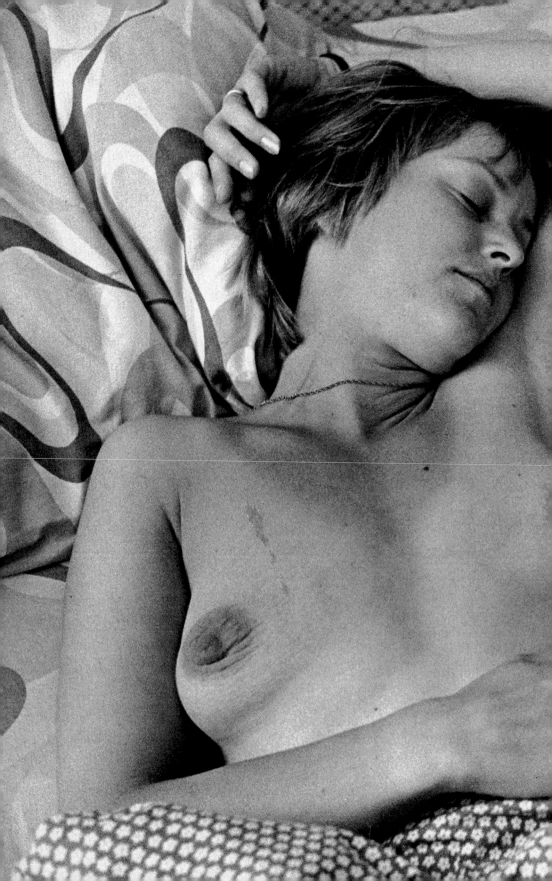

Life is a continuum and we start children's sex education by the way we handle them from birth …

First experiences

When I started writing this book I thought that the first sexual experience for most girls would probably be a romantically charged schoolgirl friendship, a "crush" on the schoolteacher or a love affair between teenagers. I had not fully realized the many and powerful negative sexual influences which jostle into children's lives – especially those of little girls – from outside and within the family, and how these may affect their later sexual development. Many women who talked about their sexual experiences in childhood disclosed how attitudes to sex were formed by things that had been done to them by an adult male, scenes they had witnessed or things they had heard, which marked themselves in their minds as "sexual", "dirty" and "bad". Mothers are rarely told about these incidents but the memory – and the shame – may last into adulthood. One of the worst things about an experience which we remember with disgust and fear is that many of us believe we are alone with it, that this awful thing happened only to *us* and that no one else can understand. If we run away from sharing these experiences, we miss out on the opportunity to explore how society puts pressure on us in defining our sexuality and sense of self-worth.

Understanding the experiences which many girls have can help us become more aware as mothers of what our daughters may be learning. As we might expect, many of the first experiences are quite simply explorations with other children which grow out of curiosity and the urge to find out for oneself. One woman, for example, said she and her sisters used to play doctors and nurses and push hairpins inside their vaginas and anuses, fascinated by the body's exits and entrances. One woman says: "I was six when I tried to make a baby with a six-year-old boy next door." Another recollects playing around with her brother's friend when she was eight: "I sat on his lap while he groped around."

The impact of negative adult attitudes

Adult attitudes to masturbation in childhood can have lasting effects. Elizabeth, for example, says she remembers she used to climb a pole in the back garden when she was seven and get a "funny feeling" which at the time she called "tickling" herself. Her friend tried it too, but one day was caught and told not to do it again "as she would do herself harm", and from then on Elizabeth says she was very anxious about what she was doing and felt terribly guilty. Ann says her mother found her masturbating when she was five, expressed her disgust and told her that if she did not stop she would take her to the doctor: "I continued to masturbate, but guiltily." Another woman says that as a nine-year-old she felt so ashamed about masturbation, but enjoyed it so much, that she devised a series of punishments for herself every time she did it. In much the same way, Elsa says that, though she cannot remember if she was ever actually spanked after masturbating as a child, she now handles the guilt she feels by having fantasies of being spanked whenever she masturbates, and then feels even more guilty because of these masochistic fantasies. Some of the excitement a woman gets from masturbation she may recognize as being because it is "naughty", and when she talks about it she may even revert to the language of childhood. Some women feel so bad about it that they cannot reach orgasm when masturbating.

These early experiences can affect adult sexual relationships, too. One woman, taught that masturbation was "a filthy habit", says she can never touch her genitals in front of her husband or make any movements which are sexually arousing because this would be like masturbating, and "sex is my husband's job". She has married a man who is very inhibited and unassertive and their sexual relationship is highly unsatisfactory. She does not feel she can ever show him how she wants to be touched and stimulated because even to guide his hand would be like masturbation.

Women often say they remember vividly the look of distaste or the shock on their mother's faces when they were discovered masturbating. Every time this happens we are giving our children powerful lessons about sex. We are teaching them that it is wrong to give yourself pleasure.

The effects of guilt

Sexual guilt learned early in life can make girls growing up more vulnerable to exploitative sex. They cannot talk honestly with us as parents about their feelings and, because they feel soiled, may find it difficult to share their thoughts and experiences with other women, too. Sometimes a woman enters a relationship with a man who seems to offer protection against still more threatening horrors awaiting in the future. Jane says she was brought up to believe that, "sex was something nice girls did not do. They had to tolerate it to get children when their rather bestial men forced it upon them. Men are pathetic creatures who have to give in to their animal instincts, but women are higher creatures who don't need such things." She led a very protected life until she left home at 19 to live in a house full of young people. Waking one morning, she found that a man who had been visiting someone else in the house the evening before had got into bed with her, but did not dare to call out or protest "as I was afraid the others would hear". A few months later she married him as she had been taught that she must marry a man with whom she had had intercourse. She was miserably unhappy and is now divorced.

To many women that must seem as yet another of the responsibilities imposed on mothers – that you must never let a child experience sexual guilt. It is obviously impossible to ensure this. Our children are influenced by the society around them, not only by our personal attitudes. If, for example, it is an exciting game in nursery school for children to shout "bottoms!", our irritation only makes matters worse. Feeling that sexual behaviour is "right" or "wrong" is part of much more widespread social values. There is a point at which we cannot entirely shield our children from values with which we profoundly disagree.

In everything I say and do, I can either attempt to package sex attractively in order to make it socially acceptable or try to see it clearly and to understand why people behave as they do. I can define sexual experience in terms of a preconceived framework of ideas or I can dare to discard the clichés and things which we are tempted to take for granted. I can deceive, distort, romanticize, and impose rules and dogma – or I can communicate to my children the value of openness and acknowledge the need for each individual to work out their own sexual identity.

7 TRANSITIONS

The girl growing up

At any time from about her ninth year the rise of oestrogen in the young girl's blood stream changes the distribution of body fat so that her hips become wider, her bottom rounder and she begins to develop a characteristically female body shape. Raised oestrogen levels also lead to breast development, which precedes her first menstrual period, and other hormones – adrenal androgens – trigger growth of pubic and underarm hair. She is now entering into puberty, a physiological stage of development to maturity which in our society is considered to be, both emotionally and culturally, one of transition to adulthood. As the girl crosses this bridge her parents often expect to find her difficult to cope with, and anticipate that she will be self-conscious, moody, vulnerable, confused, hostile to authority, acutely concerned with her physical appearance and that at some time she will fall in love with a member of the opposite sex. Perhaps the single most significant thing about adolescents in our culture is that they are not taken seriously. Whatever the girl does, whatever she believes, someone will say, "She'll grow out of it. It's just a phase." She is in a limbo in which not only is it difficult for her to find and shape her own identity as a woman, but any identity she has may be actively denied by adults as transitory, superficial and meaningless.

The first period   Parents often feel a good deal of conflict about a daughter becoming sexually mature and this may be expressed in their attitudes to her first period. Paula Weideger (*Female Cycles*) claims that adults observe the emergence of the woman from the child partly with goodwill but partly with fear. Female sexuality, the symbol of which is menstrual blood, represents not only the potential for childbearing but the threat of pollution. In many ancient and primitive societies (and a dominant theme with regard to the nature of women in the Judaeo-Christian tradition), the unleashed power of the female essence as it flows in menstrual blood is believed to contaminate crops, sour milk and even sometimes make any man who crosses the woman's path sicken and die. In the twentieth century we are more sophisticated. But we still treat menstrual blood as dirty and shameful, something a girl must learn how to carefully hide so that no man can guess that she is menstruating. The ambiguity of our feelings is expressed in the mixed message we give her that she should be proud to be grown-up now, but that she must hide pads and tampons quickly, secretly dispose of or wash soiled underclothes, and, above all, avoid letting males in the household know that she is menstruating. The shame and humiliation which are communicated, however unwittingly, to girls as they are warned to conceal menstruation insidiously prepares them for being stamped with a biological stigma and gender handicap in Western society.

The ovarian cycle, menstruation and conception are not just incidental biological processes, physical accidents which impinge on the mind, but for many women are part and parcel of the way they feel about and see themselves and are inseparable from the sense of self. Far more happens in a woman's body than ever does in a man's. When enormous changes occur in her body her sense of self is profoundly changed. Equally, when the self passes through a transmutation her body changes, too, and there is a physical expression of this change. The menstrual flow, for example, is affected: its timing, quantity, whether it occurs at all, or continues normally. When a woman is very anxious or deeply shocked her periods may come to a full stop. When she grieves this may happen too, or bleeding may continue as if it were a physiological expression of mourning. All these things the adolescent girl gradually begins to learn about herself and the discovery may make her feel uncomfortably dependent on her body and even trapped in it. One of the hardest things of all for her may be to enjoy her own body.

> "You made a fuss about it, as if it were a big thing to happen. If girls are well prepared it's not such a big step."

It is often claimed that a woman is at the mercy of her hormones, subject to cyclical rhythms which enfeeble her, make her incapable of rational thought, render her emotional and mentally confused and which may even unhinge her mind, and every month she has what is seen as a "dirty discharge" of blood. "Womanhood began with much unpleasantness", Clara Thompson wrote. ("Cultural pressures in the psychology of women")

It was characterized by feelings of body shame, loss of freedom, loss of equality with boys, and loss of the right to be aggressive. The training in insincerity, especially about her sexual being and sexual interest, has undoubtedly contributed much to a woman's diminished sense of self. When something so vitally a part of her must be denied, it is not a great step further to deny the whole self.

Girls are themselves aware of the contradictions in the manner in which menstruation is greeted and the ambiguity of its meaning. Looking back, my own daughters have described their experiences in this way: "I felt physically mature. I always associated the smell of menstrual blood with women and that was nice. You said 'Congratulations!' I realized that you wanted to give a positive reaction in a nice, liberal, feminist way. But I was just about to go riding and I couldn't get the tampon in. It was a bloody bore! And of course, it was terribly uncomfortable on the pony with the tampon not properly in."

There is an inherent conflict in the situation so that nothing a mother does is likely to be absolutely right. Another daughter said to me: "You gave me all the right books explaining menstruation, conception and pregnancy but I just wasn't terribly interested at the time. I knew about it all anyway – from biology – along with all the correct labels. But when, a long while later, I actually began to menstruate, I was appalled! Somehow I had never connected all that theory to me. I hadn't even realized I had a hole there!"

Another daughter: "You showed me pictures from a thing called the *Birth Atlas*, I remember, and explained that my vagina was almost at right angles to my cervix and things like that. I went in the bathroom and bled all over the bath struggling to get a tampon in but I couldn't. And you said, 'Do you want me to come and do it for you?' I felt awful! I was really worried you would come in."

Another daughter: "I was so afraid you would make a fuss about me 'becoming a woman' that I didn't tell you I was having periods for three months. I didn't want to make a big thing of it because I was no more interested in sex than in the inhabitants of Outer Mongolia. Girls at school spent all their lunch hours and breaks talking about it. It was a nuisance. They all got at me for being a swot. I was frightened of starting periods and that happening to me, talking all the time about boys and periods!"

The girls turned to me and said: "*Whatever* you did, it was bound to be wrong!"

Establishing a separate identity

The way in which a mother decides to react to the advent of her daughters' menstruation has to be wrong, in a way, because a major task for a girl in adolescence is to differentiate herself from her mother. The scenario in which the first menstruation takes place is just one part of that process of differentiation, and probably a highly significant one. And to differentiate she has to make boundaries, to draw back from her mother, to define herself as distinct from her with different ideas and feelings. She has to claim a right to her own sexuality and may accentuate, and make a caricature of, her distinctiveness in an attempt to define herself as separate. The more liberal and understanding the mother, the harder this task is for her daughter.

Mother, Mother, Mother-goddess,
moulding your child into beauty,
You take her by the hand
And lead her gently into life,
Your beautiful daughter
Into your beautiful life.
There is nothing she can do
That you cannot accept, understand, forgive,
There is nothing she can do.
There is nothing she can be
That you will not re-interpret into beauty
There is nothing I can be,
Mother, Mother, Mother,
I am screaming
Let me be.

Do not come into my room, Mother,
Do not come and make it beautiful and fresh
with your flowers and your love,
Do not breathe into it your love of life,
Your joy, your joyful view of life,
Here in my dark stale room I sit alone
amongst the crumbs, the coffee-cups, the smelly socks
I pick my nose, I lick my plate,
Hugging my sordid individuality about me
Like barbed wire
Keeping you out.
I am I, not she – your daughter,
I am Me.
[Polly Kitzinger]

This need to assert a separate identity may happen partially because there is nothing in our society that allows the formal and cumulative acquisition of status as a girl moves into womanhood, as in the past, when she let down her skirts and put up her hair, her father gave approval to a suitor, she plighted her troth, became a bride, managed her household, became a mother of a child and subsequently of a large family. And though a golden "key of the door" may still be emblazoned on twenty-first birthday cards, it has no counterpart in reality. The young woman has probably already been sharing a flat with friends for several years and, without her mother needing to know, has been on the Pill for longer.

*Cultural
variations*

Our view of adolescence as a period of years that is a "difficult phase" is, historically speaking, a recent one. In the past girls went straight from being children to wives and mothers, or into domestic science, teaching, nursing or other occupations. My own mother left school at 13 because money was short and by her middle teens was already in nursing. The abrupt break we have today between childhood and entry into a period in which conflict between the adolescent and her parents is anticipated and in which the young woman is treated for some years as if she were not really, or not yet "herself", is not typical of Third World societies or of Western Europe in the past. Margaret Mead has shown that adolescence is created by culture. (*From the South Seas: Studies of Adolescence and Sex in Primitive Societies*)

In many Third World societies becoming a woman, around the time of the first menstrual period, is given ritual recognition. It marks the beginning of a process when a girl is socially separated from her mother, makes new social bonds through marriage and is realigned to her family of origin, her kinfolk, as the means through which her husband's family is linked to it. In Sierra Leone a girl is introduced into the important sisterhood of the Sande society at any age between eight and 17 and from that point is considered ready to bear children. In some cultures painful, hazardous and mutilating rites, such as clitoridectomy, may be part of this celebration, making the girl ready for or marking her arrival at adulthood. Many of the rites echo wedding ceremonies. When a Tamil Hindu girl in Sri Lanka has her first period, for example, a celebration is

With puberty a girl begins to form new and tentative relationships in the search for her own sexuality and her identity as a woman.

enacted very like that of a wedding and actually goes by the same name. It includes ritual baths, a seclusion period with a special diet and a party when the house is decorated as a "wedding house", and the girl is dressed like a bride in a red or pink sari for the last ceremonial bath. After this she wears for the first time a grown-up style sari and gold jewellery and is seated on a throne decorated with flowers to receive presents from family and friends. (D. B. McGilvray, "Sexual power and fertility in Sri Lanka") An integral part of such ceremonies is acknowledgment and celebration of a girl's readiness for motherhood, her reproductive "destiny", and her sex as a means to this. In the West we have no such rites of celebration which confer status in this way.

In our culture, adolescence is treated as a time for assessment of what the individual has so far achieved. The young person is weighed in the balance. Though this is a time of school exams, passing them, however high the grades, confers a restricted kind of status on the girl. They show that she has been a good pupil and may present her with a ticket for going on to further education or, if employment is available, into a job. But exam results do not say anything about other aspects of her personality. The first job, the first pay cheque, or even drawing social security for the first time, may be powerful markers of reaching adult status, but these pale into insignificance for many girls compared with "going all the way", and with the raising of the school-leaving age are more likely to *follow* rather than precede the first act of intercourse.

Adolescent sex Though it is important that parents should not assume that a teenage girl is interested in sex, is having her *first* sexual experience, or necessarily wanting to be attractive to boys, she is subjected to a good deal of pressure from her peer group to be sexually active, with hints about all the marvels of sex from those girls who have "done it". It is vital, therefore, that she understands contraception and how to obtain it *before* she is emotionally involved with a boy.

The adolescent girl in our society may not feel she is an adult until she has had sexual intercourse, which often takes the place of the highly ritualized threshold to adulthood in Third World cultures. It is the act of penetration which, in itself, and uniquely among all other acts, symbolically represents sexual experience. And by this very act to become an adult the girl is perceived as *losing* something – her virginity – whereas the boy has gained something, even if it is only "a lay".

Information about contraception needs to be understood by girls and boys long before puberty. From the age of three or four children want to know why water comes out of a tap when it is turned, where the electricity goes when the switch is up, why people breathe and sleep and have ticking hearts and how babies are born and how they get inside their mothers. This is all part of acquiring knowledge of the day to day mechanics of how things work. Knowledge of contraception given then will not, of course, be adequate as the girl grows older, but nevertheless she needs information *bit by bit*, not in an indigestible gobbet as she is on the threshold of puberty.

A mother can never take it for granted that the girl who has been given frank and graphic information about sex and contraception can synthesize these different pieces of knowledge into a whole. We cannot assume that she will choose to apply any of this knowledge to herself or be able to relate cognitive learning to emotional processes. All we can offer is a relationship of trust and openness, our willingness to listen and share with her, when and if she wants to, and our own honesty.

Many young women have intercourse feeling that getting pregnant is something that is unlikely ever to happen to them. In adolescence, and long past it for many women, we often do not think of ourselves as able to bear a child. Susan Griffin (*Made from this Earth*) recounts a discussion with a woman who has had three abortions, the first when she was 22. She had not used contraception. "I simply did not recognize that I was a woman and capable of conceiving. In some very basic way I didn't believe in my own existence." She goes on to say that her family was very open about sex: "I had plenty of information about how to get protection if I needed it. But my carelessness was allied more to my personal development . . . as a woman."

Women often say that they used sex in adolescence to get proof that they were of value and that somebody wanted them. "I first had intercourse because it was expected of me," says one woman (everyone else in her peer group was having sex with their boyfriends), "and to be grown-up. I felt very inadequate when I was trying to prove I was attractive and to make someone love me". And another says, "Sexual feeling became an obsession; otherwise you felt you were missing out." A woman who had intercourse for the first time at 16 says it was painful but she enjoyed it "because it made me feel grown-up".

Many of the women who have told me about their feelings had a series of casual sexual encounters during adolescence, "all grope and a quick cuddle, a fun thing". Most were anxious to lose their virginity. But when it happened it was an anti-climax: "It left me totally cold. I thought, 'If this is sex, you can keep it!'" "It was sneaky," says another about that first act of intercourse, "hard to experience because it was so quick". When they faced their parents afterwards they often felt that they bore the marks of the experience like stigmata. "I felt they could see guilt written all over my face", says a woman about herself at 15, "that they would be able to see what I had done just by *looking* at me."

Though rushed and furtive, the clandestine nature of adolescent sex makes it exciting and women, perhaps now married with small children, often look back to those days with nostalgia, or draw on their experiences in adolescence as the content of fantasies during lawful intercourse in the matrimonial bed on Saturday night when the children are asleep. "Sex was more exciting when grabbed at, with the danger of being discovered, and I really got worked up." "Sex was more of an adventure than now", another says, "a time of discovery emotionally and physically, of experimentation, trying out new positions and techniques." The trouble, explains one woman, "is that the initial thrill goes away when you get to know someone really well. Sex in adolescence was *wonderful*."

During adolescence many of the patterns of later sexual activity are laid down. For most teenagers there is, for example, a clear distinction between petting and "going all the way". Mothers often reinforce these distinctions. One woman remembers being told that she must not let a boy touch her above the hem or below the waistband, but everywhere else was all right. Sexual intercourse becomes the climax to which every other kind of sexual act leads, the purpose and culmination of all this excitement. And intercourse is seen primarily as something a male does to a female, penetration and ejaculation. Even though girls may be willing partners to the fumbling, in the end, sex is a *male* achievement.

And so it remains. The goal is seen as intercourse and anything else merely "foreplay". This is why many women are dissatisfied with their sex life, for their men reduce preparatory stimulation to the minimum necessary in order to get in and, once there, ejaculate, pull out, roll over and fall asleep. The woman lies in the darkness remembering the thrill of adolescent sex or the early days of a relationship, when the emphasis was on arousing her. She feels that the journey there was more exciting than arriving.

Popular images of women

Our culture tells the adolescent girl, almost invariably, that her body is not good enough, that it is too fat, too thin, that her breasts are too small or too large, she is pear-shaped or top-heavy, her bone structure is wrong and so on. Boys are enjoined to scrub their fingernails and deal with dandruff and spots but they are not required to constantly shape, trim, adorn and disguise themselves to present their bodies as worthy of approval. For girls this starts in earnest in adolescence and continues for many women right through their lives into old age. We are taught that we dare not show our real selves and we become expert in packaging. "As a child I liked my body", one woman says, "its solidity, its capacity for pleasure and activity. I welcomed menstruation when it started. But I soon began to realize that I was not going to become what females should be: gentle, pretty, slim", and from then on she only liked her body when she was alone with it.

A girl growing up in our society is surrounded by images of sex and of women packaged and presented as objects to titillate male sexuality. Sex is offered as the reward for using a hair spray, eating a box of chocolates or wearing a cross-over bra.

The advertising industry has been quick to cash in on women's vulnerability. Unsure of our own value, we tend to seek guidance to assure us that we are fit for male consumption. Women are shown agonizing over hands roughened with domestic work, meals that do not appeal to their menfolk or laundry that is not whiter than white. "You are deceiving yourself", the message runs, "if you think that what you are is good enough. You are more inadequate than you realize." And only when they sort themselves out and emerge with softened hands, select the right instant food and the better washing machine and use the cleaning powders that destroy and purify deep down round life's hidden S-bend, do they get the reward of love and admiration from men. The woman is depicted as a confused, anxious child, needing advice from an older, more sensible friend who uses the right floor cleaner, so that the husband returning home from work smiles approvingly and is apparently sexually excited by the sight of the gleaming kitchen; from the male scientist with the fruity voice who shows her how she too can get the stains out of Johnnie's football shorts and be loved thereafter; or the uniformed professional – nurse, doctor or engineer, for example – who guides her gently but firmly into making the appropriate choice of consumer products. Once she does this, she suddenly changes from a worried drudge to a beautiful, poised, confident woman. It is, of course, all a joke. But a joke that it would not pay the ad agencies to tell if there were not hidden in such material an image of how women have been conditioned to see themselves and of how men like to see them.

There is no way a teenage girl today can avoid these images of women in magazines, on television and surrounding her on posters unless she is both deaf and blind. They are sometimes spiced with comedy, when we are able to see the plastic cut-outs for what they are, but no amount of laughter can deny their power to influence a girl's ideas of how women are supposed to be in our society.

The place of a mother's own experience

Mothers are aware that their adolescent daughters are living in a world in which they are vulnerable to exploitation and the advice they give is often an odd combination of warnings about getting pregnant and catching VD on the one hand and romantic ideas about love, finding the right man and knowing instantaneously that this is "it", on the other. The mothers who told me about the kind of guidance they planned to give their adolescent daughters nearly all emphasized the romantic aspect of this message, often throwing in a comment about having contraceptive information for good measure. The romantic message comes over in frequently startling contrast to their own sexual experiences and relationships with men. A woman who says she is "frigid and lost and desperately lonely despite being married" still intends to tell her daughter, "Wait for Mister Right to come along. You'll know when he does." Another, for whom sex is "like waiting for the kettle to boil", says, "Respect your body. It is something wonderful and should be reserved totally for your husband." Another, whose husband is "always saying I'm fat and stretch-marked", and who says of herself that she has "gone downhill" since the birth of her children, tells her daughter that, "sex is the way we bring new souls to the earth." A woman whose husband uses her "like a rubber doll for his pleasure" can still advise her daughter that "sex is an expression of deep love for one other person and not to be squandered or cheapened." The dream has been kept intact, perhaps for the woman's *own* sake, even though reality often appears to have taught her exactly the opposite. Most women seem unwilling or unable to draw on their personal experiences to guide them in knowing how to counsel a daughter. It is as if between many mothers and daughters a delicate web of deceit, spun over centuries, is being perpetuated and the adult woman, having failed to find her own Prince Charming, or having discovered that he was quickly metamorphosed back into a frog, longs for her daughter to find the romance which proved illusory in her own life. We visit on our daughters our unrealized dreams and longings. We burden them with our own unlived lives. Perhaps we have to learn to say good-bye to the asymmetry of the mother–daughter relationship and rediscover ourselves as equals, as sisters.

We need to support each other emotionally with no accusations, no recriminations, no guilt. An enormously helpful thing the Woman's Movement has done for many women is to introduce them to consciousness raising groups and to spread the idea that we can share with, and love and help each other. In such groups women of different ages can get together to grow in self-awareness and understanding of one another.

Choosing a contraceptive

If you have run through four or five different forms of contraception, are not satisfied with any of them, have tried several kinds of pill, all of which have produced side-effects, have even relied at times on "being careful", you are not alone. Many of the women who have told me about their contraceptive experiences describe what amounts to an obstacle race to be able to control fertility. Most of the books and pamphlets which deal with contraception seem to be designed to increase the contraceptive user's confidence and get her to feel that she is in control. This section aims to do something different: to describe women's actual experiences as they affect both the psychological and physical aspects of sex.

The 300 or so women, most of them with young children, who have told me about what happened to them may be exceptions, but this is rather unlikely. It sounds as if women do not always disclose to their doctors all the inconveniences and discomforts of contraception, nor their inner fears. If we feel insecure using a contraceptive technique, or anxious about whether we shall be able to conceive when we stop using this method, these worries affect our feelings about sex just as much, or even more, as a method which is cumbersome and so interferes with the spontaneity of lovemaking or one which, because it saps energy or reduces libido, makes of sex an unpleasant chore. Any doubts about a contraceptive method, whether or not they seem justified to an outsider, can detract from our sexual experience.

The Pill

Most women reading these pages will at some time or other have been on the Pill. Those who like it usually feel that it is the easiest way and that it is lovely not having to organize contraception before intercourse but be able to be completely spontaneous. They realize that it is the most reliable of methods and appreciate that under the National Health Service it is free or costs very little. Even so, a couple of women conceived while on the progestogen-only pill (the mini-pill – a pill which contains a synthetic form of progesterone), and several point out that it is important to have available another contraceptive method to use if you get any illness involving diarrhoea or vomiting.

There is a general strong feeling that when you are on the Pill you are "messing about with your body". Many women are anxious about the possible longterm effects on their bodies: "I never liked the thought that it puts your body in a constant state of pseudo-pregnancy." Some are unhappy about regularly taking drugs of any kind, whether this is aspirin, the Pill or anything else, and women who are breast-feeding often feel, with justification, that they would prefer not to administer hormones to their babies in their milk, however apparently safe it appears to be and even though there have been no apparent side-effects in babies. Many women have an uneasy feeling that the Pill can interfere with their chance of having a child when they want one and those who have never conceived in the past may feel that they simply want to know that they *could* get pregnant if they wanted to.

But the main problem is that many of us encounter major difficulties in taking the Pill, ranging all the way from forgetting to take it regularly ("I had a problem remembering but the alarm on my watch helps") to such serious side-effects as migraine, depression, extremely heavy bleeding – occasionally lasting as long as a fortnight – pre-menstrual tension, high blood pressure, phlebitis and giving birth to a deformed baby. Elizabeth had a baby who died when two weeks old from a congenital heart defect and attributes this to taking a high-dose pill for six years and then conceiving within two weeks of stopping. If you are on the Pill it is important to leave two or three months after coming off it before you have unprotected intercourse and to use some other method of contraception during this time, so that you can be quite sure that the hormones are out of your body. You will also have a much better chance of being able to date your pregnancy accurately because you will have got back into your menstrual rhythm.

Women report recurrent headaches which stop when they come off the Pill. Some say they get feelings of stress or become inexplicably irritable while taking it. Others have morning sickness or nausea in the evening and many say that it reduces sexual drive, either because they just lose interest in sex or because they are "too tired to be sexy". "I never felt like sex except during my period," one woman says, and another: "It put me right off my husband as well as sex." A woman who is on the mini-pill says: "It depressed my interest in sex and my ability to feel *anything* when making love and gave me blinding headaches." She became very anxious about this as her father died of coronary illness and she herself has a history of high blood pressure. Some women put on weight or suffer from water retention (feeling fat and bloated) which they lose when they come off the Pill. Some women say that being on the Pill has made their periods regular and less painful, though these are offset by an equal number of women reporting that the Pill has made their periods heavier, longer and more painful. Jan says the Pill suited her well physically and that she didn't have any unpleasant side-effects "except that after taking it for two years I began to come down with minor infections, such as flu and tonsillitis, very regularly. I read that the Pill might indirectly be the cause as it makes the body use vitamins faster. I don't know how accurate this is, but when I started taking once-a-day multivitamins I had no more trouble." Gill has diabetes and was on the Pill for about 10 years "but had to stop using it as it caused glaucoma and I went blind in one eye and I only have 60 per cent vision in the other eye". Rose's sister-in-law died after a blood clot when taking the Pill and though Rose was on the Pill for the first five years of her marriage she now, at 28, feels really anxious and after her baby is born will change to another method of contraception.

There are fewer side-effects with the progestogen-only pill, but many women taking it have breakthrough bleeding and it is not as reliable a contraceptive as the combined oestrogen and progestogen pill. Some women say they are so anxious that the mini-pill may not be 100 per cent effective that they avoid intercourse at the time when they think it possible they might be ovulating.

Many of the women who are no longer taking the Pill had been advised to come off it by their doctors. One, for example, had an ovarian cyst. Another developed varicose veins. Some have been switched from pill to pill because of putting on weight or because of pregnancy scares which stopped bleeding entirely. Many GPs now advise patients who are over 30, and also those who smoke, not to choose the Pill as a method of contraception.

But even though some GPs are very cautious, there are others who take little notice of side-effects reported by women. Even when a woman tells her doctor that she is unhappy about the Pill, that her breasts are hurting, she is putting on weight or has lost interest in sex, she may be encouraged to persist. Lydia told her doctor that her whole body ached, she had pain in her breasts and "achy pains" in one leg and was worried in case there was a connection with the Pill. "He replied that 'it was getting used to my body'." Stella had "lost interest in sex" and was having painful, irregular bleeding, but says: "My doctor made light of these side-effects and told me to go home and keep taking it. I finally decided that it was *my* body and I didn't want to."

Easy as the Pill is, it is not the solution to contraceptive worries for many women. In coping with fertility fairly effectively, it poses fresh problems and introduces new anxieties.

New hormonal methods

Latest developments in hormone-based contraception include methods of introducing hormones in the form of implants which can be removed before you want to conceive. There are also impregnated devices which are inserted through the vagina and can be left in for up to three months. One version of this is a progestogen-releasing ring which you put in yourself and fit against the cervix. An advantage over the progestogen-only pill, for example, is that there will be no breakthrough bleeding, as the hormone supply is steady. Nor can diarrhoea and vomiting interfere with its efficacy.

A nasal spray is now being tested which uses luteinizing hormone-releasing hormones (LHRH) which suppress the hormone that initiates ovulation. This also works in men, so it may form the basis of the first male hormonal contraceptive.

The intra-uterine device (IUD)

The IUD, or coil, has been used for hundreds of years in North Africa – but by camels, not women. Camel traders taking their camels across the Sahara inserted small pebbles in the uterus of female camels so that they did not become pregnant during the long journey across arid country. But the practice may have an even longer tradition. When I was interviewing Zulu witchdoctors I learned that it was used when the Zulu people made great treks in towards Central Africa. Since the journey was always long and hard the elders of the tribe first selected small pebbles from the river bed, blessed them in a special ceremony to control fertility, and then put one into the uterus of each woman of childbearing age. Much reduced fertility during these great treks has often been attributed to starvation, but it seems more likely that it was the consequence of this practice.

The advantage of an IUD is that, once inserted, it needs checking only occasionally. Women say that there is tremendous benefit in not having to dose themselves with hormones or fumble with latex. They claim they hardly notice it and that to be able to have intercourse without premeditation is a positive bonus.

But the disadvantages of the IUD are all too apparent. Pelvic inflammatory disease is common and many women have painful, heavy, lengthy periods or non-stop bleeding. Karen says that she "suffered the coil for seven months . . . I was in constant pain and bled all the time." An IUD does not always stay in place. Ann says she had a coil fitted which was trouble-free for 12 months, but that she then had to have a D and C (dilatation and curetage). A different coil was fitted and this caused great pain and finally had to be taken out because it had lodged in the wall of her uterus. The failure rate is also high and women either conceive because it has fallen out undetected, or conceive with it in place. This is what happened eventually to Jane who had had trouble with the coil from the very beginning. She says that it was "disastrous as it was incorrectly fitted". She endured a great deal of pain and heavy bleeding. "But at the check-up they assured me that this was quite normal." After six months she and her husband decided they wanted another baby so she went to have it removed. The doctor refused to do this as she had not had a period because she was breast-feeding. So she weaned the child, but her periods still did not arrive. She had a pregnancy test, which was positive. Unfortunately this finished in a miscarriage but there was still no sign of the coil. On X-ray it showed up as having pierced the uterus. It had lodged between it and her abdomen and she had to have a laparoscopy to have it removed. Many of the accidental pregnancies that occur with an IUD in place end in miscarriage. Many women are very concerned about the failure rate and also about the increased incidence of ectopic pregnancy (pregnancy in the fallopian tubes), while using an IUD.

Some women find the IUD uncomfortable or painful and occasionally severe pain during intercourse is reported. One woman said: "It played havoc with our sex lives." Men may also find the thread causes discomfort to them. But if this happens with intercourse it is worth having the thread shortened.

Even though they may have no discomfort at all, though, and be completely unaware of its presence, the risk of pelvic infection, uterine perforation and the chance of getting pregnant makes many women decide that an IUD is not for them and a large proportion of those who have told me about their experiences with the IUD have moved on to other kinds of contraception.

The sheath

In a cave at Combarelles there is a drawing of a man and woman dating from prehistoric times. The couple are having sexual intercourse and it appears that the man is wearing a sheath. Minos, King of Crete, was said to use a sheath made from the bladder of a goat. In Ancient and Imperial Rome it is recorded that the bladders of several different kinds of animal were used, apparently in order to protect against venereal disease. It has been suggested, however, that the use of the sheath as a method of contraception was unknown. (Hania W. Ris, "The essential emancipation: the control of reproduction")

Nowadays, the sheath, or condom, though for some women their primary method of contraception, tends to be used as a good method on which to fall back when something else is not working well, or at times when another contraceptive method is ill-advised. Couples use it after having a baby before going on to their chosen type of contraception, during breast-feeding, after the man has had a vasectomy and before they get the "all clear", sometimes when semen seems to be the cause of slight spotting from the cervix during pregnancy and occasionally as part of the treatment for premature ejaculation (since stimulation is decreased).

Those women who prefer the sheath as their main method of contraception point out that they do not have to "do any mopping up" or have semen "dribbling out of the vagina down my legs for hours afterwards". In fact, its main advantage is seen as saving "mess": "It's very clean and I don't have to get up to wash afterwards." Some like the man to have the main responsibility for using contraception because they think it important that he is prepared to do this for the woman he loves. Occasionally a Catholic wife is happy for her non-Catholic husband to use sheaths so that it is not a decisive act on her part: "I would always feel guilty at the back of my mind if I used anything." The sheath is simple and easy, needs little forethought, does not interfere with a woman's hormonal balance and is not a foreign body permanently inside her.

But very few women like it and their partners often dislike it too, mainly because it reduces stimulation for both of them, and because they are afraid it may split or slide off. Women are sometimes allergic to a spermicide used with the sheath and if they do not use enough spermicide, find the rubber very uncomfortable: "I seem to go dry as soon as my husband uses them". Some women say it is "smelly and awkward", "messy and sickening" and that it interrupts lovemaking: "When I am very excited, my husband stops to put it on. Then it seems to put me off . . . ."; "It dulls feeling a little for both of us. . . . our sex life has diminished to almost nil." Wendy says that her husband likes her to roll the sheath over his penis as part of lovemaking, but that she dislikes doing this, finds it interrupts the flow of pleasure she is experiencing, so is a "turn-off", and that this may be partly why he hurts her when he penetrates. "There is," she says "a loss of sensation for both of us, but it's better than nothing." Gail agrees that it is uncomfortable and says that her husband is not keen on it because it reduces stimulation and she dislikes it because she gets itching afterwards, but says that it is the best method she can find because "it does not interfere with or affect my body".

Over the world as a whole, only about one-third of people using contraception rely on male methods. And the proportion of those doing so has decreased steadily as the Pill, the IUD and female sterilization have gained acceptance. One major problem with these recent developments is that such methods do not protect against sexually transmitted diseases. Various US Government Select Committees have explored how to increase the marketing appeal of condoms for that very reason. In 1978, for example, at a hearing of the House Select Committee on Population, it was suggested that condoms should be marketed in three sizes:

In men who are petite, they fall off, and in men who are extra well-endowed, they burst. Women buy brassières in A, B and C cups and pantiehose in different sizes, and I think it would help condom efficiency, that we should package them in different sizes and maybe label them like olives . . . jumbo, colossal and super colossal so that men do not have to go in and ask for the small . . . . (B. Seaman, US Congress House Select Committee on Population)

It will probably need more than this for condoms to gain in popularity over the Pill.

The cap

The cap dates from the early years of the last century, though it first became well known in Holland and so became known as the "Dutch cap".

The major advantage of the cap or diaphragm is the absence of serious side-effects and for many women this compensates for the disadvantages of messiness and inconvenience: "I use the cap and I'm not really happy with it. I find it's a nuisance putting it in and getting it out. The spermicide I use with it is messy – dribbling out for hours afterwards – so I often use it without spermicide and then worry about it."

Getting the cap in takes a bit of learning. It tends to spring out of your hand and can seem to have a life of its own. One woman says she knocked herself out on the loo pan while lying on the bathroom floor trying to insert it. Another found it got hooked in front of her cervix so that she could not dislodge it to take it out and she had "dreadful tussles with it, rolling around on the floor and swearing and getting out of breath".

Doctors usually advise inserting the cap routinely every evening "as if cleaning your teeth" so that it does not interfere with the spontaneity of lovemaking. Women, however, do not like all the fuss of getting it in and using spermicide when it is not going to be necessary. Some say they feel resentful towards their men afterwards if it is not used: "If you put it in and don't use it, you feel cheated and if you haven't got it in, you don't feel like going off to put it in." Victoria expresses succinctly what many others feel when she says: "It takes a lot of getting used to. All the jellies seem so messy. OK with a regular partner, but a passion stopper with someone new. Whatever the clinic says, it is *not* like cleaning your teeth." Too much gel and the disc slips all over the place, too little and you wonder whether you are running the risk of pregnancy.

Women find the spermicide extremely distasteful and some worry that if they *did* conceive, the chemicals in the spermicide could affect the fetus. So, though a woman may choose the cap as the least disadvantageous of methods, very few seem to enjoy using it. One who does, says: "It's *wonderful*. Reliable, easy to use, no side-effects, sexy, earthy."

One great advantage of all barrier methods is that they may help to protect against sexually transmitted diseases and it also looks as if they can protect against cervical cancer. New barrier methods are being developed, including a collagen sponge which does not need to be fitted, as the cap has to be, and which can be bought over-the-counter. It is the first female barrier method that women can use without visiting a doctor beforehand.

Withdrawal

The disadvantages of withdrawal are well known. Before the main spurt of semen is ejaculated there are a few drops of liquid which often contain some sperm and this is enough to make a woman pregnant. It is also difficult for a sexually aroused couple to be so aware of what they are doing that timing is accurate. What if she grips him between her knees and in her arms so that those few precious seconds are lost? What if the very struggle to get away in time triggers ejaculation? Withdrawal is a risky game and though most women have some experience of it, at least once or twice in adolescence or after, it is one that leads to constant anxiety about whether your period will come. And since "mess" seems to be an important issue for women, it comes bottom of the list in terms of comfort and cleanliness.

Natural methods

There are, however, other, "natural", methods which women who are disillusioned with the Pill and with mechanical methods of contraception are discussing more and more. The range of natural methods includes the rhythm or "safe period", temperature and Billings (Evelyn Billings and Ann Westmore, *The Billings Method. Controlling fertility without drugs or devices*) or meuco-thermal methods. Some women do not accept that sex must always involve penetration and say that during their most fertile period they prefer to make love without intercourse. They point out that sex is often equated with intercourse but that there are many other ways to enjoy each other.

Some use a combination of rhythm with the sheath when they are most likely to be fertile, but do not usually find it satisfactory as they are aware that it is not absolutely safe. Nancy has had two babies in two years trying to find the "safe period" and now uses the Billings method, with which she is "totally happy". She says "Since I have an irregular cycle 'the safe period' was not safe. This method is accurate and makes for a better marriage."

If you are to be successful in using any of the "natural" methods you need to know your body and your menstrual rhythms really well. It is not enough to rely on a calendar. But women who have got in touch with their bodies in this way, who know exactly how they feel prior to and during ovulation and understand the changing physical sensations of the cycle, are enthusiastic about it. They have an almost evangelical zeal. They combine calendar rhythm, basal body temperature and vaginal mucus examination with persistence, intellectual fervour and imaginative flair! "I am the type of person who likes to be in control of my body and know what it is doing all the time, and the meuco-thermal method goes along with that", one woman says. And another: "It taught both of us self-discipline and more respect for each other." Many emphasize that it teaches their male partners, too, more about a woman's body: "I use the Billings ovulation method and am quite happy with it. Indeed, it is a shared thing with my husband, who helps to keep a record. We often observe the changes in my vaginal mucus together. He is very familiar with my mucus"; "I'd always enjoyed keeping a record of my menstrual cycle and now I felt I was really getting to know my reproductive system. It was exciting to know when I ovulated, to see the changes in my mucus and see my temperature rise and fall according to the cycle. Abstinence was never a problem as Guy and I both found it exciting. When we decided to try and conceive, it was great to be able to pinpoint virtually the exact day we were likely to make a baby."

But counselling and supervision of the charts by someone skilled who knows all the pitfalls to be avoided is necessary while you learn an effective method and this is not always available. Daisy says that when she decided on the meuco-thermal method after having her first baby she never "felt 100 per cent sure that I was safe, and this affected my sex life. . . . The method is very good if you get continued counselling and careful supervision of your charts until you are aware of all the elements of the system. I moved to an area where there was no counselling at a time when I wasn't fully confident of the method and so I got caught. This has dwindled my faith in the method and I know after I have my second child I will go on the Pill, but I would like to say that the method can work and does work for a lot of people."

It cannot work, either, unless you and your partner are willing to incorporate into your life together regular phases when you do not have intercourse, and are meticulous about this. Some couples use alternative ways of making love during these times and enjoy occasions when they have anything *but* penetration. Some find a period of abstinence exciting. But it is obviously not a method that works if you succumb to the thrill of the moment without forethought, nor if you are moving between different partners who do not share your enthusiasm for the system.

New developments in natural methods

Since it can be difficult to read a thermometer absolutely accurately and to assess the state of cervical mucus with certainty, research has been taking place into electronic apparatus to eliminate human error. So-called "computer contraception" has been invented in the form of a fertility indicator that records the temperature and analyses it in a minute computer. Because this device identifies a woman's fertile phases it can be used equally well for contraceptive purposes or to find out when your fertile period comes if you want to conceive. One version has three lights: when the amber light switches on it shows that it is the right time of day to take your temperature. This is in the early morning only. You then take your temperature by putting the thermometer in your mouth, at which point one of the two other lights will switch on: it may be a continuous red light, which signals that you are in the pre-ovulation phase and that there is a possibility of conception, or a flashing red light which signals that you are highly fertile at this time; or a green light which shows that you are infertile. By pressing a button on the first day of your period you programme the computer to record your cycle in the form of a temperature chart. This can then be put in a special printer at the doctor's and a graph is produced to show your cycle. One computer tested for two years by the World Health Organization and the International Health Federation, was found to have a less than two per cent failure rate if intercourse took place only when the light was green.

Another system is based on identifying the increasing chloride content of cervical mucus during the follicular phase of the cycle. You push a specially treated tampon into the vagina until you can touch the cervix, where the mucus reacts with substances in the tampon. You then compare the colour of this with the shades on a reference card which will tell you whether you are entering the fertile period or not. The system is widely used in the United States and Japan.

Preventing implantation

When there is contraceptive failure women are often unaware that there is action they could take to avoid implantation of the fertilized ovum. Some doctors believe that women should be given a first-aid pack of morning-after pills if they rely on the sheath or when they are not having regular intercourse but suddenly find themselves in a situation where they have had unprotected intercourse. To be effective the postcoital pill has to be taken within 72 hours of intercourse. If you do this there is only a one per cent failure rate. The pills are the ordinary combined oestrogen-progestogen contraceptive pills (*not* mini-pills) and you should take two as soon as possible and another two 12 hours after. Side-effects are nausea (60 per cent) and vomiting (30 per cent) but this does not last long. Some women experience headache, dizziness and tenderness in their breasts. (*British Medical Journal*, Volume 285, pages 322–4, 1982) Another method of preventing implantation is to have an IUD fitted, and this would be the obvious thing to do if you have let 72 hours go by before taking action. Used in this way, the IUD has a very low failure rate and no pregnancies were reported in nearly 700 postcoital insertions. But you may have a lot of pain and some bleeding and as many as 20 per cent of women fitted with an IUD suffer from pelvic inflammation.

The important point about these methods is that you do not have to wait to discover whether or not your period comes, with all the anxiety that this entails. There is action you can take to stop implantation and both methods, even though they have disadvantages, enable women to have more control over their own bodies than ever before.

No ideal method

When all is said, there is obviously no perfect method of birth control at the moment – certainly no single one that is right for everybody. It is more a matter of finding out what is available and then working out your personal equation. Whatever their current method of contraception, few women are really happy with it. Of the hundreds who have talked with or written to me about their sex lives, only a tiny minority express no reservations about their current method of birth control and these are about evenly spread over all the methods.

Many women seem to spend much of their reproductive life in search of the perfect contraceptive, trying one thing, finding it unsatisfactory and going on to try another.

Progress in male contraception

Research is taking place to try to discover an effective male contraceptive. Men are less than one per cent of family planning clinic clients, according to the US National Institute for Community Development. One of the problems with developing a male contraceptive is that whereas women usually only produce one ripe ovum each cycle there are millions of sperm in each ejaculation. Most of the chemical methods so far produced have lowered this sperm count but have not killed all the sperm.

The hormone nasal spray which has been devised for use by both women and men is unlikely to be a widely accepted method, because it reduces men's sex drive. Though women taking the contraceptive pill often experience reduced libido they continue to take it because it is an effective contraceptive. Birth control experts consider men would not find this acceptable in their case.

Women often feel bound to put up with unpleasant and dangerous side-effects of contraception because there is no alternative to avoiding pregnancy. Since men do not bear babies they are less likely to tolerate headaches, loss of libido, weight gain, reduction in the amount of semen, retarded ejaculation and other side-effects of hormone treatment. There was hope for Gossypol, the male contraceptive derived from cotton seeds, which was developed in China. But one-third of the subjects experienced side-effects which included fatigue, anorexia, reduced libido, muscle weakness and potassium loss, and 20 per cent remained infertile long after they stopped taking it.

Little is known about cultural variation in male reactions to side-effects of contraception and it has been taken for granted that men are less willing to tolerate side-effects than women are, but it might be that retarded ejaculation, for example, would be seen by some men as having advantages, and even reduction in the amount of ejaculate may not put some men off using a hormone-based contraceptive. (A. E. Reading, D. N. Cox and C. M. Sledmere, "Psychological issues arising from the development of new male contraceptives") We still seem a long way off, however, from having a really reliable contraceptive which men are willing to use.

In a spoof report, "Breakthrough in male contraception", Dawn Bracey described a new contraceptive in the form of an intra-penile device (IPD) developed by Dr Sophie Merkin and marketed under the trade name of "Umbrelly". It is like a minute umbrella, the underside of which is coated with a spermicidal jelly, which is plunged into the tip of the penis and through the scrotum.

Experiments on 1,000 white whales proved the Umbrelly to be 100 per cent effective in preventing production of sperm, and eminently satisfactory to the female whale since it does not interfere with her rutting pleasure. The device is safe; only two of the 763 students tested with the IPD died of scrotal infection.

Side-effects were few; only 20 had tissue oedema. Complaints included cramping, bleeding and acute abdominal pain, but Dr Sophie Merkin considered that these symptoms should disappear within a year. One complication caused by the IPD is scrotal infection which sometimes necessitates surgical removal of the testicles, "but this is a rare case," said Merkin, "too rare to be statistically important." And the report goes on to say that: "she and other distinguished members of the Women's College of Surgeons agreed that the benefits far outweighed the risks."

This satirical report is not so different from the kind of studies published by male gynaecologists about the insignificance of the side-effects of contraceptive methods used by women. And it is difficult to imagine that men would readily submit to taking pills, which, though they effectively eliminated potency, had multiple side-effects, including weight-gain, loss of sex drive, crashing headaches, hypertension, depression, and continual nausea. They would be even less likely to do so if warned that during the 10 years or so in which they would be taking them they should not smoke lest they increase the risk of side-effects, and that there was a possibility of sudden death or permanent cerebral damage from a blood clot. If the man went to a doctor to voice his misgivings he would be told: "You mustn't believe everything you read", be given another brand of the pills with reassurance that if he just kept on taking them his body would eventually adjust to them, and if he persisted in expressing his anxiety would be offered tranquillizers because of his evident symptoms of neurosis.

Sharing responsibilities in contraception

Only when women take action can there be some development towards fully shared responsibility for contraception. This is made more difficult because women are often accused of being ignorant about the working of their bodies, of not listening when doctors tell them what to do, and being imbued with superstition. "How can another woman make you pregnant?" the Health Education Council asks in an advertisement. The answer is all too obvious: if you listen to "old wives' tales" instead of obeying your doctor.

Women are also often told that they cannot hope to understand such matters, which only doctors with a lengthy specialist training can possibly know. And the accusers are often women themselves. A senior physiotherapist – a woman whose job it is to teach other women about their bodies – tells me that suggesting that a woman should introduce her fingers into her own vagina to feel her cervix is "unwise". Why? I ask. "Because they would not be sterile." (But nor is a penis.) "And because a woman could not understand what she feels. A doctor has been doing vaginal examinations for *years*. Only a doctor should do it."

Today the Women's Health Movement, strong in North America, Europe and Australia, is questioning the old attitudes and acting as a catalyst for change. Groups of women are finding out about their bodies, taking on responsibility for their own health, questioning doctors, challenging medical authority, breaking through the mystique of professionalism and learning from sharing personal experiences. Women are beginning to take control of their sexuality and their lives.

When it's difficult to start a baby

Sexual spontaneity goes out of the window the moment you start being concerned that the baby you wanted is not coming and that you need to have intercourse on special days of the month or change your techniques if you are going to conceive. Sex then becomes a means to an end.

Intercourse a duty

This is bound to affect your feelings about lovemaking and bring with it a whole range of other emotions: hope, frustration, irritation, guilt, despair – for *both* partners. If you are not sure when you ovulate, or even *if* you ovulate regularly, you take your temperature first thing in the morning and keep a chart and also, perhaps, examine your mucus. When the right moment comes intercourse is required, but he is away on a business trip, is tired out after a strenuous working day, or has 'flu. Or you have had a row and the last thing you really feel like is making love. Intercourse in these circumstances becomes a duty which has to be performed, a proof that you want a baby enough to take the trouble, a gamble in which you are taking your chances against an obstinate fate.

It can be more complicated than that, too. For if you want to give a baby the best start in life you have probably become very environmentally conscious. You have learned that smoking and drinking heavily produce more inactive sperm, that hot baths and tight underpants and jeans may also immobilize sperm, that potency and fertility are directly related to good nutrition. But your partner cannot stop smoking, had to skip lunch and called in at the pub on his way home. The man, in his turn, gets to feel that he is being treated like a stud bull, allowed to have intercourse only when the time is right and perhaps not to have intercourse in the whole second half of the month when you might possibly be pregnant, lest he dislodge the minuscule fertilized cell cluster. This is bound to put stress on a relationship.

Medical intrusion on sex

When doctors get involved, starting a baby also becomes a clinical exercise. It is almost as if the woman and her doctor become the procreating couple. The couple may be asked to have intercourse within a specified time before the woman attends the clinic so that she arrives with semen in her vagina. The man may be asked to go to the clinic to masturbate and produce a semen specimen so that it can be examined under the microscope to discover the ratio of live sperm. Healthy semen is reckoned to contain a minimum of 20 million sperm to each cubic centimetre. This test is often done after a series of investigations have taken place in the woman, though it is one of the simpler and most obvious ones that ought to be done early on in the process, since in at least 20 per cent of the cases of infertility the problem is with the man.

A man sometimes feels that not only his sperm are being called into question, but his very masculinity. He is being told he is inadequate. This may affect the way he makes love and even his capacity to have and sustain an erection.

A couple are both under stress and often in a state where the strain they feel finds an outlet in accusations against each other – that perhaps he does not really care or genuinely want this baby or simply that they do not understand each other's feelings.

Anxiety and ovulation

Anxiety about having intercourse at the precise time of ovulation and not to have it until that time can sometimes stop ovulation taking place altogether. A specialist in fertility treatment (Sherman J. Silber, *How to get Pregnant*), tells how a woman who was instructed to take her basal body temperature, to abstain from intercourse for five days before her temperature went up and then to have intercourse, found that her cycles became completely unpredictable, 20 days one month and 45 days the next. She had stopped ovulating. He suggested the couple should not gear lovemaking to the temperature chart and have intercourse whenever they felt like it. In two months she was pregnant. This, apparently, is quite a common pattern.

Seeking help can often alleviate anxiety, however. Twenty per cent of women get pregnant between their first consultation with a specialist about infertility and the doctor actually initiating treatment. This may be because the couple can at last relax in the knowledge that they are doing something about it.

Openness with each other

If you both realize that you are likely to be under emotional pressure when it takes a long time to start a baby, you can help each other by talking openly about your feelings before they build up to become a barrier between you. Then the procedures involved in trying to conceive that elusive baby may bring you closer together, so that you can understand each other better.

Loving closeness *after* intercourse is vitally important, too. Ejaculation and the reception of semen is not just a job of work to try to make a baby. Both partners need to know that they are loved and wanted *for themselves*. A woman may have been advised to lie in one position, perhaps on her back with a pillow under her bottom, for 20 minutes or half an hour after intercourse, to give the sperm the best chance of progressing through the cervix, but she should not have to lie alone and hoping while her partner turns over and goes to sleep. It can be a time for loving and close tenderness. She may seek further stimulation to have an orgasm during this time.

Sex during pregnancy

Nausea and vomiting in the first three months of pregnancy may be a sexual turn-off. Many women never experience this, but those who do may feel sick not only on waking in the morning but also in the early evening. Some feel sick right through the day.

Even if you feel rather better by bedtime, constant nausea makes it difficult to feel erotic. One woman, on what was supposed to be a romantic second honeymoon which coincided with the sixth and seventh weeks of her pregnancy, remembers the details of the lavatory bowl in the hotel and the tiles and plumbing around it with much greater clarity than anything else about the holiday. Her husband lay in bed reading thrillers while she retched and vomited in the bathroom.

A woman may have nausea with one pregnancy and not with another. Tiredness and "overdoing things" often play a part in it. Eating regularly is important to avoid letting your stomach become empty. Small, frequent meals seem to be better than large ones further apart.

Many more women feel nauseated than ever actually vomit. If you do vomit, anxiety about how this may be affecting the baby may add to your dis-ease with your body. These combined feelings mean that you are most unlikely to enjoy sex during this time. "I felt really mucky," one woman said. "Drained of all vitality, smelly, with a tinny taste in my mouth. I wondered where this much vaunted pregnancy radiance was. I felt ghastly! And sex was out of the question." Looking back on their pregnancies, most women who have had early pregnancy sickness seem to feel that during this time they were preoccupied with keeping control over their bodies and of avoiding situations in which the sensations became overwhelming. Until this phase has passed sex is just another nuisance which threatens to tip them over into further nausea.

It rarely lasts past the first three months and a woman usually wakes up one morning feeling quite different or realizes with surprise, as she gets to the end of the day, that for the first time she has not felt sick. It is as if the curtain goes up on a whole new experience of pregnancy.

Breasts

But there are other things which may inhibit lovemaking in those first weeks. One is breast tenderness. Changes in the breasts, which make them ready for later feeding of the baby, are some of the first obvious ways in which a woman's body can be seen to adapt to pregnancy. The little bumps around the nipples, called Montgomery's tubercles, get bigger and the breasts themselves become larger. A bra may feel uncomfortably tight and in some women the breasts are so sensitive that they feel almost bruised. What is often called "a good uplift bra" is necessary and even though this conjures up a picture of some monstrous contraption hoisting you into a different architectural shape, all that it means is that there should be firm support *under* the breasts (around the midriff) and straps wide enough to take the extra pull of weight. Some women feel so uncomfortable in bed at night that they wake up with pressure against their breasts and they prefer to wear a "sleep" bra as well.

When this happens a woman cannot easily think of her breasts as erotic objects or as playthings for her man, even though a small-breasted woman may like them being larger and may be proud of her new figure. The newly pregnant woman is very easily hurt by a lover who likes to pummel, bite or suck energetically, as some men do. Any nipple stimulation must be done very gently, therefore, and stroking of the breasts should start off by touch which is as light as thistledown and only becomes firmer if it feels good to her.

In fact, this is one of the most obvious things about sex in pregnancy. A partner needs to be gentle at all times. Even if you enjoyed rough love-bites and a bit of sexual grappling before you became pregnant, you are most unlikely to now.

In a state of sexual arousal the breasts swell by as much as 25 per cent. So when you yourself get sexually excited you top up your already enlarged breasts as more blood rushes into the veins and the tissues become further engorged. This is why even when you are highly aroused, you may flinch as he touches you and then suddenly feel very much on the defensive.

Anxieties about miscarriage

Fear of miscarriage also has a marked effect on the physical expression of sexual feelings and even on the capacity to be aroused in the first place. If you have already lost a baby in the first few months of a previous pregnancy, or have any bleeding at the beginning of this one, you may feel very apprehensive and be almost "holding on", both physically and emotionally, to this pregnancy. The result is that you may see sex as a direct threat to the baby and also feel far too tense to relax and enjoy lovemaking. A woman who is anxious tends to hold her muscles in a state of contraction, not only those in her face which give her an anxious expression, but others all over her body. The man, too, may be very nervous and feel that he is a danger to the pregnancy, and a couple who feel like this interact negatively, each triggering off further anxiety in the other. They may even avoid cuddling and caressing because they are so fearful of sexual arousal.

Learning to relax is a way of helping yourself to enjoy pregnancy.

This is a pity, because they both need to relax. The stress of worrying about miscarriage may actually increase the chance of

miscarriage. Little is known of the effects of stress on early pregnancy, but it is reasonable to assume that physiological changes which are known to occur under acute stress – changes in the biochemistry of the blood, for example, and the way it flows through the blood vessels in the uterus – can affect the developing embryo.

No studies have been done to show whether not having intercourse in early pregnancy helps to avoid miscarriage, though many people think this must be so. Doctors usually advise against intercourse if a woman has any spotting of blood in the first 12 weeks or has miscarried in the previous pregnancy. Most women probably feel safer avoiding intercourse if they have any bleeding, though up to one-third of women in any ante-natal class say that they have a slight blood-stained discharge somewhere around the time when the first or second period would have been due – and go on to have a normal pregnancy and a healthy baby. They often do not tell a doctor about this, so doctors may not realize just how common it is.

A doctor who has advised against intercourse sometimes forgets to say: "It should be OK, now. You are past the time when you are most likely to miscarry," and the couple continue not only to avoid intercourse, but often any form of lovemaking as well, right through pregnancy, or feel terribly guilty about it if they *do* make love. This seems to be another way of "medicalizing" pregnancy and making it stressful for a woman and her partner. Since nothing is known for sure of the effects of lovemaking on miscarriage in the first three months, it might be better for the advice not to have been given in the first place.

Tiredness

Many women feel incredibly tired in the first weeks. They worry that they will be like this until they have the baby. This physical exhaustion is associated with the major adjustments the whole body is making in those first few weeks, things you cannot see, but which are of far-reaching importance. The baby is fully formed in miniature by three months and by this time, too, every cell in the mother's body is directly or indirectly involved in adapting to meet the challenge of pregnancy. No wonder she is tired!

Moreover, all this is happening at a time when she may have told very few people about being pregnant, so no concessions are made when she feels under some pressure at work, for example, or feels she ought to finish off something she has started by the time she is going to leave to have the baby. A woman who has not got a job outside the home, but who is busy with older children, may want to prove to herself that she is going to be able to handle the toddler and a baby, too. The result is that she drops into bed with relief and falls asleep as soon as she can. Sex is the last thing she wants.

A woman who feels confident about her sexuality and who normally enjoys it is more likely to take all this in her stride. Studies also show that a woman having her first baby tends to be less interested in sex at the beginning of pregnancy, whereas women having second and subsequent babies often notice very little change in libido.

Some women actually enjoy sex more immediately they know they are pregnant. It may sound odd, but they find it easier to give themselves to their feelings when they are pregnant because there is

When we realize that pregnancy is not primarily a medical condition, we can discover new aspects of our sexuality.

no longer the *risk* of getting pregnant. For these women the whole business of contraception is associated with "holding back", "being careful", "remembering" – to take the Pill, for example; with concern about whether they are inserting a diaphragm correctly, making sure that a condom hasn't slipped off as the man withdraws; with recording the menstrual cycle and having intercourse only when it is "safe", or even gambling with getting the man out before he ejaculates. A woman who is constantly anxious about getting pregnant discovers that, once pregnant, she can forget all these things and relax and enjoy it.

Even so, this is more likely to happen after about 10 to 12 weeks. Sometimes it takes even longer to start to enjoy pregnancy. But once the period of nausea and vomiting, anxiety about possible miscarriage and extreme lassitude is over, many women say they enjoy sex more than ever before. The middle months of pregnancy are a time when they feel happy with their bodies and glow with a kind of pregnancy radiance.

This probably will not happen if you are under great pressure at work or if having a baby means that you are constantly worrying about money. In that case the fatigue felt in the early weeks tends to continue and you never get "turned on" in mid-pregnancy. Nor is it likely to happen if you feel angry about being pregnant in the first place, or trapped by all sorts of obligations at work or in the family. Though some women actually enjoy "angry" sex and repressed hostility seems to give lovemaking an extra zip, in pregnancy this kind of fighting lovemaking does not seem to work for most women and becomes merely painful. Your partner must change his way of making love or you may want to avoid it altogether.

The second three months

By the beginning of the fourth month the tissues around and inside the vagina have "ripened" and remain like this throughout pregnancy. William Masters and Virginia Johnson (*Human Sexual Response*) describe them as engorged in a way similar to that during sexual arousal. They have become thicker and swollen, rather as a soft fruit ripens. Even the colour has changed from shades of pale pink and red to purple, violet and blue as a result of the increased blood supply. This means that the woman is in a permanent state of gentle sexual arousal. She also feels much more moist. Extra vaginal lubrication, which seeps through the convoluted walls of the vagina, may make her much more conscious of her vagina. Some women say they feel juicy and sweet.

The pressure on the genital organs from about the fourth month is so great for some women that they say they feel "randy", like Jane, who admits "I can't wait for my husband to get home, poor man!" or Rosie, who says "I couldn't get through the day without masturbating, I felt so sexy. I thought I must be very peculiar till I talked to my sister-in-law about it who'd had a baby last year and she said she felt just the same."

A woman who is feeling super-charged like this can be aghast to discover that her partner does not want to have intercourse or that he cannot get or maintain an erection. Many men are anxious that they can hurt the baby. This concern may have very good effects, because they become more thoughtful and considerate about lovemaking than before. But a man who is really frightened may refuse even to touch the woman. Some men have told me that they were terrified of breaking the bag of water. Others have believed that they could damage the baby. Others that if they let themselves go everything can get out of hand and labour may start forthwith. It is almost as if they feel that to keep themselves under restraint will help make the pregnancy go well; as if their self-control will somehow "guard" the pregnancy. These beliefs are remarkably similar to those held in Third World societies, where taboos are enjoined on a father in order to ensure the well-being of a baby while it is still in the uterus.

Most couples probably find that they want to adapt lovemaking techniques as pregnancy advances. Any weight on the breasts feels extremely uncomfortable and the "missionary position" is a very bad one unless the male partner is careful to take all his weight on his forearms. A side-lying position in which the woman has her back to the man as she nestles into his "lap" is often comfortable for this reason. Some women enjoy being on all fours or kneeling with the man behind.

Once the fetus has engaged in the pelvis, with its head fitting neatly into the bony cradle like an egg in an egg cup, it may feel as if the baby is about to drop out and there is no spare room. Even if she did not want it before, the woman may then prefer a position in which her partner enters her from behind. She may like to lie, crouch or kneel with her back to him so that the uterus, which lies almost at right-angles to her vagina, is free from pressure and she can use her buttock muscles to grip the penis, so controlling the depth of penetration.

The last three months

By about seven months indigestion and heartburn may be a problem when the woman lies flat, so she needs to have her head and shoulders well raised with pillows. This means that she may prefer making love in a sitting position, using a big floor cushion, a chair or the side of the bed.

A woman's fantasies about her body – her body image – subtly affect her sexual feelings. The body is going through such vast changes during pregnancy that some women get a very distorted view of their bodies. They feel far bigger than they really are or believe that their partners must find them ugly, when, in fact, men often delight in pregnant women and find the physical changes exciting and beautiful. One woman described herself as like "a hippopotamus wallowing in the mud" and said she felt completely sexless right through her pregnancy. Another said she felt like "a goddess, queen of all dark growing things stirring deep in the earth", was in a state of erotic arousal until the moment she went into labour and kept that feeling right through childbirth.

Modern ante-natal care can make it difficult for a woman to enjoy her body in pregnancy. It does this by conveying the important message that the ordinary ways of knowing about and trusting our bodies are no longer valid and that we must defer to medical opinion and accept a medical view of what is happening to us. Women often go to an ante-natal clinic with a sense of well-being but come out feeling anxious, depressed or ill. The

POSITIONS FOR INTERCOURSE DURING PREGNANCY

Here no pressure is put on the woman's back or abdomen and she is able to move freely while her partner stimulates her breasts.

In this position the weight of the baby is suspended on the abdomen. It may be comfortable if you get backache. Your partner gives clitoral stimulation with his hand.

This may be a good position if you do not feel dizzy when you lie on your back. It can be varied with more cushions behind your head and shoulders.

A position which may be difficult in advanced pregnancy because of the bump, but has the advantage of being upright and active.

Your partner's joy in your pregnant body can help you develop a sense of confidence.

image of our bodies that we receive from medical care affects our sexual feelings and for some women puts an invisible brake on pleasure in sex during pregnancy.

This is particularly the case for a woman who is undergoing a series of special tests in pregnancy, including, for example, amniocentesis, serial ultrasound scans, oestriol tests and other investigations. She is more likely to have her whole pregnancy "medicalized" when it has been difficult to get pregnant in the first place or to hang on to a pregnancy. Then her relationship with her partner may seem to come second to that with her obstetrician. It is as if the doctor and his pregnant patient form a new procreating couple and that the health and life of the baby depends on the success of this important relationship. The baby's father may come to see himself as unnecessary and even as a danger to the fetus. It is vital that a couple talk about this together and that expert professional care is not allowed to usurp or intrude on the special relationship of the man and woman who are becoming parents. Their responsibility for the child continues long past the pregnancy and birth and anything which adversely affects them as a couple can have longterm consequences for the child. Expectant parents need to be able to nurture each other in order to grow into being a mother and father capable, in their turn, of nurturing a baby.

A loving sexual relationship can actually contribute to the well-being of a pregnancy not only because the woman knows she is cherished and because the ordinary stresses of life are temporarily dissolved away whenever she turns towards her lover, but because when she is sexually aroused oxytocin is released into her blood stream. Doctor Michel Odent calls this "the happiness hormone". Oxytocin is important in contributing to the good tone of the contracting uterus. Uterine sensitivity to oxytocin builds up in the last few weeks and this leads to a spontaneous start of labour.

When obstetricians induce labour they often use a synthetic form of oxytocin – syntocinon. Or they may use prostaglandins in the form of a pessary inserted near the cervix. The highest natural concentration of prostaglandins in the human body is in the semen.

When a baby is due to be born but labour has not been triggered off spontaneously at the calculated date passionate lovemaking can sometimes further soften the cervix and start the contractions which initiate labour. Yet, faced with what they see as the threat of induction, many couples feel too intimidated to experiment with their own ways of inducing labour naturally.

Anxiety about induction also means that a woman may not feel like making love. It is as if she has already become the object of medical care, a uterus, a pelvis and a birth canal to be acted on obstetrically, just at a time when lovemaking – and feeling a whole person – could contribute most to the natural flow of the birthing process. She may also draw back from intercourse because when the baby is deep in the pelvis it is often uncomfortable. It can feel as if the penis is perilously close to the baby's head. "I felt that any violent, thrusting penile movements might be injurious to myself or my child," one woman says. "I felt increasingly protective for the well-being of my baby, so much so that I felt the child's well-being far more important than whether my partner was satisfied or not after lovemaking." In fact, the baby is well protected inside a membrane-walled bubble of water and the soft tissues of the cervix act as a cushion in front of its head, too.

Encouraging labour to start

There is a special way of having intercourse if you want to use it to start labour. It has not been subjected to controlled research, but experience shows that many women, either coincidentally, or as a result, go into labour during the night following this kind of lovemaking. It will not always work, but gives you the best chance of starting naturally:

Lie on your back, head and shoulders well supported by as many pillows as you like for comfort, your partner facing you and kneeling between your parted legs. Lift one leg so that your foot is over his shoulder, then the other. Though this position is not comfortable, it allows the deepest penetration so that the tip of the penis can touch the cervix. The Japanese have invented a special vibrator to provide stimulation of the cervix in order to induce labour in a similar way, but it hardly seems necessary to manufacture a device when a loving partner can do the same thing.

Though it is not necessary for you to have an orgasm, and being determined to achieve orgasm can make it more difficult to have one, if your partner knows how to touch you so that you become excited, too, and have an orgasm, this may start contractions which later settle into the rhythmic pattern of early labour. When he has ejaculated he should stay inside you for five minutes or so and you should stay in the same position, with legs raised, for 10 to 15 minutes, so that the cervix is bathed in semen.

*Nurturing one another
enables you both
to nurture the
new life ...*

The other important thing is to follow intercourse with manual and oral nipple stimulation. This in itself is often effective, even without intercourse. It is also helpful in labour if progress is very slow, or if contractions come to a stop, since stimuli received from the nipples trigger off uterine contractions. About 20 minutes of nipple caressing, interspersed with other kinds of loving touch, seems right for most women.

Do not lie awake waiting for labour to start. Let yourself relax and drift off into sleep. Even if you do not start contracting, you have probably helped the cervix to ripen further.

One man described what happened in these words: "Weak, irregular contractions started immediately we had made love. When I sucked her nipples they got much stronger. I worked out that I could keep the contractions going by touching or licking her nipples about every ten minutes. Then she got up and walked about a bit and I think that helped. But she was tired and wanted to get some sleep before starting, so I kept contractions going with nipple stimulation and she dozed between them. It was quite hard work, but I enjoyed it. I felt really useful because it was so obvious it was helping the labour."

When we realize that pregnancy and birth are not primarily medical conditions, but part of a woman's psycho-sexual experience, we begin to discover the relations between different aspects of our sexuality and gain new understanding because we are in touch with our bodies and our feelings.

The sexuality of birth

If you have had a painful labour or one which was distressing because you felt trapped (even if it was not particularly painful), you may think that sexual excitement and feelings during birth have no connection at all with each other. The sensations of labour are obviously nothing to do with being sexually titillated. Yet in a strange way the energy flowing through the body in childbirth, the pressure of contracting muscles, the downward movement of the baby and the fanning open of soft tissues, can be powerfully erotic.

The rhythm of labour

The locus of almost all the sensations experienced in labour is an area about the size of your hand, deep in the pelvis. If you rest a hand above your pubis you will find the right place. The cervix opens beneath this area and most of the pain felt comes from it as it opens and is pulled up and over the baby's head. It may feel like a glowing fire which bursts into flames as if from the action of a bellows as a contraction builds up. The pain spreads from the cervix right round into the small of the back until it is as if you are held in a tight grip from front to back for half a minute or so, after which it fades away again. This tightening is not haphazard. It is firm, regular, rhythmic. There is a definite pattern which in itself is satisfying. A woman who is enjoying her labour swings into the rhythm of contractions as if her birth-giving were a powerful dance, her uterus creating the beat. She watches for it, concentrates on it, like an orchestra following its conductor.

All these sensations are at their most powerful in her sexual organs. Feelings pour through her genitals. In ante-natal classes you may never learn this, or, because medical language often obscures what women really feel, it may never be put into words which enable you to anticipate this intense sexual sensation. The uterus, the vagina, the muscles enfolding the vagina and rectum, the lower back, the rectum itself and the anus, the buttocks, tissues around and between the vagina and anus, and the clitoris are all suffused with heat as if with liquid fire or as if brimful and pouring over with glowing colour. It can be the most intensely sexual feeling a woman ever experiences, as strong as orgasm, even more compelling than orgasm. Some women find it disturbing because it is sexual and they feel out of control as the energy floods through them and they can do nothing to prevent it.

The place of birth

The intense sexuality of natural birth stands in startling contrast to the institutional setting usually provided for the experience. It is as if we were required to make love, pouring ourselves, body and mind, into the full expression of feeling, in a busy airport concourse, a large railway terminus, in a gymnasium or a tiled public lavatory. Today birth is treated as a medico-surgical crisis. Women tend to be fed into the hospital system at one end, to be processed through it and come out at the other with a baby. Instead of being a personal, private, intimate experience, it is as if the mother is on an efficient assembly line. Even the way she sits or lies is dictated by the position of electrodes and catheters attached to her body and long tubes tethering her to machines. And though professionals may be kind, labour becomes an ordeal, not only because of pain, but because she feels imprisoned in a situation outside her control.

Women who have discovered that birth is a passionate and intense sexual experience are likely to have given birth in their own homes or in maternity units where there is unusual flexibility to enable them to behave with spontaneity and without inhibition. In an increasing number of hospitals and in birthing rooms inside them, a woman can have her baby without unnecessary intervention and in an atmosphere of peace and close intimacy with helpers who have become her friends. The sexuality of birth is for the first time being experienced by women who are less concerned to remember all their breathing and relaxation exercises learnt in ante-natal classes, than to get in tune with their bodies and to allow the energy of labour to flow through them. Even 10 years ago a woman who cried out or grunted or groaned in labour often thought that she had "failed". She was concerned to "keep control". This stemmed from the teaching of "psychoprophylaxis" which introduced a barrack-square discipline into preparation for childbirth and emphasized raising the pain threshold by keeping alert and using distraction techniques under the direction of a labour "coach". It is not surprising that women inculcated with such teachings, though they did well in labour and had a tremendous sense of triumph at delivery, were unlikely to experience childbirth as a psycho-sexual process.

Even if a pregnant woman came to feel that birth could be sexual and sought to let her body come alive in labour in the same way as it does in happy lovemaking, in the last 20 years or so she would usually have found that she was up against so many obstacles to this in hospitals that it was easier just to give in and let the professionals take over. There are very few institutions in which a woman can feel free to be herself, to let emotions sweep through her and do whatever she wants to do. A woman in labour becomes, in effect, an object on which doctors act. Many of the procedures which are an accepted part of childbirth today and which make it so difficult for a woman to discover anything sexual in labour, have been introduced to formalize the relations between professionals and patients and to repress and inhibit their expression of emotion. They have become part of the hospital institution, sanctified in the form of unquestioned routines and practices which are justified on the grounds that they are for the safety of the baby, though in many cases no research has been done to prove or disprove this claim.

A process of depersonalization

In the late nineteenth century there was much discussion among doctors as to how they could remove the sexuality from pelvic examinations and from the relationship between the male gynaecologist and his female patient. Should the doctor look away from the woman while doing a vaginal examination or stare with concentration at her face so that she could be quite sure that he was not looking at her genitals? Should a female chaperone always be present? (Wertz and Wertz, *Lying-in*) The gynaecologist had to rely upon "the touch" and must never uncover the patient's genitals. In the training of doctors the emphasis was put on rituals by which a woman's modesty might be maintained. The Victorian doctor's role was that of guardian with ward, father with child, teacher with pupil and father confessor with supplicant. The obstetrician-as-scientist did not come on the scene until the twentieth century, when women started to give birth in hospitals.

In the maternity hospital the doctor is on his own territory. He has the power, equipment and machinery and the supporting staff to turn each birth into a medico-surgical procedure. This enables him to treat a woman's body as if it were separate from herself as a person. As hospital birth became the norm, more and more women gave birth on narrow, hard delivery tables under bright lights with their legs raised and fixed wide apart in lithotomy stirrups. In the USA the upper and lower ends of the patient's torso were divided by sterile drapes, the isolated lower section designated as the obstetrician's "sterile field", which only he could touch. This was always a fiction, as the proximity of the vagina to the anus means that it cannot really be sterile. Doctors and nurses wore sterile garments, gowns, caps, overshoes, masks and surgical gloves.

Childbirth became increasingly mechanized after the Second World War. In the 1950s and 1960s women often laboured for long periods alone, without their husbands or other family members. What had been a personal, intimate and passionate act of creating life, became a process in which a woman was treated with cool, brisk efficiency or one in which she was left to "get on with it" until the obstetrician put in an appearance just before delivery, anaesthetized her, applied forceps and pulled out the baby like a rabbit from a hat.

In North America the obstetric delivery became a caricature of normal childbirth. Not only were the woman's legs suspended in stirrups but her wrists, too, were often bound. Her body became the passive object on which the doctor acted to effect delivery. She lay flat on her back while he got on with his job at the lower end of her body. Her perineum was shaved as bald as an egg and the doctor's view of her was of a heavily draped, lumpy object, like a settee shrouded in dust covers, with a central window in the cloth with an opening in which the ball-shaped mass of the fetal head could be seen descending through the smooth, shiny, bulging balloon of the perineum. It seemed that the doctor was no longer doing things to a woman's body, but was servicing a reproductive machine.

Another theme in the relationship between obstetrician and patient which runs parallel with the emergence of doctor-as-scientist is that of the deliverer who has the drugs which can take away pain, who promises the woman "Trust me, do what I say and you need not suffer."

A package deal

There is a price to pay for such solicitude. Effective anaesthesia makes more intervention possible. And because it interferes with a woman's normal physiological functions and usually also affects the fetus, it makes this intervention more likely. As a result women may be offered a package deal of pain relief plus a forceps lift-out and whatever else may be necessary – intravenous uterine stimulants, a catheter to drain urine, a surgical cut to open the vagina and stitches in it afterwards, pain-relieving drugs and sleeping pills in the week after delivery, and so on.

It started in the USA in the 1920s with Dr Joseph De Lee's system of "prophylactic forceps". This entails sedation, an episiotomy (the cut) and the introduction of forceps to pull the baby's head out over the perineum. Since this method made delivery much more painful, general anaesthesia was used in the second stage of labour. And to cope with the pain which occurred before then, a mixture of mood-changing, pain-relieving and sleep-inducing drugs was used for the earlier part of labour. One of the most notorious of these, scopolamanine, was widely employed in the USA and is still in use in many hospitals. It makes the woman confused and restless, often so much out of her mind that she has to be nursed in a high-barred and padded cot or wear a kind of straitjacket or baseball helmet in case she injures herself. From the delivery room she goes straight to the "recovery room", where there is another set of equipment to resuscitate her if necessary.

To increase efficiency, birth has also become a production-line operation. Tasks are divided up between different professionals. A woman being processed through labour is admitted by one member of staff, supervised in the first stage by others, delivered by yet another group and cared for subsequently by a different post-partum team. Often she has never met any of these people before. It is task-centred rather than woman-centred care, and, especially for the poorest and the least educated, takes place in an alien environment among total strangers, without explanation, regardless of a woman's own wishes and feelings, and without anyone there who can understand what she is going through.

It was not till the beginning of the 1970s that it became normal practice in most hospitals for the baby's father or another close family member to be present during labour and delivery. The battle for one of the most natural rights is still being fought in some American hospitals more than a decade later.

Active management of labour

The innovative strategies devised by obstetric efficiency experts culminated in a method known as "the active management of labour". There are different interpretations of what this actually means, but in many hospitals it involves induction of labour if a woman is more than a week or so past her date, electronic monitoring of the fetal heart with an electrode stuck through her vagina into the baby's scalp and the control of uterine activity by a hormone intravenous drip so that labour does not exceed 12 hours, 10 hours, eight hours, or whatever consultants in that unit have decided is the correct norm for dilatation and expulsion. If the baby is not born within the time limit set, delivery is effected with forceps or by a caesarean section.

The vogue for induction, with artificial rupture of the membranes and on intravenous oxytocin drip, reached its peak in the early 1970s when, in many hospitals, nearly half of all births were started off artificially in this way. This is now being replaced by the use of prostaglandin pessaries inserted against the cervix. It has yet to be seen whether there will be the same fervour to initiate labour with prostaglandins in the 1980s.

The other great development towards what is literally, for some women, painless childbirth has been the introduction of epidural anaesthesia. With an indwelling catheter in her spine, a woman can have all sensation removed from her waist down. If she chooses, and her anaesthetist times it correctly, feelings can be allowed to return for the expulsive stage of labour so that she has more chance of being able to push her baby out. Even so, the need for forceps delivery, though it may be only a simple "lift-out", is increased with an epidural and one study reveals that women are five times more likely to have an operative delivery after this kind of anaesthesia. (I. J. Holt and A. H. MacLennan, "Lumbar epidural analgesia in labour") As techniques have developed, epidural anaesthesia has been given with more discretion, so that, for example, a woman may be able to retain feeling in her legs and with more experience with epidurals, forceps rates have gone down. An epidural is the most efficient method, for most women, of removing pain, with minimal effects on the fetus. The mother can read a magazine or do crosswords through contractions and deliver while watching the birth as if on a TV screen. She is calm, cool, collected – a fully "co-operative patient". And that is how epidural anaesthesia is advertised to obstetricians: it "preserves the morale and co-operation of the mother" though they are warned that "facilities for supportive measures to maintain vital functions such as maintenance of the airway, oxygenation with or without assisted ventilation, maintenance of blood pressure, etc., are essential", and side-effects such as a sudden drop in blood pressure, "tremor, tachycardia (a speeded up heart rate), bradycardia (a slowed down heart rate), malaise, vomiting and, rarely, convulsions or coma" result. (Sales blurb of Duncan Flockhart and Co.) But there is a price to pay for this, too. When physical sensation is obliterated in this way, birth is also drained of any sexual feeling.

Electronic fetal monitoring also contributes to the de-sexing of childbirth. The equipment may be fixed to the woman's body, both outside and inside. She is tethered by catheters and electric wires to equipment standing round the bed. She cannot move freely or even shift position without risking interfering with the print-out of the monitor or detaching an electrode or indwelling catheter. It is almost as if it is the monitor which is having the baby and all eyes are fixed on it.

Seeking to experience childbirth

It is against this background of the progressive depersonalization of care, the take-over by machines and a cultural de-sexing of birth, that women are seeking today to experience childbirth as a life-enhancing personal experience in which they can get in touch with their own feelings and can give glad expression to the energy sweeping through their bodies. They are no longer so concerned to be "in control" or to prove that they have learnt their exercises well. They are reclaiming the sexuality of childbirth.

This is highly disconcerting for those doctors who see their main service to patients as having "a live mother and live baby" and reducing the pain of labour. They are bewildered by women who want to move around, to rock or crawl or dance, to be held in a lover's arms and embraced and kissed during labour, to be stroked and massaged, and to make whatever noises come naturally, whether it is to groan or sing, to moan, or cry out. They may feel rejected, as if the woman's complete involvement with what is happening implies hostility when they most want to help and to offer the patient their professional expertise.

In hospitals today there is much more flexibility than even five years ago about what a woman does during the whole first stage of labour, when the cervix is dilating and midwives often encourage her to walk around and to get in any positions in which she is comfortable. It is obviously impossible to do this if she has continuous electronic fetal monitoring but it is being increasingly recognized that there is a physiological advantage – the uterus contracts better, the woman experiences less pain and the oxygen supplied to the fetus is improved – when she can move around freely.

Approaches to the second stage

The second stage of labour, however, when the baby is being pushed down the birth canal, is still treated as a time when a woman is supposed to battle with her body to get a baby born and to follow the instructions she is given by her attendants. It is when we look at the second stage of labour that we realize just how far women in Western society have been turned into objects on which male doctors act. For it is then that the basic lack of confidence in our bodies, intrinsic in the attitude of many professionals, is expressed most clearly. The second stage is often turned into an athletic contest in which the woman struggles to push the baby down through the barriers of flesh, spurred on by everyone present. They form a cheer-leading team urging her to greater effort, more sustained and deeper breaths, more energetic straining.

This not only makes her feel that she is falling short of a standard impossible to attain, but imposes an unnecessary stress on the second stage which can sometimes adversely affect the baby. When a woman is exhausted with straining, when she bursts blood vessels in her face and eyes and tries to hold her breath for as long as possible, there is a real risk that the cardio-vascular disturbance created in her own body will affect the baby's heart rate, its oxygen supply and its acid base balance. (Roberto Caldeyro-Barcia *et al.,* "Bearing-down efforts and their effects") When a woman holds her breath and strains for a long time her blood pressure drops. This reduces the oxygen available to the baby. Then, when she can push no longer, she gasps for air and her blood pressure suddenly shoots up above normal. Yet long before this stage is reached the flow of oxygenated blood to the fetus may already be reduced. What often happens then is that the dips in the fetal heart rate which persist after the end of the contraction are the signal for staff to urge her to push still harder and to hold her breath still longer. This has the effect of cutting down the baby's oxygen supply still further.

Childbirth education classes must bear a good deal of responsibility for the strenuous pushing and prolonged breath-holding imposed on women in labour. They have actually been trained to do something which is quite unnatural. They have also often been taught how to strengthen and pull in their abdominal muscles. A woman who is pulling in her abdominal muscles very often also pulls in her pelvic floor muscles, resisting the descent of the baby's head and causing herself unnecessary pain. For the pelvic floor muscles are completely released only when the lower abdomen is allowed to bulge out, the very opposite of the muscular sucking-in movement which is still taught in some ante-natal classes.

Other mammals do not behave like this. They do not get into the extraordinary positions which are often required of women in labour, lying flat on their backs with their legs up in the air, for example. They do not go in for all the huffing and puffing and breath-holding which women are taught to do. A cat or a dog will often push its young out with short, rapid breaths and with an open mouth. They also tend to choose a semi-upright position and with the pelvis tilted and to move around and shift position frequently during the expulsive stage.

When a woman does what comes naturally she tends to breathe in very much the same way as other mammals giving birth. It is a breathing pattern which corresponds almost exactly with that of sexual excitement and orgasm. And she does this quite spontaneously. Masters and Johnson point out that during orgasm breathing is at least three times faster than the normal rate. As a woman reaches the peak of orgasm her breath is often involuntarily held and she gasps, groans, sighs or cries out. When the orgasm fades away her breathing gets slower again. If she is experiencing a multiple orgasm (waves of desire and fulfilment, with intervals between each), her breathing accelerates as each fresh wave rises in crescendo and then, as it peaks, she holds her breath for a few seconds – and may do this between one and five times at the height of orgasm. She then continues quickly again and the breathing gets slower as the orgasm wave passes.

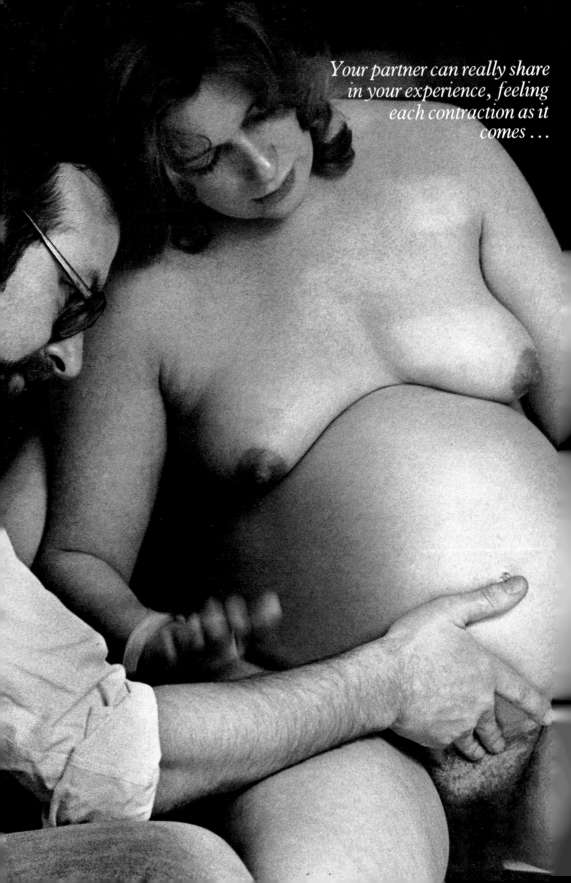

Your partner can really share in your experience, feeling each contraction as it comes …

This is exactly how a woman breathes when she behaves spontaneously in the expulsive phase of labour. If she has never been to ante-natal classes and is not told at the time how she should breathe or what she should do, she breathes quickly, holds her breath only for a few seconds, breathes out, continues to breathe quickly, holds her breath again for a few more seconds, and so on until the contraction starts to fade. And just like a woman having an orgasm, she tends to want to hold her breath like this between one and five times at the height of the contraction.

All this is quite different from the pattern usually imposed on women by instructions and the kind of encouragement they are given: "Push! Push! Don't waste your contraction! . . . Take a deep breath, hold it. Now come on, you can do better than that! Don't let your breath go! Take another one! Hold it for as long as you can! . . . Breathe in, block, fix your ribs and diaphragm and push, 1–2–3–4–5–6–7–8–9–10–11–12–13–14–15." The idea behind this is that she should be pushing right through a contraction, using every second of it, and putting her utmost strength into it.

It is the exact opposite of what happens during a woman's orgasm. What has happened is that a *male* model of physiological

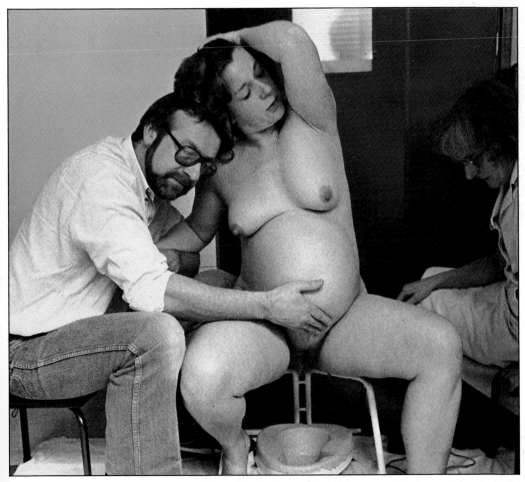

activity is being imposed on women in childbirth. It is as if the pattern of male orgasm – stiffen, hold, force through, shoot! – is distorting our own spontaneous psycho-sexual behaviour. Instead of the wave-like rhythms of female orgasm, bearing-down is treated like one long ejaculation. A woman is supposed to carry on as long as she possibly can and then to sink back, exhausted.

When a woman is pushing because it is insisted she does so, or because she herself believes it is the only way to get a baby out, a great deal of stress is often put on the tissues of her perineum as the ball of the baby's head is forced down through tissues which have not yet fanned out. And she herself is under great psychological stress as she struggles to expel the baby as if she were trying to get out a large, hard, constipated motion.

The spontaneous second stage

When a woman is helped to do whatever she feels like doing in the second stage, adopting positions, moving and breathing in any way she wants to, the second stage can become an intense sexual experience. Rhythms are unforced, she is not striving to reach what appears an unattainable goal or to put on a performance, but listens to and trusts her body. She pushes only when the desire is urgent and overwhelming. She feels the extraordinary and intensely sexual sensations as the baby's head presses first against her anus and then down through the concertina-like folds of her vagina until it feels like a hard bud in the middle of a great, open peony. Perhaps she puts her fingers down to feel the hard top of the baby's head as it presses through spreading tissues. She is in touch with what is happening. There is no need to use counter-pressure against the baby's head, to tell her to pant, to rotate the head externally or to do any of the other manipulations which are often necessary when guiding a desperate woman, and which have become part of the routines of delivery. Her face lights up as she realizes that this is her baby being born, a living being from her body, and she can see its head and reach down and feel it as it slides into life. Suddenly she is full, stretched to her utmost, as if she is a seed-pod bursting. There is a moment of waiting, of awe, of a kind of tension which occurs just before orgasm and then suddenly the baby passes through, the whole body slips out in a rush of warm flesh, a fountain of water, a peak of overwhelming surprise and the little body is against her skin, kicking against her thighs or swimming up over her belly. She reaches out to hold her baby, firm, solid, with bright, bright eyes. A peak sexual experience, the birth passion, becomes the welcoming of a new person into life. All the intense sexual feelings of labour and delivery have culminated in the passion, the hunger and the fulfilment of a mother with her newborn baby.

Because she has been able to act spontaneously in giving birth, she acts spontaneously now, too. There is a flow of feeling which opens her arms to cradle her child, causes blood to rush to warm her breasts, and makes her nipples firm so that she is ready and eager when the baby starts to seek her breast, latches on and presses out the rich colostrum.

Sex, birth and motherhood are not really different, conflicting experiences. They are part of a continuum and what we learn from each, deepens our understanding of other aspects of our lives.

After childbirth

One of the most dramatic changes that can ever occur in a woman's body comes with the birth of a baby. Before, she was full. Now she is empty. There was another living being inside her. Now that baby is outside and is someone that she has to get to know and care for. In the process of labour the body has been like the stage on which a drama has been played, or, for some women, more like a battlefield on which a contest has been fought out. The new mother may feel aching and tender all over – soft, open and terribly vulnerable. Women say they feel "fat, leaky, tired", "lost", "fragile", "as though my femininity had been taken away", "like an old woman", "a mess", "overweight", even, for one who enjoyed having the baby inside her, "let down because I missed being pregnant". A woman may feel like this even after a straightforward labour. When the birth has been difficult she may be really frightened of and alienated from her body and alarmed by the changes that have been forced on it. "I felt I might tear open at any moment"; "after the poking and prodding I wanted time to recover and have my body to myself again". She wonders whether she will ever feel that it is hers again to experience with sexual delight. She may be in pain, stiff, bruised and sore, and when she shifts from one buttock to the other stitches in her perineum make her think that she is sitting on embedded thorns or slivers of glass.

The way labour is managed

It is not surprising that childbirth can profoundly affect a woman's feelings about sex. But it is not only a matter of whether labour has been easy or difficult, short or long drawn out. Fundamental to how she feels about her body after childbirth is the way in which it has been treated by those caring for her. If she has been treated as a person, her body handled with consideration, has been kept fully informed about what is happening and been able to share in all the decisions made about her care, she has retained her autonomy. Her body still belongs to her and she is likely to feel she has used it in an exciting and splendid way. But if she has been processed through labour as if on a conveyor belt, with little or no choice about what happens to her, if she was probed and examined roughly and treated as the object of a medical exercise rather than a person going through an experience of deep emotional significance, she is very likely to feel at first that her body no longer belongs to her but to the hospital, and later on to find it very difficult to express herself through her body without inhibition. She holds herself rigid, protectively guarding her body from pain, invasion and injury. It can be a long, painful journey to get on good terms with your body after such an alienating experience, to begin to like it and allow sexual passion to sweep through every pore.

Women's feelings about their bodies

In the first few weeks after childbirth she may be bleeding as much as if she had a heavy period. Her pads stick to skin which may have been nicked and is exquisitely tender because her pubic hair has been shaved and is beginning to grow again.

Many women embark on motherhood feeling strangers to their bodies. June, for example, had a forceps delivery and says: "I was devastated by the birth. My body felt so abused. My vagina, stitched back together, was black with bruising and I couldn't sit down. It didn't seem like my body. I didn't recognize it as mine. Sex was unthinkable. I completely retreated into myself. Whenever my husband touched my vagina I immediately thought of the birth, the doctors, the examinations, and got very upset." It is not only that so many things have already happened to the mother during childbirth, but that further changes take place in the six weeks or so after birth. The uterus is contracting and returning to its pre-pregnancy position and size. She loses the body fluids she stored in later pregnancy, partly from her bladder, but most of all through her skin in the form of sweat. She feels hot, smelly and sticky. Her breasts start to lactate and become heavy and swollen, with veins like rivers and tributaries etched all over them. They are aching and tender and milk oozes or spurts from her nipples. Before feeds she may feel that both breasts are blown up like balloons about to burst and after feeds they are sagging and empty.

"I was frightened things might be odd inside afterwards."

As the main flow of bleeding is reduced it gradually changes from brown to pink and then becomes merely a clear discharge. Some women feel dirty throughout this whole period, as if all their body orifices are open and leaking, as if this flow of fluids represents a kind of puerperal incontinence. It is no wonder that they hate their bodies, feeling them ugly and soiled.

Moira says that long after her soreness and bruising had disappeared she continued to feel like this. For her it was because her self-image seemed inextricably linked with her memories of her mother, who had died when she was nine: "She was extremely large, overweight and looked far more than thirty-seven at the time of her death – probably an exaggerated image, but an utterly unsexy pattern of motherhood." It may be that many of us identify with our own mothers' bodies at that time. We may find them distasteful because they are for us an indication of aging and of the sexlessness which, in Western culture, motherhood represents.

Others feel quite differently about this new softness and openness. Even the odour of puerperal blood may be exciting and the capacity to produce milk so abundantly and unexpectedly seems like a miracle. "My body felt *delicious*", one woman said, "comforting, sensual, sexy", but not, she added, orgasmic. It may be a simple matter of feeling back in shape again, the sort of shape you feel you were meant to be. "I felt great about my body after the birth," Fiona says, "because the bump was gone and my stomach was flat again." For Marion it was much more than that: "I felt in touch with natural forces – more sensually and sexually aware." It seemed to her mystical, as if she had had an ecstatic religious experience.

"I felt what a marvellous job my body had done."

Some women feel a flood of vitality which they long to express sexually even in the first days after delivery. It was like that for Viv. She hated being separated from her husband in the 48 hours after the birth because she was feeling so sexy. "The birth amazed me! I was proud that my body could produce my lovely baby. How nature can work! Afterwards I felt like running round a football pitch! I was amazed how quickly my body returned to normal. I couldn't *wait* to get back home to my husband – and bed! I was *very* randy!" This period of six to eight weeks after the delivery can be one in which there is an entirely new sense of harmony between mind and body, of psycho-physical efficiency and co-ordination, astonished awareness of biological power and, for some women, what amounts to reverence for the energy and detailed and precise patterning of natural forces in the female body. There is a glad surprise, a sense of triumph and something which can only be described as physical radiance. Birth has been life-enhancing. Some women even experience a permanent state of languorous satisfaction after childbirth which is like that felt after orgasm. It is as if your body has been gathered into waves of passion in labour and is now like a little boat tossed on a peaceful beach after a storm.

Birth can affect men in this way, too. If they were not only present at the birth, but shared in preparation for it and were fully involved right through labour and delivery, they may become more aware of the subtleties and intricacy of a woman's body and have gained a new understanding of female sexuality. John feels this happened with him. Ellen went through several weeks after the birth when she felt "unclean" and very "clinical" about her body: "I felt it didn't really belong to the 'me' I knew from before." It was John's love and his pleasure in her which made her feel very different. He had been at the birth and says he felt a deep awe for all that her body could do and was suffused with love and tenderness for her. Before the birth he had been a rather aggressive, high-speed lover. Afterwards he became gentle and caring and Ellen experienced orgasm for the first time during intercourse.

Some women think that the experience of birth brings them to the point where they can surrender conscious control of their bodies so that they enjoy orgasm, sometimes for the very first time. Others attribute this to the man's changed attitudes and new tenderness. Whatever the cause, it is not unusual for women to find that sexual experience has a new depth and diversity, though some months often pass before they realize this.

Episiotomy and sex

Any woman who has had an episiotomy is very unlikely to feel relaxed about sex until the wound has healed. After suturing of the perineum, tissues will be swollen between the stitches. Many zealous doctors – and in particular medical students – pull stitches so tightly that they do not allow any space for the inevitable swelling that follows tissue injury. The new mother may also be aware of a knot of scar tissue.

If stitches were supposed to dissolve but fail to do so they may become deeply embedded and be the cause of constant irritation and pain. Some women have to go back into hospital to have a surgical operation to remove these stitches. Rowan said she felt in the first weeks after delivery as if she would never be able to have intercourse again. She was resutured nine months after the baby had been born and now wishes that she had taken action sooner and seen a doctor. The problem, though, was that she never dared to look at the scar: "I was afraid it would look so awful." If she had examined it she would have seen the black stitches still in the skin and realized a week after delivery that they were not dropping out as they should. At that stage they could have been removed almost painlessly so it is better to pluck up courage and look.

When scar tissue becomes infected the stitches may break down completely and the whole wound gape open. The woman has antibiotic treatment and then has to be resutured. Here again, it is important that a woman is aware of what has happened and the best way to know is to *look*.

In Britain episiotomies are usually done laterally, as a straight cut from the base of the vagina out to the side of the perineum or in the form of a "J" shape. That is, they are made across tissues and muscles which do not normally divide at that point. When tears occur they are in a different place: either grazes or small lacerations in the labia if the woman was in an upright position at delivery or a laceration in the midline from the vagina down towards her anus. Though painful at first, first degree tears in the labia heal rapidly and many do not need stitching. A laceration in the midline occurs at a point where tissues naturally divide and so healing is usually quicker and there is less pain than after an episiotomy made in a physiologically less suitable area.

In many hospitals today episiotomies are done more or less routinely for first-time mothers and are also performed for women having subsequent babies if they have had a previous episiotomy. This means that in some hospitals 80 per cent, or more, of women get an episiotomy, whether they like it or not. Many women are feeling angry at this Western way of female genital mutilation and are questioning its routine use.

Making love again after being stitched

The chances are that if you have had a tear, and provided your partner is gentle and considerate, once the tissues have healed you will feel very little discomfort apart from a little tightness if lovemaking includes penetration. On the whole these tears, though painful at first, heal very speedily. As you relax and gain in confidence even this will go, though it may take about three months after the birth for you to feel perfectly comfortable. A great deal depends on how you were sutured, of course. If the doctor has done too intricate an embroidery you may have been stitched too tightly. This can be an alarming feeling and you may wonder if you will ever be able to have intercourse again. But this feeling will pass, and you can help yourself by taking some of the measures which I suggest later in relation to episiotomy wounds.

Sometimes a woman is very uncomfortable after a small tear, which may be only a graze, because it has occurred in a place where it is continually bathed in urine whenever she goes to the lavatory. It stings terribly and some women even find they put off emptying their bladders because they cannot face the pain. This only lasts about two weeks, at the most. If the tear and suturing was in the midline, down from the base of the vagina towards the anus (a very common place for it to occur), pressing a witch-hazel soaked sanitary pad against it as you empty your bladder, can alleviate this. If you use a small disposable pad (and your drains can stand it) you simply drop it into the lavatory pan when you have finished. Some women use a few drops of arnica oil, a homeopathic remedy, stroking it into the bruised or tender tissues, and say that this helps a good deal. Letting a warm stream of air from a hair dryer blow on to the affected area also aids the healing process.

**POSITIONS FOR INTERCOURSE
AFTER CHILDBIRTH**

*A cushion under the hips
may enable penetration to
occur without pressure on
scar tissue after suturing of
the perineum. The man
should support himself with
his arms so that no pressure
is put on her breasts.*

*If both partners enjoy a
face to face position, but
the woman is uncomfort-
able lying on her back she
may like to lie above her
partner where she can
easily control the degree of
penetration.*

*After a Caesarean section it
is important for a man not
to put pressure on the scar.
Not only is it uncomfort-
able, but a woman may be
anxious that the line of
stitching will burst open.*

When you first want to have intercourse it is a good idea to have
some oil or a proprietary gel available so that your partner can stroke
the tissues very gently, with a feather-like touch, and make them
more flexible before he attempts penetration. He should not come
in until you feel deliciously slippery and juicy.

Whether you have had an episiotomy or a tear, or are simply
feeling rather bruised, it is important to make love at least for the
first few times *without* penetration. Anxiety to "get back to normal"
or "do it properly", or even to have intercourse because you want to
show your man that you love him, will make it far less likely that
you enjoy lovemaking. A light touch, tenderness and sensitive
awareness of how you both feel about lovemaking are vital after
having a baby (as they are at all other times).

If you have had an episiotomy you are more likely to meet real difficulties. You will need to be very patient and it may take four months or more before you can really begin to enjoy intercourse, and even then you may much prefer it without penetration. For some women it takes much longer than that. One problem may be that there is a knot of scar tissue to one side at the bottom of the vagina which feels large, nobbly and very tender. You may not be able to tolerate any pressure or pulling against this area which, when you feel it with your fingertips, can seem much larger and harder than it is, like a walnut rather than a raisin.

When you make love you will want to avoid touching this scar tissue. There are several ways to do this. If you want penetration you can use pillows to tilt yourself or your partner at such an angle that it is less likely that he touches this part. You can also use your own buttock muscles, tightening them firmly so that your buttocks are drawn together, to protect this area as your partner slides in. But you need to be able to do this without contracting your pelvic floor muscles. It is easy to practise this: press your buttocks towards each other as if they were two tight little Danish pastries. Then move your pelvic floor muscles up inside you and bulge them out again, exploring ways in which you can make your muscles go up and down while your bottom is held rigid like this. Once your man is inside you will not need to keep the buttocks tight, provided he is at the right angle and the weight of the penis is directed towards the root of the clitoris and is not dragging down on the base of the vagina. You may find that a firm pillow under your buttocks is enough to do this. Alternatively, having intercourse on top of your partner may give you more control and the freedom to shift position.

Some women like the lubrication given by the man's semen when it is spilled outside them and over the sore, tender tissues. Others hate this because they think it is messy. However you feel about it, semen is probably better than anything you can buy.

Fear that you are going to have pain is very likely to make you tense up inside, which then produces the constriction which causes you further pain. So it is important to be able to release your pelvic floor muscles and make them soft, loose and velvety as your partner comes in. Some men think that the only way to penetrate is to push. This is not so. If a man has a strong erection he should be able to wait at the entrance of the vagina, only the tip of his penis between the outer folds of your labia, and you come down to meet him with your muscles. You will discover when you have bulged the muscles out you can then make little movements with them, alternately contracting and releasing, so that you stroke him lightly. *He avoids all thrusting* and leaves the action to you.

Occasionally there is pain deep in the vaginal vault. This usually means that trans-cervical ligaments have been torn or sometimes that there has been a tear high up inside the vagina which has not yet healed. The body's capacity for spontaneous healing is remarkable and you may discover that simply changing the position in which you make love is all you need to do. But if you are still having pain six months after childbirth, and there are no signs that things are getting better, it would be sensible to see a gynaecologist. You can arrange this through your general practitioner.

Breast-feeding

Some women choose not to breast-feed because in their heart of hearts they do not like the idea of the close and unremitting physical contact with the baby. A woman may be quite frank about this, or simply know that she feels uncomfortable about breast-feeding but not be able to put her feelings into words, or may be unwilling to admit, even to herself, how she feels.

Many women who start to breast-feed with some trepidation, not knowing whether they are going to be able to tolerate being tied to the baby's needs so intimately or to give their bodies with such unreserved love, grow to enjoy breast-feeding. It often takes six weeks – sometimes longer – before this stage is reached. But when they do get there they take sensuous pleasure in feeling a baby sucking at the breast.

Different reactions to breast-feeding

Breast-feeding is a sexual experience. It is not just that the mammary glands are organs of sexual arousal, but that the rhythms of breast-feeding – the build-up to breast fullness as the baby gets hungry, the speed with which the breasts respond with warmth when the baby cries, the erection of the nipple as the baby seeks it with an urgent, searching mouth – have an intensely sexual quality.

This sexuality embarrasses and distresses some women. Others enjoy it. Nipple stimulation, both during and after birth, results in uterine contractions. In the days following delivery this means that putting the baby to the breast leads to strong contractions which may be painful, but which do the good work of tightening the muscular walls of the uterus so that blood vessels are gripped, bleeding is reduced and the uterus returns quickly to its former shape and tone and almost to its pre-pregnancy size.

In the same way nipple stimulation given by the baby, the touch of the little hands against the breasts and of the firmly rounded cheek against the areola, may not only be a generally pleasurable sensation, but actually result in genital stimulation, though for many women this is a gentle feeling of warmth and openness and not something they would associate with sexual arousal. But for some this is so exciting that they experience orgasm.

And here, too, reactions vary. One woman delights in the unexpected sexuality of breast-feeding. Another shies away from it because its sexuality confuses her and she feels that two ways in which she uses her body which ought to be kept completely separate are getting mixed and confused. This may even bring a sense of moral outrage and revulsion from physical contact with the child, as if the baby is responsible for seducing her.

The first phase

During the early weeks of breast-feeding your nipples may feel very tender. Even women who go on to breast-feed happily often get nipple sores and cracks. So it is not surprising that your breasts do not feel part of your erotic self at that time. Some women continue to have very sensitive nipples throughout breast-feeding because they do not know how to get the baby well latched on and off and a hair-line crack develops where the nipple joins the dark circle around it. Some catch thrush from inside the baby's mouth, which makes the skin itchy. If this is the case, feeding is probably painful for the baby, too. The nipple will recover only when the baby's mouth is treated.

Sensitivity

The feeling of acute sensitivity to a lover's touch can remain all the time you are breast-feeding for other reasons. For some women this increased toughness of the nipples means that they become more responsive to their partner's touch. Maggie says that her husband has "his share of my milk" and that she often has an orgasm as he sucks at her nipple. Juliet also says that she "relates better" to her breasts while feeding, partly because they are fuller, firmer and "altogether sexier". But there is more to it than that. The year after the birth has been one of growth in Juliet's sexual relationship with her partner because he is spending much longer arousing her whole body and does not home in on her genitals so quickly. She attributes this partly to their having changed their contraceptive technique, since she has come off the Pill and he is using a sheath.

Yet many women draw back from breast stimulation from their partners for psychological reasons. Though there are some who enjoy milk spurting out when the breasts are stimulated ("it was great fun because all foreplay involving breasts resulted in fountains of milk!"), for others – and some men too – this is very off-putting. Women who talk about the "mess" of milk spurting out tend to use exactly the same words that they also use to describe the "mess" of semen dribbling out of the vagina.

The increase in breast size which comes with breast-feeding is exciting for some couples. A woman may feel that her breasts are much more attractive and long to enjoy them more in lovemaking for this reason. But a man, as we have seen, may not respond in the way she expects him to. Stephanie, whose breasts were very small before pregnancy, but who now has a 40-inch bust, says she feels neglected by her partner because she wants him to suck her nipples and he refuses to: "the idea of feeding my husband is very sexual, but he isn't interested."

The impact of breast-feeding on a relationship

Though research shows that women who are breast-feeding are more likely to resume intercourse earlier and to enjoy it more after childbirth than those who are not breast-feeding, many find that sex takes on a new dimension which draws the interest away from genital sex. They feel fulfilled, that they are doing what their bodies were made for, but it has nothing to do with intercourse. A successful and unhurried breast-feeding experience can enable a woman to get in touch with her body in a new way.

When breast-feeding is not going well the relationship with the partner is always affected, directly or indirectly. Equally, the couple's relationship always affects the breast-feeding experience. One of the ways in which this occurs is when the man is anxious about the woman breast-feeding openly and naturally in the presence of other people. Peggy's husband was very enthusiastic for her to breast-feed. This was all right until her plan to feed on demand meant that she sometimes breast-fed in front of other men, though she says she was very discreet. She knew that Mike felt very uncomfortable about this and it inhibited her from "letting down"

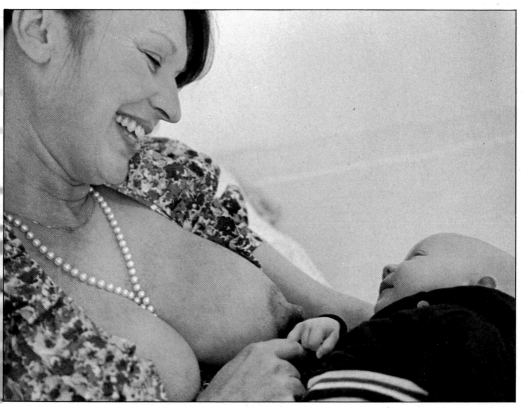

As well as communicating with your newborn, breast-feeding can put you in touch with your body in a new way.

the milk. Breast-feeding became less and less satisfying for both mother and baby and she began to lose her milk and gave up after three months.

Sometimes a man is jealous of a baby having unrestricted access to the breasts. It is as if the baby has stolen the woman's body. Luke said he found it irritating to always come across his little son glued to the breast with the tenacity of a mollusc sticking to a rock. Luke is a doctor and at that time was studying hard for exams. He felt *his* needs were paramount and really wanted Joan to mother *him* as he struggled through this difficult passage of his life.

She realized that Luke felt shut out and jealous of her intimacy with the baby, and felt torn between both their needs. Unable to cope assertively with this and to discuss it with Luke, she hoped the problem would go away. She was often alone in the flat and since Luke was working so hard, found solace in her closeness to the baby. Luke passed his exams and is now a doctor. Joan is training to be a breast-feeding counsellor. The couple have separated.

Tiredness and anxiety

Sheer exhaustion plays a part in the new parents' sex lives, too. Anxiety about whether breast-feeding is going to be successful and if the baby is getting enough milk interferes with any thoughts of lovemaking: "I had so much milk and was so tired and fraught when she cried at night", says Judith, "and then she began to bite me and it really hurt. I cried and felt guilty, pressurized, all mixed feelings, but hoped we could pull through." Even when things are going well

227

babies tend to wake up at inconvenient times, almost as if with a sixth sense that attention is directed elsewhere: "We are usually half-way through when Daisy wakes up!"

In attempting to meet the needs of a small baby daily patterns of life have to change, too, and you may discover that the time, the partner and feelings of sexual arousal never seem to coincide. Daphne says: "I felt very tense all the time I was feeding and worn out from the demands of a baby depending entirely on me to be fed every three hours." She began to feel exhausted and depressed, and she and Noel got into the routine of going to bed at different times. She was so tired by the time he came home from work that she went upstairs as soon as they had finished the meal and they never had a chance to make love. She did not want him to penetrate but did crave physical affection. But since Noel thought sex meant intercourse he was careful not to touch her as if he expected her to make love. He did not think it would be fair when she was so busy with the baby and was doing such a good job as a mother. As a result they stopped making love entirely. Looking back on it, Daphne thinks her misery during that awful first year was largely because she did not have the emotional sustenance of an old love and physical closeness. She felt he was holding her at arm's length: "I did go off sex in one way," she says "as I needed every ounce of energy just to cope with the baby. I wanted affection and support, not sex." But she missed out on both.

Breast-feeding can be a highly sexual experience, not only for the mother but also for the father and the baby...

Conflicting feelings

Some women find it hard to get aroused all the time they are breast-feeding: "I psychologically set my breasts aside for my baby and they were a means of food for him and nothing else." Some do not experience a return of erotic sensation till several months after they have stopped breast-feeding. Other women feel a highly-charged sensitivity from then on and enjoy their breasts in an entirely new way. If a woman's partner enjoys touching and sucking her nipples during this time she may find it disturbing, but difficult to tell him about this in case he feels he is rejected. Women often say things like: "Breast-feeding makes me very touchy about that area being handled." Sometimes a woman insists that before her partner touches her breasts he must wash his hands, or makes a pointed demonstration of washing her breasts afterwards. A woman who feels that the primary biological link with her baby has first claim on her and who, even though she wants to be able to respond to her lover, is unable to do so while she is lactating, may feel guilty about it: "I can't let go completely. I still have this feeling of my body belonging to the baby. I couldn't let my husband touch my 'working' breasts."

Sharing the experience of breast-feeding

A couple are often concerned that breast-feeding will mean that the man cannot get to know his baby intimately and that the relationship between mother and child is bound to be an exclusive one. We have seen already in Chapter 6 that a father has many other opportunities to get to know his baby – bathing, massage, just plain cuddling and holding can all be important parts of the relationship between father and child. Some women who really would prefer to breast-feed decide that they will bottle-feed after all because it is not fair on the father who wants to be fully involved with his baby. One woman said: "I can't help feeling that it would be selfish of me to breast-feed when John is so longing to be able to give the baby the bottle."

There are ways of taking your partner into the circle of your love when breast-feeding. It is obviously difficult to do this if you are struggling through the early stages, learning how to get baby "on" and "off" and not at all confident that you are doing anything right. The first six to eight weeks of feeding are often not straightforward. A woman is learning new skills and her attention is focused on the baby. But for most of us, there comes a lovely time when we can open up our arms and enjoy the sensuous pleasure of breast-feeding in the sure knowledge that it *works* because the baby is thriving and our bodies feel good. Some women say they feel "in touch with natural forces", and "more sexually aware". A father, too, may feel a surge of warmth and pleasure in the breast-feeding relationship.

Your lover can then become part of this experience of tenderness and sensual fulfilment, lying beside you as you feed or with an arm round you both.

Little hands explore the curve of your breast and the father spontaneously sucks a finger as the baby suckles. Or excited little feet pummel as the thrill of sucking and feeding sweep through the baby's whole body. As you drop off to sleep he takes the baby and nestles her against his own chest or lies with his arms enfolding you both. Breast-feeding *can* be a shared experience.

The menopause

Even those of us who think we know pretty well what happens to our bodies, who understand the ovarian cycle and childbirth and feel in touch with these rhythmic processes, may know little about the menopause and approach it in a much more negative way.

In biology lessons at school, and later when we read about sex, learning about the menopause either gets left out or we do not take it on board because it seems irrelevant and so far off in the future. It is something that happens to our mothers, not to us.

And then suddenly a woman discovers that her periods are not coming regularly or she has hot flushes – and there she is in the thick of it, disconcerted by what is happening to her and perhaps also rather frightened of getting old.

The menopause has had a bad press. It is treated as another of those inscrutable female mysteries in which women are trapped by their hormones, subjected – body and soul – to a flood of chemical substances which cause them to lose any control over mental processes they may once have had to be de-sexed and turned into wrinkled "senior citizens".

Prophets of doom

Robert A. Wilson (*Feminine Forever*), the American popular messiah of hormone replacement therapy (HRT), writing in "Menopause – the loss of womanhood and the loss of good health" claims that menopause is "a serious medical condition endangering the health and happiness of any woman", but that it is curable by HRT. Wilson is very sorry for the doctors of menopausal women:

What can the poor doctor make of the woman who complains to him of nervousness, irritability, anxiety, apprehension, hot flushes, night sweats, joint pains, melancholia, palpitations, crying spells, weakness, dizziness, severe headache, poor concentration, loss of memory, chronic indigestion, insomnia, frequent urination, itching of the skin, dryness of eye, nose, and mouth, and backache?

A chemical imbalance results in "menopausal castration" and "a mutilation of the whole body. . . . No woman can be sure of escaping the horror of this living decay. Every woman faces the threat of extreme suffering and incapacity." David Reuben, in his bestseller, *Everything You Always Wanted to Know About Sex but Were Afraid to Ask*, is another prophet of doom:

As the oestrogen is shut off, a woman comes as close as she can to being a man. Increased facial hair, deepened voice, obesity and the decline of the breasts and female genitalia all contribute to a masculine appearance. Coarsened features, enlargement of the clitoris and gradual baldness complete the picture. Not being a man, but no longer a functional woman, these individuals live in a world of inter-sex. . . .

To many women the menopause marks the end of their useful life. . . . Having outlived their ovaries, they may have outlived their usefulness as human beings. The remaining years may be just marking time until they follow their glands into oblivion.

It is hardly surprising that many women protest that nothing is going to change them.

For each woman the menopause has its own meaning ... and even if it is often a time for self-assessment, it can be seen as a fresh beginning ...

What really happens

In fact, the menopause does bring change. We have the choice of either denying these subtle changes, pretending they have not happened, or of finding out about our bodies and adapting to them as a swimmer adapts her strokes to the power of the current. Life carries us onwards and we flail around resisting the inevitable or learn how to adjust to what is happening.

The menopause is, in fact, only the cessation of periods. The whole process by which a woman moves out of her potential reproductive functioning into a state of being in which she is no longer fertile may take up to five years and goes by the name of the "climacteric". During this time enormous hormone changes are taking place in her body and a new balance is being found, one which is natural and right for an older woman. It is not the beginning of the end, but a process similar to that of adolescence.

Irregular periods

The menopause is preceded for many women by a phase of irregular periods. This is often associated with raised levels of the follicle stimulating hormone (FSH). When menstrual periods become irregular these levels of FSH and luteinizing hormones (LH) become higher and often triple. One year after ovarian function has stopped entirely – that is, when the menopause is over – FSH levels are 10 to 15 times higher than when a woman was menstruating. The maximum LH level is reached two to three years later, after which it declines (see section on hormones on page 52).

Ovulation ceases

The ovary is the main source of oestrogen secretion in a woman's body. So once the ovaries have ceased to work oestrogen levels drop. There is, however, another hormone, testosterone, which is thought to be the hormone primarily associated with sexual arousal in women (though this has yet to be proved). This, which the body continues to secrete, in itself is a source of oestrogen. So women past the menopause still produce oestrogen, but from a different source. There is a gradual fall in oestrogen production from the mid-twenties. For most women, the menopause is not a question of a sudden withdrawal of oestrogen. This only happens after surgical removal of the ovaries, and results in an abrupt surgical menopause unless the oestrogen is chemically replaced.

New hormonal balance

What is really happening during the menopause is that the endocrine system is reorganizing itself and the body adjusting to cope with the lower levels of oestrogen produced by testosterone. Once this adjustment has been made, the signs of the menopause which some women find so distressing – hot flushes, night sweats, palpitations, either flooding or scanty periods or both, and loss of libido – cease and the woman is able to be on better terms with her body.

Hot flushes

Most women, but not all, experience some hot flushes. There is a sudden wave of heat which spreads through the face and neck, and sometimes the rest of the body too. It can happen anywhere and at any time and is independent of the outside temperature. Some hot flushes are simply mild feelings of warmth. Others make the woman break out into sweat and afterwards she feels drenched and cold. Many women find hot flushes highly embarrassing because they draw attention to their menopausal condition. It is almost like a public declaration of parting with one's youth and femininity.

In fact, a hot flush can look very attractive. I did not realize this until one day, as I had one, I went to a mirror and attempted to observe myself dispassionately. Though I felt odd, I liked the rosy glow. From that moment on I decided that hot flushes were life-enhancing. Once you can think positively about a hot flush, the sensations experienced may change their quality too. Each flush is wave-like, rather like a contraction in labour or like a wave of sexual feeling sweeping through the body. It is possible to go *with* it rather than resisting it or trying to pretend that it is not happening. You can greet it with your breathing and continue to breathe, flowing as it rises in crescendo, peaks and then gradually fades away. It helps if you let the breathing flow right down into the pelvis so that not only the abdomen, but also the pubis, moves slightly, rising up as you breathe in and descending a little as you give a long, slow breath out. One way of rehearsing this is to rest a hand over the pubic mound and to practise breathing with full, slow breaths, emphasizing the breath out and allowing the breath in to look after itself. Feel the subtle movement of the pubis under the palm of your hand as you do so.

Not only can a hot flush feel sexy, but breathing in this way actually opens up the vagina, too, till it feels almost as if you could "breathe with" your vagina. Instead of tightening up as if you could somehow restrict and block the hot flush by muscle tension, closing the body and denying what is being experienced, you release and open, letting whatever sensations come sweep through your body.

Even so, some women still have uncomfortable hot flushes and there are other things you can do. One woman I know has a Japanese fan and wafts it slowly in front of her face whenever she feels a flood of heat coming. The slow movement probably helps her to breathe slowly then, too. You can also keep a small water spray handy, either the commercial kind or the type that is used for spraying indoor plants. Women often stress that it is a good idea to wear layered clothing, so that you can discard a cardigan or big scarf, or whatever, whenever you feel too hot.

Some women get night sweats which mean that they have to change the bedclothes as many as four or five times in the night. For most women it is not anything like as awful as that, but having a change of bed clothes at hand, together with iced water, toilet water or eau-de-cologne and talcum powder and an electric fan which can be switched on in an instant is a good idea. Kicking off a duvet is easier than struggling with blankets, too.

Changes in vaginal tissues

Another aspect of the menopause which can be distressing is discovering that your vagina is very dry and that the tissues have become thin, fine and easily damaged. This, of course, affects your feelings about intercourse, though it does not affect your libido.

Normally the vagina is slightly acid. There are special bacilli which turn the carbohydrate released from dead surface cells into lactic acid. With the menopause the vagina often becomes neutral or alkaline. At the same time, when the ovaries stop functioning and oestrogen levels are lowered, there is a decrease of vaginal blood flow, a reduction in the quantity of the vaginal fluid and a reduction in transvaginal electropotential (the transport system for electrolytes and water). These four things together dry out the vagina and cause sexual problems. The withdrawal of oestrogen makes the lining of the vagina more easily torn and also subject to infection. Tissues at the neck of the bladder may respond in the same way. The result is that the woman is more prone to vaginal and urinary infections. Gynaecologists doing research in the United States say that: "Most sexual problems experienced by menopausal women are due to the physical status of the vaginal mucosa." (James P. Semmens and Gorm Wagner, "Estrogen deprivation and vaginal function in postmenopausal women")

Treatment for vaginitis

All these changes can be reversed with oestrogen. Moisture is restored to the vagina and lovemaking and intercourse are no longer painful. The first line of treatment is to use a vaginal lubricant during lovemaking. If this is not enough to help, you can have an oestrogen cream prescribed, which you introduce into the vagina with a small plastic plunger. Vaginal tissues, however, absorb oestrogen readily. If you use this constantly you are increasing the risk of cancer of the uterus. Among women as a whole, one in 1,000 develops uterine cancer. If you use oestrogen, depending on the length of therapy and the dose, the risk increases 10 times.

It may be that one tube of oestrogen cream will soften and thicken the vaginal tissues enough to have intercourse again without pain. The treatment of choice after this is regular intercourse, since the flow of semen itself bathes the vagina in nutrients and helps to keep it flexible and plump.

Lesbian women, however, have this problem too and they find that even loving fingers are uncomfortable. If a simple lubricant gel or, as some women prefer, vitamin E oil, does not work, the only alternative is the course of oestrogen cream.

When oestrogen is taken orally it is usually now combined with progestogen in order to counteract some of the effects of oestrogen, and reduces the risk of cancer. Progestogen acts to protect the lining of the uterus. It is taken during the last 10 to 13 days of the month. But high levels of progestogen are associated with changes in blood cholesterol levels and with hypertension and thrombosis. If you decide to try HRT it is important that your health is carefully monitored all the time you are on it. You should have the lowest dose of supplementary hormones you need in order to treat your condition and should not continue the treatment longer than necessary. If you have already had a thrombosis or suffer from high blood pressure or heart disease, have diabetes or anything wrong with your liver, or suffer from migraine, there are special risks with HRT and you will need to discuss these fully with your doctor.

Calcium deficiency

Osteoporosis is thinning of the bones and it can affect women past the menopause. It results in three common kinds of fracture: compression fracture of the spine, fracture of the femoral neck and fracture of the wrist. It occurs because calcium is metabolized in a different way after the menopause. You cannot replace the lost calcium in bone, though hormone replacement therapy (HRT) prevents further loss. Most women do not suffer from osteoporosis and it may be related to nutritional deprivation earlier in life. So preventive measures which involve hormone replacement therapy (taking oral oestrogens three weeks out of four at the time of the menopause) are probably unwise. Research shows that you have to keep the oestrogen up all the time and that if the therapy is stopped, bones can still become porous once oestrogen is withdrawn. (Jean Hailes, "Sexuality and aging")

There is some evidence, too, that nutrition can play a part in preventing bones becoming fragile at the time of the menopause and after. Vitamins C and D are important, together with calcium and supplementary fluoride. A diet rich in vitamins and minerals is better than pill-popping, since the body can absorb them more easily. Possibly the dosage of fluoride should be adapted to individual needs and related to the amount obtained in drinking water.

The pros and cons of HRT

Hormone replacement therapy was hailed in the 1960s as a panacea for all menopausal problems. If a woman in her fifties could not sleep, if she was irritable, her hair or skin became dry, she had headaches or felt tired, found it difficult to concentrate, was depressed or did not want sex, HRT could cure it! It was almost as if it were the elixir of youth, as if it could obliterate wrinkles, restore vitality and stave off old age and death itself! The salesmen of this "miracle cure" inculcated fear as they preached. Claiming that the menopause was "a preventable and curable deficiency disease" (Robert A. Wilson, *Feminine Forever*), they warned women that without HRT they would become like eunuchs and be crippled by what was happening to them. Although the exponents of HRT were careful not to claim that HRT restored libido, their publicity material included statements like: "Now almost every woman, regardless of age, can safely live a full sex life for her entire life." The press picked this up and HRT was plugged in the pages of fashion and beauty magazines:

It restores a feeling of confidence and well-being, makes your skin smooth and resilient, bounces up your hair, firms your breasts, sparks your interest in sex – a real package deal that spruces up your vagina, uterus and clitoris. In no time at all, everything is exactly as it should be: your whole body is primed for sex. ("Sex begins at forty", *Harpers*, quoted in Rosetta Reitz, *Menopause: A positive approach*).

HRT cannot restore lost youth and it is not an aphrodisiac. It can prevent hot flushes, if taken at the onset of the menopause, can prevent thinning of the bones for as long as it is taken, and is highly effective in restoring the elasticity of the vagina.

This is what one woman, who is grateful for HRT, says about the effects of her treatment:

I started on Cyclo-Progynova and it changed my life. I get no side-effects at all. At the Older Feminists there seems to be an incredible amount of fear and prejudice about HRT. This is *my* experience – I have been taking it for more than two years and haven't regretted it for a second. You women who light up your twentieth cigarette of the day and tell me I'll get cancer – give up the fags and improve your life with HRT!

In contrast, another woman says she found it hard to disentangle the effects of the menopause and her mother's death and the emergent adolescence and adulthood of her children. She was deeply distressed and also had acute and painful physical symptoms, including pain in her limbs, headaches, water retention and heavy bleeding. Her lover was a woman and she feels that her constant support and care helped her through this stage and that she was fortunate in not being expected to have sexual intercourse. She goes on to say:

I feel lucky that being a lesbian, my partner was able to identify and sympathize with my condition. . . . The certainty that I was a whole person, friend and lover to my partner was a real life-line. Most women of my age have unluckily missed the sisterly support of the Women's Movement. . . . I certainly failed to find any medical help or advice. The assertion frequently made by doctors, and by women too, even in books purporting to be about the menopause, that looking after oneself, keeping fit, slim and active will adequately see one through this time, doesn't help. In my case such advice only created more guilt and self-doubt. . . . I have been forced to reconsider myself – in every sense. Brought face to face with my feelings I had to search to find my qualities. . . . Losing my youthful body I had to learn to love my aging body in which I genuinely began to feel a new ease. Looking back, too, I now see that in spite of everything it was a highly productive time.

The meaning of the menopause

For each woman the menopause has its own meaning. For many it is a symbol of getting old. It may bring such physiological disruption that a woman is alienated from her own body so that there is an end to all sexual feeling and experience: "I have dried up. My clitoris has disappeared. I feel angry with myself. I hate my body. I am ashamed of it and want to hide. And everything connected with sex I want to push away."

For some the menopause is experienced as bereavement: "When my periods came I felt, 'I am now a woman'. Exit periods and I am now a non-woman." The way in which the menopause has been written about by predominantly male doctors who describe "vaginal atrophy", "degenerative changes", "oestrogen starvation" and "senile pelvic involution" conditions women to see each sign of the menopause as a stigma by which they are labelled as aging and "past it". Rosetta Reitz (*Menopause: A Positive Approach*,) says that if she believed these words were applicable to herself she would feel she had to commit suicide:

Yet these absurd descriptions of us are a functioning part of the literature of menopause. By exploring the language of menopause we learn about how we, as menopausal women, are viewed, for language is one of the major methods of communication and it mirrors the culture. In communicating meaning, the question of *whose meaning* presents itself.

She goes on to say that when men experience changes in physiological and sexual function that come with age they are not described in the same sort of language:

We do not have "testicular insufficiency" to match "ovarian insufficiency" or "senile scrotum" to match "senile ovaries". In the *Merck Manual of*

Diagnosis and Therapy, the common physician's handbook, in describing premature menopause, specific medical directions are given for the "preservation of a serviceable vagina". Do you think there is equal discussion of a "serviceable penis"?... Of course there isn't! When a doctor injects testosterone in a man, it is not for the purpose of preserving or creating a "serviceable penis"... Men do not serve. Women do. The purpose is to increase his libido, to raise his hormone level.

Social attitudes to growing older

But this is not just something that doctors have done to women. Social attitudes to growing older and the emphasis on women being attractive and young may in themselves impose on us or exacerbate an existing sense of loss at the time of the menopause. This feeling of losing something is the basis on which women evaluate themselves in self-deprecating and derogatory terms. We see ourselves as if reflected in a distorting mirror erected by society.

A distinguished man with silver hair and a bit of a paunch escorts a slender, glamorous woman in her twenties. They are conducted to their table in the restaurant by the head waiter. The man's face is wrinkled, his jowls heavy, but he has the smell of opulence about him, a subtle mixture of cognac, lime and cigars. She wears a clinging, low cut dress and is looking at him adoringly. All eyes are on them: "That's the shipping magnate." He wears the girl like a medal. She is one of his acquisitions, an outward sign of his success. Other men envy his wealth, charisma, his possession of such women. The virility which is an implied part of this presentation of self, this public act he is performing, is an important ingredient of the money and power on display.

A woman enters with a much younger attractive man. She is obviously in her fifties, her hair dyed, slightly too dark against her wrinkled skin, her pancake make-up stopping abruptly at her hair roots. Around her eyes carefully graded blue and silver shadows form an aquatint landscape as over a delta of branching rivers. The man must be about 28. She is holding his hand across the table. Mother and son? The messages passing between their eyes are obviously erotic. This is an aging woman who has captured a much younger man. Disgusting! Or, perhaps, ridiculous. There is something almost obscene in thinking of that flaccid, sagging female body naked beside the young man's. The marks of age, which in a man can be signs of success, distinction, power are in a woman signs of the loss of femininity and of any power she may have once possessed. Her task is to retire and "grow old gracefully".

In peasant societies old women control the lives of younger ones and, indeed, often hold sway over everything that happens within the territory of the household and the extended family unit. Matrons in their fifties are dominant and powerful in the village community. The menopause releases them from the social obligation of reproduction and they become political dynamos, wheeling and dealing, plotting and scheming, organizing their families, economically powerful – with complete control over the distribution of food, and often directing the lives of the men. Getting older means power, for women as well as for men, and the transition from relative powerlessness to the acquisition of power is much more marked for women. To be past the menopause is to enter into a new

Attraction is not bound by age . . . it is social attitudes which impose constraints

and freer phase of life. The effectiveness of women in Chinese political and work cadres has been attributed to the traditional power of older women in Chinese society and the manner in which this sparks off political awareness in younger women, too, in order to cope with dominant grandmother figures. Traditionally in Japan a woman passes through different phases from childhood to maturity until, at 61, she enters the oldest and most venerated age group (John F. Embree, *A Japanese Village*). There is a party and from then on she can wear a crimson petticoat. Being older is not treated as a disability to be ignored or apologized for, but as a triumph.

Making changes

The social setting for an easy progression through the menopause and into old age is absent in Western urban–industrial culture. Even when the menopause is not confronted as bereavement of youth, it may be threatening for other reasons. For some women the menopause means getting like their mothers, seeing themselves in the image of their own mothers, and they cannot cope with the hostility and anxiety this arouses: "Oh, God! The beginning of the menopause! My mother was a very difficult woman going through the menopause. I remember Father being upset. She was irrational, hysterical, neurotic. I was fourteen when it all started. It coincided with an awful part of adolescence for me. I think, 'God! I mustn't get like my mother'. She broods over me like a terrible ghost."

The menopause may seem like a day of reckoning, a time when a woman looks back on life already lived, evaluates it and finds it wanting: "I feel an element of failure because I haven't had a special relationship." But though it is a time for self-assessment, the emphasis can be on how you are going to use the rest of your life. Some women see it as a fresh beginning, opening the door on a new phase of existence. Many say that they are forced to ask themselves who they are and what they want to be and do and that though the process can be painful it results in exciting change and possible developments. They start on a different kind of work or get training for jobs which are often quite different from those they had in their early twenties. They stress that this enables them to cope better with the physiological problems of the menopause. One woman told me that she was sure that work outside the home had kept her sane. There is often a spin-off to work, whether it is paid employment or learning a new skill – meeting other people and being stimulated by their personalities and ideas.

This is especially important for a woman who has spent many years at home engaged in the major tasks of caring for her family and housework. She may feel she has lost all ability to make new social contacts and to be stimulating and stimulated in her turn. Creating satisfying relationships brings a new sense of self-worth.

Sometimes this means a reawakening or diversification of sexual experience. Barbara says she was at the point of feeling "What on earth is in the future now?" She took an Open University course and her life changed dramatically: "It was a turning point. I met up with a group of people younger than myself. It made me feel alive." Then at a summer school she fell in love with a man of 30. They had an affair: "It was absolutely fantastic! It rejuvenated me."

She did not tell her husband because, she says, of not wanting to hurt him: "And he was so pleased at what the Open University had done that he felt rejuvenated too. He became very sexy."

An older and better lover

Other women discover that a longterm relationship blossoms without the extra stimulus from outside. Sometimes this is due to sexual changes in the male partner. As a man gets older he takes longer to climax and there are times when he is satisfied without ejaculation. This makes him a better lover. Where a relationship is a going concern women often comment on the way in which it is enriched and diversified once fertility is behind them and there is no worry about contraception: "Our understanding and love for each other has gradually increased and strengthened over the years. Sexually, we know what gives us most pleasure."

It is not like this for all couples. Even in a good relationship, sex may no longer have the central place it did in earlier years. Social pressures to be sexually active sometimes make couples anxious about not having intercourse but, as one woman put it: "We don't need to go on having intercourse to prove we are any good. We have found a new way of loving, without intercourse."

Menopause is not the beginning of the end. By the year 2000, in the world as a whole, one in every three women can expect to live 30 years after her menopause. The average life expectancy will be 75 to 80. What we do with those years, our physical and emotional well-being and how we feel about ourselves as women who are growing older, with or without sexual partners, is vitally important. Those 30 years can either stretch out into a waste land or be a time of extra productive life.

Growing older

When sex is seen as therapy, as an important kind of preventive medicine, like jogging or incorporating poly-unsaturated fats into a fibre-rich diet, it can be very threatening if either partner goes "off" sex as they grow older, or both experience less sexual arousal. Maintaining a healthy body – perhaps life itself – seems, according to much present teaching about sexuality and aging, not only to entail regular genital sex, but also sex with orgasm. If you cannot keep your sex life going you are warned that you risk all sorts of illnesses and wasting conditions and, ultimately, senility. The older woman who has become less interested in intercourse, who is well past the passionate stage when conflict with her partner was terminated by exciting lovemaking (at least till the curtain went up on the next row) and who knows just about everything she can know about her own and her partner's body and ways of making love, may feel under pressure to keep up sexual performance as a kind of health insurance.

Society's pressures

Any dogma about how we should feel and express ourselves through our bodies can degrade sex. Contemporary teaching about the necessity of genital activity traps women in a culturally imposed mould equally as much as when, in the past, the female orgasm was considered a symptom of mental illness.

Active sexuality, which is invariably equated in our society with having intercourse, is supposed to keep your eyes bright, your skin smooth, hair glistening and tissues supple – perhaps because sexual desire is associated in our minds with youth and vitality. It is a kind of sympathetic magic.

The implication is that if you are not "having sex" you have let yourself "go". In Western culture the contemporary cult of youth coerces both women and men into demonstrating that they are sexually alert. Women especially are driven to make cosmetic camouflage of the aging process and often to act out a hectic pantomime which mimics themselves when young: heavy eye make-up, slimming diets which sometimes produce elderly anorexics, aerobic exercise classes, cosmetic surgery and sojourns at health farms to bring back inner peace, outward beauty and "sex appeal". "We hang on to the idea of ourselves as 'girls'" says Katharine Whitehorn, "because the only alternative seems to be 'crone'". ("No country for old women"). There are other words for women of this age, but all of them are equally unattractive: matriarch, harridan, battle-axe and old bag (though some of these words are now being reclaimed by the Woman's Movement and beginning to have positive meaning).

It is as if the shadow of gradual dissolution, the shadow of death itself, looms near and the weapons that a woman grasps to fight it are all those bottles on her dressing table, the visits to her hairdresser, the frenetic search to keep the semblance of youth. Sexual activity, and the sometimes desperate search for orgasm, is used in order to plump up her cells, boost her confidence, tone her muscles and flood her with the hormones of everlasting youth. It is a means to an end, one more weapon in the armoury.

In a society where women are valued mainly for the support they give men – producing and rearing their children, cooking their meals, boosting their morale, showing how clever, rich and virile they are, the wife of a successful man may be used to demonstrate, by the clothes and jewellery she wears, the prestige and status of her husband. Her mink, her diamonds, the tan she acquired on the holiday in Mustique, her whole life-style, are evidence of conspicuous consumption and hence of her husband's success. Some older women, trapped by marriage to successful men like flies in amber, are taken round on selected business or professional trips and to conferences where they participate in the "ladies' programmes" and further embellish the image of their men. The presentation of the woman as a desirable sex object is all part of this elaborate jostling among men for recognition of status. If the wife is too heavily addicted to tranquillizers or alcohol, or is in any way unable to fill this role suitably, she may be replaced by a younger dollybird.

Making your own adjustments

But, of course, most of us do not live like this and have quite a different set of problems related to aging. Many women retire from work to live on a pension that entails forethought and penny-pinching about everything involving money. They may be alone, perhaps for the first time for many years, after a partner's death, or caring for one who is ill. The natural aging process puts a brake on some activities, though it may open up the possibility of others for those who are prepared to look for them. A woman who perceives her role entirely in terms of domestic responsibilities may be unable to make creative use of this new opportunity because once the children have left the home and her husband is retired she is stripped of the only role she ever had. She feels lonely, socially isolated and, since nobody seems to want her, becomes more and more depressed and encased in her own misery.

This may seem to have little to do with sexuality, but the feelings a woman has about her body and about herself as a sexual being derive from the way in which she sees herself reflected in the eyes of others. Her self-image is bound to this reflection. Throughout her life she has been trained, as a woman, to study that reflection and to value herself in terms of it. When it tells her she is old and unwanted she feels completely discarded and drained of vitality.

It does not have to be like this. A woman who has devoted her life to nurturing others may suddenly find herself with space to do things *she* wants to do. Hardly likely to take up sky-diving or wind-surfing for the first time, she may decide, however, to try yoga classes or regular swimming sessions at the public baths instead. There is a whole new space opening in her life where she can explore what she wants to do, discover new skills and develop old ones, meet different people and make new friends, link up with others who share her concern to help those in need and create a better society, and to *be herself.* For some women, growing older and relinquishing the more direct responsibilities of parenthood, for example, means that they are free to explore new aspects of their sexuality, perhaps one which they have been denying for a long time. A woman in her fifties or sixties who seeks a love relationship with another woman may find that it is difficult to come out as a lesbian and when she does, discovers that the lesbian social world tends to be young and she feels terribly out of place. Some younger lesbians, however, value having older women among them: "It's nice to look round the room and see a mixture of ages and know that lesbians have always been here and always will be."

Whether heterosexual or lesbian, a woman may find that one aspect of this process of discovery is that she now experiences sex in a way that she enjoys, without having to attain a standard or reach a goal. Masters and Johnson showed in their research that sexual activity does not usually come to a full stop with increasing age, though the rate of intercourse is often reduced. Seven out of 10 couples over 60 were sexually active.

Women themselves, talking about changes in their sexuality as they grow older, often stress that sex is not so "urgent", but much more an expression of all that a couple mean to each other. Sensuous, loving touch, tenderness for the other person, the joy of shared memories, the same sense of fun – all these play a dominant part in sex when a couple have been together a long time, and the relationship is a good one. Desire remembered, the primavera radiance of earlier lovemaking and its sweet-sharp astonishment and ecstasy, may be mellowed and muted against a more vivid backdrop of time and place. An older woman was talking about her honeymoon in Austria. She was deeply, passionately, in love. "I don't remember anything about that night", she confessed. "But oh, how I remember Salzburg!"

Yet for some women sex clearly improves with age. One doctor who directs a sexual counselling clinic in Australia tells of a woman who was anorgasmic through two marriages, began to have extra-marital relations at 72 and had an orgasm for the first time at 74.

Blodwen is 69, has been twice widowed, and now has a "part-time partner". She says that intercourse has improved with age. When young she always wanted to get rid of the man's penis from her body as soon as she had had an orgasm. Now she can continue to enjoy her partner's penis inside her and has a second orgasm after a while. Sensations are less intense but much longer drawn out. "Once you would have given your life almost for that moment of ecstasy, taken any risk," she says. "Now, you are aware that the moment will pass." But even though this is so, she is able to enjoy her new-found sexual relationship in a way that she never could have in the past.

Writing about women over 70, Masters and Johnson said that the important things were good health and "an interested and interesting partner". For a woman seeking a male partner can be a problem. We live approximately eight years longer than men. When we marry, our husbands tend to be a few years older than ourselves. So even if a woman is healthy the second condition – the interested and interesting partner – may be absent. Most women outlive their husbands by about 11 years and among all those over the age of 60 there are four women to every three men.

It is cruel counsel to tell women that they must have intercourse in order to stay healthy if only because many, whether they choose to do so or not, have to live without a man. This concentration on intercourse as the *sine qua non* of sex means that masturbation is

Age does not have to bring inactivity or immobility – it can be a time to discover new aspects of the self

considered a kind of second class sexual outlet. Yet many older women enjoy masturbation and some first discover it after they are widowed. At the same time that older women are told that they *need* sex, they are denied the right to be sexual. Geriatric sex is considered peculiar, laughable, often disgusting and obscene. One sex therapist says:

Denial of late-life sexuality has a destructive effect that goes far beyond its negative impact upon the aging person in sex life and self image. It complicates and distorts inter-personal relations. It creates serious conflicts between children and those widowed and divorced parents who are thinking of remarriage. ... To the extent that our society defines the sexual interest and activity in older persons as deviant behaviours, persons in whom sexual interests and activities continue will suffer, so that not only sex but the marriage relationship in the later decades of life may be affected. (Dr Elsie Koadlow, "Sexuality and the elderly")

Overt sexuality in old age is far more likely to be denied to women than men. A silver-haired man like Lloyd George is admired for his voracious sexual appetite in old age. If a man has enough power, or enough money to give him power, he can get away with it. (Onassis is reported to have claimed that power is the best aphrodisiac of all.) But a woman of the same age who seeks sexual expression is comic or indecent, and somehow very threatening to the young.

Our culture puts older women in a double-bind. They are taught that they must have sex and orgasms to keep young. They are also taught that sexual relationships and the seeking of sex as they age is ridiculous. Mutton must not be dressed as lamb. The only alternative may appear to be a lace cap and to model yourself on "Whistler's Mother". But that inner serenity, when imposed on you from outside, is impossible to achieve.

Even if the woman over 60 is not expected to be in a rocking chair, it is often suggested that she should be able to stand back and not get emotionally involved. Being "sensible" is to be temperate, to see things in perspective (though any perspective must depend on where you are standing at the time). To grow older is:

Deliberately to close
Your senses to the spring
Because her wiles must bring
December round again;
To shun love's foothills even,
Fearing to reach the crest
Of joy, and see beyond
No choice but to descend
Those slopes of less-than-best
Which are most kin to pain.
(Jan Struther, "To Grow Old")

It does not have to be like that. The new space in a woman's life can offer something else. It provides an opportunity to explore who she really is and to understand the non-genital aspects of sex in a different way. If the emphasis is no longer exclusively on intercourse as the be-all and end-all of sexual experience she can see the richness to be drawn from other kinds of creative expression which derive from sexual energy, but which are often never seen as having anything to do with sex: the warmth of a relationship with any person we love deeply, the affection between close friends, being given the trust to enter into the feelings of another human being, when the barriers which separate us are dissolved and we meet each other face to face, the energy kindled by hard, creative work into which we pour ourselves, the deep emotion and inner power which flows from affirming life instead of denying it.

A woman whose husband died some years ago told me that when she took her newborn grandchild into her arms a feeling swept through her which was just as intense as any experience usually thought of as sexual: "I felt suddenly, 'This is what these arms are for'." There are women who discover painting, who take up a social cause with passionate committal, who learn new skills and ways in which to express all their experience of life lived. They seem to be few and far between and those we think of stand out as exceptional, because Western culture usually discards older women.

When older women have talked to me about their sexuality they have emphasized that the idea of "performance" in sex, seen from the perspective of age, is no longer valid and that sexual relationships are re-evaluated. Some women say that, looking back at their lives, they are aware that what is often seen as the sum-total of sex – needing and pairing with a man – made them very dependent and that this dependency patterned their whole existence till now. It was only as they became older that they were able to shed this dependency and have a clear, hard look at themselves and the meaning of their lives.

Doing this, painful as it often is, sometimes gives fresh life to the partnership and where the woman finds herself, or chooses to be, alone she expresses her vitality in a new, uninhibited and deeply satisfying way.

Nutrition and aging

An older woman living alone may allow her nutrition to deteriorate because it is so much easier to make a cup of tea and some bread and butter than to prepare a salad, and there may sometimes seem little point in fussing over cooking something when there is no one else with whom to share the meal. Yet nutrition is extremely important for the elderly. One answer to the solitary snack may be to invite a friend to share a meal on a regular basis. If you do not grow your own vegetables or know someone from whom you can get garden-fresh produce, or it is difficult to get to the shops to obtain fresh fruit and vegetables, vitamin supplementation may be advisable.

Sex and nutrition   **Vitamin B** found in wholemeal grains, peanuts, liver, egg yolk, milk, green and root vegetables and fruit, is a vitamin older people may lack if on a bland diet of highly processed foods. You can take a couple of spoonsful of brewer's yeast or wheatgerm every day (sprinkled over prunes, porridge or muesli, for example) or take vitamin B pills. Without vitamin B you get depressed, have difficulty sleeping, are exhausted and feel under stress. The earliest sign is tiredness and being unable to summon energy for anything, let alone sex. Vitamin B is not stored in the body and needs to be taken every day. If you are having any difficulty in sleeping it is well worth taking a vitamin B complex supplement every day.

Vitamin C is found in fresh fruit and vegetables, especially citrus fruit. It can be flushed away by large amounts of coffee and tea and also by alcohol. If you are having antibiotics you need extra vitamin C. Without enough of this vitamin you feel run down and under stress and catch colds and viral infections. You cannot take too much vitamin C, as it is not stored in the body, and you need it every single day. So supplements may be useful.

Vitamins A and D work together to keep bones, teeth and nails strong, hair and skin in good condition and resist infection. If you are short of vitamins A and D your skin and hair are in poor condition, nails and bones brittle, and you readily pick up colds and other infections. Vitamin D comes from sunlight on the skin and codliver oil is an excellent source. There are small amounts in milk. Vitamin A is in green leafy vegetables, liver, milk, oily fish like salmon, herring and mackerel, egg yolk, fruit and some root vegetables. It is possible to overdose with A and D supplements, so consult your doctor or a woman's health group if you think extra vitamin A and D in the form of capsules would help you.

Vitamin E helps to retain the elasticity of the skin and, with vitamin C, assists the healing of wounds. It is one of the vitamins claimed to be useful in the treatment of arthritis. It is found in soya beans, sunflower and sesame seeds and green vegetables.

Since modern processing and storage of foods often deprives them of their vitamin content, one multi-vitamin tablet taken each day may be a good idea for the older woman.

Urinary incontinence

Aging may bring physical disabilities that interfere with the way you express yourself sexually. Stiff joints, an aching back, difficulty in hearing and seeing, loss of taste and smell, may all mean that you need to adapt and experiment in lovemaking, as I suggest in pages 156–7. But the most disturbing thing of all can be incontinence of urine. This starts as "stress" incontinence and you find yourself losing a little urine when, for example, you cough, sneeze or laugh. It means that the pelvic floor muscles are not in good condition. It is very important for the woman over 60 to do regular pelvic floor exercises to keep these muscles well toned. They are described on pages 48–50.

If muscles have already become slack you should ask your doctor for the help of a physiotherapist, who will make sure that you are doing the movements correctly and can also offer faradism, a mild electrical stimulus applied to the muscles concerned which causes them to automatically contract. This gives you something to build on and the condition of the muscles can be changed dramatically with just one course of faradic stimulation. Trying to remember to keep to an exercise session is unlikely to be successful. It is much better to coax these muscles into being expressive just as muscles of the mouth are expressive, and to use them in much the same way.

8 COPING WITH DIFFICULTIES

Differences in desire

It is not surprising that any two human beings in a sexual relationship experience differences in desire. The extraordinary thing would be if they always felt exactly the same and if libido invariably waxed and waned at the same time.

In the past, differences in sexual arousal in heterosexual relationships may have been less marked because the man was seen as the initiator and the woman as someone who responded. If your task is merely to make yourself available and to show that you are pleased about what is happening, you do not have to pretend you are sexually excited when you are not. And since you do not have to get an erection, all you need do is to demonstrate that you are willing. If, however, you are supposed to be a sensuous, totally fulfilled woman, but it is one of your "off" days, the task is more difficult.

When a man is seen as the sexual aggressor any evidence of reduced libido may be welcomed by a woman who is relieved not to be "bothered". Jamaican peasant women talking about their relationships with their men often said to me: "him don't trouble me", usually welcoming this because they did not then have to worry about getting "spregnant".

Differences in desire can be particularly distressing for women in partnerships with women, for lesbian sex is sometimes imagined to offer perfect fulfilment and ecstasy, because "two women can really understand each other". This may sometimes be true, but when one woman wants sex more often than the other the problem can seem even more acute than those associated with differences in desire between a woman and a man.

Overloading the role of sex

A couple who are going for out-and-out "togetherness" and harmony make demands on themselves and each other. Sexual excitement is likely to become evidence of love and caring for the other person, and absence of excitement seems like cold rejection.

In our sex-oriented culture we have elevated sexuality to such a level of importance that we have made it the test of significance in a relationship, as if without it the bond between two human beings cannot be strong. Many couples in fact come to accept and learn to live with differences in desire and refuse to let it ruin the relationship. In our culture it can be quite difficult to do this because we are under pressure to feel that if difficulties like this remain unsolved there must be something fundamentally wrong between a couple. We are bombarded by advice in magazines and books to find the root of such problems and eradicate them – often with the assumption that a man by his very nature "needs" sex and a partnership must crack if a woman cannot satisfy his appetite.

Some couples may create a different *modus vivendi*. If both feel happy about it, one may have outside affairs or they may form a triangular relationship, with another person welcomed into their own and extending it. For many couples this does not work. They may agree that one will give the other sexual pleasure without having to pretend an excitement he or she does not feel, simply because there is love and caring in the relationship. One partner may masturbate to relieve sexual tension and they may often choose physical contact and cuddling in place of genital sex.

We need to look beyond our sexual difficulties to the feelings we have about ourselves and our relationships.

The important thing is that you work out what you really want from the other person. Sex often represents for us things we are asking for which are only indirectly related to anything happening with the genitals. Many difficulties in a partnership get labelled as

sexual problems which are really something quite different. If you want more sex than you are getting it may be that you feel you are lacking physical contact with the other person, that your partner never has enough time for you, or that when you are together the other person's mind is somewhere else; he or she is just "not there".

There are times, phases in a relationship, when we may have to recognize that emotion is going elsewhere and must draw back so that it can pour into work or go to someone else, a child or a parent, for example, who needs our care. All these things are part and parcel of any relationship that is not just a superficial meeting of bodies or an outlet for the sex drive.

There may be times, however, when we become aware that not being able to be sexually aroused is a sign of something else going wrong. Many physical illnesses reduce libido because they make us feel run down and weak. If we are in pain we cannot concentrate on lovemaking, though sometimes sex is deliberately used to try and blot it out. Just as toothache or a sore throat, for example, dampens desire, in something of the same way worries about money or the children, problems at work and other preoccupations interfere with sexual arousal and its expressions.

Libido, like the appetite for food, is affected by stress, anxiety and depression. When emotional energy is being used to cope with stress, sex may be employed simply as a distraction in an attempt to relax or sleep, or we feel too drained to enjoy sex at all.

Sexual feelings reflect and express other things that are going on in our minds and in our lives as a whole. If sex is the only or main point of meeting between a couple, they are likely to find that they get out of synchronization with each other and become hurt or anxious because they cannot understand why the other seems to be rejecting. Even with a couple whose lives are intimately shared, there must be times when one does not realize how something preoccupying the other's mind interferes with sexual arousal or the capacity for its expression.

It is clear from the way women have talked to me about sex that when communication between a couple is good about all the other things that are happening to them in their lives, there are likely to be far fewer sexual problems. It seems that when sex is approached out of context, seen as an isolated activity separate from everything else that affects us, there are most likely to be misunderstandings and obvious differences in desire between partners, producing variations which are inexplicable to them and are interpreted as signs of loss of love or outright rejection.

The effects of stress

"Stress" is a much over-worked word. It is sometimes implied that it is the cause of almost every malady from which human beings suffer. Yet stress is a normal part of living and without it there would be no excitement and no motivation to get up, get going and make things different. People seek stress to add zip to their otherwise monotonous, boring lives. Reading thrillers, seeing horror films, playing Bingo, mountain-climbing, betting on a horse, supporting Manchester United, going on a fairground roller-coaster, being spellbound by those TV games in which the final reward for correct answers is a car, a 'fridge, a three-piece suite and

Erotic feelings flow most easily when we feel confident, secure, relaxed...

a holiday for two in Hawaii, playing the stock market – even, for some, their style of driving the car – are all ways in which we deliberately introduce extra stress into our lives and the spice of gambling with the unknown, and sometimes with death.

For each of us, though, there is probably an appropriate stress level, and if we go beyond that it becomes excessive and we feel we are going to crack under the strain. And the right stress level when we are in our twenties may prove too much in our fifties. Or we may be able to cope with and enjoy an entirely different kind of stress at different ages.

Hard work, though stressful, does not necessarily interfere with sex. It may bring a sense of achievement which boosts the ego and adds to the pleasure of sex. But sometimes work is used to avoid intimacy and to escape being deeply emotionally involved. Work may be used as an escape route like this because sex entails the pain of possible rejection and failure, and the person is too vulnerable, too exposed, to face this. Flinging yourself into hard work and doing something at which you know you can be successful means that you need not reveal that vulnerability.

Dealing with rejection

If you feel that you are being sexually rejected it may help to ask yourself if there is anything your partner could be finding threatening in the relationship. Is it, perhaps, that there is an unspoken fear of rejection by you, or of reaching a high enough standard? (This standard may not be one expected by you, but an entirely self-imposed one.) Think, too, of the times when *you* have drawn back from intimacy – not necessarily of a sexual nature – with another person and from revealing yourself completely, in case you might get hurt. Then ask yourself if there is any way in which you can give emotional support so that it becomes easier for your partner to develop confidence. Some reflection about this can provide a good basis for a couple to talk together about the feelings of rejection and failure which may be at the root of the difficulty. It may be important for one partner to be able to say to the other, "I feel under pressure to have sex and this is making it even more difficult for me to be spontaneous," or even to say, "I feel I can't start making love because you seem so glad and so grateful and I feel I owe it to you to go on and have intercourse, but it's not what I want at the moment." It can be important for the other partner, too, to say "You don't have to show me you love me by having an orgasm, but I do need physical contact, so touch me, cuddle me."

Sometimes this sense of failure intrudes into a relationship from outside because, for example, in the work place one or both partners are fighting losing battles, feeling "used" by their colleagues, or are engaged in unremitting work for which there is no achievement or personal reward, e.g. housework. The feeling that, whatever you do, you cannot be effective, and that no one values it can attack an individual's sense of self-worth and this, in turn, has a profound effect on sexuality.

But it is obviously not just a question of worries at work, but of any experience which leaves a person feeling completely humiliated – being unemployed, made redundant, or retiring and feeling that you are not needed by anyone can have this effect.

*Caring and
communication*

Erotic feelings are an integral part of our whole personalities. They flow most easily when we feel confident, secure, relaxed, and are quickly inhibited when we start to doubt ourselves and are insecure and tense. Masters and Johnson (*Human Sexual Inadequacy*) have written about the way in which critical observation of one's own sexual arousal and performance, presiding over sexual experience like a judge, destroys libido. They call it "spectatoring". In sex, self-doubt – fear of failure, analysis of one's own performance – tends to result in failure, which leads to a further erosion of confidence, and therefore a couple need to talk together about how they really feel and what each of them is seeking from the other.

Communication may not swing wide the flood gates of sexual passion, but it does open the way for tenderness, caring, loving recognition of the reality and uniqueness of the other person, and, as they let the tensions go and share and explore together, understanding takes the place of resentment and accusation.

Vaginal pain

Many women have times when they experience soreness and tenderness in the vagina. This can be due to passionate intercourse which bruises delicate tissues. In the early stages of a sexual relationship it may happen because of a partner's poor sexual technique or as a result of self-centred thrusting without regard to the woman's response. The treatment is obviously to sort out the relationship and be firm about what you want and do not want.

Vaginal tenderness or vaginitis is also often the result of a minor infection. Through the centuries women all over the world have developed their own healing treatment for the vagina. You may like to try one or other of these old herbal remedies before seeking medical help. They will not be enough if you have a severe condition, and if the cause of vaginitis could possibly be a sexually transmitted disease, see your doctor as soon as possible, because then you will definitely need an antibiotic.

*Herbal
treatments*

Herbal treatment should start to work within seven days or so of regular use.

For thrush (*candida*), in its early stages, natural yoghourt may be effective. It can be introduced with a tampon of the kind supplied inside a cardboard cylinder. Pull the tampon back a little way to create a space between the tampon and the top of the cylinder and pour the yoghourt into the space. Insert the tampon in the vagina and then withdraw the tampon, leaving the yoghourt in place. You can leave the tampon in for a while, but not for more than four hours or so, lest you run the risk of toxic shock resulting from infection. If a tampon is left in for too long, bacterial reaction creates toxins which are absorbed through the vaginal walls into the blood stream. Yoghourt can also be sucked into a bendy straw and then squeezed into the vagina by pressing the end of the straw.

Another remedy is a peeled clove of garlic wrapped in fine, sterile gauze (to get it out easily). It should be removed after four hours or so and replaced with a fresh one.

You can also bathe your vagina with a herbal solution and soak a sanitary pad in the same mixture so that it can be applied externally. A solution made from dried calendula (marigold) flowers is an old remedy. Steep a large breakfast cup full of calendula in a pint of boiling water for 15 minutes. Strain it and dilute with boiled water to make two pints. Store in a covered jar in the 'fridge.

If these home treatments are having no effect after a week's use, go to see your doctor. An antibiotic will probably be prescribed.

Post-menopausal vaginitis

Vaginal tenderness after the menopause results from the natural withdrawal of oestrogen once a woman's reproductive life is over. The vagina gets dry and intercourse becomes painful. Application of an oestrogen cream may prove useful in this case. Oestrogen cream has fewer side-effects than having hormone replacement therapy in the form of a pill but you will need to see your doctor for such a cream to be prescribed. You will probably not need to use it for a long period of time (see page 235), since the post-menopausal body is still producing testosterone which itself secretes oestrogen.

Finding the cause

Sometimes women experience pain in the vagina when there seems to be no obvious physical reason.

The first thing you should do if you are suffering pain in the vagina for no apparent reason is to consult a doctor so that you can have a swab test to find out if you have an infection. If you have an infection it can be treated with cream and pessaries and possibly an oral antibiotic as well.

If you are told that there is nothing wrong but you know yourself that there *is*, you may need to do a bit of detective work in order to track down the cause of the trouble. Start by keeping a record of times you notice the pain. Discovering when you get it can help you understand *why* you get it. For vaginitis can be a condition in which you are really expressing feelings of conflict.

One woman, for example, had severe vaginitis only at weekends when she was alone in her bed-sitter. Another noticed that it started in mid-afternoon before she left work to go home to a partner with whom she hated to have intercourse. Another knew that her mother strongly disapproved of her boyfriend and her vaginitis was so bad that she was physically unable to have intercourse. In her case the vaginitis went when she felt herself strong enough to refuse to lie to her mother about going on holiday with her lover.

Some psychotherapists believe that the most common reason for vaginitis is that a woman is angry with her male partner but is unwilling to face up to that anger. (Joan Woodward, "The diagnosis and treatment of psychosomatic vulvovaginitis") This anger often goes unrecognized. One woman who had had an incestuous relationship with her father was terribly afraid that if she conceived she might have a daughter who could, in turn, be incestuously involved with her father. It was not till she was able to talk through these fears that her vaginitis started to improve. A newly married woman who was feeling great resentment towards her husband said that she wanted to go home to her father where she felt "safe" After counselling she decided to talk to her husband about all the things that were upsetting her and they agreed to make love without penetration. Her vaginitis cleared up in a few months and they began to enjoy intercourse together.

It is not surprising that our minds affect our bodies. If you are experiencing vaginal pain and there is no organic reason for it, it is worth considering what your body is saying to you. You can either choose to continue with the symptom or you can find out *why* you are feeling like this. If you can locate the reason for your reaction it may then mean that you have to go on from there to confront a challenge in a relationship that needs changing. It can, of course, be very difficult to do, but this may be more effective than using creams or medicines in an attempt to eradicate the symptoms without understanding the cause.

Vaginism

Some of the conditions which are called sexual dysfunctions or abnormalities are simply a matter of a woman or man not liking certain sexual practices. We would not define people as suffering some eating abnormality if they did not like oysters or had to force themselves to eat them. To a certain extent this applies to sex.

Diagnosing a "dysfunction"

Vaginism is a spasm of the muscles around the vagina which makes intercourse painful or impossible. If you do not like oral sex no one is going to accuse you of having a sexual dysfunction. If you do not enjoy penetration, however, or if you like it only occasionally and usually prefer other ways of making love, you may be labelled by a doctor, marriage counsellor or psychotherapist as suffering from the clinical "condition" vaginism. You may be convinced yourself that there is something wrong with you.

Fear of penetration

A leading American sex therapist, Helen Singer Kaplan (*The New Sex Therapy: Active Treatment of Sexual Dysfunctions*, Chapter 20) says of vaginism:

Anatomically, the genitalia of a vaginistic woman are normal. However, whenever penetration is attempted, the vaginal introitus literally snaps shut so tightly that intercourse is impossible. . . . In addition to the primary spasm of the vaginal inlet, patients with vaginism are also usually phobic of coitus and vaginal penetration

What Helen Singer Kaplan is saying is that a so-called "vaginismic" woman does not want a penis inside her vagina and that if someone tries to force it inside her she contracts her vaginal muscles to "close up" her vagina. Doctor Kaplan goes on to say that:

Many women who seek treatment for vaginismus are sexually responsive. They may be orgastic on clitoral stimulation, enjoy sexual play, and seek sexual contact – as long as this does not lead to intercourse.

So there is a sexually responsive and active woman who has orgasms but who does not like penetration. This situation is seen as a "problem" only when the woman or her partner thinks that she *ought* to have penetration and that this is the whole goal of all

257

lovemaking. It is because sex is defined in such a way that a woman who does not enjoy this is called vaginismic.

Gynaecologists often make a diagnosis of vaginismus during the course of an internal examination. Masters and Johnson (*Human Sexual Inadequacy*, p. 251) describe the doctor's experience with a vaginismic woman:

The patient usually attempts to escape the examiner's approach by withdrawing towards the head of the table, even raising her legs from the stirrups, and/or constricting her thighs in the midline to avoid the implied threat of the impending vaginal examination.

Many women will be aware that they have had some symptoms of what doctors call vaginism during a pelvic examination. It is not pleasant to have cold metal objects pushed inside you by a strange doctor. Women who tighten their vaginal muscles in a reflex response in this situation may still be very happy to have fingers or a penis inside them during lovemaking. On the other hand, some women tense up during sex, too, and make it impossible for a man to penetrate. It sometimes happens that a woman remembers an unpleasant physical examination and fears that her lover's approach will be similar. Or intercourse may be attempted soon after childbirth when she is still sore from stitches or following a traumatic delivery which is still fresh in her mind.

Many women, in fact, let a man "get on with it" rather than protest and if their bodies respond in such a way that it is obvious that they do not enjoy penetration they may feel guilty and ashamed. Women sometimes surrender their bodies like this because they are conditioned to believe that men must never be frustrated lest they seek their pleasures elsewhere. They may sincerely believe that they want to be penetrated but find that their bodies are somehow betraying them. It is as if a loving human relationship between a man and woman depended entirely on showing each other that you enjoy eating oysters, but whenever you try to swallow an oyster you gag on it. However many other things you like, even though you are a veritable gourmet concerning other kinds of food, there must be something wrong with the relationship because you cannot swallow oysters.

Different theoretical approaches to vaginism

Women who believe they are suffering from what is defined as a sexual dysfunction often visit marriage guidance counsellors, doctors, psychiatrists, psychologists and other sex therapists in an effort to be "cured". These cures are sometimes effective – at a price. Sometimes vaginism is even treated by surgery. Helen Singer Kaplan tells how a patient came to her who had had a perineotomy (cutting open and enlarging the vagina) that she was told needed 75 stitches. Before the surgery she had been unable to have intercourse but enjoyed sex and had multiple orgasms with clitoral stimulation. After the operation she could have intercourse. But she was no longer capable of achieving orgasm and progressively lost all interest in any sexual activity at all, including the clitoral lovemaking she had enjoyed before.

Psychoanalytic therapy is based on the theory that the woman is unconsciously trying to castrate the man with her vaginal muscle because of penis envy. There is no evidence at all for this assumption. Though a woman may dislike her partner, or be angry because he has subjected her to repeated attempts to have intercourse when she doesn't want it, it is a long way from this to demonstrating that she has a deep, unconscious hatred of all men and is trying to get revenge on them because she feels castrated.

Desensitization and flooding

Behaviour therapists base their treatment on systematic desensitization. They get the woman to practise relaxation and then to imagine the painful situation, starting by thinking of a partner undressing only, then coming towards her, then getting into bed, then having an erection and so on, all the time staying relaxed. Once she can avoid tensing up in these imagined situations she is taught how to put graded plastic dilators inside her vagina beginning with slim ones and working up through bigger and bigger sizes.

Some therapists believe in "flooding". They ask the woman to imagine the most terrible thing that could ever happen and once she can stay relaxed whilst thinking of being aggressively penetrated by her partner's penis, she is considered on the way to recovery. Masters and Johnson and other sex therapists working on these lines involve the partner in the therapy from the beginning. They get him to put on rubber gloves and teach him how to do a pelvic examination and then how to insert dilators in the woman's vagina. Helen Singer Kaplan warns that

the fact that the wife has become physically capable of having intercourse does not carry with it the guarantee that she will automatically respond adequately to sexual stimulation; similarly, once the long-waited opportunity to have intercourse becomes a reality, the husband may experience potency or ejaculatory problems.

Helping yourself

If you find that your muscles contract involuntarily when your partner is about to penetrate, or even when you think about it, the first thing for you to do is to talk about it together and tell each other what you most enjoy in lovemaking. Because a man is very likely to enjoy penetration, it does not follow that a woman enjoys it. As discussed earlier, penetration is usually an ineffective form of lovemaking to stimulate the clitoris. There are many other better ways of doing this. They include the woman being able to rub against her partner's body or other firm surface, drawing up her knees and pressing her thighs together, or her partner using hands or tongue for direct clitoral stimulation.

Take time together to explore these ways of making love, using massage and whole body caressing, too, and avoiding any attempt at penetration. As you do so, talk about what pleases you.

Show your partner with your own fingers the kind of touch that excites you most. Suggest to him that he watches exactly what you do when you touch the vaginal lips and clitoris or stroke your buttocks or thighs. Then take his hand in yours and guide his fingers to do the same movements. His hand should move only where you put it.

When you feel you are ready for it, ask him to place both his hands anywhere on your body where they feel good. This might be your buttocks, the small of your back, the sides of your hips or your breasts, for example. Then show him how you can slide one finger into your vagina, curving it so that it slips in easily. When your finger is inside, suggest that he uses any form of stimulation which you enjoy very much. This might be sucking your nipples, licking your tummy, kissing or giving clitoral stimulation with a butterfly-like touch. As you get excited you will feel with your finger that the concertina-like lining of the vagina unfolds deep inside and that the innermost part opens and balloons out, while the part nearer the outside plumps up and gets hot and firm.

When you are assured of this spontaneous vaginal response, ask your partner to continue lovemaking by caressing other parts of your body. Keep your finger inside and you will probably become aware of the rhythmic contraction and release of the vaginal muscles as you become more and more excited. *At any point you can ask your partner to stop* and you should make a firm agreement about this beforehand. Or you can decide to return to an earlier exercise.

When your partner gets very excited, hold his penis and guide it to wherever he can be firmly clasped, but is not inside you. Hold him in your hands or nestle him between your thighs or feet, under your arm or between your breasts. You may feel you want to keep your own finger inside you whilst he reaches orgasm himself. Do whatever feels right for you at the time.

When you are able to enjoy this together, you can decide to go on from that and show him how he can slip his finger inside you, in exactly the same way as you did your own. You may find that there are certain movements he can make once his finger is inside which you find pleasurable. If so, tell him. It is as if you are the conductor and your partner waits patiently and accepts your guidance about what to do and exactly when to do it. Everything depends on this carefulness and sensitivity to your wishes. There is no need to hurry or to put on a demonstration of how it is working. Take it all in your own good time. The important thing at this stage is that he only does what you ask him to do, nothing else at all, and that you feel in control.

Once you are happy with this, suggest that he slides two fingers in very gently. You may like him to do this so that the palm of his hand is over your pubic mound and clitoris, or in such a way that he can caress your clitoris very delicately with his thumb. Do not attempt to have intercourse until you have reached this stage *and are enjoying it*. You must be the one to decide. Not every woman who does this, however systematically and carefully, and even though she accepts the *idea* of penetration and is sexually aroused, will enjoy the feeling of having her lover inside her.

You may discover that you always prefer lovemaking which does not involve penetration to conventional sexual intercourse. There is nothing wrong with you if you feel like this. Exploring different kinds of sensory awareness in lovemaking will help you be more flexible about what you do and will probably reveal new ways in which you can enjoy sex. But the important thing is that neither of you should feel constrained to engage in any sexual activities which you do not really like and that a loving relationship enables you to invent ways of giving each other pleasure in a mutually acceptable way. For each couple it is a journey of discovery.

To cope with difficulties a couple need to explore feelings at leisure.

Premature ejaculation

Any couple who agree that they would both like to prolong intercourse can learn how to extend the pre-ejaculation part of lovemaking from a few minutes to an hour or more.

Sometimes a man becomes so excited he ejaculates before his partner is ready for it. Like vaginism in women, this is often treated as if it were a pathological condition and is called premature ejaculation. But in most sexual relationships it is something that occurs from time to time and usually simply means that you could not both get into the same rhythm of arousal. It may happen when you are tired, have other things on your mind or are anxious.

The conventional view is that any ejaculation that occurs before a man has come inside a woman is "premature". But from another point of view, an ejaculation that occurs before a woman feels exactly ready for it, even if it is inside her, can be considered "premature". Perhaps the easiest way to define it is to say that premature ejaculation exists whenever a couple believe it does.

Both partners' reactions

There is a wide range of reactions to discovering that your partner has ejaculated before you were ready for him. Perhaps you feel he has been incompetent and cannot help resenting it; it can seem as if he has been using you merely as a sex object and spilling over you regardless of your feelings. If he ejaculates over your body or into your hair or face you may experience disgust, feel in a sticky mess and your one thought be to have a bath. Or your emotions may be quite different – the semen is like a lover's gift, the scent erotic, and, drying on your skin, still there to remind you when you wake from sleep of the passionate lovemaking before. Or you may feel that you have failed in some way because you were not sufficiently aroused to have an orgasm when he did. Or you might be rather pleased that you were so exciting he could not hold back.

In the same way, a man's reactions vary widely. He may apologize abjectly or imply that you are to blame because you are "frigid", may carry on making love as if nothing has happened, or may suddenly lose interest in you.

Many couples enjoy lovemaking even if the man ejaculates before the woman has an orgasm, because it does not affect their capacity to express delight in each other's bodies in other ways and he can stimulate her with his fingers or his mouth. If lovemaking were just a matter of an erect penis juxtaposed to a receptive vagina our sexual behaviour would be simpler, but much less interesting.

Some men are actually quite nervous of female sexuality and may feel in some way that they are going to be sexually attacked by the woman and required to demonstrate their virility. We often assume that men are insatiably sexual and demanding; historically in Western culture they are supposed to seek out conquests and be active and dominant, whereas women are passive, receptive and the compliant receivers of the semen forced on them by men. In fact, many men are far less confident than this and doubt their own sexual prowess or feel that a woman cannot really want them. A man may believe his penis too small, or his erection not big enough, or think that the woman is bound to be put off by his body when she actually looks at him naked. Feeling that he has to prove himself, he then may get so excited at having achieved erection and penetration that a bit of friction added to this provokes ejaculation.

If this happens frequently and you are disturbed by it there are a few things you can try.

Start/stop method

There is no need to engage in any elaborate psychotherapy. You are more likely to change ejaculatory behaviour by a very simple technique you can adopt yourselves. It is a carefully regulated start/stop method of lovemaking. Give yourselves three weeks or so to play things a different way and talk about the different techniques you try in an open and relaxed manner. Both of you stand to benefit from being able to spend longer in lovemaking.

The essence of achieving control is for you both to learn to recognize when a surge to orgasm begins and then to stop it before it reaches a crescendo. Wait a little and when control has been achieved, pick up the lovemaking where you left off, but observe closely and as soon as the next wave of excitement starts, stop again and allow a pause before beginning stimulation. Your aim is to find the same place together in the "sexual dance".

Some couples run into difficulties with this method. Lying still and not touching each other may avoid premature ejaculation but the problem is that being careful not to move or seem aroused in case the other partner gets overexcited is sexually depressing. There is another method: the squeeze technique.

The squeeze

This is a method which can be exciting for the woman at the same time as it delays the man's ejaculation, perhaps because of feeling the thrill of power to control his sex.

When he begins to get too excited, hold his penis very firmly with two fingers and a thumb near the top where there is a hard bulge all round, with your thumb pressing on the underside of the penis. If you hold him lightly it will stimulate him further. It has to be a firm grip. Your hand is bigger than the area of the ridge, of course, but that does not matter. Just squeeze quite hard, keeping your hand still. Three or four seconds is long enough.

You will be aware that his excitement comes under control. His penis may be a little less rigid and throbbing, his breathing easier and he will look more relaxed generally. He may lose up to 30 per cent of his erection. Then take your hand away. You can do this any number of times during lovemaking. Masters and Johnson devised this technique as a variation of the start/stop method of treatment and claim that, from their experiments, it is almost 100 per cent effective. (*Human Sexual Inadequacy*)

Using the squeeze enables you to show your partner that you are not a predatory, demanding woman before whom he has to demonstrate his virility; or that he has to live up to some "macho" image of masculinity which has been inculcated in him as he grew up; he can allow an erection to subside, and it will come back again. He learns that you love to tease his penis and that it is responsive to you in a much more subtle way than simply going hard because he is pressing against your body. And together you develop a delicate control which adds new flair to lovemaking.

9 SEX AND POWER

Sexual harassment

"Sexual harassment" is a term which has little meaning for many women. In fact, many say they have never experienced any, but then add things like: "Only the usual bottom pinching and sexual innuendo in the office", or something about men brushing up against them in crowds. Some think that harassment means attempted rape, and that nothing else qualifies.

It is impossible for a woman to live in Western society without encountering harassment, even if it is only what Margaret Atwood has described as the looks on strange men's faces "from truck-cab windows and construction sites; a speculative look, like a dog eyeing a fire hydrant." (*Lady Oracle*)

Harassment as threat

We stand waiting for a tube surrounded by posters depicting female crotches, cleavages and thighs, parts of our own bodies detached, packaged and presented in order to titillate and so sell a product. A woman walking without a man on the street is leered at by men who look her body up and down as if it were theirs for the taking. Sex may be used in the work place as a condition for a woman's advancement. From adolescence on, most of us have to run the gauntlet of harassment in our everyday lives. The words used – "wolf whistles", "being touched-up", "flashing" – often sound quite jolly, redolent of Nell Gwynn and "Merrie England" and Restoration comedy, with plump breasts falling out of corsages, lecherous dandies and assignations in the rose arbour. The reality behind the words is a good deal uglier. Take "flasher", for example. Though the term sounds fairly innocuous, and flashers are often excused as being merely inadequate personalities, a woman only realizes that an incident was "flashing" in *retrospect*. Afterwards she can breathe a sigh of relief and give way to anger – but not at the time. At the time it *could* mean rape.

Harassment as "approval"

Harassment of any kind carries with it the implication that a woman – any woman – exists only for male sexual pleasure, that she is a female object, not a person – and ultimately has no rights over her own body. Yet some women clearly *enjoy* it. They feel that they do not really exist as individuals unless they can see from men's faces that they are appreciated. They get a kick out of being whistled at and the knowledge that they are whipping up a bit of sexual excitement.

Some get so accustomed to it that they miss it when it is withdrawn. In advanced pregnancy a woman sometimes says she feels a loss of value when a man comes up with that appraising look in his eyes and then looks away rapidly as he sees the swollen curve of her abdomen: "Pregnancy has no place in the sexuality that pervades everything. Once you are pregnant you are 'obviously another man's property' and rape – physical or verbal – has so much to do with the threat of impregnating the innocent, the vulnerable, or with punishment for being available – and I'm not. So for a long time I have been free from sexual innuendos, grabs at my tits, attempted pick-ups. Men who walk up to me turn away from my womb with a mixture of guilt, fear and disgust on their faces. Strangely, once I was no longer bombarded with sexual advances, it struck me how in one way it gave me a sense of power, of attractiveness, and more importantly, a sense that I existed." (Tessa Weare, "Round in a flat world", *Spare Rib*)

Exerting power

Why do many men harass women? It is obviously not intended to arouse us sexually. It gets a glance, perhaps a giggle, and often evokes a response of embarrassment or outright fear. This is its function – to provoke fear or submission. The issue is one of power. The boy who calls out something suggestive as a girl passes by does so because he wants to show his peers in the group lounging on the street corner that he can evoke a response in a woman. It is an exercise in power, not only over her but *vis à vis* the other youths.

Coping with sexual harassment

1 *On the street*

The most difficult thing can be not so much coping with the harasser as with your own feelings about what is happening. Shula was on a tube late at night when a man sitting opposite her exposed himself and started to masturbate: "I was very frightened and for some time after felt that all men were in the same plot to 'get at' me. I also felt rather ashamed of myself – I was a serving police-woman at the time (not in uniform, of course) and I felt I should have done something heroic, or at least laughed it off. However, I felt violated and dirty somehow in that I knew I had been a part of this man's fantasy. This feeling of having been affronted and invaded is what I remember most."

A woman may blame herself for attracting the man's attention in the first place and ask herself "What have I done?" She may worry that she is making a fuss about nothing, or be paralysed with fury. Much of the anger that boils up may, in fact, be inturned against yourself and you feel sick or emotionally drained for hours after. It is important to develop techniques for handling these situations.

Some women find that drawing attention to what is happening in no uncertain terms is enough to scare off a persecutor. It is often difficult to summon up the courage to do this but it is probably the most effective thing you can do. If a man is following you, for example, you can shout loudly: "Stop following me! Leave me alone! Go away!" But, however angry you feel, it is *not* a good idea to explode into bad language. One young woman who did this was grabbed by the man who was hovering around her making obscene suggestions, and told off for being unladylike!

2 In education

Mothers are often not aware that their daughters may be subjected to harassment from primary school on. It goes by the term "teasing". Horse-play often occurs around the lavatories: "The loos were separate from the main classroom blocks. The game was for little boys to invade the girls' loos and to drag girls into the boys' loos where they could show them their 'things'."

Parents are unlikely to be able to stop this behaviour entirely. But they can acknowledge what is happening and the confused feelings it arouses in the child. A mother can validate a girl's half-expressed anger about it by saying, "Yes, I expect you feel very cross about that." The tendency for us is to dismiss it by saying, "They'll grow out of it", or "They're only being silly little boys." This makes it difficult for a girl to face up to her feelings of anxiety, fear or anger. You could also get together with other parents, including those of the boys concerned – perhaps through the PTA – to see if there is anything you can do about it. Parents are often unaware that their sons are involved in this sort of thing.

In secondary schools boys harass girls at a stage in their lives when the girls feel self-conscious about their changing bodies. A girl discovered, for example, that boys had stolen a packet of tampons from her desk and had festooned her study with them. Girls try to change for games with boys tapping at the windows or peering through frosted glass.

Male teachers are sometimes unaware that they are harassing girls by resorting to sexual innuendo and smutty jokes either to be "trendy" and gain acceptance from the boys or in a misguided attempt to break down the barrier between teacher and taught.

All this may seriously affect a girl's capacity to concentrate on her studies, too. The sharp fall in academic performance at this time and the frequency of anorexia may sometimes be symptoms of the harassment that girls endure during adolescence.

A mother can point out to a daughter of this age that what she is experiencing has a name: sexual harassment. Offering her the phrase and linking it with adult experience may help her cope.

Teenage girls may also want to talk with other girls about what is happening. It takes courage to do this, but if they do so they can share their experiences and present a united front to the boys.

A girl who goes on to further education usually enters predominantly male territory. Though there may be as many female as male students, there are few female staff at the top.

Boys and girls are often seen as having very different motivations for going on to polytechnic or university in the first place. Whereas boys go to study for a career, girls are still thought of as preparing for a job before they find a good husband and in order to have "something to fall back on". Whereas for boys college is seen as the first step on a career ladder, for girls it is often seen as almost a holiday interlude before entering into marriage and motherhood.

If you are going to college you need to sort out your priorities beforehand. Exactly how important is it for you to get a good qualification and how much do you want to have a vigorous social life? Here is how one woman worked out how to be self-assertive about her priorities:

She was determined to get her work done as well as enjoy being with her boyfriend: "I told John that it wasn't fair to expect me to be free whenever he was available and to fit into his working time-table. I had to sort out how much time I wanted to spend on work and how much with him. I got him to sit with me and discuss it, though he was very resistant at first. When he saw I was serious he agreed. I think a girl may have to show her boyfriend that she takes her work as seriously as he does his own. John used to drop in for meals for example and I enjoyed making them but it took ages and it was always me who did the shopping. So we had to agree that it was one evening at my place and I'd cook and another evening in the week he'd be responsible for the meal. Of course, the answer was that he usually took me out, so he didn't have any work."

Some male tutors make sexual advances to women students. The student is often flattered by the attentions of a man who is, or appears to be, a brilliant academic. The tutor, for his part, sees sex with female students as a fringe benefit. Perhaps it also offers one way of hanging on to youth. For though an academic ages, students are always 18 and some women think sex with a tutor will help their work. Occasionally this is so, but it is more likely to detract from it: "Ken had a different girl every year. Always first year students. He was no longer interested in them by the second. At the time every girl thought she was the special and only one. He was married, of course. You can imagine him doing this for twenty or thirty years as long as he could get away with it. He didn't intend to leave his wife. I suppose he stood a fair chance of getting virgins if he picked them carefully. I think that's what he fancied."

These women also have practical suggestions to cope with men's unwelcome attentions. Most colleges have women's groups now and you can join or, if it does not exist, start one. This is a good basis for collectively putting pressure on university authorities to make the campus a safe place for women against the unwelcome attentions of prowlers. There should be locks on all windows and all paths should be well lit. Disabled women are particularly vulnerable because they are usually in ground floor rooms. They also often have to go a longer way round to get to places, sometimes along inadequately lit foot paths.

3 At work

The Pennsylvania Commission for Women defines harassment as "any repeated and unwanted sexual advance, ranging from looks, innuendoes, verbal offers, threats, to actual physical contact or coition . . . It may be implied or requested or demanded; it may come from a direct confrontation or from the persistent undertone . . . (*Not for Fun, Not for Profit: Strategies for ending sexual harassment on the job*, Helen Seager, Pennsylvania Commission for Women 1981) It is quite distinct from mutual flirtation in that it is a one-sided and unwelcome attention and the "victim does not have the power to end the harassment".

Research shows that women most likely to be subjected to this behaviour are in low status and service jobs: low level clerical jobs, factory operatives, waitresses – and also air hostesses. It is usually the most economically vulnerable women who are most harassed, particularly those with few skills and little chance of getting another job, women recently divorced and those supporting young children. Though some women hope that "laughing it off" will stop harassment, you cannot rely on this working. It may, in fact, encourage a man to offer more of the same to get a further reaction.

Women need to learn survival skills to cope with harassment. The most important element in coping is that you feel you have the *right* to object. Ignoring behaviour like this is not enough to show your disapproval of it and is often interpreted as a licence to continue. You do not need to apologize for what you are saying, nor to smile while you express your objections to the behaviour. If you *do* smile, you may cancel out the force of what you are saying. We all tend to smile in a placatory way in these situations and it needs a good deal of determination not to do so.

If your harasser continues unchecked, find out if other women have experienced the same treatment. Do not expect their support. They may say, "Yes, but it's a bit of a giggle" or "Don't take it so seriously. He doesn't mean any harm." On the other hand, victims are often harassed in isolation and do not realize that other women are subjected to the same behaviour.

If you are being really bothered by continual harassment it may also be a good idea to keep a diary. Record carefully when the harassment occurs and what it is. Write down how you felt at the time. If you were under psychological stress and it affected your behaviour, or your ability to concentrate at work, record this. You may need this evidence later if the harassment is investigated, so it is important to be specific. Concentrate on working well and keep any records that you can as evidence of your good work.

4 *In the home*

Home may seem a haven of security compared with these other places. But sexual harassment does occur there. Children may be molested or raped by relatives and adult women sexually abused by the men with whom they live.

Most incidents of sexual harassment in the home are far less damaging but nevertheless can be a source of irritation. The behaviour and remarks made by service engineers and visiting tradesmen is sometimes offensive. A woman says: "The plaster came down and a man came to repair it. It was a huge hole and I offered him tea and said that it looked like a difficult job. He leered at me, winked and said, 'I *like* filling holes'."

If you find a workman's behaviour objectionable, write to the company stating this and saying exactly why. Keep a copy of your letter and if you do not receive a reply write to the Managing Director. In large cities it may be possible to ask a firm specifically to send a woman worker. Not many women are employed to do plumbing, decorating or electrical repairs, but increasing numbers are going into this sort of work and in some cities there are women-only firms. Your local Women's Centre will be able to tell you about them.

The telephone offers another means of access to the home for men
who want to frighten women. It is sometimes claimed that we
should feel sorry for men who make obscene phone calls because
they are frustrated and unhappy.

A telephone counselling agency at one time catered for such men
by providing the "Brenda" service. A man wanting to make an
obscene call could ask to speak to Brenda while he masturbated. A
woman working with another counselling agency says: "The men
who phoned sometimes expected me to do this and were surprised
when I told them I was there to help with serious problems. I said
that while they were on the phone somebody else who was in
distress might not be able to get through. They saw it as their *right* to
have me talk to them while they jerked off. When I objected they
sometimes claimed they were paraplegics in wheelchairs or something like that and that their balls were turning blue. It made me
feel I was being treated like a prostitute." This service allowed men
to see obscene phone calls as legitimate sexual expression.

It is a frightening experience to get obscene calls if you are alone
in the house. You may not realize at first that it *is* an obscene call
and keep listening because you cannot actually believe what he is
saying and do not want to be rude. When you do realize what is
happening and have slammed the phone down there is the additional fear that he may come to the door, since he obviously can get
the address from the telephone directory. If you have children you
may be anxious that a child could answer the phone.

To prevent obscene calls, do not put your first name in the
directory or any title that indicates your gender. If you get an
obscene call you can arrange to have calls intercepted for a time,
but if it persists you can get your number changed.

In the meantime, if you are dealing with a persistent caller, you
can keep a whistle by the phone and send a shrill blast straight into
his ear. Liz Stanley and Sue Wise (speaking to the British Sociologi-
cal Conference, April 1982) found that the most effective method
is to pretend that the line is very bad and you cannot hear what he is
saying: "You've got a twelve-inch *what*? I'm sorry, this is a terribly
bad line." They say that the man often decides to ring off and when
he puts down the receiver the woman feels that she has defined the
situation and gained the upper hand.

Sexual assault

Far from being just to do with what happens in our private lives sex
is a political matter. Heterosexual relations are commonly the
expression of social inequalities of power.

Sexual abuse of children

Most women can remember an incident in childhood when they
suddenly became aware of male sexuality in a negative way. The
most common of these vignettes of male sex is a man exposing
himself. The girl sees male sex as nothing to do with kisses and
cuddles and fondness, but possession of an organ that a man sticks
out of his trousers and tends and does strange things to as if it were a

puppy dog or other pet. Little boys expose themselves, too, of course. I remember one when I was in nursery class who showed off his "little thing" under the table. Though some girls were admiring and curious, my friend Sybil and I both had brothers and were scathing in our denunciation of this exhibitionism.

It is quite a different experience for a little girl to come upon a man masturbating in a dark doorway or country lane. One woman remembers: "There was something pink there. It was stiff and he was holding it. I thought he'd hurt his hand." Looking back on it the man concerned may seem merely pathetic and the whole scene mildly funny. But for some girls it is a traumatic experience and may leave an emotional scar. One, for example, describes how when she was six a man exposed himself as she was on her way home from school. It was not until she was an adult and looked at the sex of her newborn son that she suddenly remembered the incident, and it forced its way into her mind in the form of a recurrent nightmare. Seventeen months later, though the dreams have stopped, she says she cannot bear her husband to wear pyjamas lest he is "sticking out at me like a dirty old man". Many girls never reveal to their parents what has happened. They say that they did not tell their mothers because they knew it was "dirty" and it seemed as if they had been contaminated by the dirt. *They* felt guilty. This is one expression of a much more general pattern in which women feel responsible for arousing male sexuality.

When a child does tell a parent about such an occurrence the response seals the flavour of the whole incident when it is remembered. In our society the girl child is often held obscurely responsible for what has happened. Especially if the girl is on the threshold of puberty she may be seen by adults as a budding Lolita who breaks down men's control so that they cannot really be blamed for whatever ensues. One of the most striking aspects of women's descriptions of these experiences as children is the sense of humiliation they feel simply because of being female. This emerges clearly in Frances's account of a sexual assault when she was riding her bike along a country footpath at the age of 10. She had just started her first period and was wearing what she calls "an awful sanitary pad". A man appeared from some bushes and "after a friendly chat put his hand up my skirt and fiddled about, especially with my anus. He told me there was no point in screaming. No one would hear me. By some miracle I struggled free and pedalled home as fast as I could." She says she was "terribly frightened and humiliated *because of the period and pad*". Unfortunately when the police are contacted it often sets in motion a train of events which means more trauma for the child. In Frances's case her parents saw that she was distressed and after hearing what had happened called the police and "I had the further humiliation of being examined by a policewoman and reporting all the details."

Many women say they never talked about these incidents until they spoke to me. Sometimes 20 years or more have passed. Often they had apparently forgotten what had happened but as they talked the intense emotions experienced at the time came back with a rush. Susan, for example, remembered that a friend of the family "kept putting my hand on his penis and one night carried me to bed", where he managed partial penetration and ejaculated all over her. She is now married but the sexual relationship is far from happy. She is not able to experience orgasm and is unwilling to masturbate because it is "disgusting". She adds, "I have no desire to touch myself except when I am washing." And this attitude has spilled over into mothering, too. Midwives at the hospitals persuaded her to start breast-feeding her baby, but she stopped at six weeks because she found the whole experience embarrassing.

Women are often so ashamed that they do not talk about these things with other women, either. They try to push them to the back of their minds and pretend they have never happened. Yet they may colour a subsequent sexual relationship in a way which, because it is not acknowledged, produces confusion and distress.

Incest

Incest is not just something that happens in the Appalachians or on Otmoor, a weird but anthropologically fascinating practice. The numbers of reported cases of incest suggest that one in every 20 girls may have been sexually abused as children. Incest occurs in educated middle-class families, not only in slum conditions among the poor and illiterate. The offender is usually a girl's father or stepfather. Up to a quarter of cases of incest probably occur with little girls *under the age of five* (R. and C. H. Kempe, *Child Abuse*) and victims are most likely to be around 10 or 11 years old. (V. de Francis, *Protecting the Child Victim of Sex Crimes Committed by Adults*) The men tend to be in their late twenties. (A. Jaffe, L. Dynneson *et al.*, "Sexual abuse of children: an epidemiological study") Kinsey revealed that almost a quarter of the white, middle-class children in his study said they had sexual experiences with adult men in childhood. Six per cent of these were with a relative. (A. Kinsey *et al.*, *Sexual Behaviour in the Human Female*)

Attitudes to incest

There is a lot of muddled thinking about incest and confusion about what to do about it, if anything. Some people think it should be left well alone and that intervention can do more harm than good. They claim that the consequences of trying to deal with an incestuous relationship, punishing the man and separating the child from him, are a good deal worse than quietly letting it continue. L. Schultz ("The child sex victim, social, psychological and legal perspectives") believes it is not the assault that causes trauma, but the parents' behaviour upon discovery: "In most cases sexual trauma, unless reinforced by court testifying or parental over-reaction, produces few permanent consequences."

There is strong evidence that the way the mother reacts to what has happened and her attitude to her daughter can have longterm consequences. It is difficult to isolate the different strands in what is a complicated emotional situation, but when a mother rejects her daughter for making what she considers must be a false accusation against her father, it is not surprising that the girl may feel "dirty" and ashamed for a long time after. When she had been sexually molested by her father, at the age of 13, Karen wrote to a women's magazine asking for advice. The magazine passed the letter to the police who arrived on the doorstep. Her mother accused Karen o "breaking up the family" and of being "mad": "Her attitude was, 'You shit. Look what you've done to this family. Dad could go to jail.'" Karen says she was "terrified and confused". Her parents often had dreadful fights: "Every time they rowed it seemed to be about me or directed at me." Eighteen years later Karen has just felt able to tell her husband about what happened and has started to get therapy for her psycho-sexual problems and depression. Because of their concern that the consequences of doing something about incest can be worse than the incest itself, social workers and others may be slow to take action. Sarah Nelson, in her succinct and important analysis, *Incest: Fact and Myth*, asserts that, "either incest is damaging and undesirable, or it is not. If professionals take the first view they should work to surmount the barriers to having it reported and stopped, not simply collapse in front of them." Freud believed that girls fantasized about incest with their fathers. It didn't really happen, or not very often. Since he found it impossible to believe that "perverted acts against children were so general" "Letter to Wilhelm Fliess", he concluded that these were fantasies. As a result many girls have been disbelieved when they have been victims of incest. One girl who was questioned by police admitted in the end, "Perhaps I dreamt it." Looking back at this from the vantage point of many years she says, "Of course I didn't. But if it was not *possible* for it to have happened – and that's what everyone said – what else could it be? So I said I made it up. It was the only way I could get out of it."

Explanations of the causes

Incest is sometimes explained and the man exonerated by reference to a little girl's "seductiveness". Schultz claims that the child and the offender form a "co-operative dyad" (L. Schultz, as above). Adele turns to daddy for a cuddle and it accidentally turns into intercourse because the child is so highly sexed. It is she, by implication, who is really responsible:

These children undoubtedly do not deserve completely the cloak of innocence with which they have been endowed by moralists, social reformers and legislators. . . . [They were] charming and attractive in their outward personalities. . . . The child might have been the actual seducer rather than the one innocently seduced. (L. Bender and A. Blau, "The reaction of children to sexual relations with adults")

In fact, as Sarah Nelson points out, children are often given treats, sweets, money, a ride in the country or the chance to stay up late. A man who does this must be fully aware that the girl is a child. We should not absolve adults from responsibility for children.

In our society little girls are often coaxed into being "feminine" and flirtatious and rewarded for it. People laugh at their winning ways and say a child can "twist her father round her little finger". We put girls under pressure when we condition them to be submissive, charming and winsome but at the same time expect them to be able to cope with male adult sexuality.

Sandra, looking back at the age of 31 to the experience of being sexually molested in her home as a child, says: "Ever since I was five I was branded a sex-pot. Mum always said it about me. When I went to school the kids wrote rude notes to each other, pictures of men

273

with large penises urinating and they always ended up in my cupboard because I didn't have the wit to know I should get rid of them. The teacher hauled me up and complained to my parents. From then on I was the guilty one. I was branded as over-sexed. So whatever happened to me was *my fault*."

Children are understandably curious about sex. Many of them soon learn that it is something to be discussed in dark corners, a source of smutty jokes, and such an exciting topic for everyone that they can draw admiring or shocked attention to themselves from other children by being able to show they have some special "inside" knowledge. But the fact that a child is curious about sex and highly motivated to find out more, or that she is cuddly, adores her father and will always do anything that he asks, are inadequate excuses for her sexual exploitation by an adult. It is also often asserted that ultimately the mother is responsible. She is too dependent or too independent, promiscuous or frigid. She is unable to have any mature, affectionate relationship with either her husband or her daughter because she has "emotionally abandoned the family" who are forced "to seek emotional refuge with each other". (S. Forward and C. Buck, *The Trial of Innocence: Incest and its Devastation*) She goes out in the evenings and at weekends, takes a job or plays bingo. "She keeps herself tired and worn out. This is an open invitation to the daughter to take over." (B. Justice and R. Justice, *The Broken Taboo: Sex in the Family*)

Many researchers claim that mothers collude over incest, either abdicating the responsibility, or pushing their daughters into it because they are hostile to them, identifying with them and making their daughters live out their own incestuous fantasies with their fathers. This seems to be part of a general tendency to blame mothers for everything that goes wrong with their children and some of the arguments are very far-fetched. But it may be important to realize that for some women the only power they have is the power to "shop" a man whom they know, or suspect, is in an incestuous relationship. Approximately three-quarters of all mothers in families in which incest is known to have been committed are themselves physically abused by their partners. (C. Dietz and J. Craft, "Family dynamics of incest: a new perspective") The "profile" of an incest family is similar to that of the family of a battered wife. Both mother and daughter are victims of male violence. Perhaps social workers appear to blame mothers because they feel so frustrated about the whole awful set-up.

The damage

Sarah Nelson is highly critical of professionals who allow incest to happen, or even condone it, because the family is sacrosanct and they think they should not do anything to interfere with it. She claims that they implicitly accept the belief that men cannot help what they do because they are naturally highly sexed and aggressive and have urgent needs that must be gratified with whoever is at hand. Women, in contrast, are stereotyped as masochistic by nature. We ask to be battered. We enjoy having violent things done to us. We like to see a daughter sexually abused by her father (Erin Pizzey and Geff Shapiro, *Prone to Violence*) Ros Coward, in an intellectually sharp and very caring critique of Erin Pizzey's view that women in violent relationships are addicted to pain because of their own violent childhoods, says: (*Guardian*, 21 November 1982)

... when we return again and again to destructive relationships, be they physically violent or just emotionally undermining, it is not the expression of a defeated and masochistic personality but perhaps the desire to return and work over contradictory and conflicting feelings. Perhaps it is a feeling that somehow, this time, something can be ... changed.

We need to rethink relationships in the family, and especially the role of women. Sarah Nelson believes that incest, like wife-beating, is most likely to happen not when the family system has broken down or is irretrievably damaged or sick, but when *tradition-al* ideas are taken to extremes – "when the family members are seen as the husband's property, and sex is among the services they are expected to provide." (Sarah Nelson, *Incest, Fact and Myth*)

Helping a victim

If you know a girl who needs help it will probably be very difficult to decide what you should do. If this is happening to your daughter, you may want to go to your doctor to talk about it or to a social worker. Some family doctors are very understanding. Others feel completely out of their depth. And many people have a GP who does not really know the family. If you ring up the Children's Office they will arrange for you to see a social worker who is usually very sympathetic. The important thing is that you contact *someone*. You need a chance to talk about how you feel and what to do about it. And the child needs someone with whom to talk who is not directly emotionally involved. Support for incest survivors is often vague and uncoordinated. Professionals disagree about whether a man ought to be put in prison or hospital, removed from the home or psychoanalysed. The central issue ought to be how best to protect and help *the child* in each particular situation.

The Mother Courage Press have published a book for girls, *Something Happened to Me* by Phyllis E. Sweet, to help reduce a child's feeling of shame, fear and confusion. This is what the authors tell the girl:

If something bad happens to you, don't think you are the only one or that something is wrong with you. Tell someone so that they can try to help you, so that you can talk and not feel so scared and alone.

If a child does tell you anything which suggests sexual abuse, avoid over-reacting – but acknowledge the pain and confusion just as if she was telling you about having been badly hurt in any other way. There are some organizations listed on pages 312–13, that may be able to help you.

Rape

Sex with violence is a common experience for women. The man who assaults a woman is rarely a stranger. He is more likely to be a member of the family, the husband of a friend or her own boyfriend. Of the women who have told me about their experiences of being raped, one in three were subjected to sexual assault as children, often by a relative or a close friend of the family, a grandfather, older brother, uncle or, particularly, a stepfather.

By a family member

Within the family network a man may be able to seduce a young girl without much difficulty. Physical violence may not be involved. One woman says she was "talked into sex" by an "uncle", a close friend of her mother's, at 14. "I liked being kissed, cuddled and stroked. I didn't like him touching my vulva – it hurt – but I pretended to like it. I suddenly realized that he was *old* and *smelly* and had rolls of fat, and there he was chug-a-chug inside me."

About half the women who told me about being raped as adults were assaulted by their own sexual partners. Rape by one's husband is not a legal offence and is, therefore, rarely reported to the authorities. Kim, for example, said, "My husband is sometimes aggressive if I refuse too often. The last time he caused a haematoma (blood clot) at the base of my skull." (These and the other accounts in this section were coincidental to more general discussion about sex with a group of women who were not specially selected for having experienced sexual violence.)

Some women expect to be raped whenever their husbands come home drunk and there is a regular pattern of being knocked about and then sexually assaulted. The incidence of marital rape may be far higher than women describing their sexual experiences to me have reported, because they are often not sure whether being forced to have intercourse with one's husband is anything out-of-the-ordinary or something to which they have a right to object.

Women who are assaulted by members of the family rarely report rape. In fact, *none* of those who shared their experiences with me who had been assaulted by brothers, uncles or fathers ever told the police, and most of them say they never told anyone else, not even – or especially not – their mothers.

Attitudes to rape

Rape is only indirectly related to uncontrollable sexual feelings. It is above all an act of violence and does not result simply from an over-spill of lust, as is often thought. It is to do with power over a defenceless victim. It is sometimes claimed that rapists must be psychologically disturbed and that no normal man would behave that way. Yet most rapists are not psychopaths. In any prison population they seem to be among the most "ordinary". In the public imagination the rapist is often considered not really responsible for what he was doing because he was sexually aroused. Men, it is implied, cannot "help it" when they are excited. Some men believe that it is impossible to rape a woman unless she is willing to co-operate. They think that, however shocked and injured a woman is, basically she gets a thrill from being raped.

Women are often held partly responsible for what happens, because they have dressed in a way to make a man lose his self-control, have behaved indiscreetly, have teased or flirted with him. In a famous legal case in 1982, a woman who had accepted a lift in a car was held guilty of "contributory negligence". It may also be suggested that she must have invited rape because she was drinking, walking alone, had not locked the doors beforehand or had been seen talking to the man who later raped her. In this way a burden of guilt is placed on the victim of rape that she has contributed to or, in some unconscious way, even *wanted* it. Just being a woman can be construed as provocative.

Fact and fantasy

Women themselves sometimes harbour the feeling that they might enjoy being raped. It would be evidence, perhaps, that they are irresistibly attractive to men. When talking about their fantasies, as we see on pages 83–5, women often describe rape, but hasten to point out that they would not enjoy it in practice, or add a note to the effect that it would be rape "with love", so that it would never cause pain. They are not, in fact, talking about rape at all, but about an erotic confrontation which is morally permitted because they are overpowered, a sexual encounter from which they are absolved from responsibility. The fantasy of being forced to have pleasure is one way of dealing with guilt about sex.

Rape, as distinct from fantasies of being forced to have an erotic experience, is violence, just as much as being knifed, and often involves other forms of violence. Rapists frequently batter the woman, cut her up or gnaw and bite her. One woman talking to me about her experience of rape at the age of four mentioned that the man had bitten off her nipples, which a surgeon had then sutured too low on her body so that as an adult they are now on the undersides of her breasts. (Her boyfriend calls her "floppy tits".)

My fault?

Once a woman is known to have been raped she may be considered "fair game" by other men. One who was raped by several boys in her teens says that this occurred after she had been forced into a back alley by a youth when she was 10 years old and raped. She had been too frightened to tell anyone about this, but he had boasted of it to the other boys and they in turn "availed themselves" of her. The dominant and pervasive feeling a woman has after being raped is of being "dirty". She may be numb with shock, in a state of terror, and afraid not only of the man who raped her but of *all* men. She often feels ashamed, as if she herself has somehow caused the rape. She has become someone different, both in her own eyes and in the eyes of others who know about it: a rape victim.

The woman who has been raped cannot always even expect sympathy from women friends, especially if the man was a relative or close friend of theirs. They are likely to think of a rapist as a kind of maniac and cannot comprehend that a brother, son or husband could commit rape. Because they feel embarrassed friends may also avoid her as if she had some highly contagious disease.

Yet she needs the support and understanding of other women. And often, too, a place of sanctuary where she can get completely away from men.

There are powerful forces in society which tell us as women who we are. So persuasive is the constant and insidious pressure of that view of women that we tend to evaluate ourselves in those terms, too. And when a man touches us up in a crowded place, or exposes himself, when we get an obscene phone call or are trapped, threatened at knife point and raped – the ultimate extension of all these other acts of sexual violence – we tend to blame ourselves and to ask, "What have *I* done?"

Getting help

If you have been through the experience of rape and need help and counsel, or know another woman who does, contact one of the Rape Crisis Centres listed at the end of this book.

277

Pornography

Pornography does not only cause violence. It *is* violence.

Film titles suggest the sadistic nature of much of what is offered: *Angels in Pain*, *Love Gestapo-Style* and *Slave Girl*, for instance. Photographs show a woman slicing her breast with a knife and smiling as she does so, or inserting a sword into her vagina – and still smiling. Not only is pornography the "celebration of male power over women" (Diana E. H. Russell, *Lorna Lederer Take Back the Night*), it is also a kind of sexual terrorism.

Arguments in favour

The case *for* pornography may seem strong. It has its supporters not only from a wide range of men of different social classes and educational backgrounds, but also among women and male and female members of the medical profession. Some believe that nothing should be done to restrict it because in a free society adults should have a choice about what they read or watch.

If we are opposed to censorship and restrictive and puritanical attitudes we may ask, "If they are only looking at pictures, what does it matter?" Men often believe that a little bit of pornography "never hurt anyone", recalling their own first encounters with porn behind the bicycle sheds at school with fond nostalgia.

Some sex therapists and psychiatrists claim that pornography "therapy" is useful in treating sexual dysfunctions. One therapist, Patricia Gillan, advises GPs to have soft porn around in their waiting-rooms so that male patients can receive "treatment" even before they go in to see the doctor. The Maudsley sex clinic has a list of recommended pornographic films and videos for "stimulative therapy". Dr Gillan shows stills from the *Story of O*, depicting a woman tied up and beaten, as part of a cure for impotence. But any cure that makes men potent at the price of using women as impersonal sex objects should be questioned. Potency is less important than being able to relate to women as human beings.

Arguments against

Pornography treats women's bodies as packages of anatomical parts, rather like cuts of meat arranged on a butcher's slab.

Some defenders of pornography protest that women are free to consent or refuse to model sex scenes and that we should not limit their freedom to choose any kind of employment they like. They do not realize that women and young children are often coerced to take part in pornography. This industry is closely linked with hard drugs and much of it is under the control of organized crime. Girls are sometimes sold by their parents to take part in pornographic films and pornographers may use their own children in this way. Horrific things are done to make pornographic pictures and films. A woman may have substances introduced into her vagina for dogs to lick off; she may be hung upside down and whipped; paint may be sprayed on her body or boiling wax dropped on to her breasts.

Some people feel that pornography is useful because it directs men's uncontrolled sexual excitement to pictures so that they are less likely to employ sexual violence against "real" women. But these *are* real women. It cannot be right to direct men's hostility on to women shown in pornographic pictures to save others from it.

The "safety valve" argument is untenable, anyway. Recent studies show that pornography actually incites otherwise fairly non-aggressive men to attack women. Even the kind of sex and violence shown on TV may have this effect. Edward Nelson at the Maudsley has demonstrated how in normal men impulses towards sex with violence are inhibited but can easily be released by showing them sexually violent films. (E. Nelson and M. Yasse, *The Influence of Pornography on Behaviour*) Such films conditioned a sample of liberal and tolerant undergraduates to feel sexually violent. Pornographic films really are *not* cathartic.

Soft porn

When pornography involves cruelty it is obvious that a great many of us must find it objectionable. But there is an undercurrent of violence in "soft" porn and pin-ups, too. Pornography sets out to shut women up, to silence them, to plug their mouths as well as their vaginas. An advertisement for a life-size plastic doll describes it as "the bed partner that doesn't talk back, just obeys". Susan Griffin (*Pornography and Silence*) quotes a caption to a picture of an apparatus for caging in a woman.

It sculptures her breasts and it narrows her waist. And it shows off her gorgeous behind. And the helmet which over her head has been placed keeps her deafened and silent and blind.

In just one issue of the magazine *Forum*, which is advertised as "The International Journal of Human Relations", there are photographs of: women encased in leather suits and helmets, a woman unable to part her legs because they are laced together through studs perforating her thighs, labia with a chain link stuck through them, a woman's torso with metal rings passed through her nipples, under the title "How it feels to be nipped in the buds", and advertisements for, among other things, soap "guaranteed to satisfy the dirtiest man in town" on which there is a picture of a woman whose clothes rub away and then her skin, to reveal a skeleton.

Pornography in the mass media

But it is not only a matter of being confronted by pornography in magazines. We do not really have any choice about whether or not we see pornography because it is all around us, in newspapers, on television and in advertisements, but we can take action in our personal lives. If there are calendars, pin-ups and other offensive material in your work place, get together with other women to find out how they feel about it. You may be surprised at how many find it distasteful. Technicians in one university department stuck pin-ups along the corridor. The secretaries distributed a petition which was signed by large numbers of staff and students and presented to the head of department. They were immediately taken down.

Women often find it difficult to take action when pornographic material is brought into the home. Men may accuse them of being "up-tight" or sexually inhibited, and a son may tell his mother that she is "past it" and that is why she is objecting.

You can point out how these pictures make you feel humiliated and degraded. Many men are genuinely surprised that you should react this way. If you have a daughter, bear in mind that this kind of image may affect her sense of what it means to be a woman.

10 LOSS AND GRIEVING

Grieving

Any strong emotional state affects our feelings about sex, whether it is joy, depression, anxiety, anger – or grieving. Sometimes these emotions make us feel more sexually aroused. Sometimes we become sexually frozen. Or they change the way in which we experience sex and the meaning it has for us.

In this chapter I want to explore the different ways in which women respond to loss, the experience of losing a valued part of the body, or that of losing a special, loved person – a sexual partner, a child or a parent. Most of us, for example, either know already, or will know, what it is for a parent to die. Death is a very unaccepted part of our culture and holds more taboos even than sex. To the small child in each of us, our parents seem tremendously powerful and strong. Deep down we may believe they will never die.

The shock of death

For a woman, the death of her mother, who gave her life and from whom she has had to differentiate herself, often painfully, in order to grow into an adult, can seem as if it is the death of part of herself. Much of her life may have been passed as if in unspoken conversation with her, trying to please her, wanting her approval. When her mother dies, her sense of her own value as a woman may be threatened. And for a man something of the same may occur when his father dies. It is like an amputation of part of oneself.

Even when we acknowledge the intensity of emotions that come after death and loss, we are rarely prepared for the ways in which grief affects sex. It can come as a total shock. We feel bewildered and confused about what is happening.

Grieving is not a static state. It is a process that goes through different phases and affects you physically and emotionally in different ways at different parts of the journey. Patterns of response to the impact of loss can, to some extent, be foreseen. It can help to realize that you are not the only person feeling like this and that it is not a totally bizarre and peculiar reaction. Knowing that other women have gone through similar experiences and have come out of them, and hearing how they coped, does not make the suffering any less, but enables you to feel that you are part of a fellowship of suffering and that there are people with whom you can share what you are going through. It will also help you actively to plan to meet challenges rather than being swept about like a leaf in the wind.

The phases of grief

Grieving is often like an illness which is at first acute but never really goes away. There is no point at which we can say, "That's it! It's finished." Its flavour, its essence, becomes incorporated into our lives, a part of ourselves.

The first phase of grieving brings with it shock, numbness and sometimes even a denial that the loss has ever happened. As we come out of that first acute stage there is full and painful recognition of loss, but at the same time we may have a feeling of unreality, that we have somehow lost personal identity. In this stage the person who is grieving is often very frightened by the strength of her emotions and may feel she is going mad. She may have dreadful nightmares or hallucinations when, after the death of a loved person, she seems to hear or catch a glimpse of them or suddenly senses their presence. She is likely to be very agitated and restless and to move between states of weeping and despair and feel generally confused, bewildered and disoriented. After the death of someone who is loved, she may also feel guilty about things she said, did or neglected to do or say, to the person who has been lost. She may even feel guilty that she is still alive. Some women go into a state of "automatic control" because, whatever they do, family members have to be fed, clothes cleaned and children got to school on time. They may clear up, clean and even throw out the dead person's belongings as if they were robots. Because she is unable to concentrate at this stage, a woman breaks off things she's doing because she cannot remember why she is doing them and has to keep on trying to "unscramble" her brain in order to complete the simplest tasks. It is quite normal for someone to be in this phase, when grieving is like an illness, for several weeks or even months.

"I cling to things as they were when he died – can't shave under my arms – a futile gesture."

It gradually gives way to a calmer state, at first just for short periods, but then, perhaps, for days at a time. You may sense a person you have loved as a living presence, almost as if the essence of the loved personality is flowing in your blood stream and has become part of you. This may be punctuated by feelings of anger, even of rage, when you want to blame someone or something for what has happened – perhaps a doctor or the hospital staff. You may also feel inexplicable anger at the person who has died, for daring to leave you. This is followed by intense feelings of guilt that you should have allowed yourself to have such thoughts. You may be guilty about any momentary pleasures and the times when you completely forget your loss, because you do not feel that you should let yourself enjoy life. You want to hold on to your grief as your last link with the loved person. It is during this stage of grieving that bad dreams often begin to give way to comforting ones about the lost person and he or she seems to become part of your life again. You feel that you have not been abandoned. And gradually you are able to pick up the threads of your life, to tackle new challenges and find pleasure in all the everyday things, the excitement or beauty of which was previously completely blotted out by intense grief.

Yet even in its different stages grieving is not a permanent emotional state. It comes in *waves*. Each wave can last as long as an hour, so it is almost as if you have a breathing space of calm in which you can rest before the next one builds up.

The grieving body

Like all forms of depression, grief involves our bodies as well as our minds. This is recognized when we say that someone has "turned white" with shock or sorrow. There is often a tight feeling in the throat. You may feel as if there is a lump there. It is difficult to eat and, when you do, you may bolt your food without even noticing what you are eating, and your whole digestive system may be upset. Breathing is often irregular. Sighing and sobbing are all part of this, but you may also find that you are holding your breath or breathing very shallowly and rapidly. There is a tremendous feeling of weakness and exhaustion, together with emptiness as if there is just a shell of a person left with nothing inside. It is difficult to get to sleep or you may sleep heavily and then suddenly wake in a cold sweat, facing the full reality of loss. And because we are "run down" and our whole bodies are involved in the grieving process, we are susceptible to viral and other infections and grieving may also find expression in physical form in an allergic reaction such as eczema or migraine-type headaches, an illness like shingles. Research shows that within months of the death of a partner the survivor is much more likely to suffer a serious illness.

When a woman is grieving the menstrual cycle is often disturbed. She may suddenly have a period when she was not expecting one and flood with blood as if her body were pouring with misery. Shirley's father had a heart-attack after he had taken her and the children to the pantomime. His death was a complete shock. She felt numb at first, but the week after she started a period and bled for a whole month: "My body grieved by literally bleeding for him." Or the periods may stop altogether as if she were frozen, fixed in her grief and unable to function normally. For someone in her forties or fifties the menopause can come suddenly, along with all the feelings that a door has closed irrevocably on that stage of her life. In men, nocturnal emissions which are disturbing for them and their partners are related to stress and grieving.

We are often completely unprepared for these physical expressions of grief. We can understand weeping, wanting to sleep and "get away from it all", and the outward signs of mourning as they are expressed in restlessness and irritation or in drooping shoulders, misery on our faces and in our bodies. But it is difficult to accept that our basic physiological systems may cheat on us or take us over so that our rational selves are powerless to battle against them.

Grief and eroticism

Reduced libido is often part of this physiological process of grief and depression. Whatever your mind seems to want, your body will not come with you. As a result a man may be unable to get or maintain an erection and though a woman may want to have sexual feelings – she may even start to be aroused – her body seems to say "No", her vagina does not soften, moisten and unfold and she cannot achieve orgasm. On the other hand, grieving and loss sometimes makes a woman feel almost driven to sex. She may be distressed by this

because it adds to her sense of being "out of control" and she does not understand this reaction and is likely to feel ashamed about it. Sex in the face of grief can be a striving for reassurance, a determined affirmation of life when confronted by death or loss.

Sometimes women say that words of comfort were meaningless and that sex took their place. When Sarah's father died she wanted sex with a desperation she has not known before or since, but had less pleasure out of it than at any other time. Her lover talked about her feelings of helplessness, since though she wanted to give Sarah reassurance she was very uncomfortable with what seemed like her rapacious demand for sex, and her own inability to give pleasure.

After the death of a parent or child each person in a sexual partnership may react in a different way and be unable to understand the other's response. One woman, for example, says that after the death of someone she loved very much, her husband was eager for intercourse, while she felt that any joyful experience was an insult to the person who had died. Knowing that these diametrically opposed reactions are both natural parts of grieving can help a couple begin to talk together about what they are going through.

A solitary experience

No two people pass through the grieving process at the same speed. In a partnership one person may be stuck in the initial stage of shock and emotional paralysis while the other cannot stop crying, or one be living and reliving the experience over and over again and needing to talk about it while the other is trying to take constructive healing action through energetic activity in order to move on from the intensity of the grief experience. You are unlikely both to feel the same. This is why, even if we are in a loving partnership, in one sense all grieving is something we have to do alone.

One of the hardest things for anyone else to understand is that grief itself protects us from the utter emptiness which it seems must be there if we allow the grief to fade. It is like a cape with which to hide from worse terrors, a cape that we draw round us for comfort. "I don't *want* the pain to go away!" one woman said.

Constraints imposed by others

Prolonged, or what appears to be excessive, grieving produces a sense of desperation in other people. This often happens with those in day-to-day contact with the person who is grieving, other family members and those closest to you, for example. They may long to tell you to snap out of it, to "pull yourself together". They set time limits on grieving. Their expectations of what is appropriate impose themselves on your grief. Yet there can be no moral imperatives about grieving. Grief simply "is", just as an illness "is". You can only accept what you feel, just as they, despite their discomfort and impatience, need to accept what you feel.

The healing effects of time

There is no formula for living through grief. Something may help one day but be useless the next. It can be difficult to believe that you will ever stop feeling the pain, but grief mellows over time and as it does you discover that you are able to function more effectively, mentally and physiologically, and that you have held on to your identity, even though at the time of sharpest agony you may have felt split in pieces.

Even when we acknowledge the intensity of emotions that come with bereavement, we are rarely prepared for the ways in which grief affects sex …

Because thoughts about the person you have lost or an awareness of what has happened to you come in waves, and with them the keenest grieving, one woman says: "treat them like contractions and labour. Go *with* them". She discovered that when she was feeling most submerged by grief she tended to hold her breath, hold *back* and freeze into stiff immobility just as she wanted to do during tumultuous contractions in childbirth. She knew that this made labour pain horrific and impossible to cope with and willed herself to breathe out and to go on breathing when this happened. Only when she did this could she let herself weep freely. Breathing led to sobbing, her grief could flow and this *expression* of grief was itself healing. It can be a relief to get away from other people so that grief can pour out like this, not any longer to have to put a brave face on it, or be cheerful for the children's sake. The woman who is grieving needs time when she can just be herself.

A unique experience

Susan Le Poidevin, a psychologist working in a hospice for the dying who also does research into how people experience grieving, believes that it is important for anyone who is grieving to have "a confiding relationship", someone with whom to talk about the most intimate and disturbing feelings, who will listen and understand, who can be trusted and who respects your identity and does not impose judgment on you or try to give advice. This person needs to acknowledge your feelings and not to diminish the experience by offering easy reassurance or meaningless words of comfort, to be someone who is able to resist the temptation to say: "I know exactly how you feel. That is how I felt when my husband died. . . ." or "When I had *my* operation. . . ." Each grieving experience is unique. No one else can possibly hope to understand exactly how you feel, however much they may long to.

Repressing grief

If grieving is blocked or denied it may be put off until years after when another loss makes it erupt like the lava from a volcano. This happened to some women who talked to me about their sexual problems after a death.

Anne's mother died when she was six. No one told her about it until after the cremation and her aunt, who brought her up, never mentioned her mother to her. When, 40 years later, Anne's husband died, the flood of grief about her mother's death poured out, too, and she mourned both her husband and her mother.

Another woman miscarried, dropping the fetus into the lavatory. Her partner fished it out and put it in a bucket. Afterwards she suffered a severe grieving illness, during which she left him. She could not understand her own reactions and was obviously very angry inside. I asked her to tell me about how she learned about death as a child and the full force of her grief suddenly burst out. She told me that she had a guinea pig which she often forgot to feed. "I was supposed to collect dandelions or grass every day. My mother said there was something wrong with it. I brought it into the house and it got colder and colder and died in my hands. I think about it a lot. I felt as if I had murdered it. Mum and Dad took it and chucked it in the bin – Oh my God! – like the baby down the toilet!" She had made no connection between these two events.

When we are grieving it may be for something over and above the ostensible object of our grief and we may be doing some unfinished grief work from the past. When the work of grieving comes to a full stop because it is evaded or cut short, there is a price to pay, even though the pain may cease. A woman whose mother died when she was four and whose father and new wife never spoke of her mother, so that she could not fully accept that she had died and grieve for her, says: "The price to be paid for the avoidance of pain is a diminution of the capacity to feel *anything*." She feels that the sexual problems in her marriage stem from this.

Enormous conflicts can build up between a couple when one person is trying to cope with a grief that the other does not realize is there or the intensity of which the partner cannot understand – and it invariably affects their sexual relationship. Whether a woman has a sexual partner or is alone, the way in which she responds sexually to grief often shocks and bewilders her. Yet death and sex are intertwined. Death and the surrender of self in orgasm are inextricably bound up with each other.

Death of a loved one

When a partner dies a woman may be so emotionally frozen that she is unable to think of herself as having any sexual feelings for a long time after, perhaps for ever. The loss of her sexual identity seems insignificant beside the loss of the person: "You keep on making tea for two, buying food he likes and remembering things to tell him"; "I missed an arm round my shoulder and somebody to confide in, the moment we both saw a joke, somebody to laugh with."

In this frozen condition, women describe physical sensations, times when it was difficult to swallow or breathe, for example: "I worried I wouldn't be able to swallow. My throat seemed to seize up"; "I felt in a state of panic, had feelings that I couldn't breathe properly"; "I was terribly tense, shoulders up by my ears"; "There was a permanent dull ache in my stomach. I remember thinking the poets and doctors had got it all wrong. When poets write of the pain of the breaking heart what they really mean is pain in the gut." (Quoted in *Widowed – What Now?* Valerie Austin and Charles Clarke-Smith.)

A woman's periods may suddenly stop or become very painful. One whose lover died in a mining accident said that her next period was the most painful she had ever had in her life. A woman of 47, who had no previous signs of the menopause, suddenly stopped having periods. One younger woman says that she did not menstruate for seven months after her husband's death. Grief can be like a shell separating a woman from someone else. Norma says she feels somewhere outside the human race, beyond normal happy or sad experience.

Feeling apart

There can be a feeling of being cut off from human contact, and that your grief is threatening others like a highly contagious disease. One woman says she felt like a "pariah", unable to face people, and this developed into agoraphobia: "It's a terrible effort facing

While we grieve the other person still seems not to have disappeared, and in clasping grief it seems that we can hold on to the reality of the lost person.

everyone you know (in a small town, that's most people)", and she found it helpful to go shopping with someone else to start with and so made herself get out of the house. A woman may draw back from any intimate human contact because she is afraid of the pain it can bring. Maggie, for example, says that she withdrew even from her children and now feels that it meant unnecessary suffering for them: "It was very difficult for me to cuddle them at first. I was afraid of the feelings that could come. If I let go I'd break down. So I was more distant than I've ever been." Because she was so frightened of human contact, she sought comfort by having a hot bath and then lying in bed wrapped in a blanket with a hot water bottle. She even bought a soft toy to cuddle. Some women find they cannot cherish themselves in this way and are concerned only to hold back the pain. "If you start to feel at all", one woman says, "it brings back all the other feelings, whereas if I feel nothing. . . . It's like being permanently under an anaesthetic. So I think it's best to have the lid on everything."

There is a paradox in that a woman who feels she cannot face intimate human contact in another, caring relationship may feel sexually aroused and seek sexual partners without any possibility of closeness or commitment. Either because this promises release from tension or because she is in an anaesthetized condition, it is at least a reminder that she is still alive. One woman said: "I wanted anonymous men to make love to me and disappear afterwards. couldn't imagine ever having emotional ties with a man again. I was scared I would become attached to someone for the wrong reasons.

"I began to feel randy. . . . What I wanted was just sex."

Many women find that there is a conflict between sex and a caring relationship and that they cannot cope with a mixture of the two. Some go for sex without love. Others seek love and tenderness without sex: "It was just that I desperately wanted to be held." A woman may be disappointed because the other person thinks the relationship implies sex. Friendships can be destroyed by sex and a grieving woman without a man is sometimes seen as threatening by other women because she is thought of as exploiting male compassion. If she is attractive and a "suitable" age she may also be seen by men as "available" and the proffered friendship comes with ties.

The force of anger

Women often describe one powerful emotion which breaks through even when they feel most frozen. It is anger – against other people, against themselves and against the person who has died: "He *shouldn't* have died. What a terrible thing to do to anybody!"; "I felt angry when he was dying. Why me? It wasn't fair. I was angry against his first wife. It was totally unfair that I should have had such a short time. I felt cheated"; "As I saw him dying I said, 'Don't leave me! Don't leave me!' Afterwards I felt angry with him. I thought, 'How could you have left me with all these children? You were always the one that went off, anyway!'" and a woman who was left with three teenagers says, "My husband got the 'good' years and left me with the grotty bits." Alison had lived for nine years with Virginia when she was told that her friend had only a year to live: "It was what people think of as marriage. You just know it's right and it gets better all the time." Alison says: "I didn't expect to feel violently angry for much of the time, for no reason. I was completely unstable for about two years, with people being very embarrassed to talk to me in case I shouted at them."

Feelings of guilt

Betty's 17-year-old son had just passed his driving test, took his car out immediately, crashed and was killed. She was overwhelmed by both anger and guilt, "that there was no time to say good-bye, to say the *important* things", and that the last thing she said to him was "For God's sake wash your hands!" She felt that the accident was in some ways her fault. And there was guilt of a deeper kind, for all the times she felt she had "failed" him.

Guilt and depression are forms of inturned anger. Many women say that they asked themselves over and over again whether there was not something they could have done to prevent the death and thought of all the things they wish now they had said or done, or omitted to say or do. One woman, the father of whose baby died during her pregnancy and whose husband died of cancer of the liver four years ago, says: "I'm still bedevilled by the terrible fear that my love and sexual need must be a killing thing."

To enjoy my body at all feels like infidelity."

When erotic feeling returns it may come suddenly, erupt in a completely uncontrolled way and be accompanied by profound guilt. The woman may feel that she has no right to sexual pleasure, or even to be alive, now that her lover is dead.

The thaw

As the emotional thaw comes there may be menstrual flooding. Some women feel as if their bodies are weeping blood. This may occur with the very first period after the death, or sometimes months after, following a phase of menstrual irregularity. With other women the body goes on working as regularly as clockwork and they may resent the machine-like smoothness of their physiology because it does not reflect their emotional distress.

With the thaw comes fresh pain, but now you can reach out and touch other people and begin to communicate physically and in words. One woman, who had drawn back from her children initially, took her little daughter in to bed with her and they cuddled and comforted each other. Another says: "What I missed most of all was not sexual intercourse but cuddling and I found myself touching everyone I could. My family indulged in a lot of hugging and hand-holding at this time." A woman who does not have this and cannot find it may turn to casual sex to give that physical contact as she is emerging from the frozen state. One woman who is alone says: "People often behave as if you shouldn't mind being without a man. The joy of going to bed with somebody, not just for intercourse, but to put an arm round them, to talk intimately, this is important – and I miss it. There is no one to touch, to kiss, embrace, express physical affection to."

> "Sex builds up all my feelings of grief and loss. I don't like to get too close to people any more."

The quest for physical closeness

When a woman comes out of the initial paralysis she may be brimming with intense feelings. Peggy, whose husband died suddenly at the age of 42, says: "Once I had done all the 'firsts': the first birthday alone; the first Christmas; the first wedding anniversary and so on, I began to live again. My body responded by becoming almost on fire with sexual longing – swinging to and fro between the two extremes of numbness and longing. I fell desperately in love with the first man to put his arms round me." Fortunately he was a good friend who was already married and the relationship could not develop in that way. She now feels it would have been disastrous.

Anna says she slept with anyone she was fond of because she needed warmth and friendship: "With each I began to hunt for the relationship I had with Jim. It was never there." She was desperate to be held, to have her own identity as a survivor confirmed and prove to herself that she was still alive. She discovered that she could enjoy sex much more if she had nothing in common with a lover. If it was someone she admired and respected the emotions proved too dangerous at that stage of her grieving.

New relationships

When a partnership has been destroyed a woman often comes to a point when she tells herself from now on that she has to go out and create relationships, and work at them. If she is now living alone and has no job outside her home she may find it difficult even to talk to other people. Simple pleasantries about the weather or prices in the shops, speaking to someone sitting opposite in a train or bus, may involve painful effort. Cruse, the organization for widows, advises the widow to wash her car as often as possible in the street or paint the front gate so that someone will stop and pass the time of day. Anything that breaks the isolation and enables her to communicate at even the most superficial level can begin to break down the barriers.

One woman who had been very happily married and now made great effort to meet people says: "When he died it was like the en of a chapter. I had my hair highlighted. I lost weight. I had affairs. They gave me a tremendous sense of self-confidence. Now I don't have to prove anything any more. But at that stage I was trying to prove that I was still attractive. I told myself, "You had a fabulous life with him, it's time to move on. Now, off you go!" A woman has to be tough to handle short-term casual affairs like this and for many women it may not be the answer.

When a woman seeks new relationships, her children may be one factor in an often very difficult equation. They may remain loyal to their father and find it impossible to accept that she could want anyone else. To a child it may seem like treachery. So women with families who go on to make new sexual partnerships often have to work out careful strategies.

Grieving after separation

When a relationship breaks down and a lover leaves, a woman may go through the experience of grieving as after a death. Mary was in a convent from the age of 13 until she was 25. She fell in love with a priest who resigned the priesthood. They became lovers, but intercourse was difficult because of the terrible guilt she felt and she decided she was not yet ready for marriage. He met someone else and married her. He had become, she says, "the centre of myself". She is emotionally paralysed. She can neither weep nor express her anger. She is, she feels, "in a deep freeze".

The woman with whom Pat was deeply in love revealed that she had another lover: "I just went rigid. I was stunned." Then she wept and the thaw was followed by tumultuous anger: "I threw myself around on the bed and screamed and kicked and shouted. I was terrified I was going to fall apart."

Jane is 59. She has been married for 30 years, but her husband has had a mental breakdown and is "like a difficult child". At first she felt no emotion of any kind. "There was only aridity. There were times", she says, "when I thought how good it would be to have a car crash. I wanted to vomit to get rid of the misery inside." She has now come out of the frozen state, lived through the anger that followed, is doing a university course and has taken a lover.

Coming to terms with your loss

The freeze, the physical sensations of constriction, of wanting to throw up and eject the misery, the gradual thaw and coming to life again which also brings acute pain and anger at what has happened, working through the grief, are all part of the grieving process after death or separation from someone who is loved.

Grieving itself can be an experience through which a woman feels she has grown. For some it is simply that the worst has happened and now they can cope with anything. They have a new, and often astonished, faith in themselves. One woman, with strong Christian beliefs, feels her religion is stronger: "I was in a tunnel but there was always a light at the end."

In a strange way, completely giving oneself up to grief is sensual in itself. "Allowing it to run its natural course," one woman says, "is a sensual experience."

As a woman comes through it she has a new sense of self: "A big point of healing came the day I sold the double bed and moved into a single one. I stopped being half a couple and became me. . . ."

Death of a baby

The death of a baby brings a special kind of grieving because it is an intensely *physical* experience. Being a mother involves not only heart and brain but a physical response which is part of sustaining and nurturing a baby's life, at first in the uterus and later in your arms. When a baby dies a woman may feel that the grieving is centred in her gut, uterus and entrails and as if these organs have been torn from her living body.

This is no lavender and lace mourning, but a grief that can be passionate and raw and that feeds on itself like an animal gnawing its own body.

Before the child is delivered, a baby is like part of a mother's body. In some ways she cannot distinguish the baby from herself. A stillbirth or late miscarriage is both the death of a child and also a physical mutilation of the mother. After the baby has been born it is as if there is an invisible umbilical cord through which the mother's life seems to flow, as well as the baby's. When that is cut by death there is a festering wound in the centre of her body.

The effect on a woman's identity

The death of a child can strike at the root of sexuality and at a woman's own sense of herself as a person and leave her with a desperate longing for a baby in her arms. For the hunger to have a child is just as powerful as the hunger for sexual satisfaction.

A woman may need to mourn a baby not only if it has never had life, but even if it has never moved inside her and was only a tiny embryo or a cluster of cells. She mourns her idea of that child, all the changes the baby would bring with it and, especially if it would have been her first child, the loss of herself as a mother.

She may meet other people – at a party, in the hairdresser's, over the garden fence – and they invariably ask "How many children have you?" She is confused and not sure what to say because she really does not know. Is a dead child still your child? Was a stillborn baby ever a reality? And if she is to disclose her tragedy, will this not put a barrier between her and other people? For any woman who has lost a baby has been through the experience of seeing other women recoil from her as if she suffered from a communicable disease.

The mourning couple

Each woman who mourns the death of a baby does so in her own way and in her own time. It is impossible to weigh grief in any scales, or even to say that an early miscarriage is always less traumatic than a late one, or that a miscarriage holds less pain than a stillbirth, or that a cot death is more agonizing than the death of a baby around the time of birth, though all these things may be true for some women. It can be very difficult for a man to understand this, perhaps because however much he grieves the father does not have the same intimate physiological link with the baby. This is why to a man a woman's grieving may seem completely out of proportion to what has happened.

Yet it may also be that she is so wrapped up in her own grief that she does not realize the magnitude of his. It is often said that grieving brings a couple together. It can have the opposite effect, with each living in a private world of misery. "A loss doesn't have to

The death of a child can split a relationship or become an ineradicable part of a couple's love.

be earth-shatteringly obvious to anyone else", one woman says, talking about a mid-pregnancy miscarriage that occurred five years ago. There was not really a person to grieve for, yet it resulted in such emotional distress that she left her husband.

The death of a child at the end of a pregnancy, at birth or afterwards is inevitably a shattering experience for any woman who goes through it. Her whole body has been working to nourish that budding life. She is turned towards the reality of the child like a magnet to the north, but now her arms are empty. At the same time that she is grieving for her baby she is having to cope with the physical effects of what may have been a difficult birth, with stitches following an episiotomy, blood and lochia pouring from her uterus and milk from her breasts. Her whole body may feel sore, bruised and tender. She may also feel physically mutilated by things that were done to her. One woman whose baby was stillborn says: "I felt like an animal, not like a human being. You are stretched out in there and there is nothing you can do." The midwife told her to push but she could not do so: "I thought it was my fault that the baby died." She felt as if she had been violated and also terribly guilty that because she did not submit and do exactly as she was told she caused her baby's death. Even though rationally she accepts that she is not responsible, there is still a lingering doubt in her mind and emotionally she is consumed with guilt.

Most women who have talked to me after the death of a baby say that they needed to be comforted and held, in close contact with someone they loved. Kitty's baby died when a carry-cot turned over in the night, trapping the child underneath. She describes her conflicting feelings about sex:

Body alive with pain, deep inner ache, bright surface pain – *raw*.
I do not want to be touched.
At the same time a desperate need to be held firmly, tightly, strongly because I am in uncharted seas,
tossed about by emotions and completely at their mercy.
I might vanish in these waters.

Yet I cannot bear to be cuddled, treated tenderly, made love to,
as that brings on emotions and those that come are full of pain.
I feel only strongly or not at all.
Sex equals violence equals death.

After the baby's death her husband initially found his sexual feelings intensified. He reached out to touch her, but her breasts were full of milk, throbbing and painful, and she flinched from him. She also speaks of the sense of isolation which grief brings:

Blot the world out.
I'm not part of the world at all;
I'm cut off from all normal activity
and watch it through glass. I watch myself and can see my performance.
Everything goes on without me.
Yet the world ought to stop for such an enormity.

Another woman describes the sense of unreality of everything except her baby's death: "I could not understand why everyday life outside our house continued as before. I was offended by the unfeeling normality of the milkman delivering and the sun rising. How could this atomic explosion not devastate everything around me?" (Wendy Valerie Harman, "Death of my baby")

At first a couple may cling together. They may be too numbed to do anything except hold each other or weep uncontrollably. There is a dreadful clarity about each detail of that time that may be remembered many years later.

Yet along with the clarity there is a sense of unreality about everything that is happening and they may be so stunned that they cannot yet really accept the baby's death. A mother described what happened after her little son's cot death: "I just held him, thinking could somehow warm him up with my body . . . when we saw the undertaker coming up the drive. We knew he was going to a morgue. We knew he was going to be cut up. Adam took him from me and gave him to the undertaker. He said, 'Keep him warm won't you.'"

The comfort a couple give each other from their closeness and shared grieving may be short-lived, or may never come at all because in Western culture there is still, for men, a taboo on tenderness and on the open expression of grief. A man is brought up to feel that he must be strong and that a woman should be able to lean on him. He is ashamed to weep, except in private. He must not "crack up". He is afraid that if he talks about what has happened or about his feelings he will break down, so he gives her a quick pat on the hand and turns away.

It can seem as if he is colluding with all the other people who deny the reality of the baby who has died. Yet she feels she should be grateful for his strength. One whose baby died during labour and who then had a hysterectomy because she was haemorrhaging and would otherwise have died, says: "David has remained so calm and positive. . . . He has been tremendous. I shouldn't have been surprised really, but of course no one wanted to talk about the baby. Even David was just going to deal with all the funeral arrangements and tell me about it when it was all over. I want to go to the funeral because I couldn't see the baby and I ought to see him buried."

In trying to control his own emotions, a man may become very irritated by a woman's unchecked grieving and seem to be not only denying her grief but rejecting *her*. Cathy describes what happened between her and Mark after the cot death of their four-month-old baby: "He was a rock. He was wonderful. But he doesn't know how to talk about it. He has been brought up to have a stiff upper lip. When I am really down he won't have anything to do with me. I long to be held, to be physically close, but he is just . . . not there."

Another woman says of her partner: "He is just like a robot. It is me who says, 'Come on, give me a cuddle. I need it!' But when I hug him he shrinks or bends his shoulders and looks at his feet." She goes on to say: "We never resolved it together. We never worked it through. We each went off into our own little worlds and it got pushed out of the way. I realize that he is very frightened that I could get pregnant and we would go through it all again. I was very angry when I found out he had been to the doctor to see if he could get a vasectomy."

After the cot death of their baby daughter, Elaine says: "My husband just wanted to be on his own. He cut himself off from everybody." A year later he has still never been able to tell work mates that the baby is dead.

Coming to terms with your grief

Either partner, or both, may have a desperate desire to replace the lost baby. A few days after their baby died in her cot at six months, both Joan and Matt experienced "a terrible urge to have another baby". They had intercourse and she experienced orgasm: "But afterwards I felt guilty. It was almost as if I had slammed the door on my dead baby, I had been able to forget the pain for a few minutes. I feel very mixed up about it all, too, because I don't think I could face the pain of another cot death."

Though desire for another baby is often the initial reaction, when they think about it more carefully both will come to realize that this particular baby can never be replaced and that they need time to grieve and to say good-bye to that baby before they are ready to welcome another. "Only when a place has been found for the dead baby, can space be made for a new one". (Valerie Harrington, "Look, listen and support") Making this space for the dead baby is a process, not an act, and it may take six months to a year or more for that to happen. It is very difficult to have to work through grieving for a baby who has died while at the same time you are preparing to welcome the new baby. There is often a terrible fear that you cannot possibly love another child as much as the one who has been lost and that to replace that baby is an act of treachery.

"We were so close. I wanted sex, I wanted comfort, but I felt terribly guilty."

A woman may seek sex because it produces powerful sensations that can fill a vacuum. Describing how she feels after her baby was stillborn, one says: "I'm frantic, mad for sex. I've got to believe that I'm alive and feel it. I need to know I'm not worthless. I want to produce life again. I feel, 'The baby's dead and I must be dead.'"

Sometimes this urge to affirm that you are alive and have the power to fight against death is the source of action and protest. Rosalind's baby had died three weeks before she talked to me. Those weeks had been filled with activity: "It came to me that I had to do something constructive. I went to the graveyard and pulled all the coloured ribbons off the flowers on her grave. I dried them and went to the missile base at Greenham Common and tied them to the wire mesh fence surrounding it. They were for all the babies who will die if there is nuclear war; all the babies who will never have ribbons, only bombs."

After the death of a baby lovemaking can become very mechanical, either because it is used to try and fill the emptiness or because a couple are desperately trying to make a baby: "We wanted another baby. We put that before any thought of enjoying it. I couldn't get any pleasure from lovemaking still after three months and I knew *he* felt I should have got over it." One woman says that grief makes her feel very old and very tired so that while sex is reassuring it is also too much for her to cope with.

A woman who has given birth to a dead baby may find penetration produces a terrible onslaught of grief and horrifying physical feelings. If the baby died before labour started there may have been a time during which she knew that she was going to deliver a dead baby and had to wait for labour to start. She may feel as if she was "a walking coffin". Penetration is like lifting the lid of that coffin.

The physical sensations she had as the body of her dead baby slipped out may also be aroused by penetration: "When his penis comes inside me it is just like the dead body coming out."

When a baby has died at or shortly after birth the last thing that has been inside the mother's body has been her baby. Anything else coming inside seems to rob her of the baby and, especially when she has milk in her breast and blood is still coming from her uterus, she feels, with a very strong *physical* sense, that her body still belongs to the child. In something of the same way, a woman may hold herself apart following an abortion. One who has had a termination because amniocentesis revealed that the fetus was severely handicapped may feel that she can only produce something that is damaged and imperfect and that her body is a place of death. It is very difficult to feel spontaneous sexual arousal and to make love when it was this that started the sequence of events that culminated in the death, very difficult to let feelings flood through you when you know that, in the end, they can result in such pain.

"Weeping together brings us closer now than sex."

If you have lost a baby it is important to take *time* for grieving. You may have to go on as near normally as possible in your work or with the family, but you still need to allow yourself space for grieving freely. This means delaying starting another baby until you are ready to greet a new child, who is not merely a replacement for the one you have lost but is wanted for itself. It means making time when you can lose control and weep. A man and woman may each be in such pain that they cannot trust themselves to do this in the presence of the other and there are times when they may need to be by themselves to grieve.

The need to confide

Finding someone who will be a confiding friend, who will listen without passing judgment or trying to eradicate your pain, can give you strength to go on and help take some of the pressures off each other. A woman who is alone, or whose partner has become absorbed in work as a way of blotting out the pain, needs this other person most urgently. We all need each other. It is not weak to need help. There will be times when you will be able to reach out and help someone else, too.

The dangers of repressing grief

If the work of grieving is delayed or blocked, grief can emerge later and poison a relationship in a way which, because it is then so long past the death of the baby, it can be difficult for a couple to identify or understand. A leaflet produced by the Stillbirth and Perinatal Death Association (Sue Burgess, *Sexual Problems Following Stillbirth*) points out that some couples are bewildered to find sexual problems recurring several years after a stillbirth, once they have completed their families. The sense that the stage of childbearing is finished and confrontation with that feeling of finality brings fresh grieving for the failed pregnancy or the dead baby.

Communicating grief

It may help to set aside some time each day, however short, when you both discuss and share feelings. Some people fear this is self-indulgent emotion, but if you were suffering from a severe physical illness you would take it seriously and make time to ask the sick person how he or she felt. We can have the same care for grieving. Bereaved parents also need a regular time when they can get out together and are able to make contact with the world outside their own grief, perhaps a walk in the countryside, a film or play, a visit to an art gallery or museum, or a jog together. Gradually the space between the pain will get longer and the death of a baby becomes woven as one vivid strand in the whole texture of life.

Mutilating operations

Losing any part of the body in a mutilating operation, however necessary and however life-saving the surgery, involves grieving. This process is long and painful for some of us. It can profoundly affect our view of ourselves and our sexuality.

Hysterectomy

Hysterectomies are performed not only for cancer but for a wide variety of conditions: for example, for general gynaecological problems involving the uterus, ovaries, fallopian tubes or the cervix. Sometimes a hysterectomy is carried out when a gynaecologist cannot work out what is really wrong. An analysis of hysterectomies in the USA revealed that one in seven of those done between 1970 and 1979 were probably unnecessary. (Report in the *General Practitioner*, 22 January 1982) Going by the figures for 1975 – a year in which 750,000 hysterectomies were performed – one half of American women will eventually have had a hysterectomy. In Britain, proportionately far fewer hysterectomies are performed. Even so, by the time we are 75 one in five of us will have had the uterus removed. The readiness with which hysterectomies are performed in the USA as compared with Britain reflects a fee-per-service system based on private medicine. It pays a surgeon to take out a woman's uterus. More than half of all uteruses excised are discovered afterwards to be physically normal.

Hysterectomy is a major operation, not just a matter of whipping out what one gynaecologist has called "a useless, bleeding, cancer-producing organ" which should be removed once it has served its reproductive purpose. Like all such operations, it demands a big emotional adjustment afterwards, which is more difficult if you are not convinced that the operation was really necessary.

Post-hysterectomy patients differ from other post-surgery control groups in being prescribed more anti-depressant drugs, and having more headaches and sleeplessness and experiencing more untreated depression. Richards revealed a 33 per cent incidence of depression in women after hysterectomy, compared with a seven per cent incidence after other abdominal surgery. (D. H. Richards, "Depression after hysterectomy")

If you are advised to have a hysterectomy for a non-cancerous condition, therefore, it may be worth exploring whether there is a less drastic treatment available. You will have to be assertive about asking questions, especially if you are offered mere reassurance, and may want to get a second opinion.

Many women do not know what will happen with hysterectomy or, after the operation, exactly what and how much has been removed. They are given minimal information about after-effects and usually none at all about sex, except to be told to "take things gently" for six weeks afterwards. They often find it difficult to know what questions to ask. When the gynaecologist tells a woman that he suspects cancer she is often in too great a state of shock to take in any details of information. Many women would like the opportunity to talk to another woman about the way in which the hysterectomy is likely to affect them emotionally and sexually, but psycho-sexual counsellors, whether male or female, in hospitals are few and far between, and nurses on the ward rarely have the information sought. Some are young and inexperienced or see their function as being mainly that of "cheering-up" the patient and either do not understand what a woman is asking or avoid discussing possible problems.

Reactions to hysterectomy

The first emotional impact of the operation for a woman who is still in her thirties or forties is the acceptance that losing her uterus removes all possibility of ever having a child. Some women welcome this as the most effective birth control method. "In getting rid of my womb I got rid of a nuisance. The surgeon may have taken away the 'nursery' (my womb) but he left the 'playpen'!" says Monica, who explains that she had three children in her early twenties "because, quite honestly, it never occurred to me not to! I was brought up to view myself as 'a wife and mother'. I was

HYSTERECTOMY
OPERATIONS

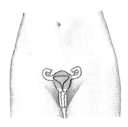

Sub-total hysterectomy
The uterus is removed, leaving the ovaries, fallopian tubes and cervix. Pre-menopausal women will continue to menstruate.

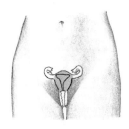

Total hysterectomy
The entire uterus and cervix are removed and the woman will no longer menstruate.

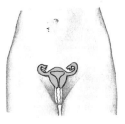

Total hysterectomy with a salpingo-oopherectomy
In a complete hysterectomy the ovaries, fallopian tubes, uterus and cervix are removed.

immensely relieved (after the hysterectomy) that I was no longer fertile and delighted to think I was never going to have to mess about with periods anymore. My feelings about my body have never been better and I feel more 'female' without a womb than ever before – a person and not merely a possible baby carrier."

Other women are unable to react this positively. Even if they did not plan to have a baby, losing the uterus may bring a shocking sense of finality. Even if you have finished your family, the thought that you cannot have another child, by accident or if you changed your mind, can mean for some women that they feel that a special quality of being, something to do with the essence of womanliness, has been removed. (It is interesting that though there is a term which expresses this for men – feeling emasculated – no such term exists for a woman's experience.)

Looking back on the time before the operation, women often describe very unsatisfactory consultations with gynaecologists who refer to the uterus as "a useless little bag", "an unnecessary and potentially pathological organ", or "an obsolete piece of plumbing". The wife of a GP, whose gynaecologist is a close friend, says that nevertheless she felt very resentful and "aggressively feminist as the two men discussed the removal of my womb, speaking of it as having 'served its purpose'. I tearfully explained that I had never minded menstruating. The gynaecologist implied that I was somewhat peculiar to want to hang on to my womb, as most women were only too eager to be rid of theirs." He also suggested that she would have "no escape" from her husband if she surrendered the sexually evading process of menstruation and that this was why she must be reluctant to lose her uterus. It is difficult to imagine surgeons speaking like this if they were proposing to cut off a man's testicles. The way a woman's uterus is referred to, often in language more appropriate for a small child (for example, talking about your "tummy" and "water-works"), is one way in which the female body, and female experience generally, is trivialized.

Janet had three children and decided she didn't want any more, so her husband had a vasectomy. Later, she developed fibroids and was bleeding three weeks in every month. So she had a hysterectomy. It suddenly hit her that she could not possibly have another baby: "I had nightmares, thinking I had a baby and waking up and it wasn't there. All my friends seemed to be pregnant at once and were thrilled to bits. When I saw a baby in a pram outside a shop I wanted to pick it up, just for a cuddle." She says this state of acute mourning for her fertility lasted for about three weeks. She was better able to cope with it because her sister had had a baby a month before her hysterectomy. Janet helped to look after her little niece and this eased the pain. It took three months for her to work through her feelings about this and to realize that having a baby is "not just the nice bits, a pretty baby in a pram, taking it for a walk in the park. Being with a baby day after day like that you remember the grotty bits, the nappies and the crying at night."

Women for whom the operation is an unqualified success, as it is for many, may find it difficult to understand how unhappy others can be after a hysterectomy and condemn them as lacking in courage or as moral reprobates. On hearing how another woman was mourning her uterus Margaret said: "What rubbish! I couldn't wait to get rid of mine!" For many years she had been bleeding two weeks out of every four and she now felt reborn. Barbara, too, says she is "furious" at women who are miserable after the operation: "My hysterectomy was the best thing that ever happened. I have never been healthier in my life. My 'femininity' is not centred between my legs. I feel more feminine not worrying about whether I'll bleed or spot through my white skirt."

Hysterectomy and sexuality

Yet many other women with whom I have talked about their emotions after hysterectomy stress that they needed to have their confidence restored in their sexuality and in their value as women. Though initially they are anxious about whether penetration will hurt, whether the vagina will be lubricated and if they will have any sexual feelings at all, for many this is not just a question of being able to get sexually excited, or of having orgasms, but of something much more fundamental about their capacity to give and receive love with their whole bodies.

When a hysterectomy is performed, the external genitals and those parts which you can easily touch with your fingers all remain as they were before the operation. But if you push your forefinger deep inside the vagina to touch the cervix, which feels like a plump, rounded cushion at the top end, you do meet a part which is changed by the operation. This cushion is removed along with the uterus in most cases and the vagina is stitched up over the area where it was before. This often has the effect of tightening the innermost part of the vaginal barrel. Some women welcome this, but for others it can pose problems. The suturing of the vaginal wall may also result in a shortening of the vaginal barrel. Both these things may mean that a woman experiences pain with deep penetration and feels the pressure of the penis against a tender area, or even as if it is "stubbed" against the end of the vagina.

Having intercourse again

Eleanor, who is 52, says she was never "keen" on sex but that after a hysterectomy she experienced pain deep inside: "When I told the doctor he said 'It can't hurt' and that I'd better use a cream." Since the gynaecologist denies that she feels any pain, she does not feel able to go back to him to ask for help.

The shortening of the vaginal barrel, on the other hand, sometimes provides a new sexual stimulus with penetration. Betty says that she enjoys intercourse more than before the operation. Her hysterectomy was done because of enormous fibroids stretching the uterus to the size of a 28-week pregnancy. This probably put pressure on trans-cervical ligaments, since before the operation deep penetration was uncomfortable. She has now discovered that she enjoys penetration. Other women have found that once the wound has healed they like more thrusting of the penis than before. Lisa, who is a lesbian, has experienced something of the same change. She says that knowing that the area involved in orgasm is now smaller makes her keen to have intense sensation. She finds that she likes her vagina "stretched hard" now: "I can no longer have good orgasms through clitoral manipulation alone. I now need something to go deep inside and actually push against the top."

"For me, sex is much better than before. Feelings are heightened."

When the ovaries remain

Women who have the uterus removed but have at least one working ovary intact still have a monthly rhythm which, though it does not produce menstrual bleeding, makes them aware of cyclical changes in their bodies at different times of the month. Helen says she could not at first understand these "odd feelings". Her breasts get sore, she feels thick-waisted, tends to be irritable and may feel rather faint at times which she supposes correspond to the week before the period she no longer has. Vicky says: "For three or four months I had to check that I wasn't menstruating as the 'ghost' feeling of doing so was so strong. It was rather as people describe the phantom feeling of losing a limb." She became more aware of pre-menstrual tension than ever before and felt very confused by this.

A woman may also experience mid-cycle feelings associated with the ripening of the ovary. Some have pain then. Kathleen has "dragging pains in my tummy". These middle-of-the-month sensations indicate that ovulation is occurring. You still have a woman's body, the rhythms of which are controlled by hormones pouring into your blood stream in moon-like time patterns.

Slack muscles

After hysterectomy some women feel the vagina is "loose". Physiologically this is very unlikely to be the case and what they seem to be describing is a lack of tone in the pelvic floor muscles. When there has been a large tumour in the uterus, it has pressed down on these muscles surrounding the vagina and subjected them to strain. You have probably not found it easy to contract them firmly and they have stretched and sagged. An important part of post-operation rehabilitation is to exercise these muscles so that they become mobile and expressive and you have good internal "posture". These are invisible movements that you can do anywhere and some are described in Chapter 2.

You may discover that you need well-toned pelvic floor muscles in order to feel fully sexually stimulated. Though the clitoris is the organ in which arousal is usually centred, muscles around the vagina are involved in the total activity of wave-like movements which bring you to orgasm. Not all women are aware of these movements deep inside, but for those who are something seems to be lacking when the muscles are flabby and unresponsive. Vicky says that she found that she had lost all sensations inside her vagina after the operation. She was left with clitoral sensation, but it seemed petty and superficial compared with the orchestral interaction of different organs she had felt previously: "It was necessary to do pelvic floor exercises for some months to restore these sensations, as the whole pelvic floor took a considerable battering."

Toning the pelvic floor not only restores an active vagina but increases a woman's general sense of well-being. It can even show on her face. A woman whose pelvic floor muscles are slack tends to have the same slackness in the muscles around the mouth. There may be a marked difference, too, in the way she walks. One with very poor pelvic floor tone walks as if she is carrying a heavy load between her legs (and it may actually feel like this for her). One with good tone has a spring in her step.

Intercourse, masturbation, intense sexual arousal and orgasm can all result in some bleeding in the first three or four weeks after the operation because as we become excited the tissues around the vagina are plumped up with blood. The pelvic floor muscles contract spontaneously in a burst of rhythmic activity when we are sexually excited, too. The combined effect of the extra blood supply and the muscular activity can produce some bleeding from the scar. This kind of bleeding is harmless, though it obviously delays complete healing, but can be very frightening. It is always difficult with vaginal bleeding to know how much is "normal" and whether what you see as just a little is in fact too much, or vice versa. It takes about six weeks for the stitch line at the top of the vagina to heal.

You may also notice that some black stitches come out with the blood. These are supposed to dissolve or fall out and once the tissues are healing well you will be more comfortable with them out.

A yellow vaginal discharge is a sign of infection. This sometimes occurs because stitches have irritated the surrounding tissues. It can be quickly and painlessly dealt with by cauterization, followed by treatment with antibiotic pessaries. If you are anxious because you are bleeding, in pain because you have a discharge like this, or for any other reason, consult the doctor.

The sexual relationship

The fact that a woman has had a hysterectomy obviously influences her sexual partner's behaviour, too.

It often happens that a man starts to think about lovemaking more from the woman's point of view and develops a more sensitive understanding of her needs. Appalled by the idea that she has had surgery, he slows down, gives more general body stimulation and is more gentle. Some men learn to be much more skilful lovers during this time. Sometimes it can be a breakthrough for a couple who were having a boring sex life for years before the operation.

Some couples, who never did get much out of sex anyway, welcome the opportunity to stop. "He is very understanding", a woman may say, or "He doesn't trouble me." One woman who had always disliked sex told me that she preferred to bring her husband to orgasm with manual stimulation and she obviously welcomed the operation as a means of avoiding intercourse. There are probably many women who welcome the chance to "finish with all that".

"I am empty."

For some in their fifties continuing to have intercourse is a symbol of youth. And it may be important for them to have orgasm with intercourse in order to prove to themselves and their partners that they are not "past it". Sexual difficulties after hysterectomy can be very threatening when intercourse and orgasm have to prove the value of a relationship in this way.

"I feel neutered."

Many of these problems are the direct result of depression and are only indirectly related to the changed physiology. If a uterus is important to a woman, she needs time to mourn its loss. She goes through a process of bereavement and grieving very like that following the death of a loved person. It is herself she mourns, herself as she once was. Loss of libido is a well-known symptom of depression and is one of the earliest signs. Vicky says she was in this state for several months because she felt incomplete as a woman. She was 33 when she had her hysterectomy and could not help "resenting women friends discussing their periods in front of me".

The comfort of a close relationship can help ease depression.

About one woman in 10 experiences depression after hysterectomy which is similar in effect to transitory post-natal depression, the kind often called the "baby blues". This can come as a shock if you are not prepared for the possibility. "I was the more upset because I felt it was so inappropriate", one woman says. When she told the Professor of Gynaecology about it he said: "Oh, yes, ten per cent of all patients experience it post-operatively, but we don't mention it in advance, as it doesn't seem worth worrying the other ninety per cent." The best treatment for this depression is loving and cherishing from someone dear to you, your partner or a close friend, and, since depression is always associated with extreme tiredness, plenty of rest. Someone who took over housework entirely and three hours on the bed in the afternoon, helped one woman most.

When a woman has had a hysterectomy because of cancer the initial feeling after the operation is usually one of relief that it is over and gratitude that she is alive. The feeling that every day is a bonus is often the dominant emotion, but because everything has often happened very quickly – the shock of disclosure of the disease and arrangements for the operation following on each other in quick succession – the time for mourning may be delayed. Some of the women who had to face up to cancer with whom I have talked have said that they needed that time in which to grieve, but that they could not really start doing so until several months after the operation was over.

A woman who has had a hysterectomy because of prolonged and heavy bleeding may feel rejuvenated once she has got through this grieving phase. She has often been through a long period of debilitating ill health and anaemia. Elizabeth, for example, had such heavy bleeding that she had to wear several pads to prevent bleeding through her clothes on the hour's journey to work. She says her sex life was unexciting because she felt so drained: "You can't be bothered." After the operation she felt very low and tired for a while, but one day looked in the mirror and realized that she looked different: "Not grey any more. It made me feel I wanted to buy new clothes and dress up." Her sex life is now better than it ever was before and she says she feels "absolutely marvellous! It was the best thing I ever did!"

Some women feel highly sexually aroused four to six weeks after the operation. This happens particularly if they were very run down because of heavy bleeding before the hysterectomy and now feel revitalized. Even women who still find ordinary household activities tiring at this stage may long to make love. For some women this may be because their partners have taken time off work to look after them and are showing their love in very practical ways, so that there is a new closeness. Even though she feels weak, it can be for a woman like a second honeymoon. When in addition a man who previously concentrated on genital contact discovers how to make love by caressing her whole body and learns to adapt himself to her rhythms and timing, a couple's sexual relationship is enhanced.

"Before the operation everything was too much effort. I plodded along. Now I'm taking great gulps of life."

Mastectomy

Mastectomy is in a dramatic sense a mutilating operation because of the obvious external evidence of amputation of a part of the body symbolic of femininity. There is no possible way in which a lover can avoid becoming aware that a breast has been amputated.

From puberty on, we may tend our breasts, pushing them into the right shape, worrying whether they are too small or too large, lop-sided or drooping and trying to firm them up, develop or reduce their size or disguise them accordingly. The first thing a man does if he is dressing up as a woman is to stick on imitation "boobs". Yet breasts are not only important sex symbols for men and in how we see our bodies reflected in men's eyes. They are a vital part of being a woman. When Daphna Ayallah and Isaac Weinstock were collecting material for their book, *Breasts*, they said that they were amazed "at how basic and profoundly fundamental the experience of having breasts was to a woman's personality and life-style. We realized that our book was not only about women's breasts, but also about women's lives today, and the experience of being a woman. As one of the women interviewed so eloquently put it, 'I can't talk about my breasts without talking about being a woman.'"

Treatment of breast cancer

For nearly 70 years the main treatment for women with breast cancer has been extensive and mutilating surgery. The breast has been removed together with the lymph glands underneath the arm and sometimes pectoral muscles, too, so that any movement involving the shoulder is reduced. There is little scientific evidence that a radical mastectomy of this kind is more likely to cure cancer than a simple mastectomy involving only the removal of the breast tissue itself and trials started in the 1950s have revealed that the most effective treatment may be less surgery and the use of radiotherapy. Some women are exploring holistic therapy, including herbal medicines and changes in diet.

The need for emotional support

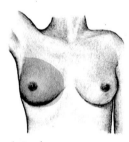

A simple mastectomy

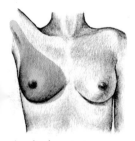

A radical mastectomy

Little psycho-sexual counselling for women who have had mastectomies is available in most hospitals. Yet 25 per cent of women who have mastectomies eventually need some sort of psychotherapy, and for some women sex comes to a stop. The Health Education Council produces a leaflet which gives a very sunny view of life after a mastectomy, with photographs of radiant women and couples holding hands. It is good that it can be like this for some women. But to superimpose this image of how one *ought* to be on a woman who is feeling depressed and who is not adjusting to the loss of her breast can only make matters worse. It seems that everyone else can cope except herself. Many women find that there is nobody they can talk to about their feelings. GPs tend not to follow cases up, reckoning that if a patient has emotional problems she will seek an appointment. Nurses are often reluctant to touch on any aspect of sexuality, saying: "We don't ask people about their personal lives. That would be intruding. And we're not psychiatrists." Consultant surgeons are usually male, filter the information they are giving women and may be evasive about using the term "cancer". They sometimes give the impression that when a breast is removed all risk of cancer goes with it. Yet the mortality for breast cancer has not been reduced in the last 40 years or more. (Rose Kushner, *Breast Cancer*) A woman is sometimes shocked to learn that she needs further treatment after the amputation of a breast: "I thought when my breast came off that was the end of it. I only agreed to have it off to get rid of the cancer."

Each woman who has spoken to me about her mastectomy has emphasized the importance of having someone to talk to, a "confiding tie", who is not necessarily anyone who has gone through the same experience herself but who is close and generous in her loving and who is not herself emotionally swamped by the experience. Sometimes this person is a man, but many women value the emotional support which can come from an understanding woman friend. If you are about to have a mastectomy it may be a good idea to seek out the right person before you actually have the operation and keep in continuing contact with her.

The after-effects

A mastectomy scar varies according to the type of surgery performed. With a radical mastectomy it may extend well below and above the area where the breast was sited. With a simple mastectomy there may just be a curve where the underside of the breast was attached to the chest wall and a vertical depression in the centre of the chest. When the bandages are first taken off this whole area is tender and swollen. Audré Lorde, writing in *The Cancer Journals*, says that when she peeped under the bandage "the scar still looked

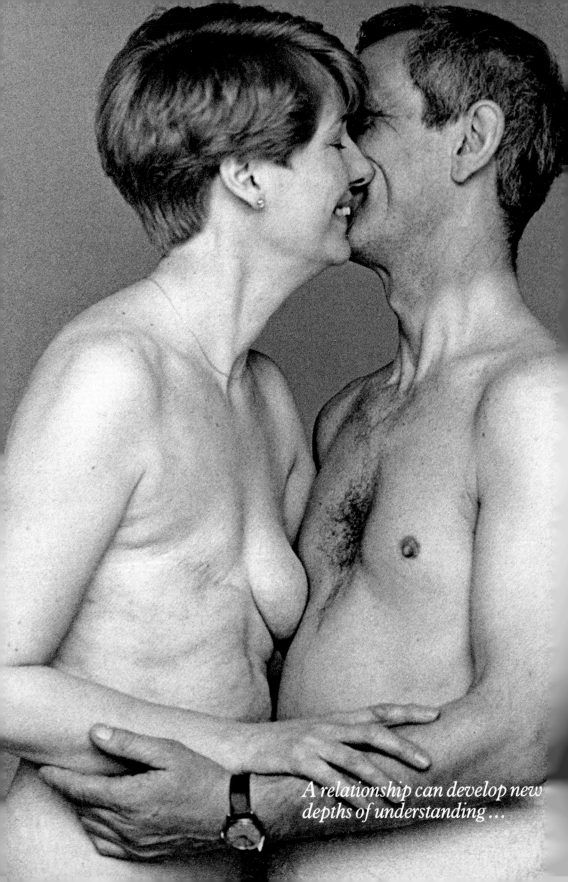

A relationship can develop new depths of understanding ...

placid and inoffensive, like the trussed rump of a stuffed goose, and once the stitches were out, even the puffiness passed." At first there may be a good deal of pain: "fixed pains, and moveable pains, deep pains and surface pains, strong pains and weak pains. There were stabs and throbs and burns, gripes and tickles and itches". Some women feel a numb, armour-plated rigidity: "the feeling that you are bound by steel, as if you are wearing a steel corset where they operated." (Laura, quoted in Daphna Ayallah and Isaac J. Weinstock, *Breasts*)

The need to grieve

Women recovering from mastectomy often feel that those around them – nurses, friends, relatives – impose on them a standard of cheerfulness to which they themselves are eager to conform to prove that they are "all right", that they are still their normal selves. It is as if the woman who has lost her breast has to reassure everyone around her. A good many facile, though well-meant, attempts to comfort are conveyed. A woman who has small breasts may be told, "Oh, you've nothing much to lose." And one who is usually capable and out-going is encouraged with "You'll bounce back again, dear!" "So I bounced back" one woman said. "Everyone was terribly positive and said, wasn't I lucky? Twice I broke down in hospital and wept and wept. I felt awful about it because it was very uncomfortable for everybody. *I wasn't allowed my own feelings.*"

"Friends couldn't face talking about it or talked about it too much. Either way, I felt I had to put on an act."

Some women find that people, both professionals and friends, are willing to discuss practical matters, like the discomfort of having a drip in the wound to drain it, but steer clear of talking about the implications of having a breast off – what it really means to a woman. "I trotted through each day thinking 'Gosh, yes, I'm so lucky!'" For three months she went on like this, intent on showing everybody that she was "getting back to normal", refusing to allow herself to grieve. Then she became deeply depressed.

Sexual relationships

Many women say that in the early weeks after the operation a sexual relationship becomes more precious and develops a new depth and understanding. A partner may reveal a capacity for cherishing and protecting greater than a woman thought possible. "When I came out of hospital sex was very reassuring and good. He made tremendous efforts and took me off for a weekend. He was especially tender when making love, much more than before. I had an awful worry about looking a freak and not being the person I was and his loving me like that and saying it made no difference helped me to accept that everything was all right for us sexually." Even so, a woman may find it hard to take off all her clothes and may be happy only with making love in the dark. Some women even get into the bath wearing a prosthesis (a dummy breast).

Lovemaking goes through subtle changes. A woman who enjoyed all the feelings in her breasts finds that the focus of her sensuality shifts to other parts of the body. Another may be so shocked, hurt or angry at what has happened that she dislikes her partner touching her remaining breast at all.

If you take your lover's hand in yours you can guide it to where it feels good to be touched. You may need to show that you want your other breast to be stroked and kissed. You may also want to try positions of intercourse which are different from those you enjoyed before. For a long time it can be painful to lie on the wounded side, especially if muscles have been cut, because your shoulder gets squashed. You will probably be unable to rest any weight on that arm or make a backward or downward thrust with it. If in the past you liked to kneel over your lover you discover that you cannot any longer lean downwards and support your weight with that arm. So sex becomes less spontaneous, more careful, but for some couples for whom sex has become rather dull over the years exploring ways of doing things and being experimental about it has not only brought a new closeness but introduces fresh spice into the flagging sexual relationship.

But as time passes a woman may need more than this. "It's all very well for your husband of ten years' standing to say having a breast off doesn't matter, doesn't make any difference to his love for you. . . ." A woman who has had a mastectomy may need the reassurance that she is sexually attractive, which can only come from a new sexual relationship, however temporary. Women who have told me of their experiences have sometimes said that an important part of the healing process came between a year and two years after the operation, when they had an affair.

The challenge of normal life

Louise had muscles removed from under her arm and found it very difficult to start driving again. She has not been able to play tennis since, but was determined to swim and forced herself to relearn this: "I was being a very good girl and saying, 'Aren't I doing well?' It made others much more comfortable to see that I was coping." She came face to face with her grief and a sense of intense inner coldness and isolation six months after the mastectomy when she was on holiday with her husband in the Mediterranean. "On the beach with very few clothes on I realized that I was different and always would be. You can joke up to a point." Her prosthesis slipped out of her bikini top into the sea. "For everyone else I tried to make a joke of it in case they were embarrassed. I had to spare people's feelings." Increasingly she felt that she needed her husband to give a parental type of support. She developed a fear of crowds and says she started to "fall apart". A man can understand why a woman may need protecting and caring for like a child in the time immediately after the operation. It is less easy for him to see the need for this six months or so later. He tends to feel that she should be getting better. Louise's husband had a very demanding job and was under great pressure at work. He spent more and more time in the office. The marriage started to crack under the impact of what she calls "appalling rows". "I kept getting thrown up against things that hurt me, a photograph of myself as I was before, the problem of trying to find summer dresses. You have to wear things with sleeves. I wept over my old summer dresses as I folded them and put them away. It was like putting away a stage of my life." Some women go through agonies in communal changing rooms and other women's embarrassed reactions to their stigma.

After a mastectomy a woman in her thirties or forties may also feel that she has suddenly grown much older: "It made me heavily middle-aged, forced me to throw away that part of my life in which I enjoyed my body, with all its connotations of sexual freedom. I couldn't feel grateful for life. I realized I had been snatched from death but I still didn't feel grateful."

For Louise, two things happened to bring her back to life. The first was when she realized that her husband was attracted to a friend and it was clear that the friend was excited and responding too. It jolted her into seeing how attractive he was. She says she realized that she had become dependent on *him* like a child on a loving father and that this kind of dependency relationship could not possibly fulfil all their sexual needs. She had to become less clinging and strike out on her own. Soon after she met a man with whom she had an affair. She did not tell him about her breast amputation until "the crucial moment", when he assured her that it could not possibly make any difference to the longing he felt for her. This was the final stage in the long process of healing. From then on she felt positive about her body.

Using a prosthesis

For many women the cosmetic treatment of a good prosthesis is an important part of recovery after mastectomy. Some treat the prosthesis almost as a part of themselves and are unwilling ever to look at the scar or to let it be seen by a sexual partner. Others see the prosthesis as a kind of self-deception. They point out that artificial arms and legs and false teeth and spectacles help you function, but that a breast prosthesis merely pretends that you have something which is missing. Audré Lorde describes how a woman from Reach for Recovery, an organization in the USA which helps women after mastectomy, visited her with a lamb's wool puff enclosed in a pink breast-shaped pad. "You'll never know the difference," she said. Audré Lorde says that however she seemed to other people, *she* would always know the difference. "Either I would love my body one-breasted now or remain for ever alien to myself. . . . For me my scars are an honourable reminder that I may be a casualty in the cosmic war against radiation, animal fat, air pollution, Macdonalds' hamburgers and Red Dye number 2, but the fight is still going on, and I am still a part of it. I refuse to have my scars hidden or trivialized behind lamb's wool or silicone gel. I refuse to be reduced in my own eyes or in the eyes of others from warrior to mere victim."

The important thing is that a woman comes to her own decisions about whether or not to wear a prosthesis and does not merely accede to the expectations of others. We are conditioned to see our bodies mainly in terms of how they look to men. Our ideas of who we are should be based on how our bodies *feel* right to us, and not become a passive reflection of the media image of how the female body ought to be.

The experience of grief

Grief can be a shattering experience. Whether from a mutilating operation or from the death of a person who is loved. It may leave an ache which is always there but at the same time it can reveal things about ourselves, make us reassess the things that matter and get a new perspective on life. And in a strange way the loss gives something and does not only take away.

Postscript

Writing this book has been for me a journey of discovery. I feel rather as if, like Alice, I had to walk straight through the mirror in which I saw my own reflection as a woman to find a strange, unmapped country and which, with the help of countless women, I have been able to explore.

I am astonished that I was so out of touch with what goes on in women's heads and bodies that I was ready to accept a predominantly male view of sex. I took it more or less for granted that sex therapists must be right when they talked about "female sexual dysfunction" and when they often used therapies to help women adapt, without questioning the social values and codes which impose on us particular kinds of sexual behaviour and assumptions about sex. Man has been taken as the model for health. Men's bodies have been accepted as the basis for anatomy and physiology and sexual behaviour and women's bodies and behaviour as deviations from this.

I have learned, as I suspected when I started out on that journey, that women's sexual lives are marvellously more complex than most books about sex would have us believe. I hope I have reflected some of that richness in these pages.

Working on this book has made me more aware than ever before of the importance for us as women of knowing and understanding ourselves and of not taking for granted anything about what we are told concerning female sexuality. All knowledge must be able to prove itself against the touchstone of personal experience and all that we can learn from other women. We need to share with each other and to build up a fund of knowledge from which all women can draw. The profession of gynaecology is controlled and dominated by men and has outlawed what women can learn about their own bodies and their sexuality. What we know cannot be dismissed as anecdote or as female "intuition". It may be very different from the information that men have about women's bodies and minds and about our sexuality, but it is precisely because it is different from their knowledge and because it flows in from first-hand experience that it is of such great value.

To each woman reading this book I want to say: Question all received knowledge, however authoritative it may appear. Trust your feelings. They are valid. And share what you discover about yourself with other women. Gradually we shall be able, as if piecing together fragments of mosaic, to learn more and more about who we are as women.

Resources and information services

There may be areas covered in this book which are of particular interest to you and which you will wish to pursue further. Alternatively, you may need help or advice with a particular problem, and be unsure where to turn. Below is a list of additional reading material and some addresses which you may find useful.

BEREAVEMENT

Addresses

CRUSE (The National Organization for the Widowed and Their Children)
126 Sheen Road
Richmond
Surrey PW9 1UR
(01) 940 4818

The Foundation for the Study of Infant Deaths (Cot Deaths)
The Fifth Floor
4 Grosvenor Place
London SW1X 7HD
(01) 235 1721/245 9421

Society of Compassionate Friends
5 Lower Clifton Hill
Clifton
Bristol
(0272) 292778

Stillbirth and Perinatal Death Association
37 Christchurch Hill
London NW3 1LA
(01) 794 4601

CHILD ABUSE AND INCEST

Addresses

British Association for the Study and Prevention of Child Abuse and Neglect
56 Bagslate Moor Road
Norden
Rochdale
Lancs. LL11 57H
(0706) 43112

Incest Survivors Group
c/o A Woman's Place
Hungerford House
Victoria Embankment
London WC2
(01) 836 6081

Parents Anonymous (support for parents who feel they may harm their child)
29 Newmarket Way
Hornchurch
Essex RM126
(04024) 51538

FAMILY PLANNING

Brook Advisory Centre Birth Control Clinics
Central Office
153a East Street
London SE17
(01) 708 1234

Family Planning Association
27–35 Mortimer Street
London W1N 7RJ
(01) 636 7866

HYSTERECTOMY

Reading material

H. June Kuczynski "After the hysterectomy" (*Nursing Mirror*, 11 August 1982)

S. H. Zervos and A. C. Papaloucas, "Psychosomatic disturbances following hysterectomy performed at a premenopausal age" (*Internal Surgery* 802, 1972)

LESBIANISM

Reading material

Gay's The Word Bookshop
66 Marchmont Street
London WC1 (01) 278 7654

Sequal write to
BM Sequal, London WC1N 3XX

Sisterwrite Bookshop
190 Upper Street
London N1 (01) 226 9782

Spare Rib is a feminist magazine available from some newsagents, or from:
27 Clerkenwell Close
London EC1 0AT (01) 253 9792

Sidney Abbot and Barbara Love, *Sappho was a Right-on Woman* (New York: Stein and Day 1973)

Betty Fairchild and Nancy Hayward, *Now that You Know: What every parent should know about homosexuality* (New York and London: Jovanovich 1979)

Dolores Klaich, *Woman Plus Woman – Attitudes towards lesbianism* (New York: Morrow 1974)

Ginny Vida (ed.), *Our Right to Love: A lesbian resource book* (New Jersey: Prentice-Hall, Inc. 1978)

Groups

Black Lesbian Feminist Network
c/o A Woman's Place
Hungerford House
Victoria Embankment
London WC2
(01) 836 6081

Gemma (for lesbians with and without disabilities, to lessen isolation)
BM Box 5700
London WC1N 3XX

Young Lesbians Group (under 21 years – social group, trips, films, information)
(01) 263 5932

Lesbian Mothers Group
c/o The Gay Centre
61a Bloom Street
Manchester

Kenric (international, non-political organization for gay women, social activities in London area) write to:
The Secretary
Kenric
BM Kenric
London WC1N 3XX

Women-only switchboards

England
Bradford *lesbian line Thurs 7 – 9pm*
(0272) 305525
Cambridge *lesbian line switchboard Fri 6 – 10pm*
(0223) 346113
Colchester *lesbian line Last Tues of month 7 – 9pm*
(0206) 870051
Lancaster *women's line Wed 2 – 9p*
(0524) 63021
Leeds *lesbian nightline Tues 7.30 – 9.30pm*
(0632) 463588

Liverpool *women's line Tues and Thurs 7.30–10.00pm*
(051) 708 234
London *lesbian line Mon and Fri 2–10pm*
(01) 837 8602
London *Friend women's line Thurs 7.30–10pm*
(01) 354 6305
Manchester *lesbian line Mon to Fri 7–10pm*
(061) 236 6305
Newcastle *lesbian line Fri 7–10pm*
(0623) 612277
North Staffs *lesbian support group (check for correct times)*
(0782) 266998
Nottingham *lesbian line Mon 7–9.30pm*
(0602) 410652
Oxford *lesbian line Mon and Fri 8–10pm*
(0865) 42333
Preston *lesbian line Mon and Wed 7.30–9.30pm*
(0772) 51112
West Midlands (B'ham) *lesbian line Wed and Fri 7–10pm*
(021) 6226580
Ireland
Belfast *Cara friend Thurs 7–10pm*
(0232) 22023
Dublin NFG *Switchboard Thurs 8–10pm*
(01) 71 06 08
IRGM Munster Cork *Thurs 8–10pm*
(021) 505394
Scotland
Aberdeen *lesbian line Wed 7–10pm*
(0224) 572726
Dundee *lesbian line Tues 7–10pm*
(0382) 21843
Edinburgh *(Scottish young lesbian line) Mon and Wed 7–10pm Sat 12–4pm*
(031) 557 3179
Glasgow *lesbian line Mon 7–10pm*
(041) 248 4596
Wales
Cardiff *lesbian line Thurs 8–10pm*
(0222) 374051
Swansea *lesbian line Fri 7–10pm*
(0792) 467 365

MASTECTOMY

Addresses

Mastectomy Association
1 Colworth Road
Croydon
(01) 654 8643

Mastectomy Centre
12 Henrietta Place
London W1
(01) 580 1602

THE PHYSICALLY CHALLENGED

Addresses

Gay Care (for homosexual men)
84 Burton Road
London SW9 6TQ

Gemma (for lesbian women)
BN Box 5700
London WC1 3XX

Sexual and Personal Relationships of the Disabled
25 Mortimer Street
London W1
(01) 637 5400

Sexual Problems of the Disabled (SPOD)
Brook House
2–16 Torrington Place
London WC1 7HN

Reading material

Nicole Davoud, *Forum* (The Multiple Sclerosis Society of Great Britain and Northern Ireland, 1981) Obtainable from:
4 Tachbrook Street
London SW1V 1SJ

Wendy Greengross, *Entitled to Love* (Malaby Press with National Fund for Research into Crippling Diseases 1976). Obtainable from: Vincent House, Springfield Road, Horsham, Sussex (0403) 64101

Glorya Hale (ed.), *The New Sourcebook for the Disabled* (London: Heinemann 1983)

Thomas O. Mooney *et al.*, *Sexual Options for Paraplegics and Quadraplegics* (Boston: Little, Brown 1975; Croydon: Quest Publishing) Obtainable from: 145a Croydon Road, Beckenham, Kent BR3 3RB

RAPE CRISIS CENTRES

Belfast *Tues and Fri 7–10pm*
(0232) 49696
Birmingham *24-hour line*
(021) 233 2122
office Mon to Fri 10am–6pm
(021) 233 2655
Bradford *Mon 1–5pm, Thurs 6–10pm*
(0274) 308270

Brighton *Tues 6–9pm, Fri 3–9pm, Sat 10am–1pm*
(0273) 699756
Cambridge *Wed 6–12pm, Sat 11am–5pm*
(0223) 358314
Cleveland *Thurs 7–10pm*
(0642) 813397
Coventry *Mon 7–10pm, weekdays 11am–3pm*
(0203) 57709
Dublin *8pm–8am*
(01) 601470
Edinburgh *Mon and Wed 1–2pm, Mon, Wed and Fri 6–8pm, Thurs 7–10pm*
(031) 5569437
Glasgow (Strathclyde) *Mon, Wed, Fri 7–10pm*
(041) 221 8448
Leeds *10am–12pm daily*
(0532) 44058
Liverpool
Mon 7–9pm, Thurs 2–5pm, Sat 2–5pm
(051) 734 4369
London *24-hour line*
(01) 340 6145
office hours
(01) 340 6913
Manchester *Tues and Fri 2–5pm, Thurs and Sun 6–9pm*
(061) 228 3602
Nottingham *Mon to Fri 11am–5pm*
(0602) 410440
Portsmouth *Fri, Sat, Sun 8pm–8am*
(0705) 739366
Sheffield *Mon and Fri 10am–1pm, Thurs 8–10pm*
(0742)755255
Tyneside *Mon to Fri 10am–5pm every eve 6.30–10pm*
(0632) 329858

Women Against Rape
Bristol c/o Caroline Barker
23 Fairlawn Road
Bristol (0272) 556554;
London PO Box 287
London NW6.

Rape in Marriage Campaign
c/o 374 Grays Inn Road,
London WC1.

Scottish Women's Aid
(031) 225 8011

"Women Against Violence Against Women" at:
A Woman's Place
Hungerford House
Victoria Embankment
London WC2
(01) 836 6081

Bibliography

Adams, C., *Ordinary Lives: A hundred years ago* (London: Virago 1982)

Alther, L., *Original Sins* (Harmondsworth: Penguin 1981)

Atwood, M., *Lady Oracle* (London: Virago 1982)

Austin, V. and C. Clarke-Smith, *Widowed – What Now?* (New Zealand: Mallison Rendel; available in England from Cruse House, 126 Sheen Road, Richmond, Surrey TW9 1UR)

Ayallah, D. and I. J. Weinstock, *Breasts: Women speak about their breasts and their lives* (London: Hutchinson 1980)

Beauvoir, S. de, *The Second Sex* (Harmondsworth: Penguin 1972)

Belliveau, F. and L. Richter, *Understanding Human Sexual Inadequacy* (London: Hodder & Stoughton 1971)

Bender, L. and A. Blau, "The reaction of children to sexual relations with adults", *American Journal of Ortho-psychiatry*, vol. 7 no. 4, 1937

Billings, E. and A. Westmore, *The Billings Method: Controlling fertility without drugs or devices* (London: Allen Lane 1981)

Bracey, D., "Breakthrough in male contraception", *Spare Rib*, vol. 93 (April), 1980

Brothers, J., *What Every Woman Should Know About Men* (New York: Simon & Schuster 1981)

Burgess, S., *Sexual Problems Following Stillbirth* (Stillbirth and Perinatal Death Association, 37 Christchurch Hill, London NW3)

Butler, P., *Self-Assertion for Women* (London: Harper & Row 1981)

Caldeyro-Barcia, R., *et al.*, "Bearing-down efforts and their effects on fetal heart rate, oxygenation and acid base balance", *Proceedings of First International Meeting of Perinatal Medicine* (Berlin: 1979)

Cole, M., "The use of surrogate sex partners in the treatment of sex dysfunctions and allied conditions", *British Journal of Sexual Medicine* (March) 1982

Comfort, A., *The Joy of Sex* (London: Mitchell Beazley 1972)

Denfield, D. and M. Gordon, "The sociology of mate swapping or the family that swings together clings together", in J. S. and J. R. Delora (eds), *Intimate Life-Styles: Marriage and its alternatives* (California: Goodyear 1972)

Dickson, A., *A Woman in Your Own Right* (London: Quartet 1982)

Dietz, C. and J. Craft, "Family dynamics of incest: a new perspective", *Social Casework*, 1980

Douglas, M., *Purity and Danger: An analysis of concepts of pollution and taboo* (London: Routledge & Kegan Paul 1966, paperback 1975)

Ellis, A., *The Journal of Sex Research*, vol. 5 no. 1 (February) 1969, pp. 41–9

Ellis, H., *The Psychology of Sex* (London: Heinemann 1933)

Ellis, S., *The Women of England* (London: Fisher, Son & Co. c.1850)

Embree, J. F., *A Japanese Village: Suye Mura* (London: Routledge & Kegan Paul 1946)

Faderman, L., *Surpassing the Love of Men: Romantic friendships between women from the Renaissance to the present* (London: Junction Books 1981)

Fairchild, B. and N. Hayward, *Now That You Know: What every parent should know about homosexuality* (New York and London: Harcourt, Brace & Jovanovich 1979)

Forward, S. and C. Buck, *Betrayal of Innocence: Incest and its devastation* (Harmondsworth: Penguin 1981)

Foucault, M., *La Volonté de Savoir* (trans. Meaghen Morris), quoted in "A review of Michel Foucault's *La Volonté de Savoir*", in Mike Brake (ed.), *Human Sexual Relations: A Reader in Human Sexuality* (Harmondsworth: Penguin 1982)

Francis, V. de, *Protecting the Child Victim of Sex Crimes Committed by Adults* (Denver: American Humane Association, Children's Division 1968–9)

Freud, S. (trans. J. Rivieri), *Collected Papers vol. 2* (New York: Basic Books 1959)
"Letter to Wilhelm Fliess", in ibid.

Friday, N., *My Secret Garden* (London: Quartet Books 1979)

Giese, H., Paul H. Gebhard, Jan Raboch (trans. Colin Bearne), *The Sexuality of Women* (London: André Deutsch 1972)

Graffenburg, E., "The role of urethra in female orgasm", in *International Journal of Sexology* vol. 3, pp. 145–8 Bombay 1950

Greengross, W., *Entitled to Love: The sexual and emotional needs of the handicapped* (London: Malaby Press for National Marriage Guidance Council with National Fund for Research into Crippling Diseases 1976)

Griffin, S., *Pornography and Silence: Culture's revenge against nature* (London: The Women's Press 1981)
Made from this Earth (London: The Women's Press 1982)

Hailes, J., "Sexuality and aging", *Social Biology Resource Centre Bulletin*, vol. 4 no. 3, Melbourne 1980

Harman, W. V., "Death of my baby", *British Medical Journal*, vol. 282, 1981, pp. 35–7

Harrington, V., "Look, listen and support", *Nursing Mirror* (13 January), 1982

Heiman, J., L. LoPiccolo and J. LoPiccolo, *Becoming Orgasmic: A sexual growth program for women* (London: Prentice Hall 1977)

Hemmings, S., "Horrific practices: how lesbians were presented in the newspapers of 1978", in Gay Left Collective (eds), *Homosexuality: Power and Politics* (London: Allison & Busby 1980)

Hite, S., *Report on Male Sexuality* (London: Collier Macmillan 1976)
Report on Female Sexuality (London: Corgi 1981)

Hoeffding, V., "Dear Mom", in Jay Karla and Allen Young (eds), *Out of the Closets: Voices of gay liberation* (New York: Jove Publications 1977)
"The flight from womanhood: The masculinity complex in women as viewed by men and by women", *International Journal of Psychoanalysis*, vol. 7, 1926, pp. 324–9

Holt, I. J. and A. H. MacLennan, "Lumbar epidural analgesia in labour", *British Medical Journal* vol. 1, 1977, pp. 14–15

Horney, K., "The problem of feminine masochism", *Psychoanalytic Review*, vol. 12 no. 3, 1935

Hurcombe, L. and S. Dowell, *Dispossessed Daughters of Eve: Faith and feminism* (London: SCM Press 1981)

Jaffe, A., L. Dynneson *et al.*, "Sexual abuse of children: an epidemiological study", *American Journal of Diseases in Children* 1–9:6 1975

Johnston, J., *Lesbian Nation: The feminist solution* (New York: Simon & Schuster 1973)

Jong, E., *Fear of Flying* (London: Secker & Warburg 1974)

Justice, B. and R. Justice, *The Broken Taboo: Sex in the family* (London: Owen 1980)

Kaplan, H. S., *The New Sex Therapy: Active treatment of sexual dysfunctions* (Harmondsworth: Penguin 1978)

Karla, J. and A Young, *Out of the Closets: Voices of gay liberation* (New York: Jove Publications 1977)

Kempe, R. S. and C. H. Kempe, *Child Abuse* (London: Fontana 1978)

Kerr, C., quoted in Eleanor Stephens, "The moon within your reach", *Spare Rib*, vol. 42 (December), 1975

Kinsey, A. C., W. B. Pomeroy and C. Martin, *Sexual Behaviour in the Human Male* (Philadelphia: W. B. Saunders 1948)
Sexual Behaviour in the Human Female (Philadelphia: W. B. Saunders 1953)

Koadlow, Dr E., "Sexuality and the elderly", *Social Biology Resources Centre Bulletin*, vol. 4 (3 December) Melbourne 1980

Kushner, R., *Breast Cancer: A personal history and an investigative report* (New York: Harcourt, Brace & Jovanovich 1976)

Ladas, A. K., B. Whipple and J. D. Perry, *The G-Spot* (New York: Holt, Rinehart & Winston 1982)

Lecky, W. E. H., *A History of European Morals from Augustus to Charlemagne* (2 vols), (London: Longmans & Co. 1911, first printed 1869)

Lewis, S. G., *Sunday's Women: A report on lesbian life today* (Boston: Beacon Press 1979)

Lorde, A., *The Cancer Journals* (New York: Spinsters' Ink 1982)

McGilvray, D. B., "Sexual power and fertility in Sri Lanka", in Carol P. McCormack (ed.), *Ethnography, Fertility and Birth*, (London: Academic Press 1982)

Marcus, S. *The Other Victorians: A study of sexuality and pornography in mid-nineteenth century England* (London: Corgi 1969)

Masters, W. H. and V. E. Johnson, *Human Sexual Inadequacy* (London: J. and A. Churchill 1966)
Human Sexual Response (Boston: Little, Brown & Co. 1966)

Mead, M., *From the South Seas: Studies of adolescence and sex in primitive societies* (New York: William Morrow 1939)

Midelfort, H. C. E., "Witch hunting in South Western Germany", in M. Daly, *Gyn/ecology: the metaethics of radical feminism* (London: The Women's Press 1979)

Nelson, E. and M. Yasse (eds), *The Influence of Pornography on Behaviour* (London: Academic Press 1982)

Nelson, S., *Incest, Fact and Myth* (Edinburgh: Stramullion 1982)

Oakley, A., *Sociology of Housework* (Oxford: Martin Robertson & Co. 1974)

Pizzey, E. and G. Shapiro, *Prone to Violence* (London: Hamlyn 1982)

Pomeroy W. B., *Dr Kinsey and the Institute for Sex Research* (London: Nelson 1972)

Reading, A. E., D. N. Cox and C. M. Sledmere, "Psychological issues arising from the development of new male contraceptives", *Bulletin of the British Psychological Society*, vol. 35 1982, pp. 369–71

Reitz, R., *Menopause: A positive approach* (London: Unwin Paperbacks 1981)

Reuben, D., *Everything You Always Wanted to Know About Sex but were Afraid to Ask* (London: W. H. Allen 1970)

Rich, A., *Compulsory Heterosexuality and Lesbian Existence* (London: Onlywomen Press 1981)

Richards, D. H., "Depression after hysterectomy", *Lancet*, vol. 430, 1973

Ris, H. W., "The essential emancipation: The control of reproduction", in Joan Roberts (ed.), *Beyond Intellectual Sexism: A new woman, a new reality* (New York: David McKay Co. Inc. 1976)

Russell, D. E. H., *Lorna Lederer Take Back the Night, Women on Pornography* (New York: Bantam 1980)

Schultz, L., "The child sex victim, social, psychological and legal perspectives", *Child Welfare*, vol. 52 no. 3, 1973

Seager, H., *Not for Fun, Not for Profit: Strategies for ending sexual harrassment on the job* (Pennsylvania: Pennsylvania Commission for Women 1981)

Seaman, B., US Congress House Select Committee on Population: Hearings on Fertility and Contraception in America, 95th Congress, III, 150, 1978

Semmens, J. P. and G. Wagner, "Estrogen deprivation and vaginal function in postmenopausal women", *Journal of the American Medical Association*, vol. 248 no. 4, 1982

Shuttle, P. and P. Redgrove, *The Wise Wound* (London: Gollancz 1978)

Silber, Sherman J., *How to get Pregnant* (New York: Scribner 1980)

Stevens, E., "The moon within your reach", *Spare Rib*, vol. 42 (December), 1975

Struthers, J., "Growing Older", in Walter de la Mare (ed.), *Love* (London: Faber 1953)

Sweet, P. E., *Something Happened to Me* (Wisconsin: Mother Courage Press 1981 (224 State Street, Racine, WI 53403, USA)

Szasz, T., *Sex: Facts, Frauds and Follies* (Oxford: Blackwell 1981)

Thompson, C., "Cultural pressures in the psychology of women", in Jean Baker Miller (ed.), *Toward a New Psychology of Women* (London: Allen Lane 1978)

Thompson, C., "'Penis envy' in women", *Psychiatry*, vol. 6, 1943, pp. 123–5

Weare, T., "Round in a flat world", *Spare Rib* (January), 1979

Weideger, P., *Female Cycles* (London: The Women's Press 1978)

Wertz, R. W. and D. C. Wertz, *Lying-in* (London: Collier Macmillan 1977)

Whitehorn, K., "No country for old women", *Observer* (16 January), 1983

Wilson, R. A., *Feminine Forever* (London: W. H. Allen 1966)

Wolfe, L., *The Cosmo Report* (New York: Arbor House 1981)

Wood, C. and B. Suitters, *The Fight for Acceptance: A history of contraception* (Aylesbury: Medical and Technical Publishing Co. 1970)

Woodward, J., "The diagnosis and treatment of psychosomatic vulvovaginitis", *Practitioner*, vol. 225, 1981, pp. 1673–7

Yates, A., *Sex without Shame: Encouraging the child's healthy development* (London: Temple Smith 1979)

Index

317

Acknowledgments

Dorling Kindersley would like to thank the
following for their special assistance:
Sally Smallwood, Polly Dawes, Flo Henfield,
Faith Haddad, all the staff at Vantage
Photosetting; and for photographic services,
Bill Rowlinson and Ken Hone.

The photographer, Nancy Durrell McKenna,
wishes to thank the many people who devoted
their time and interest to being photographed
for this book.

Artists
David Ashby
Alicia Durdos
Edwina Keene
Kevin Molloy

Howard Pemberton
Jenny Smith
Lucy Su
Kathy Wyatt